ORGANIZING AND FINANCING BUSINESS

ORGANIZING
AND

JOSEPH H. BONNEVILLE
Professor Emeritus of Finance, New York University,
Visiting Professor of Finance, University of
California, Los Angeles

LLOYD E. DEWEY
Professor of Finance, New York University

HARRY M. KELLY
Professor of Finance, New York University

FINANCING
BUSINESS

SIXTH EDITION

PRENTICE-HALL, INC.

Englewood Cliffs, N.J.

Organizing and Financing Business
Sixth Edition
by
Joseph H. Bonneville, Lloyd E. Dewey,
Harry M. Kelly

© 1932, 1935, 1938, 1945, 1952, 1959 BY
PRENTICE-HALL, INC.
ENGLEWOOD CLIFFS, N.J.

LIBRARY OF CONGRESS
CATALOG CARD NO.: 59–10559

First printing .... *June, 1959*
Second printing .... *December, 1959*
Third printing .... *September, 1960*

PRINTED IN THE UNITED STATES OF AMERICA

64189–C

Preface

New practices, changes in emphasis in the teaching of business finance, changes in laws, and the great impact of federal income tax upon financial planning have required substantial changes in, and additions to, *Organizing and Financing Business.*

Comments from users in schools and colleges throughout the country, coupled with the authors' experiences in their own classrooms, have resulted in the inclusion of new material and modification and rearrangement of sequence and content. Readers familiar with previous editions will find that the chapter dealing with credit and collections has been omitted. Part of the material has been incorporated in the chapter on financing working capital requirements and in the chapter on business and the banks. Because of the importance of banks as suppliers of short-term funds, the chapter on business and banks now immediately follows the chapter on working capital, so that both may be conveniently assigned and discussed as a unit, if desired. Because some teachers do not wish to spend much time discussing uncommon types of business organization, the material presented has been reduced somewhat, and all organizations except the corporation are covered in one chapter instead of two, as formerly. A more teachable arrangement has been achieved by including the discussion of liens and mortgages in the chapter which deals with the general principles of financing with borrowed capital.

Although some of the problems at the end of each chapter have been retained, either in original or revised form, many have been replaced by new ones, all of which have had two years trial in the classroom. An innovation is the addition of a special problem for written assignment at the end of most of the chapters.

The authors of the previous editions welcome Professor Harry M. Kelly as a co-author of this, the sixth edition. Professor Kelly has had more than a decade of experience in the use of *Organizing and Financing*

Business in his classrooms, and the authors feel that his contributions to the present revision have greatly increased the usefulness of the text.

The authors are indebted to many teachers all over the country for useful suggestions. They acknowledge with gratitude the many contributions from their colleagues at New York University. Dr. Hobart C. Carr, Chairman of the Banking and Finance Department, made many suggestions for the inclusion of new material. Dr. Gordon McLean contributed many of the new problems and made helpful contributions to the text. Professor Frank Angell brought the chapter on insurance up to date. Dr. Anne Hulse of the Department of Economics, Hunter College, critically reviewed the entire manuscript and assisted in getting it into final form for the publisher.

J.H.B.
L.E.D.
H.M.K.

Contents

VI. FINANCING BY MEANS OF STOCK . . . 93

The owned capital of a business · Capital stock, capital, capitalization · The act of capitalizing · Basis of stock financing · The transfer agent and the registrar · Features of stock financing · Dividends · Classes of stock · Common stock · Preferred stock · Nonparticipating and participating · Types of participation · Non-cumulative and cumulative stock · Redeemable or callable stock · Convertible stock · Protected preferred stock · Prior preference stock · Deferred stock · Guaranteed stock · Voting and non-voting stock · Vetoing stock · Par value and no-par value stock · Negotiability of certificates of stock · Names defining stock statue · Authorized stock · Issued stock · Unissued stock · Full paid stock · Part paid stock · Outstanding stock · Treasure stock · Creation of treasury stock · Forfeited stock

VII. FINANCING WITH BORROWED CAPITAL 113

The use of borrowed capital · Trading on the equity · Effects of trading on the equity · Secured and unsecured loans · Liens as security · Security and equity · The mortgage · Statutory form of mortgage · Operation of foreclosure claims · The corporate mortgage · Mortgage bonds · The trustee · Parties to the corporate mortgage · Form of the bond · Types of mortgages · The closed end mortgage · The open end mortgage · Limited open end mortgage · Restrictions or escrow provisions · The after-acquired clause · Avoidance of the after-acquired clause

VIII. CLASSIFICATION AND TYPES OF BONDS 132

Corporate bonds · Rights of individual bondholders · Classification of bonds · Purchase money and similar bonds · Consolidated or unified bonds · Adjustment or reorganization bonds · Funding or refunding bonds · Prior lien bonds · First, second, third, etc., mortgage bonds · Bridge, terminal, dock, and divisional bonds · First and consolidated, first and refunding, etc., bonds · Debenture bonds · Subordinated debentures · Trustee or receiver's certificates · Collateral trust bonds · Equipment trust notes · Assumed, guaranteed, indorsed, and stamped bonds · Bonds of stipulated interest rate · Income bonds · Profit-sharing bonds · Participating bonds · Tax-exempt bonds · Registered bonds · Coupon bonds · Registered coupon bonds · Interchangeable bonds · Gold, silver, and legal tender bonds · Callable bonds · Convertible bonds · Serial bonds · Sinking fund bonds

ORGANIZING AND FINANCING BUSINESS

CHAPTER I

Visualizing the Field

The study of business topics. Only in comparatively recent years has it been generally acknowledged that valuable preparation for business careers can be obtained through classroom instruction and the study of textbooks. In the past, business ability was acquired through what might be called an apprenticeship system. One learned to do business by doing business. Today, however, it is recognized that the organization, financing, and management of business, together with such special business activities as financing, advertising, merchandising, accounting, purchasing, office management, personnel management, and credit management require much more general and specific knowledge than can be "picked up" by observation alone. A careful and specialized study of the codified experiences and practices of thousands of businessmen will produce greater business capacity than will any amount of mere observation within any particular business house. Of course, there occasionally appears a business genius whose entire development has been attained through observation and practice, but how much more rapid, how much more substantial his development might have been if his inborn ability could have been built upon a solid foundation of organized knowledge and a full understanding of basic principles, successful practices, and governing laws. There is no doubt that a combination of the two is required to produce the best results.

The organizing and financing of business embraces broad and complicated activities, requiring a wide, general knowledge, as well as much specialization. The course, of which this book forms the base, attempts to present, in a comparatively brief manner, those underlying principles of organizing and financing that may be acquired by reading and study.

To get at the very bottom of the subject of organizing and financing business, one must have a clear conception, first, of what the term *business* actually embraces, and then the details of organizing and financing as applied to it. To that end, we begin with a general description of business.

What is business? Business is a commonplace term but, in taking up its definite study, it is well to have a realization of its vast significance. To many it connotes merely merchandising, the operation of some kind of a shop or store, large or small. This is entirely too narrow a concept. Business must be understood to embrace every human activity (usually activated by the hope of profit) whereby man's wants are supplied. Lumbering, mining, fishing, farming, manufacturing, trading, transporting, shipping, building, merchandising, and many other activities are businesses that help to supply material wants. The practice of law, medicine, dentistry, teaching, accounting, nursing, entertaining represent a few of the types of business activities that supply desired services.

Business is often divided into two main groups: industrial businesses and commercial businesses. Industrial businesses are those that actually produce commodities either by manufacture or by some definite treatment of materials, or that produce and supply the raw materials, which may be used in their original form or from which marketable commodities can be manufactured or prepared. Commercial businesses are those that have to do, not with the actual making of commodities or the procuring of them from nature's stores, but with the distribution of them through various channels from the producer to the final consumer. It must be noted, however, that all commercial businesses do not deal in commodities. Railroad and steamship companies, doctors, dentists, lawyers, bankers, brokers, accountants, teachers, actors, musicians and others provide their services instead of tangible commodities, but they are, nevertheless, considered to be in the commercial field. There are, of course, many firms engaged in both industrial and commercial activities. These must be classified as combinations of the two kinds.

Too often the layman thinks of business and the study of business as a dry and uninteresting subject. To him, business is a necessary evil since man must eat and live. To him, it represents a long ride to work in the morning when it would be far more pleasant to sleep or to play golf or fish. Nothing could be further from the truth. A business is what you make it. It can be dynamic and exciting, or dreary. A Ringling Brothers' clown once said that he felt he was cheating the management because he was taking pay for doing something he wanted to do anyhow. When a man or woman finds his work is play, then that person is usually a success in business. We are fortunate in living and working in a time of great and wonderful development. New products are being invented every day. Monsanto Chemical Co. adds about fifty new products each year to its already large list of products. Its Treasurer will be counting money five years from now earned from the sale of products that the company has not even thought of yet! Television, radar, jet planes, have all been developed since most of the readers of this book were in elementary school.

Engineers, designers, economists, writers, but, most of all, men and women engaged in finance, play a glamorous part in this ever-widening horizon of new products. Nothing moves in business without money and credit, and it is unfortunately a sad fact that many new products die without ever seeing the light of day because no one was available who would finance the new venture. It takes vast sums of money to bring a new product into being; it takes even more money and credit to keep it alive and healthy after it has been started. How does a businessman raise a million dollars? The banks will lend a new business only a small percentage of such an amount, and then not for what is called venture capital. Venture capital will have to come from other sources. And for expansion, where does the businessman go for the next million, and the next after that? As a concern grows and becomes well known, possibly recourse can be had to the securities market. Usually neither the new concern nor the small concern offers the certainty of success that the older and tested company does. Before anyone with money will invest in business, he must be convinced of its ultimate success. Often, too, the investor will demand a high proportion of control over the management of the new enterprise and will, of course, look for a return commensurate with his risk. One of the most difficult problems of a promoter or entrepreneur requiring financing from outside sources is to accomplish this without losing control or promising too large a share of the profits in order to retain control.

Purpose and aim of business. It must be borne in mind that business is not merely a happening. Fundamentally business has an economic purpose, that is, the producing and marketing of every possible article and service that will help supply human wants, and the production and distribution of these in the most convenient and reasonable manner and at a profit. Without properly organized business, the world today would be without thousands of everyday commodities looked upon as the most common necessities. It is easy to recall how, in the recent past, World War II so seriously interfered with the functioning of business all over the world, and how difficult or even impossible it often was to obtain many of the things most easily and readily procured when business is functioning smoothly.

Finance is an important part of the organization of business. Yet when you ask the average person what he thinks finance is about he will probably reply—stocks and bonds. Or he thinks of a Hollywood type tycoon making financial decisions which will gain him millions from a luxurious office. Boswell relates that Samuel Johnson, when asked to auction a soap factory, appealed to the flagging interest of potential buyers by exclaiming that he was not here to sell "a parcel of boilers and vats but the potentiality of growing rich, beyond the dreams of avarice."[1] Business finance is not the study of stocks and bonds. And though there is the dream of becoming rich beyond the dreams of avarice, such success is usually achieved by imagination, persistence in the face of difficulty and constant study and application of sound principles of business finance. The direct aim of the businessman is to make a profit out of which to support himself and his dependents and, furthermore, to lay aside savings in as large an amount as possible to constitute a competence for his retirement or an estate for his family upon his death. He may not realize fully the importance of the economic function of business, but he does realize that the better he serves the public, the better are his chances of success and profit. This perfectly legitimate desire to make money impels the businessman to direct his business effectively.

Incidental to supplying human wants with its products, merchandise, and services, and the owner with a profit, the successful business also furnishes a living to various groups of employees working on a salary, commission, or profit-sharing basis. With all business, whether the largest or the smallest, finance is a constant day-to-day problem of planning the short-term and the long-term needs of the business and arranging for such financing. It must look forward and make financial decisions which will achieve the objective of management, whether that objective is increasing profits, maximizing dividends, or preparing for a merger or consolidation.

The financial manager has the task, too, of receiving and paying out money, not merely managing the profits of the business. In 1956, General Motors received $10,800,000,000 from sales. Of this amount, almost $300,000,000 was retained from the profits. An additional $347,000,000 was retained from the depreciation allowance. Not one dollar was received from the sale of stock or bonds. If we look at the sources of funds for all corporations during the year 1957, we find that gross saving, which includes depreciation and retained earnings, amounted to $24,500,000,000, a reduction in liquid assets another $5 billion, an additional $2.5 billion from an increase in trade payables, and only $14 billion from the sale of stock and bonds. Of this amount totaling $46 billion, $30 billion was spent on plant and equipment. When it is realized that it takes three and sometimes five years to erect a plant or build an oil tanker, it will be easy to appreciate all of the economic and financial planning that goes into the decision to acquire new plants and equipment five years in the future.

Once the initial establishment has been financed, the financial management of the smaller business is quite likely to be chiefly concerned with problems of raising and safely utilizing short-term funds. However, a

---

[1] Boswell, *Life of Samuel Johnson*, Vol. II, 380 (1791).

small business like its larger counterpart must keep itself up to date if it wishes to survive competition. It must normally grow with the community it serves. Because the small business, unlike larger corporations, does not have ready access to the public capital market, the rate of expansion often depends upon the savings of profit which the proprietors reinvest in the business. To be prepared to expand or make changes when expedient and timely requires foresight, careful planning and skill.

As in most fields of business activity, financial management is constantly trying for new and better ways to accomplish its purposes and, since other phases of business management are doing the same thing, those responsible for the raising and administration of funds used in the business have constantly to meet new problems occasioned not only by new activities within the business but by external developments brought about by competition, changed economic conditions and demand for the product or services sold.

Basic problems facing the financial management, the tools used in solving them, the adaptability of the type of business organization, need to be studied by businessmen, not only by those contemplating the beginning of a venture but by those engaged in operating a going concern. The purpose of this text is to treat, at least in a basic manner, some of these, not only to enable a student to reach a reasonable degree of competence as a result of present study, but to lay a sound groundwork for further development in the field of business finance.

Functions of business. As may clearly be gathered from what has gone before, business has two great functions it must perform: namely, production and marketing. These problems are coordinate and mutually dependent. Production without marketing is useless, and marketing without production is obviously impossible. The proper combination of these two functions, however, gives us our magnificent business system.

One might say that this is all very obvious and that business is, after all, a very simple thing. One should go further, however, and consider that the performance of each of these functions is dependent upon the intelligent operation of scores of lesser, or assisting, functions, which, though subordinate in scope, are indispensable to the proper development of the two essential functions. Among these assisting functions are such things as accounting, advertising, organizing, financing, purchasing, office management, factory and store management, transportation management and many other activities. Each of these is a complete study in itself, and it is upon the knowledge, ability, and skill of the executives and operatives in charge of these and similar departments that the success of a business is largely dependent.

This book is limited in its scope to the treatment of the elements involved in the organizing and financing of business in its numerous forms.

Organizing the business. *Organization of a business* in this text must be taken to mean the formation or original creation of a business enterprise in any of its several legal forms, and not the internal or departmental organization for purposes of operation, which is sometimes referred to by this phrase.

Faced with the problem of organizing or starting a new business in any particular line, the organizer must first select the form of business organization he will use. In this matter, there is a wide choice; the principal forms will be discussed in Chapters III and IV.

Preliminary definitions. As we go into the study of finance, we shall come to hundreds of names and terms more or less peculiar to the subject and shall learn the significance of each in turn. There are a few basic definitions, however, which we must have at the very start in order to lay a working foundation. These are the terms *funds, credit,* and *capital.*

Funds. *Funds* constitute the prime requirement in starting and operating any business enterprise, and by far the largest of all financial activities consists of the raising and management of funds.

The word has been defined as follows:

(*a*) "Cash or its equivalent; that is, checks, drafts, money orders, and so forth. The term may be used to include securities which have a ready market and which can be quickly liquidated."[2]

(*b*) "A *fund* is a collection, or store, or amount of something by means of which purchases and payments may be made. The word funds signifies any and all things which may be currently used in a community in exchange for goods or property of others."[3]

(*c*) "Funds include all the instruments and instrumentalities whereby the exchange of goods is facilitated, and include money, credit money, and credit."[4]

Credit. *Credit,* which is one of the subdivisions of funds, is the ability to buy with a promise to pay; that is, to receive or procure goods or services and obtain title to them at the present time, although the actual payment is deferred until a future date. Concisely expressed, *credit is the power to obtain goods or services by giving a promise to pay money on demand or at some specified date in the future.*

Modern business is conducted very largely on a credit basis. In a complete transaction, such as the production and marketing of a given article, there are many processes that consume considerable time, and only the continuous and successive passing and acceptance of credit all along the line enables the various business houses involved to carry out their re-

---

[2] G. G. Munn, *Encyclopedia of Banking and Finance* (Cambridge, Mass.: Bankers' Pub. Co., 1949).

[3] Frederick A. Cleveland, *Funds and Their Uses* (New York: D. Appleton & Co., 1922).

[4] Charles W. Gerstenberg, *Financial Organization and Management of Business,* 3rd rev. ed. (Englewood Cliffs, N.J.: Prentice-Hall, Inc., 1951).

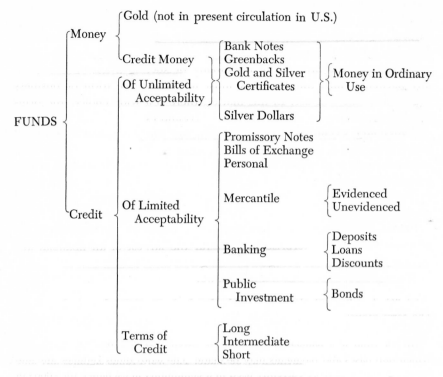

Divisions and Subdivisions of Funds

spective parts. In the diagram of funds shown above, there appears also an outline on credit, but a few words of explanation are probably in order.

1. Personal credit, as the name implies, is the credit used by an individual, but not in a business capacity. The credit on which one carries a monthly account with the grocer or butcher is usually based solely upon one's personality. Likewise, a person's ability to borrow small amounts at the bank on an ordinary note is due to his personal credit. As we shall see later, the credit of a partnership is often based largely upon the personal credit of the members of the firm, rather than upon the business strength of the firm itself.

2. Mercantile credit is that employed in general by business firms of all types in carrying on their activities. It aids in all production, manufacturing, and mercantile transactions from the time raw materials are gathered until the finished product is received by the retailer. This mercantile credit may be *evidenced* or *unevidenced*.

3. Evidenced credit means credit in which the creditor holds some kind of document or paper from the debtor acknowledging the debt or promising to pay. Holders of such credit instruments may frequently negotiate or discount them before maturity, thus making available to themselves the cash represented by the credit item, less interest to maturity. *Unevidenced credit* is credit in which the creditor has no credit instrument, but rather carries the claim as an open account. He expects to collect it at the end of the credit term, or he may assign or sell the account before that time.

Banking credit consists of the deposits, loans, and discounts of a banking house.

Public credit is that enjoyed by any political entity.

Investment credit is represented by bonds. Bonds are promises (of either corporate or public borrowers) to repay specified sums of money at some future time.

Capital. The term *capital* has been used by economists, accountants, and financiers in so many cases and with so many shades of meaning that it is practically impossible today to apply to it any fixed definition applicable to all cases. From the general point of view, however, capital means all the property of every kind employed by the business, though, accountants express it as the total ownership in the business, consisting of the amount invested, the surplus, and the undivided profits, that is, the net worth.

The word *capital* must not be confused with *capitalization* and *capital stock*, which indicate quite different things, as will be shown, later.

Capital property. *Capital property* is a term generally used to designate property of every type that constitutes the capital of any enterprise. It may be viewed as comprising two kinds: *capital goods* and *capital rights*. *Capital goods* consist of cash, buildings, real estate, inventory, equipment, machinery, rolling stock, and other such capital property. *Capital rights* embrace stocks, bonds, notes and securities in general owned by a business, which carry the rights assigned to them and which are normally convertible into goods (usually cash), either by redemption or by sale.

Capital value. The term *capital value* explains itself, but attention must be called to its several types and subdivisions.

In any company that has been in operation to any extent, there is, or should be, a great difference between the original capital value and the present capital value. The former represents the capital value at the inception of the business; the latter at the present time. It is well to note, also, that there is a distinction made between the *nominal* and *actual* original capital value. Nominally, the original capital value is the authorized par value of all stocks and bonds of the company; but actual original capital value is, of course, the amount actually paid in on those securities. The present capital value consists of the stock and bonds (original proprietorship), in addition to the existing surplus.

Fixed and liquid capital. *Fixed capital* is capital represented by fixed assets. These are assets to be used in the conduct of the business, generally without change of form: nontrading assets, such as land, buildings, equipment, machinery, furniture, and fixtures. These assets are of a permanent nature and, in the ordinary course of business, will not be converted into cash; their value would often be sacrificed if the attempt were made to convert them into cash through quick sale.

Liquid capital, known also as current, quick, or fluid capital is capital represented by cash or other assets that, in the ordinary course of business, will be converted into cash, and that ordinarily can be converted into cash by a quick sale without having their value greatly sacrificed. These liquid assets, other than cash, consist of such things as raw materials, finished goods, accounts receivable, and notes receivable.

Interrelated subjects. The study of finance is most intimately related to that of economics, accounting, business law, and business management. These five subjects overlap and interlace so persistently that it is impossible to go into any one of them without penetrating to a considerable extent into the other four. We shall not, in our present study of the organizing and financing of business, slight any principle of economics, fact of law, feature of accounting, or rule of management that may be necessary for an understanding of our subject, but we shall touch on them as lightly as possible and in a purely nontechnical manner, leaving the exposition of these subjects to their proper courses and textbooks.

Tools of the trade. We have seen that financing a business, which we may call financial management, production and marketing are not independent functions within a business. Each function depends upon a knowledge of the problems of the other functions. Combining the results of these functions into one picture is the role of the accounting statement. Therefore, to manage a business and its financial affairs wisely, at least an elementary knowledge of accounting and the method of analyzing accounting statements is necessary.

Throughout this book, reference will be made to financial reports of the business. By this term is meant the balance sheet and the statement of income, profit and loss. The latter is often referred to as the "income statement." It is from these financial reports that the businessman charts his course of action and measures his progress.

These reports, of course, must be accurate in terms of addition and subtraction—that is easy. But to serve as a chart, financial reports must be much more than accurate. Suppose you were going on a trip by auto from your home to a city five hundred miles distant. Would you appreciate it if the road map was beautiful in color, with the cities in the correct geographical location, but with the roads not marked? Would you get there? Or what would happen if a marine chart was marked with the harbors correctly placed, but without the depth of the water. A ship depending upon this chart would more than likely run aground. The same result would happen if a businessman relied upon statements that were incomplete, no matter how prettily they were dressed up. Financial statements purport to reflect the financial condition of a business. As such they are used by internal management, i.e., board of directors, officers and other key men. These men, incidentally, see and study a great many detailed reports on financial transactions which do not appear in the financial statements furnished to stockholders and creditors.

But both the management and others feel, however, that financial statements have at least two limitations. First, accounting is not an exact science like chemistry or physics. There still remains a great deal of difference of opinion among accountants how certain assets, such as inventory, buildings, and equipment, are to be evaluated, or how certain charges such as depreciation are to be computed. Even where one company's financial progress is to be compared from one year to the next, certain difficulties are presented.

Second, financial statements are made up periodically, that is, at year end, or semiannually, or even quarterly. A great many transactions involving the flow of funds, therefore, are not reported in the financial statements because they originate and are completed during the interim between statements. Movement of inventory, short-term loans, turnover of accounts receivable are necessarily only partially reported as these transactions are initiated and completed between accounting periods. These problems, however, are of more concern to the creditor, the stockholder and the financial analyst than to the treasurer who, as we have mentioned, has direct access to the accounting records.

Although a thorough understanding of accounting is of great value to the financial manager or analyst, it is not necessary to be an accountant in order to study and to understand finance or financial statements. Some familiarity with accounting terminology, as well as a knowledge of the difference between a balance sheet and a statement of income, will not only facilitate your understanding of the subject, but will, at the same time, make your study of finance much more interesting.

The financial statement. A balance sheet is a statement of the assets of the business on the one side of the statement (the left side) balanced off on the other side (the right side) by a statement of the liabilities (debts of the business) to its creditors, plus the net worth. Net worth, or capital, represents the contribution of the owners, whether it be a single proprietor, partnership, corporation, or some other form of business organization. This relationship can be summarized by saying that assets equal liabilities plus capital. From that it is easy to understand also that assets minus liabilities equal capital.

Assets may be defined as something of value possessed by the business. That does not mean in all cases, however, that the asset can be turned into cash, or even that it has a cash value. Assets may, for our preliminary understanding of the balance sheet, be divided into those assets which are current, and those which we shall call long-term or fixed assets. Students of accounting will be more precise in classifying and naming these non-current assets. Current assets have also sometimes been called circulating assets by those who wished to emphasize the changing nature of these assets as a result of the day-to-day operations of the business. Cash is used to purchase inventory and inventory, when sold, becomes cash or accounts receivable. Accounts receivable, in turn, becomes cash as the customers pay for the goods they have purchased.

The management of these assets, i.e., cash, accounts receivable, and inventory, demand close attention of the financial manager, who must at all times have funds on hand to pay the employees their wages at the end of the week, the landlord his rent, the bank its interest, and the creditors for the goods and services purchased by the firm. If the treasurer does not have funds, he must at least have access to short-term lenders of money. The sales manager and the production managers will cooperate so that there will be inventory on hand to sell. However, the treasurer will want to assure himself that there is not an unnecessarily large amount of funds tied up in excess inventory or in accounts receivable.

The planning and management of inventory is a subject in itself, involving the most efficient use of equipment, labor and capital. Inventory may cost 15 to 25 per cent of its own value in a year. That is, the cost of storage space, warehouse costs and equipment, insurance, waste and other factors account for a cost of fifteen to twenty-five cents on the dollar of inventory stored during the period of a year. Having inventory in excess of the business needs is, therefore, wasteful. The sales manager would often find it easier if the terms of credit were more liberal. Usually, more sales could be made if the customer had sixty days to pay the bill than if the customer had only ten days. But tying up funds in accounts receivable is seldom to the liking of the treasurer who must meet bills now, not sixty days from now.

Astute management of the current assets is important not only because these are the assets which form the company's trading assets and, therefore, the usual source of profit or loss, but also because they are continuously being traded. Fixed assets once acquired need relatively little attention other than proper maintenance.

Fixed or non-current assets consist of investments which the company plans to hold for more than a year. These may represent money invested in subsidiary companies or in stocks or bonds of other companies. By far the greatest proportion of fixed assets, however, is represented by land, building and equipment. Although the building and equipment account changes from year to year as new additions are made or old equipment wears out, this section of the asset side of the balance sheet

is likely to remain relatively static. That does not mean, however, that
the executives of the company need pay little attention to the management of the buildings, equipment and other fixed assets. In some industries, the railroad and the electric and gas utilities, for example, plant
and equipment constitute by far the greatest portion of the total investment. Proper management of the assets represented in this portion of
the balance sheet may vitally effect the ability of the business to produce
inventory and profit.

Other non-current assets are goodwill, patents, and prepaid expenses.
Usually these represent but a small part of the total and will be considered elsewhere in the text.

On the right hand side of the balance sheet the liabilities, or debts of
the business, are likewise divided into current and fixed. Current liabilities are those debts which mature within one year from the date of the
balance sheet. Accounts payable for goods received, notes payable for
short-term bank loans or to trade creditors, income taxes which will
shortly fall due, and wages due though not yet payable at the date of
the balance sheet, make up the bulk of the current debts. Long-term debt
is made up of debts payable some time more than a year in the future.
These debts may be in the form of promissory notes; more often they are
evidenced by bonds.

Net worth, or capital, comprises the other section of the right side of
the balance sheet. In this section is found the owners' investment in the
business. In a single proprietorship and partnership, the sum set forth is
the owners' investment. In a corporation it represents the original contribution of the stockholders plus retained profits of the business and
other surplus. The character of this surplus will be considered fully in
subsequent chapters.

The statement of income is a summary statement of the business
activity during the period covered by the statement. If the income statement is an annual report, the first line of the statement will represent
the dollar amount of sales for the year. Subtracted from the gross sales
will be any returns of merchandise or allowances agreed to by the
seller. From this net figure will be subtracted the expenses incurred by
the company in earning its operating income.

Often a company will have other sources of income either from subsidiary enterprises or from investments. Sometimes this income will be
added to the operating income and the expenses incurred in earning the
income will be subtracted from the total. At times accountants may form
this into a separate section of the income statement. It depends upon the
manner in which the management separates its activities. Expenses of a
manufacturing company would include the raw materials consumed,
wages, selling and administrative expenses, cost of power, light, heat,
maintenance of grounds, building, and equipment, depreciation, interest

costs, and other items which contributed to the salable product. The result of subtracting costs from income is profit. Of course, not all of this profit is available to the owners. Income tax must be paid. Net income after taxes is available to the owners of the business.

There must certainly be a close relationship between the profit earned by the business and the owners' investment in the business. It is a compensation for the use of the capital and the risk undertaken. If the current interest rate paid by a savings bank is 3 per cent, it is not hard to see that a small businessman would prefer to leave his money in the bank and receive this amount with virtually no risk rather than invest the same sum of money in a business risk and receive the same amount of profit. How much in excess of 3 per cent would be necessary to attract his capital depends upon the risk he takes. Naturally, the greater the risk undertaken the higher the return necessary to attract his capital. The same thoughts motivate corporate investors. If the rate of profit earned on net worth does not justify the risk, then the stockholders will seek means of improving the profits, or of liquidating their investment if possible.

Social responsibility of business. Business has grown tremendously in size since our country became a nation. In 1800 there were probably no more than 250 private corporations, and these were mostly quasi-public in nature.[5] Business concerns were mostly small, employing but a few people. Difficulties of communication and transportation tended to keep business units small and dependent upon the locality for sales. As our nation grew and transportation of raw materials and finished products at reasonable rates became feasible, business units grew in size.

Unfortunately businessmen too seldom felt a sense of social obligation. When corporations became larger and larger, monopoly, unfair business practices, fraud, and exploitation of the worker were frequently associated with them. Questionable financial practices often led to business losses and perhaps to business depression. Many terms have been used to describe this era. Materialistic capitalism, rugged individualism, or what you will, are descriptive of an era of an unrestrained seeking for power and profit by some greedy capitalists.

It must not be imagined, nevertheless, that no good came out of this period. Quite the contrary. The big steel companies, the transcontinental railroads, the unparalleled development of electrical power came about in spite of the business ethics of the times, ethical standards which would not be tolerated today. Not only do governmental agencies like the Securities and Exchange Commission watch closely the financial and other

---

[5] Only eight manufacturing businesses were incorporated in the United States in the year 1800. Danis, *Essays in the Earlier History of American Corporation,* II, Harvard Economic Studies, No. 16. Cambridge, Mass.: 1917.

business practices of large corporations, but there seems to have developed a high sense of social obligation on the part of management toward the community, its employees, and its stockholders. The growth of all three forces have been nothing less than phenomenal in the past twenty years. For example, Westinghouse Electric Corporation in the period between 1938 and 1957 increased its average number of employees from 42,402 to 128,572. Sales increased during the same period from one million, eight hundred thousand to over $2 billion. Consolidated Edison, in the post World War II period of ten years from 1947 to 1956, added almost $800,000,000 to its assets. Directors could no longer treat giant corporations as pawns in a game of power. The security and economic welfare of the country demanded otherwise.

Questions for Study and Review

1. What advantages does the study of business in modern schools of business have over the old apprentice system of training? Do you think it possible to prepare for executive responsibility in a large corporation without a college education?
2. What do you mean by the term *business?* Into what two main groups may business be divided?
3. Discuss the economic purpose of business. What part does finance play in achieving the purpose?
4. What is the function of the financial executive in a business? Discuss his relationship to the other executives.
5. Define: funds; credit; mercantile credit; capital; capital property.
6. What is the relationship between assets, liabilities and net worth on a balance sheet? In what ways can assets be increased?
7. What is a profit and loss or income statement?
8. Define: current assets; current liabilities; fixed assets.

CHAPTER II

Starting a Business

General considerations. Presuming that we admit, as stated in the preceding chapter, that "business" consists of all of those activities of every kind by means of which human wants are supplied, we must realize that these activities are widespread and complicated in nature. No longer can one person, one family, or one group produce all, or even a small part, of all the articles, substances, or services required for modern living. An inventory and analysis of the articles in a single household would show their origin in, and association with, thousands of different businesses in connection with their production and distribution. These goods are obtained by the population at large by purchase on a monetary basis, and the considerable majority of the purchasing public obtains the money by working on a wage or salary basis for these businesses. But others must organize, manage, and operate these businesses, in order that the desired goods may be produced, and that the workers may have the employment by which to earn the money wage needed for their purchases.

This study is not concerned primarily with those persons who determine to live as "employees" or wage earners, but rather with the activities of those who choose to organize, manage, and operate businesses, either individually or in conjunction with others. Many determine every year to "go into business." For these there are two primary decisions to make: First, what type of business shall be chosen, manufacturing, merchandising, mining, transportation, utilities, banking, real estate, or insurance? Second, what legal form of organization shall be used, proprietorship, partnership, corporation, or other type.

The answer to the first of these two questions is very largely preinfluenced by the prior life of the prospective business organizer. The strong tendency is to enter into a field with which the organizer has some knowledge or experience. If he has been employed in the building and construction business for some years, not only would his natural tendencies urge him to enter that or some kindred field, but he would be much better prepared to make a success of it than he would of a banking house or a retail store. There are thousands of little details of information, "tricks of the trade" so called, which come only with experience, and without them success is doubly difficult. In the great majority of cases it is the experienced shoe clerk who opens the new shoe store, the assistant pharmacist who starts the new drug store; the customers' men, economists, and experienced security salesmen who organize brokerage firms, as well as thousands of those who simply follow their fathers into their businesses.

The second preliminary question as stated above is: what legal form of organization shall be used? This has to be determined upon before any organizational activities can take place and, of course, cannot be decided upon until the organizer or his advisor know what the various forms are, together with the characteristics of each in detail. The several forms—proprietorship, general partnership, limited partnership, joint venture (syndicate), joint stock company, business trust (often called Massachusetts trust), and corporation—have their various characteristics as to methods of formation, liability of financing, distribution of profits, flexibility as to expansion and so forth.

Chapter III and subsequent chapters are devoted to analyzing and outlining the several forms so that the proper one may be more accurately selected and the remainder of this chapter will be used to discuss other preliminary activities of the organization of a business, generally known as "promotion."

Of the great number of persons who go into business for themselves, only a small number, estimated by various economists as from 10 per cent to 20 per cent, meet with sufficient success to enable them to remain in business while the others make failures of their attempts. Practically all of these failures can be attributed to a lack of business knowledge on the part of those concerned. If they knew enough of business principles, methods, and practices they could generally foresee that their business was doomed to failure even before it was started, largely because the demand which the business will serve is not large enough to insure sufficient return to pay all operating expenses, interest on borrowed capital, taxes and other expenses. Again, the prospective businessman must remember that all business consists of supplying human wants or needs and that he must determine in advance whether the goods he proposes to manufacture or deal in are those that people want or can be induced to want; that is, is there an existing demand or the possibility of creating a demand?

If it can be shown that there is a demand of substantial size, capable of sustaining production and sale of a product at a profit, it must then be determined how completely that product is already being supplied by others, that is, what competition will be encountered. As an example, let us suppose that in a certain town there is just sufficient retail demand for shoes to support four existing shoe stores. The opening of a fifth shoe store will indeed be a hazardous undertaking. This is not because shoes are not in demand, but because in this town this demand is completely filled.

If the new store should get its proportionate part of the available business, so that the trade is divided into five parts instead of four, no one of the shops will be making a profit and the one with the least reserve power, capital, or general ability must fail. This generally means failure of the new concern rather than that of one of the four old and established ones. If, however, the new store is greatly superior to the old ones, having better goods, better service, more modern and attractive equipment, better location, more convincing advertising, and so on, it may well attract from the other shops sufficient of their trade to succeed, while one of the others must fail. But this does not improve the economic situation, for we still have a failure of one store out of five caused directly by the opening of the new business.

But even in the event of ample demand with inconsiderable competition, it is highly unwise to enter business in any field without a fairly sound knowledge of business and business principles. In the not far distant past, it was generally believed that this essential knowledge could be obtained only by experience and hard knocks. Today, however, experience is bolstered up by scholastic study and it is the combination of the two that creates the successful businessman. The young men and women who are, today, occupying junior positions in the business and commercial world, and who at the same time are taking well-designed business courses in our various colleges of business administration are unquestionably destined to make our great business leaders of tomorrow. At this very moment hundreds of scouts are canvassing the universities seeking likely graduates in business courses to help fill their great demand for individuals with the fundamental training in business subjects. These graduates are being snapped up and given initial salaries which a very few years ago would have been considered fabulous.

Promoting a business. A business does not spring, Athena-like, fully formed, from the brow of some commercial Zeus, but can properly come into being only after the painstaking performance of many preliminary activities. All of these things which must be done to bring a business into existence are known under the general name of *promotion*. This term embraces such activities as the careful investigation of the entire proposition to determine (1) the probability of its being profitable, (2) the amount of funds that will be necessary to start it and continue it on a sound basis, (3) the possibility of procuring the properly qualified associates, (4) the possibility of making all of the necessary contracts and procuring the required options, franchises, and charters, (5) the methods by means of which the necessary funds for the business shall be raised, and in most cases (6) the actual raising or procuring of the funds themselves.

Let us assume that we have conceived the idea of organizing and operating a large shoe manufacturing company. The first necessity is a competent promoter. This promoter may be an individual, an associated group of individuals, or an organization whose business is doing promotional work. The work of the promoter is for purposes of study divided into three parts, discovery, assembly, and financing.

Discovery. The term *discovery*, as applied to the first step in business promotion, means more than seeing or finding what appears to be a good opportunity to start an enterprise. It means more nearly the complete uncovering of the entire proposition through careful investigation and the determination of whether or not the enterprise should be undertaken. To assure the feasibility of the proposition, this discovery must show that the business will be profitable, how profitable it will be, and the amount of funds or capital necessary to inaugurate it. Consultations, studies, estimates, tentative contracts will establish the cost of necessary land, buildings, furniture, fixtures, and equipment. To this amount must be added the funds necessary to get the business started. That is, to pay all running expenses such as wages, salaries, rents, taxes, materials, heat, light, power, advertising and scores of other items until such time as the business begins to have its own income to take care of them. This is generally known as initial working capital and will be treated in some detail in Chapter XII.

Thousands of businesses fail every year principally because the promoters have not adequately provided for this and the businesses "run out of money," as they say, before they really get going. Having determined the full and complete capital requirements, the promoter must estimate the probable income which the business may expect. This requires primarily most intense market research to determine what may be expected in sales at specified prices. Further extensive study in the production field will disclose the cost of actually manufacturing our shoes in the quantities we propose. By adding together all expenses of operation and production and subtracting the sum from total receipts we have our estimate of the profit. It is not sufficient, however, that the promoter can assure a profit, but he must assure sufficient profit, that is, the profit must be sufficient to represent a fair return on all the capital involved in the business. Therefore, the amount of profit must be applied to the amount of capital to get it on a percentage basis. The percentage which should be earned varies in different businesses, the general opinion being that the more risky the type of business the higher the rate of earnings should be. This will be discussed at some length in Chapter X, Capitalizing the Corporation, but we may say here that a 10 per cent earnings rate (capitalization rate) is considered about the lowest possible, even for exceptionally safe and well established businesses. Sixteen to 20 per cent are fairly representative rates but very risky propositions sometimes go as high as 100 per cent.

Upon the completion of this discovery step in his activities, the promoter is presumed to have definitely established whether or not the starting of the business is justified from a financial point of view and he is justified in going forward to the assembly and financial steps. If, however, the discovery shows that the proposition is not financially justified, those he represents should abandon the idea, thereby in all probability, preventing large losses through failure.

It can readily be seen how important this discovery step is, and how much depends upon the skill, knowledge, experience, ability, and honesty of the promoter who is doing it. An apparently slight miscalculation on any one of the elements involved may cause the entire findings to be incorrect and may induce large investments in a profitless enterprise or the condemnation of one that is essentially sound.

Assembly. This second step in promotion embraces the various activities, other than financial, necessary to give absolute assurance that the proposition can be developed in accordance with the plans and without any danger of hold-up, delay, or possibly complete blocking, or other disappointments. It consists largely of procuring all necessary contracts, agreements, options, permits, and so on. We may require in our shoe manufacturing company a factory building whose cost has been estimated at $500,000. Unless we have a very definite agreement with a construction company that it will build this structure for us when and where, and how specified, we may find it impossible to procure the structure at the time and price we had planned. If we have chosen an ideal location for our factory but have not procured an ironbound option on it we may not be able to procure it or at least we may have to pay an unexpectedly high price. Rights of way for railroads and franchises to operate utilities in cities must be "nailed down" well in advance.

Sometimes a promoter may deem it wise to procure a contract with a supply house guaranteeing to supply certain materials in the quantity we want at the time we want it. Promoters have been known to have had certain prominent management personnel sign contracts to accept managerial positions with our company when organized. Neglecting to make sure of some apparently small detail may cause much trouble. Care must be taken to understand that assembly does not mean the physical assembling or procuring of assets such as grounds, building, furniture, machinery, and so on (this is usually known as the "construction" of the business). The actual construction is seldom begun until the entire promotion is complete and the necessary funds have been procured or assured in accordance with the financial plan.

Financing. When the discovery and assembly have been accomplished, it devolves upon the promoter to arrange for the financing of the proposition; that is, to devise the plans and method of raising the necessary funds for starting and carrying on the business.

A promoter's activities may be centered on developing an entirely new proposition, in arranging for some type of combination of several existing companies by means of consolidation, merger, or lease, or possibly planning for an expansion of a company. In any of these cases, he must make discovery and assembly along similar lines, but the financing for the different kinds of propositions may be by quite different methods. The financial arrangements for purposes of consolidation, merger, lease, or expansion will be discussed in later chapters, and the financing spoken of in this chapter will relate to that of a new enterprise.

If the business under consideration is comparatively small and the promoter is working it up as a private business for himself, using his own funds to start it, no question of the method of raising funds is involved. He simply puts into the business the money he has saved for the purpose, and probably some that he has been able to borrow.

It often happens, however, that the discovery shows the proposed business to be a larger financial burden than the promoter can carry. In that case, he may wish to acquire one or more partners to invest with him. His sole financing problem here is to find persons satisfactory to him who can be induced to invest the desired amount in the partnership.

The term financing, as applied to the promoter's activities, however, generally covers his work in devising methods of raising funds for the larger enterprise, which will, in all probability, be organized as a corporation or perhaps some similarly financed form, such as a joint stock company or a business trust. The latter two, however, are seldom used today.

Financing an enterprise of this sort usually involves the raising of funds for three distinct purposes:

1. *Financing during the organization period.* This means meeting the cost of all intangible property from the very start until the time when the business is ready to begin actual operation. It embraces expenses for such things as investigation of the project; procuring parties who may be willing to participate; preliminary engineering, legal, economic, and accounting advice on the project; canvass of territory to ascertain whether sufficient business can be procured; an estimate of the cost of the plant, of the income, and of the profit; the incorporation of the company, if it is to be incorporated; the securing of the franchises, if franchise is necessary. The funds for this purpose are usually advanced by the promoter himself, his associates, or his employers and, unless the work is successfully accomplished, this may entail a considerable loss.

2. *Financing the actual construction.* This means meeting the costs of

all tangible property. It covers the cost of real estate; labor, materials, and contractors' fees; machinery, furniture, fixtures, and equipment; engineering costs; expenses of the company organization during construction; taxes and insurance during construction; working capital; legal expenses; stores and supplies; and the various costs of carrying on the financing such as bankers' commissions or charges, discounts on bonds, and the promoter's profits. Proceeds from the sale of the company's securities (stocks or bonds or both) are properly used to defray this expense.

3. *Financing the business* means providing the funds needed over and above the actual receipts of the business to operate it until such time as the receipts are sufficient to cover all outgo. Many businesses have to operate for many months, some for several years, before this *break even point* is reached. The entire amount by which the receipts fall short of expenditures during this early stage of the business must be provided in advance by the organizers, and the promoter must be sure that it is arranged for in his financial plan. Funds for this purpose normally come from the sale of the company's securities.

Methods of financing. In making his plans for the financing of a proposed business, the promoter is limited to a choice between only two means. He can sell part ownership in the business or he can have the business borrow money for capital purposes. Often he devises a plan consisting of a combination of these two.

The person promoting and organizing a business entirely for himself contributes his own savings, thus, in effect, selling the entire ownership of the business to himself. If he takes in partners, he sells them parts of the ownership. In either case, of course, some borrowing may be resorted to for additional capital.

Passing these simple affairs for the moment, let us consider the problem of the promoter of a company that is to be a corporation or one of the similar forms, a joint stock company or a business trust. When he sells ownership, he sells shares in the business, and the buyers (at least in a corporation and joint stock company) are given *certificates of stock* indicating their ownership. When he has the business borrow some of its capital for a long term, the lenders are issued instruments acknowledging the loan and promising to repay it at a certain time. These are *bonds,* and this process of borrowing money for the company is known as *selling its bonds.* Bonds are seldom used in the initial financing, as the company is new, untried, and has not yet built up a favorable reputation or acquired sufficient property to render it a sound investment. Later on, when the company has built up a sound history and possesses valuable property which may be pledged as security, bonds are frequently used for financing expansions.

The promoter must decide upon the total amount of capital to raise, how much by the sale of stock and how much by the sale of bonds. He thus devises what is known as the *financial plan,* and the financing of the promotion, as well as the future success of the business itself, depends very largely upon the judgment and ability he displays in forming this plan. If the financing is on the basis of a public offering of the securities, he will undoubtedly receive valuable assistance in working out the plan from the investment bankers who will undertake the sale and distribution of the issues. The methods of formulating the financial plan or capital structure are described in detail in a later chapter.

The promoter. The promoter occupies a most important place in the financial and business world. His work lies in visualizing new organizations to serve business needs and combinations and expansions of existing businesses to work in a more economical and profitable manner; the investigation and assembling of these propositions; and, finally, the work of actually bringing them into existence by obtaining the interest of bankers, financiers, and the investing public. All these are activities without which the business world would soon stagnate.

The name *promoter* has been much abused and most people inexperienced in financial matters associate the work with a smooth individual trying to sell stock in some fraudulent plan or "get-rich-quick" scheme. Of course, there are plenty of such people who call themselves promoters. There have been cases when the public has been defrauded of millions of dollars through the sale of stock in nonexisting rubber plantations, gold mines devoid of gold, and building developments under water at high tide. The stories one hears of selling to visitors to New York stock in its Brooklyn Bridge, or Central Park, or the Woolworth Building for varying amounts are not at all fairy tales. Things such as these have actually been done a number of times, and the men who do them are self-styled promoters. They are, of course, merely confidence men and swindlers. The legitimate promoter is in no way to be confused with them. To be successful, a promoter must be capable, honest, and honorable. His entire stock in trade consists of his business ability and his reputation for successful and honorable promotion in the past.

The great majority of all business propositions are promoted by bankers, lawyers, engineering firms, and business executives, who frequently are the originators of the ideas, and also the ones to whom clients and friends bring their ideas to be materialized. These are known as occasional promoters, as distinguished from professional promoters, who devote their entire time and energy to promotional work.

The prospectus. In the promotion of a small business, the preparation of a formal written statement detailing the results of the discovery, advantages of the proposition, probable profits, and so on, is generally not necessary, as such details are presented orally to those whom the promoter desires to interest. Such a statement, when written out in detail, is termed a *prospectus* and is usually designed to present the proposition in the most favorable manner possible in order to interest people in investing in the enterprise. In a business in which it is planned to sell securities directly to the public without the aid of an investment banking house, a prospectus would in all probability be written in general terms and resemble more a good sales letter than a technical discussion, leaving it to a follow-up by a salesman or by correspondence to cover any inquiry for further details. When, however, the sale of securities is handled by an investment banker, a complete prospectus, substantiated by whatever data are available, will be expected.

In the case of securities offered in interstate commerce and registered with the Securities and Exchange Commission, a complete prospectus, drawn up in complete agreement with the registration statement, is required by law and offerings can be made only through such a prospectus. (See Chapter XI.)

Promoter's remuneration. Successful promoters receive quite large payment for their services. This remuneration, however, is generally in the form of stock in the company they are promoting, rather than in cash, so that, if the business is not a success, their stock is worthless. If, however, the venture succeeds, they have a good block of dividend-paying and marketable stock.

Many have complained that the large blocks of stock often given to the promoters are out of proportion to the value of their services. In some cases, this may be true; but promoters are paid not for their services alone, but also for the financial risks they take. A promoter of his own enterprise may spend from his private pocket thousands of dollars in investigating the proposition, only to find eventually that it is unsound and must be abandoned. This expenditure, then, is a total loss to him. A promoter cannot well insist upon payment in cash, rather than in stock, for that is immediately construed as an evidence that he lacks confidence in his proposition. Stock accepted by the promoter must sometimes be held for several years before the company gets on a dividend-paying basis, or before the stock attains an attractive price on the market. A more equitable method of payment is accomplished in some cases by remunerating the promoter in cash for all expenses advanced and paid by him and paying him in stock for his actual services.

Secret profits prohibited. There is no legal restriction or limit upon the amount of profit a promoter may make on any piece of work as long as the amount is arrived at and agreed upon openly and fairly between the promoter and his employers. The promoter is, however, barred by law from making a secret profit. A secret profit means any profit over and beyond that definitely agreed on, of which the employers have not been fully and completely informed and which they have not agreed to allow. It has been ruled at law that a profit is considered secret unless the promoter renders an *actual, full* and *frank* statement of profits made on any contract between him and his employers. *Actual* means that a real and definite statement of profits must be made and that a mere absence of intent to conceal or merely refraining from concealment is not a sufficient disclosure of facts. *Full* requires a specific statement of the *amount* of profits—a statement, for instance, that the promoter is making or expects to make an extra profit is not sufficient. *Frank* requires that the actual facts be given, not merely how or where they may be obtained.

If a promoter is discovered to have made a secret profit at the expense of the organization, the latter may repudiate all dealings with him and cancel his contract. It often happens, however, that the services of a particular promoter are practically indispensable and that the contract with him is too valuable to give up. In that case, the organizers may affirm the continuation of the contract and sue the promoter for any damages resulting from the abuse of his quasi-fiduciary powers. Often the matter is compromised by the organizers' holding to the contract, but taking over from the promoter the secret profits.

After the company is incorporated and is doing business under its bona fide board of directors, the promoter is no longer bound by his quasi-fiduciary relationship and may deal with the company just as may any other outsider. This ability to act without restriction of any kind is known as *dealing with the corporation at arm's length.*

Legal status of the promoter. The promoter occupies a rather peculiar position in relation to the organizers and the prospective stockholders of the proposed corporation. He is not an agent for the corporation, because it does not yet exist in the eyes of the law and, hence, cannot be a party to an agency contract. Most of his acts and dealings, however, are like the acts of an agent dealing for a legitimate principal. It must be understood by all parties dealing with him that all contracts and agreements made with him as the representative of the corporation-to-be, are merely tentative and do not become firm contracts until adopted by the corporation upon its formation. Of course, such contracts are seldom declined by the corporation. Many express the relation of the promoter to his company as being in a quasi-fiduciary capacity, others express the same meaning by saying that he occupies a position of semi-trust.

Relations between joint promoters. Often two or more persons will unite their efforts as *joint promoters* of the same proposition. This often brings up the question as to whether they are to be considered as partners in this activity. The universal ruling is that joint promoters are not ipso-facto partners. This means that they are not considered partners simply because of the fact that they are joint promoters. Of course, if they have actually entered into a partnership contract in the matter, then they are partners. This is very important in connection with their individual liability for indebtedness or damages. (See Chapter III on part-nerships.)

Promoters are not compelled to carry a proposition through to com-pletion against their best judgment and may give it up at any time for cause, provided they do not violate the terms of any specific agreement. It is, in reality, the actual duty of every promoter to give up immediately the promotion of any business that he determines will be unprofitable. Such abandonment, of course, will often entail upon him considerable loss, particularly if he is promoting on his own account and has advanced considerable sums to carry on the preliminary stages of the promotion. Some unscrupulous promoters will, therefore, carry along a doubtful pro-motion until such time as they can unload it on someone at a price that will enable them at least to break even.

Summary. The prospective businessman, then, if he wishes to have a fair assurance of success, should have at least some business education and experience and some specific knowledge of the field he expects to enter. Many who do not have these qualifications attempt to compensate for them by employing trained and experienced managers. It is some-times possible to succeed by this method, but hired brains rarely take the place of proper business knowledge and ability on the part of the principal. And a business so conducted often fails before the owner has been able to develop sufficient ability by association and practice to conduct the business himself.

He must know the great importance of proper promotion, especially the preliminary investigation. He must decide whether he has the ability to do this promotion work or whether he must trust it to another. In case he decides on the latter course, he must know just what to expect from the relationship and must exercise the keenest judgment in selecting his promoter.

He must know, also, which *form of business organization,* as listed in Chapter III, is best suited to the needs of his business, and he must select the most desirable one. Chapters immediately following are devoted to a somewhat detailed description of these various forms of organization, showing their respective advantages and disadvantages.

Questions for Study and Review

1. Would a more general knowledge of business principles and methods tend to reduce the percentage of failures? How?
2. Explain the importance of choosing a business that will fill an economic demand.
3. What is meant by the term *promotion?*
4. Name and explain the three steps in promotion.
5. Before advancing beyond the discovery step in promotion and especially before attempting to raise funds for a proposed enterprise, of what should the promoter give unquestionable assurance?

6. Name and explain the three purposes for which initial funds are raised by the promoter.

7. In how many ways can funds for an enterprise be raised? What are they?

8. Discuss the importance of the promoter's position.

9. Discuss methods of the remuneration of *promoters*.

10. Discuss in detail the topic *Secret Profits by Promoters*.

11. Are joint promoters of the same proposition partners? Discuss.

Problems

1. John Able and Charles Able live in a small town which is rapidly growing into a city because of the erection of two factories on the outskirts and the great influx of population. John is considering the organization of a company to operate a bus line within the town and about ten miles out into the country which, although now sparsely populated, will probably build up in the next three or four years. Charles, a part-time inventor, has developed a new plastic kitchen utensil. Outline how each would promote his idea, developing your answer in accordance with the three steps in the text.

2. Mr. Smythe has $25,000 capital and is thinking seriously of opening a book, card and novelty store. He finds that he can rent a store in a shopping center in a newly established residential neighborhood and can purchase a full inventory for $18,000. At the same time, he finds he can buy an already established business in a well-settled old neighborhood for $25,000. What factors would Mr. Smythe have to consider in making his choice?

3. After two years of successful management, Mr. S. finds that if he had $5,000 additional capital he could take advantage of the liberal discount on greeting cards for anticipating payment before the due date, and also add a line of plastic ships and airplanes for the "do-it-yourself" hobbyists. To what sources might he turn for the additional funds? Discuss the advantages and disadvantages of each.

4. Messrs. Allen, Babcock and Chase retain Mr. Sloan as a promoter to ascertain the profitability of a pickle works. Mr. Sloan convinces them of the need for the product and its profitability. He finds a suitable piece of land priced at $50,000. Another piece of land immediately adjoining can be acquired for $20,000 though it is not suitable for the erection of a factory. Mr. Sloan purchases both parcels for $70,000 with his own capital. As a promoter he sells the $50,000 parcels to the organization for $75,000. A year later, Messrs. Allen, Babcock and Chase sue Mr. Sloan for earning a secret profit of $25,000. (a) What will be the result of their suit? (b) If Mr. Sloan operates the second parcel as a parking lot for employees, do Allen, Babcock and Chase have any remedies against him?

5. Mr. Samuels sells some uranium stock which he is promoting to Mr. Brown, saying, "I am told by engineers that, in their opinion, this land has uranium in it." Subsequent tests prove the engineers wrong in their opinion and, as a result of the failure of the company, the stock became worthless. Can Mr. Brown sue Mr. Samuels, and on what grounds? On the other hand, supposing Mr. Samuels told Mr. Brown that, "In his opinion, the land contained uranium," could Mr. Brown sue?

Choosing the Form of Business Organization

Forms of business organization. Probably the first business was founded in some prehistoric time when one who had more of something than he needed bartered it for some other article he desired. Eventually, certain articles desired by everyone, thus making them generally acceptable, were adopted as a medium of exchange. Then those who had acquired or who had manufactured articles in excess of their own needs sold their products, taking some medium of exchange—usually gold, silver, or some baser metal—in return. The step next taken was the acquisition of goods by those possessed of funds, to be resold at a profit, and we have the foundations of business as it exists today.

The first type of business organization was the individual proprietorship, in which one person owned his stock of trade or conducted his crude manufacturing entirely for his own profit. The individual proprietorship is the most common of all forms of business organization today; its simplicity recommends it for the small business. But as soon as men began to combine their abilities and capital in various undertakings, other forms of business organization developed. Originally, some of the forms may not have borne much resemblance to what they are today, for the process was one of evolution with adaptations to our ever-changing economic environment.

In this and succeeding chapters, we shall study those forms that are in use today. They are:

1. Individual proprietorship.
2. General partnership.
3. Limited partnership.
4. Joint venture.
5. Joint-stock company.
6. Limited partnership association.
7. Massachusetts Trust.
8. Corporation.

The student may well wonder why it is necessary to have so many forms of organization but, as we undertake the study of each, it will be seen that they represent merely a desire on the part of businessmen to find a means of obtaining for each participant the desired proportion of income, risk, and control of the enterprise.

Factors in choosing a form of organization. No form of business organization yet devised is equally satisfactory for all businesses. All have certain advantages and disadvantages, and the business organizer should select, if possible, the particular form which will show the greatest number of desirable features and the smallest number of undesirable features when applied to his particular circumstances and desires. A characteristic which is distinctly desirable from one point of view may be equally undesirable from another.

When facing the problem of deciding what form is best for a certain business, the size of the business is often the determining factor, because that one point may narrow the choice to two or three of the forms. However, in studying the various types of business organization, a consideration of the following questions with regard to the characteristics of each will help in the decision as to whether it meets the needs of the particular business.

1. Is the formation simple or difficult?
2. What is the feasibility of aggregating sufficient sums of money for the purpose of the business?
3. How is the risk shared, and what is the liability of the owners?
4. In whom shall rest the authority and responsibility of management?
5. What stability does this form offer?
6. Does it offer flexibility as to expansion, management, and movement?
7. What is the legal status of this form as applied to my business?
8. To what extent is it free from government control?
9. What is the tax status of the form of organization?

Facility of formation. Some forms of business organization require almost no effort to start, but others may involve difficult and expensive legal proceedings occupying considerable time. Some have to be most carefully contrived to be permitted to organize under the laws of the respective states. The small-business organizer will do well, if possible, to avoid complicated forms and organize in as simple and easy a manner as his type of business will permit. Of course, the more difficult forms often possess features or advantages necessary to the welfare of his business, in which case the extra trouble and expense of organization are justified.

Feasibility of aggregating capital. Many thousands of promising businesses have been wrecked because their organizers were unable to raise a few extra dollars of capital. An organizer must make a liberally adequate estimate of the amount of capital needed to make a success of his business enterprise, and he must choose a form of organization that will unquestionably make possible the raising of this amount. If he himself has sufficient personal wealth, he may start individually and independently; otherwise, he may associate with himself other individuals who are able and willing to put together sufficient funds for the purpose. If, however, he anticipates a big business, needing very large capital and probably increasing from time to time, he must invariably choose a form of organization in which ownership can be sold in small units to large numbers of investors.

Sharing of risk. The risk of loss that one may assume through liability for the company's debts in case of failure is one of the most important considerations in entering into or investing in a business. It is largely upon the risk involved that an investor will base his opinion as to the amount of return he will demand on his investment. In some forms of business organization, the personal property of the owners may be claimed by the company's creditors, and, when this is possible the expected return must be high to warrant the investment. Creditors are always the potential owners of a business; so the investor in any business must look beyond hoped-for prosperity to possible insolvency and determine who, in that event, must share the loss and to what extent the creditors can come back upon him or upon his individual resources.

Before investing in a business in which he assumes considerable risk, the investor will do well to see that the form of organization is such as to give him considerable control. The greater the risk involved, the greater is the control desirable.

Authority in management. In the various types of organization, authority is vested in different ways. In some lines of business the personal element of the owner is highly necessary; in others it is not. When such owner personality is needed in the conduct of the business, it can be obtained by choosing a form like the individual proprietorship or partnership. Conversely where a firm is large and where authority must be delegated, a form of organization like the corporation may be necessary.

Stability of organization. It is highly important to the investors and to all other persons with whom the business has to deal that the business have stability and also a certain degree of permanency; if its life is limited, it should be to some definitely known period. Some forms of organization, as we shall see later in this chapter, are subject to sudden and unexpected dissolution for many reasons beyond the control of the owners, while others have continuous and uninterrupted existence.

The flexibility of expansion, management, and movement. It is desirable at the outset to provide a form of organization that will permit expected expansion of the business without complete reorganization at some future date. As the business grows, the problems of management will also increase, and there must be adequate provision for the necessary delegation of authority. In some businesses, it is very important that the business be able to establish branches or agencies for doing business in several places or in different states. For some forms this is easy; for others it is beset with restrictions, legal provisions, and expenses. It is wise to make a study of this particular feature of each form of organization before selecting one.

Legal status. Every form of business organization is governed by laws of some kind, and there are many restrictions as to what certain forms may do. Those formed under definite statutes must live up to the very letter of the law. The laws relating to partnership are well crystallized in the uniform partnership law, but the laws of corporations differ widely in practically every state. Many occupations, such as those of medicine, dentistry, law, and pharmacy, can be engaged in only by persons with particular qualifications, proved by strict examination and attested by specific licenses. In many states, such businesses as real estate, insurance brokerage, accountancy, and teaching are also limited to persons obtaining state licenses. In most jurisdictions, physicians and lawyers are denied the privilege of incorporating and hence must operate as individuals or partnerships. Regardless of what one may know about business methods and operation, it is good practice to employ the service of a capable lawyer in establishing the true legal status of a business in any given jurisdiction.

Government control. Beyond legislating as to what shall constitute certain forms of organization, the various states, as well as the national government, exercise considerable control and regulative power over the conduct of business in general. Private enterprises enjoy far more freedom with regard to this governmental regulation than do those engaged in public service, but even certain forms of private businesses are subject to close governmental regulation and visitation. The corporation is more closely supervised than any other form, but the individual proprietorship and partnership are almost unaffected. This governmental regulation is intended to promote the economic welfare of all, but frequently it becomes irksome to the company itself. Very often, if the organizers see beforehand that it will be too much of a burden, they will seek to find, if possible, some other form or organization upon which government supervision does not bear so heavily.[1]

---

[1] Note here and in all following paragraphs concerning governmental regulation or control of any type of business, that, during World War II, the national government, in the interest of national defense, assumed a control and direction of businesses of every type theretofore unknown in this country. For a number of years past however, these government restrictions on business have been gradually relaxed so that they are now no longer particularly oppressive, but it seems very doubtful that business as a whole will regain the almost utter freedom of action it enjoyed in the prewar days.

Tax status of the form of organization. It is possible that the choice of the most desirable business organization may depend upon the tax status accorded it by both federal and state governments. For example, a corporation must pay a tax to the state at the time of its organization and in addition certain filing fees. Partnerships do not pay an organization tax. Corporations, and in some states other forms of organization whose ownership is divided into transferable shares, may be subject to an annual state franchise tax based on income or the amount of capital. Partnerships, unless they elect to be taxed as corporations (a privilege given them in the federal revenue code of 1954), pay no federal income tax, but the individual partners are taxed on their respective shares in the profits, whether or not the profits are withdrawn from the business. Corporations pay a federal income tax and, subject to a minor exemption, its shareholders pay income taxes on any dividends actually received. It may be seen, therefore, that corporation profits may be subject to double taxation. In addition, a corporation doing business in several states may find itself liable for taxes in these states. It may also be noticed that in some states and municipalities unincorporated business organizations may be subject to taxes on gross income. Today the tax status of the form of business organization is of great importance not only for those contemplating a small business venture but to those whose income is large enough to be subject to high income tax rates.

The individual proprietorship. The simplest and oldest form of business organization is the *individual* or, as it is sometimes called, *sole proprietorship*. It is, in a sense, a one-man organization, for the owner and proprietor is solely responsible for all the activities and liabilities of the business. In businesses in which the capital investment is small, this form of organization is most practical. No formality need accompany its formation. Every man has a right to engage in any lawful business without special sanction or permission from the state. There are, to be sure, special police regulations, such as the obtaining of licenses and building permits, that must be complied with in certain businesses and in some localities; but these regulations, which usually have in mind the protection of the public health and safety, are restrictions upon the business itself and not upon the right of an individual to engage in that business.

The individual proprietorship is popular today in spite of the concentration of so much of our economic activity in large business units. It is entirely flexible as to management: the owner may discontinue one form of activity and take on another at will, and he may engage in a dozen side lines totally unconnected with his main business should he so desire. It is flexible as to movement: the Federal Constitution (Art. IV, Sec. 2) guarantees the right of an individual to carry on his business in any state with all the freedom of a citizen of that state. The fact that all profits are to go into the proprietor's own pocket is an incentive to industry and close application to the business.

The personal nature of the individual proprietorship has other advantages. The reputation of the owner for honesty and integrity is the reputation of the business itself. In some businesses, people like to deal directly with the proprietor. This is splendidly illustrated by the ability of some independent stores to withstand the competition of the large chain stores, even though the chain offers lower prices.

In some businesses, it is important that trade secrets be maintained. The close contact of the sole proprietor with his employees and his close supervision of his business affairs help in keeping the affairs of the business secret from competitors. There are no stockholders to whom statements of income, profit, and loss must be submitted. No submission of reports to government bureaus, where they become matters of public record, is necessary. There are no special taxes upon the individual proprietorship as an organization. There are no organization taxes to be paid, no matter how much capital is put into the organization at the beginning. The owner is, of course, as an individual responsible for property and income taxes, but there are no federal taxes upon the business as an organization.[2]

The individual proprietorship is, however, strictly limited in the amount of outside capital that can be brought into the business. While real estate and chattels owned may be mortgaged, the general credit of the business is limited to the personal resources of the proprietor and funds cannot be borrowed for long periods of time. This is due to the obvious lack of stability or continuity of the business as an organization. The business, as such, ends with the death, insanity, or bankruptcy of the owner. Even though the activities be carried on by a successor, it is now a different business, and the personal credit of the new owner is the credit of the new organization. This inability to obtain large amounts of capital usually prevents the growth of the business to a large size. Expansion is largely dependent upon the reinvestment of earnings by the proprietor.

A further limitation upon the expansion of the business is the inability of one man to supervise the detailed operations of a large business. True, the owner may delegate his authority to employees, but it must be remembered that he alone is responsible for any debts of, or claims arising against, his business. Hence, for his own protection, he is compelled to maintain a careful watch over all its activities. As the business grows in size, it is necessary to delegate more and more authority to others and, as a result, it is difficult for him to keep close control. It is nothing unusual

---

[2] New York State has an Unincorporated Business Tax that is in the nature of an income tax and applies to individual proprietorships, general and limited partnerships.

to see large and prosperous proprietorships change into corporations to facilitate the raising of funds and to provide a more practical large size management.

Chief advantages of the individual proprietorship are:

1. Ease of formation.
2. Simplicity and flexibility of control and movement.
3. Presence of the personal element; a strong incentive to industry.
4. Secrecy.
5. Freedom from organization and franchise taxes.
6. Freedom from governmental control.[3]

Its disadvantages are:

1. Difficulty in raising very large sums of capital for starting or for expansion.
2. Unlimited liability of the proprietor for all debts of the business.
3. Lack of stability or permanence.
4. Limitations upon the extent to which its powers can be delegated, preventing great expansion.

The general partnership. A *partnership* is an association of two or more persons to carry on, as co-owners, a business for profit (Uniform Partnership Act, Part II, Sec. 6). It is reasonable to assume that the development of the simple general partnership followed quite closely upon the beginnings of business enterprise. The need for the help of another, either in skill or capital, led to the formation of a general partnership in which the ownership and participation in the business are enjoyed not only by one but by more than one person.

Simple as this form of organization may seem, the relationship among members of a partnership and the dealings of such firms with one another have been subject to much litigation. The laws affecting the general partnership have developed through such litigation, and the practices followed by organizations of this type have grown through more than three centuries and have been codified in the Uniform Partnership Law, which was adopted in New York State, October 1, 1919 (see N.Y. Laws 1919, Chapter 408). At the present writing, the Uniform Partnership Law has been adopted by thirty states and territories.[4]

Contractual nature of the general partnership. The partnership does

---

[3] See footnote No. 1, p. 30.

[4] Alaska (1917), Arkansas (1941), California (1929), Colorado (1931), Delaware (1947), Idaho (1920), Illinois (1917), Indiana (1944), Maryland (1916), Massachusetts (1922), Michigan (1917), Minnesota (1921), Missouri (1949), Montana (1947), Nebraska (1943), Nevada (1931), New Jersey (1919), New Mexico (1947), New York (1919), North Carolina (1941), Oregon (1939), Pennsylvania (1915), South Dakota (1923), Tennessee (1917), Utah (1921), Vermont (1941), Virginia (1918), Washington (1945), Wisconsin (1915), Wyoming (1917). Most states that have not adopted the Uniform Partnership Act have so amended their respective partnership laws as to make them almost identical with the terms of the act.

not require a special charter or franchise from the state, but is formed by a simple contract between two or more persons. Such contracts may be oral, if they can be performed within a year, or in writing. The Uniform Partnership Law states that "persons who are not partners as to each other are not partners as to third persons," but the absence of any written contract or evidence of an oral one does not necessarily mean that a partnership does not legally exist. The existence of the partnership relation may be *implied in law* from the acts of the persons involved. The law states that the "receipt by a person of a share of the profits of a business is prima facie evidence that he is a partner," unless such profits are received as installments on a debt, wages, rent, interest on a loan, or as a consideration for the sale of the goodwill of a business.

As a general rule, something more than mere sharing of profits is required as evidence of intent to form a partnership. The existence of a partnership will be implied in law when some, or all, of the following are present (1) a joint interest in a business (as distinguished from any other activity, for example, a philanthropy), (2) a common investment, (3) a sharing of the profits as such, (4) a control of the business on the part of each.

There is also a situation wherein, even though no actual partnership exists, a person may be held liable as a partner by third parties. In the words of the Uniform Partnership Act (Sec. 16):

. . . when a person by words spoken or written or by conduct, represents himself, or consents to another representing him to anyone, as a partner in an existing partnership or with one or more persons not actual partners, he is liable to any such persons to whom such representation has been made, who has, on the faith of such representation, extended credit to the actual or apparent partnership, and if he has made such representation or consented to its being made in a public manner, he is liable to such persons, whether the representation has or has not been made or communicated to such person as giving credit by or with the knowledge of the apparent partner making the representation or consenting to its being made.

This is called *partnership by estoppel* in legal terminology. It means that, having led third parties to believe that he is a partner to their injury, the person making the misrepresentation may not later deny liability on the ground that he is not a partner.

Legal status of the partnership. It his been noted that the formation of a partnership does not rest upon any special grant of authority from the state but upon the common-law right of one individual to contract with another. The partnership firm is not an entity.

Real estate owned by the partnership may be held in the firm name, in the names of all the partners, or in the name of one partner, who in such case holds it in trust for the firm. The equitable interest in real estate held in the firm name may be conveyed by a deed signed by one of the partners in his own name, if such an act is done in carrying on the business of the partnership. (See Uniform Partnership Act, Sec. 10; or N.Y. Laws 1919, Chapter 408, Sec. 21, for full details with regard to the conveyance of partnership realty.)

For many years, one of the outstanding characteristics of the general partnership was that it could not sue or be sued in the firm name, but only in the names of the several partners. This has caused a great deal of trouble and inconvenience in partnership litigation, both in suits brought by its partners and those brought against the partners. In recent years there has developed a tendency among the states to pass "permissive statutes" providing that under specific conditions, partnerships may sue and be sued under the firm name. States that have already adopted such laws are: Georgia, Hawaii, Idaho, Nebraska, New York, North Dakota, Ohio, Oklahoma, and Vermont. In other states, however, in which such specific laws have not yet been enacted, the old rule of suing only in the name of the individual partner still prevails.[5]

Taxation of general partnership. The partnership does not have to pay an organization or franchise tax. It is liable for property taxes upon property held in the firm name. Partnerships as such do not pay Federal income tax, but the partners are individually liable for the taxes on the distributive shares of the profits for the taxable year or upon the profits during the accounting period ending within the taxable year. Nevertheless, the partnership is required to file a return showing its gross income and allowable deductions, the names and addresses of the partners entitled to a distributive share of the net income, and the amount of each share.[6]

Authority of each partner. Each partner is an agent for the partnership for the purpose of its business and may bind the partnership firm by any act that is apparently for the carrying on, in the usual way, of the busi-

---

[5] Illustrative of this new concept in partnership suits, the new law of the State of New York is pertinent. New York has effected this new proceeding by inserting in the "Civil Practice Act" a new section (Sec. 222a, Chapter 842, Laws of 1945, effective September 1, 1945), which is as follows: "Two or more persons carrying on a business as partners may sue or be sued in their partnership name whether or not such name comprises the names of the persons. If the persons be defendants in an action or proceeding, the summons or other process may be served upon any one or more of them with like effect as though all of the persons had been named as defendants by their own respective names. Where a judgment is taken against the defendants, the clerk with whom the judgment-roll is filed, must enter upon the docket opposite the name of each defendant upon whom the summons was served, the word "summoned"; and a like entry must be made by each county clerk with whom the judgment is afterward docketed. An execution upon such judgment may be collected out of the real and personal property of the persons summoned, whose names shall be indorsed on the execution."

[6] See footnote No. 2, p. 32. Also for taxable years starting after 1953 a partnership may make an irrevocable election to be taxed in the same manner as a corporation provided there are no more than fifty partners (professional partnerships such as for medicine, law, etc., generally excepted). See Sec. 1361 *et. seq.*, Internal Revenue Code, 1954.

ness of the partnership. This does not prevent agreement among the partners themselves, which may limit the authority of any one of the partners. Such limitations, however, are not binding upon outside parties in dealings with a partner, unless the party has knowledge of such a limitation. Should the act be one not apparently within the scope of the partnership business, the firm is not bound by the partner's acts; and, unless the business has been abandoned by the other partners, no partner, without the consent of the other partners, has the authority to:

1. Assign partnership property in trust for creditors.
2. Dispose of the goodwill of the business.
3. Sell at one time all the partnership property.
4. Do any act that would prevent the carrying on of the usual business of the partnership.
5. Confess a judgment.
6. Submit a partnership claim to arbitration.

The filing of general partnership agreements in some office of public records is not sufficient notice to outsiders of the terms of the agreement. There is no statutory requirement that such agreements be filed; hence, there is no obligation on the part of anyone to look for them. However, common prudence ought to dictate that, when a partner attempts to do something in the firm name that is unusual, the person dealing with him should question his authority.

As between the partners, any breach of the partnership agreement limiting the powers of a partner may be treated by the other partners as an act of bad faith, which might justify proceedings in a court of equity for an accounting and dissolution or as a breach of contract, giving rise to damages that could be sued for at law.

Liability of partners and sharing of losses. The common expression is that general partners are jointly and severally liable for the debts of the partnership. Joint liability means that all of the partners together as a group are liable to the creditors. Their agreement may set forth how they wish to share this liability. They may specify equally or in some other proportion. If no method of sharing is specified, it will then be equal parts to each partner. Beyond this joint liability, however, a several (separate) and individual liability for all the debts rests upon each one of the partners. If one or more cannot pay his or their shares, then the others have to make it up. Thus in a partnership of three, two can make no payment, thus the third partner can be made to pay it all. If, however, one partner thus has to pay more than his equitable share, he is considered to have contributed the excess amount toward the debts of his partners and, under what is known as *The Right of Contribution,* he can obtain a court order directing his partners to reimburse him for the amount he has paid in excess of his legal share.

If firm creditors cannot be satisfied by the assets of the partnership, they may proceed against the personal assets of any or all of the partners. Thus in the case of a business failure a partner may lose not only his business but also everything he has on the outside not otherwise exempt by law.

In a bankruptcy or dissolution proceedings against a partnership and partners, certain precedence of claims must be observed. Creditors of the partnership firm have first claim against assets of the partnership, while creditors of the individual partners have first claim against their personal assets. This principle of lining up separately the business and personal assets of the debtor to determine the order in which they shall be available to the creditors is known as the *marshalling of assets.*

The sharing of partnership profits. General partners may agree upon any desired methods of sharing profits. Often the partnership agreement provides that profits shall be divided equally among the partners, or in proportion to their investment in the company, or in any other proportion. But it is most important to realize that if the agreement fails to specify some particular manner of sharing the profits, then they will be shared equally among the partners.

This equal sharing of both profits and losses, unless otherwise provided by specific agreement, is a dangerous pitfall of partnership. Under this law, a partner who makes a very small capital contribution, perhaps giving only his name or services, will receive a share of the profits, or must bear a share of the losses, in as great a proportion as one who has contributed the greater part of the capital. One of the most undesirable features of the partnership is its lack of stability or liability of dissolution. It will be seen that upon occasion a partnership may be dissolved not only contrary to the wishes of the members but even contrary to their interests. A general partnership may be dissolved in any of the following ways:

1. Contract
   a. Lapse of agreed period.
   b. By mutual agreement to dissolve.
2. Bankruptcy of a partner.
3. Bankruptcy of the partnership.
4. Withdrawal of a partner when no fixed term has been agreed upon.
5. Death of a partner.
6. War between nations of which partners are citizens.
7. Court decree in cases of:
   a. Misconduct that prejudicially affects the carrying on of the business.
   b. Insanity.
   c. Breach of the partnership agreement.
   d. Partners' inability to carry on the business except at a loss.
   e. Court's finding dissolution necessary and equitable.

The withdrawal of a partner and the conveyance of his interest in the partnership does not, of itself, dissolve the partnership when the partnership is for a definite term. All that the purchaser obtains is a right to the share of the profits distributable according to the partnership agreement.[7]

In the dissolution of a partnership, the order of the payment of claims against the partnership assets is as follows:

1. Those owing to creditors other than partners.
2. Those owing to partners other than for capital and profits.
3. Those owing to partners in respect of capital.
4. Those owing to partners in respect of profit.

Delectus personarum. Since every general partner, on account of the agency power of partners, is liable for obligations made by his associates, even without his knowledge or consent, it is of the utmost importance never to enter into a partnership with any person who cannot absolutely be trusted to act wisely, conservatively, and in the interest of all the partners. One must be protected also against the possibility of having undesirable partners taken into the firm after its organization. To accomplish this end, there is the legal principle of *delectus personarum, or the right of "Choice of Persons."* In effect this means that each partner can choose his own partners, and that no new or additional partner can be taken into the partnership without the consent of every one of the existing partners.

The law looks upon the contract of partnership as a personal one and the right to participate in the control and management of the firm cannot be assigned by one partner without the consent of all. Upon the conveyance by one partner of his partnership interest, the only right received by the purchaser or assignee is the right to profits mentioned in the preceding section. He may not interfere in the administration of the partnership business affairs during the continuance of the partnership, nor may he inspect the partnership books. Should he believe himself unfairly treated, he must have recourse to a court of equity where he may ask that a receiver be appointed and an accounting made. It is, of course, up to the court in the light of all the facts to decide whether such a course would be equitable. Even should a partner die and the remaining partners decide to continue the business, the heir of the deceased partner may not of right demand admittance to the partnership. The old partnership has ceased and this is a new one, with a new agreement, and difference in membership. A partner may sell or dispose of his *interest* in a partnership, but he cannot sell his *membership.*

---

[7] When dissolution is caused in contravention of the partnership agreement, the other partners are entitled to damages and may continue the business in the same name by putting up a bond to secure payment of the withdrawing partner's interest, or may pay him the value of the interest, less damages and goodwill. The retiring partner must be indemnified against future partnership liabilities. (See Uniform Partnership Act, Sec. 38, par. [2].)

General characteristics of the partnership. The partnership form of organization offers better opportunity for the aggregation of capital than does the individual proprietorship, for additional capital can be obtained through the contributions of members of the firm. Then, too, there is the additional credit gained through the combined personal credit of the several partners. From the point of view of the creditor, the unlimited liability of the partners lends an element of strength to this form of organization. However, this same feature deters many from investing as partners in the enterprise.

Against the possibility of aggregating greater sums of capital through the admission of new partners, there is the unwieldiness of an organization consisting of many members. The constant likelihood of dissension and disagreement among a great number of persons, when each has the same authority in the management of the concern, is a decided detriment to the obtaining of large sums of money in this manner. The lack of stability due to the ease of dissolution of a partnership prevents borrowing for long terms on the general credit of the business.

In business in which it is desired to be free from statutory limitations, the partnership has a decided advantage. This has led to the adoption of the partnership organization in preference to that of the corporation in the cases of the New York Stock Exchange and other exchanges throughout the country. The partnership is free to engage in any business it wishes to, and there is no obligation to make reports to the state or disclose the partnership affairs to anyone.[8] Since the partnership, as such, is not distinct from the individuals who compose it, it may conduct its business freely in any state of the Union without restriction with the express permission of that state.

The partnership agreement. There are so many questions that may arise after the formation of a partnership that an agreement should be drawn in writing at the outset. Although no two agreements will be alike in all particulars, the following points ought to be covered:[9]

1. *Nature of business.* The scope of the business and the relation of each partner to the business should be clearly stated; also, whether a partner is permitted to engage in outside transactions, and whether or not each partner is required to devote all of his time to the business.

2. *Capital.* Specify the amount to be contributed by each partner, and how it is to be paid. If partners agree to contribute equally, the agreement should state whether cash or its equivalent is to be paid in and the penalty, if any, for the failure of one partner to contribute as much as another.

---

[8] Owing to Federal Security and Exchange regulations, this is no longer true of stock exchanges.

[9] J. L. Bogen, *Financial Handbook* (New York: Ronald Press Co., 1952), pp. 372-73.

3. *Changes in capital.* If undrawn profits automatically increase and losses decrease the capital accounts of the partners, the agreement should cover the point fully, since the interests of the partners in capital and profits may not be the same.

4. *Interest on capital.* Unless provided for in the agreement, capital contributions do not bear interest. If interest is to be allowed, the rate should be fixed.

5. *Withdrawals.* Since this is frequently a matter of dispute, explicit provision should be made to cover the manner and extent of withdrawals and the penalty for overdrafts.

6. *Undrawn profits.* If profits are allowed to accumulate, the agreement should state whether such amounts are to be treated as loans or additional capital. This provision is important, since the agreement may provide (see below) that profits are to be apportioned on the basis of capital contributed.

7. *Interest on loans or withdrawals.* If it is desired that interest should be allowed on loans or charged on withdrawals, the agreement should be so stated and the rate specified.

8. *Distribution of profits or losses.* The method of apportioning profits and losses should be stated and each partner's percentage specified; also, any contingency that may affect the share of any one should be included.

9. *Approval of accounts.* There should be some agreement as to the approval of the individual partners' accounts in respect to withdrawals, as well as in respect to the income and capital accounts.

10. *Salaries of partners.* If any partner is to receive a stated salary, the amount, also, should be specified, when it is to be credited, whether or not interest is to be allowed thereon if undrawn, and whether the amount is to be charged as an expense of the business before the profit or loss is ascertained.

11. *Dissolution.* The procedure should be stated in regard to the death or withdrawal of a partner; whether the books shall be balanced at once or allowed to run on to the end of the month or other period; whether, in case of dissolution, the partners are to share losses in the same proportion as each one's capital bears to the entire capital.

12. *Special causes for dissolution.* If the partnership can be dissolved for any reason other than death, such as disability or intemperance, complete details should be stated.

13. *Settlement after dissolution.* It is important not only to arrange the method of determining each partner's share upon dissolution, but it is equally important to fix the details of payment. The most equitable way is to provide for full payment within a fixed period, or to pay a certain proportion annually or semiannually. The rate of interest on the balance should be stated.

14. *System of accounts.* To obviate subsequent differences of opinion

as to the system of accounts, the agreement should specify the type of accounts to be kept, that they be balanced regularly, and that they be audited annually or oftener by a professional accountant. It is desirable that the method of selecting the auditor be stated.

15. *Disputes about accounts.* An arbitration clause should be inserted to the effect that if any dispute arises involving the accounts, it is to be submitted for settlement to a certified public accountant to be mutually agreed upon. Since disputes occur with respect to other matters, as well as to the accounts, in such cases, the reference should be made to a certified public accountant and a lawyer, with power lodged in them to select a third party in case of disagreement.

16. *Firm insurance.* If life insurance for the benefit of the firm is to be carried on the life of one or more partners, it should be stated how the premiums are to be paid and the disposition of the proceeds if collected. Also, it is well to state the disposition in case the partnership is dissolved while the policy is in force.

17. *Goodwill.* If withdrawing partners or representatives of deceased partners are entitled to goodwill, based on profits or otherwise, the method of calculation should be stated in detail. For instance, if salaries of partners are treated as business expenses in determining annual distributions, it must be stated whether or not such salaries are to be likewise treated if goodwill is based on *average net profits.* Salaries of partners and interest on partners' capital are in reality divisions of profit—not expenses—and it requires a clear and affirmative agreement to deal with them as expenses. When no agreement exists as to how the profits are to be divided, the law gives each partner an equal share in the profits and assumes that the losses will be borne equally by each partner.

The advantages of a partnership are:

1. It is easy and inexpensive to organize.
2. The unlimited liability of partners makes it reliable.
3. The direct gain to its members is an incentive to close attention to business.
4. The personal element in the characters of the partners is retained.
5. It is generally free from government control.[10]
6. It is free from organization taxes.

The disadvantages of a partnership are:

1. It has the danger and lack of stability that come from liability of dissolution.
2. It has divided authority.

---

[10] See footnote No. 1, p. 30.

3. It has instability, due to the need for constantly harmonious action.

4. Personal liability for firm debts deters many from investing capital in it.

5. Its borrowing power is usually limited.

Limited partnership. The limited partnership is in reality a legal partnership and fits under the definition given in the Uniform Partnership Act: An association of two or more persons to carry on, as co-owners, a business for profit. But it differs from the general partnership in several important ways. Primarily it is said to be composed of two *kinds* of partners, general partners and limited partners. There may be any number of each but there must be at least one of each kind. In other words a limited partnership is not a partnership composed entirely of limited partners.

General partners in a limited partnership have exactly the same characteristics, rights, liabilities, as those in a general partnership but the limited partners characteristics, rights, and liabilities are quite different. They are not agents for the firm, and, in fact, have no voice whatever in the management of the business. They have no liability whatever for the debts of the company beyond the possibility of losing their investment, and their personal assets are in no way liable for firm debts. They have no power to withdraw from the partnership. Withdrawal of one or more of the limited partners may be effected only with the consent of the general partners and then only if the firm is solvent and the withdrawal will not cause insolvency. The limited partnership agreement, as stated above, provides for the freedom from liability of the limited partners. Since contracting parties cannot free themselves of obligations by simple agreement, this must be accomplished by some governmental authority. Therefore the limited partnership cannot, like the general partnership, be formed by a simple common law agreement. It must be formed by a statutory agreement authorized by the law of the state. State statutes governing the organization and operation of limited partnerships were for many years quite diverse in character and content, but this condition is now fairly well remedied by successive state adoptions of the Uniform Limited Partnership Act.[11]

The chief characteristics of limited or special partners that differentiate them from the general partners are:

---

11 The Uniform Limited Partnership Act has been adopted in the following states and territories: Alaska (1917), Arizona (1943), California (1929), Colorado (1931), Florida (1943), Hawaii (1943), Idaho (1919), Illinois (1917), Iowa (1924), Maryland (1918), Massachusetts (1923), Michigan (1931), Minnesota (1919), Missouri (1947), Montana (1947), Nebraska (1939), Nevada (1931), New Hampshire (1937), New Jersey (1919), New Mexico (1947), New York (1922), North Carolina (1941), Pennsylvania (1917), Rhode Island (1930), South Dakota (1925), Tennessee (1919), Utah (1921), Vermont (1941), Virginia (1918), Washington (1945), Wisconsin (1919).

1. Their liability for the firm debts is limited to the amount invested or agreed upon by them to be invested in the business.

2. The withdrawal of their capital is prohibited, except under exceptional circumstances.[12]

3. They have absolutely no voice in the management or control of the business.

4. They must be bona fide part owners of the business and not merely lenders of money. As such, they are entitled to share in the profits of the business.[13]

If the names of the limited partners are used or displayed in any manner in connection with the business, it must be made plain and clear, beyond reasonable possibility of misconception, that these members are connected with the firm in a limited capacity; otherwise, they will be liable as general partners for the satisfaction of the debts of the firm. The business may be adjudged a general partnership and all the members general partners if the limited partners overstep their legal restrictions in any manner, or if the stipulations of the state statutes are departed from in the slightest degree.

Although the limited partner who interferes in the management of the partnership in any way may be held liable as a general partner, it must not be inferred that he may not be employed by the partnership to transact partnership business. Any participation on his part, however, must be clearly subject to the direction and control of a general partner. Further, a limited partner may lend money to the partnership and may lend his name as security for the partnership on the partnership's negotiable paper, as long as the statutes as to noninterference in the management of the concern are complied with.

A limited partnership formed in one state has no legal standing as such in any other state; it has simply that of a general partnership. The only way to give limited partners full protection is to organize the business as a limited partnership within, and under the laws of, each separate state in which the firm is to do business.

This form often enables owners to obtain capital investment from men of wealth who would not consider entering a general partnership with the unlimited personal liabilities for firm debts that are attached to it.

Until recent years suits brought by and against limited partnerships had to be brought in the names of the general partners. Today, however,

---

[12] See Uniform Limited Partnership Act, Sec. 16.

[13] A limited partnership agreement may provide that a limited partner is to receive interest on his investment, either in lieu of or in addition to a share in the profits. Such interest cannot, however, be paid if its payment would reduce the amount of the limited partner's investment. Such so-called "interest" is, therefore, not interest in the true sense, but simply a special sharing of the profits, something similar to the preferred dividends of a corporation.

states are beginning to adopt new statutes that permit limited partnerships to sue and be sued in the firm name.[14]

The joint venture. A temporary association of individuals or firms for the purpose of carrying through some particular business transaction or deal (this association ceases upon the successful termination, or upon the failure, of its purpose) is known as a *joint venture,* or sometimes as a *joint adventure.* It is formed by a simple contract agreement, as is the general partnership; and, as in the partnership, each participant assumes unlimited liability for the debts of the concern. This form lacks stability because of the danger of dissolution, but not to such a great extent as does the general partnership. With the following exceptions, a joint venture may be dissolved through the same contingencies as the partnership:

1. A member cannot withdraw without the consent of all the other members; but if he does withdraw with such consent, his withdrawal does not dissolve the organization.

2. The bankruptcy of a member does not necessarily dissolve the organization, though it may do so. Such action depends upon the nature of the venture and the duties and importance of the bankrupt member.

3. Its continuance is not affected by the death of a member; his personal representative may take his place.

4. War between nations represented in the nationalities of the members would not dissolve the concern if it could be shown that intercourse with an enemy alien was not essential to the enterprise.

The title to the property of the organization is usually vested in one member known as the *manager.* Unlike his power in the partnership, a member in the joint venture cannot bind the other members of the association by his acts, although the manager is, by the contract agreement, usually given practically unlimited powers to act for the other members.

One of the principal differences between the joint venture and the partnership is that, in the former, one member may sue the other members at law for his share of the profits. This is not permitted in the partnership. Suits are brought and sustained in the names of the members; but if one member has conducted the business in his own name, he may sue and be sued in his name.

The joint-stock company. The joint-stock company form of business organization has never been important in the United States. The corporation, much as we know it today, while slow to gain popularity, evolved and developed after the Revolutionary War. It has since kept pace with the needs of the country for such an organization. The joint-stock company is, however, of great interest to business and legal his-

---

14 See footnote No. 5, p. 35, for details.

torians for it was undoubtedly the form of organization which, with various changes in legal concept and business practice, became eventually our modern corporation. Its origin is often placed in England in the early seventeenth century. Probably, however, the first joint-stock company was formed much earlier. There is a record of a company formed in the fourteenth century by creditors of the city of Genoa who, unable to obtain payment of their debts, in effect assumed the debt, receiving certain privileges such as construction of public works and trade. Transferable shares were sold at that time. Even in England, where there is no certainty that the Italian experience was an influence, a joint-stock company known as "The Russia or Muscovy" Company was formed by John Sebastian Cabot in 1553 to survive for a century. Certainly by the middle of the seventeenth century they were well known and some of them, such as the East India Co. and the Hudson Bay Co., played important parts in early American and Canadian colonial history.

The joint-stock companies of the seventeenth century were sometimes given royal charters giving powers and special privileges, even the power to govern parts of the New World. However, many were merely contractual organizations having no governmental sanction and operating much as any private partnership. Fraudulent promotions and excessive speculation in the early eighteenth century and a "stock market" crash in which many people lost heavily resulted in the Bubble Act of 1720. Companies with transferable shares thereafter required the consent of the government for their formation much as corporations must do today both here and in England.

The American express companies used the joint-stock company form, probably because of their interstate and interterritory business, avoiding, thereby, possible legal difficulties with the slowly developing corporate laws. The Adams Express Co., which has not been in the express business since 1918, when it sold out and became an investment company, was organized as a joint-stock company in 1854 and still operates as such. Its shares are bought and sold on stock exchanges, the same as shares of a corporation, and perhaps by some who do not know the difference. However, to all practical purposes, the corporation has replaced the joint-stock company in this country.[15]

Characteristics. The usual characteristics of a joint-stock company may be summarized as follows:

① Management is in the hands of a board of managers or directors which may be either self-perpetuating or elected periodically by the shareholders.

---

[15] A student interested in the early development of the joint-stock company should read W. R. Scott, *Joint Stock Companies to 1720*, probably the most authoritative work on the subject.

(2) Ownership is divided into transferable shares. There is normally no right of *delectus personarum.*

(3) Stockholders are liable for debts as in a general partnership.[16]

(4) It is not a legal entity and in the absence of statutory authority cannot be sued as an organization (a few states treat it as an entity).

(5) Generally considered a common law organization enjoying the same freedom of management and movement as a partnership.

(6) Has continuous succession, only losing its status should all the shares be acquired by one person (it then becomes an individual proprietorship).

Tax status. Some states, such as New York, require that the joint-stock company pay the same annual franchise tax as a corporation, although it does escape the organization tax of the latter. The Federal Government treats it as a corporation for income tax purposes.

Advantages and disadvantages. The advantages of the joint-stock company form of organization are many and in point of number, at least, overbalance the disadvantages. If an absolute limitation of liability of the members could be brought about, this form would be preferred to that of the corporation by a great number of concerns now using the latter form. The most important points of comparison may be tabulated as follows:

Advantages of the joint-stock company:

1. It is easy and inexpensive to organize.

2. It makes possible the raising of a fairly large amount of capital by the sale of stock and by borrowing on long-term credit.

3. The unlimited liability of members (when it is not avoided) adds financial strength to the company.

4. The centralization of control in a board of managers avoids danger of lack of harmony among the agents.

5. The organization possesses considerable stability; it has continuous life.

6. It has flexibility as to expansion, management, and movement.

7. It is not legally complicated.

8. It is practically free from government control.[17]

Disadvantages of the joint-stock company:

1. The unlimited liability of the members cannot universally be avoided; hence, the uncertainty deters some prospective investors.

2. The valuable personal element of the individual proprietorship, present to some extent in the partnership, is lacking.

---

[16] Attempts to avoid this liability are usually made by placing a clause in each contract to the effect that the shareholders or directors are not to be held personally liable. See also p. 51 for similar clauses used by Massachusetts Trusts.

[17] See footnote No. 1, p. 30.

3. It is generally subject to the same Federal and state taxes as are corporations.

Limited partnership association. This peculiar hybrid between the partnership and the corporation is provided for by the statutes of only five states, Pennsylvania, Michigan, New Jersey, Ohio, and Virginia. As it is of practically no use outside of its state of origin, it will not be encountered often in general business. It is created, like a corporation, by filing a certificate of association with the state and by paying an organization tax. It is usually responsible for other state taxes on the same basis as a corporation. Its ownership is divided into shares, represented by stock, and the stockholders elect directors to manage the business.

The limited partnership association differs from the joint-stock company and the corporation in this way: Upon the transfer of any of its shares by an owner, the purchaser must be elected to membership in the association before he has any rights. He may demand election to membership, and if this is not granted, he may compel the association to pay him the value of his shares as agreed upon or as determined by appraisers appointed by the court. The transfer of shares does not, however, affect the life of the association. The laws of both Pennsylvania and Michigan governing these associations provide that every contract involving more than $500 must be signed by two of the directors. Unless it is so signed, the association is exempt from liability on it.

In the state of its organization, the members of a limited partnership association are not personally liable for the association's debts. The members will, however, be held liable unless the organization strictly complies with all the terms of the statute authorizing the organization. Outside the state of their organization, courts are inclined to treat these associations as general partnerships. This form of organization, therefore, is suited only to a business conducted entirely within the state of its organization. Except for the smaller initial expense of organizing, it has little, if any, advantage over the corporation.

The Massachusetts Trust. This organization, sometimes referred to and usually calling itself a voluntary association, business trust or common law trust, is another form of organization of some historical interest but of no present importance as far as this country's business is concerned. It originated in Massachusetts where corporations could not be formed primarily to hold and deal in real estate until 1912. There was a fear that if corporations operating under perpetual charters were permitted to engage in the business of acquiring and holding lands they might become too powerful to be controlled. To make it possible to engage in the real estate business on a large scale, the common law trust was adapted to this purpose. Its early freedom from governmental control, corporation taxes and the freedom from personal liability on the part of beneficiaries, generally called shareholders, made it attractive for a time to other types of business. Most of the original advantages have disappeared. It is required, if engaged in business, to pay federal income tax and some states such as New York apply to it the regular corporate franchise tax. In many states, it must qualify to do business within the state as a foreign corporation if formed outside of the state, and in some states it is treated as a general partnership. Lack of familiarity with its intricacies and fear of possible future legal difficulties compels lawyers to advise their clients against using it for business purposes and to recommend the use of the corporate form.

Since the Massachusetts Trust is based entirely upon the legal principles of the trust, it will be well to look into these principles briefly before studying its application to business ownership and operation.

Trusts. First of all, it must be clearly understood that, in speaking of *trusts* in connection with business, we do not mean the monopolies or combinations of big business brought about by *voting trusts*, which were so prevalent some years ago and which were given the name *trusts*—a word that has developed an undesirable significance.

By the term *trust*, in its financial and business sense, we mean the holding and care of the property (either real property or funds) of one party by a second party, for the benefit of a third party. The first and third parties may be the same person, *e.g.*, the case of a person who places his property in the hands of a trustee for his own benefit at a later period.

The principal parties to the formation of a trust are: (1) the *trustor* (also known as the *grantor* or *donor*), who is the party placing his property in trust and thus actually creating the trust; (2) the *trustee*, who receives, takes legal title to, and is charged with the management and preservation of the property that constitutes the trust estate; and (3) the *beneficiary*, for whose benefit the fund is established and who holds equitable title to the property.

When a person, by means of a deed of trust, places property, including the legal title thereto, in the hands of a trustee to be held by him for a specified time and then to be delivered by the trustee to some certain beneficiary, who may be the trustor himself, he creates a *living trust*. If the party, however, provides in a will that, upon his death, certain of his property shall be held in trust by a trustee for a beneficiary during a stated period, he creates a *testamentary trust*. It is often arranged that the income from the trust fund shall go to a certain person during the life of the trust, and at the expiration of the trust period, the principal shall go to a different person. In this case, the person receiving the income during the duration of the trust is known as the *life tenant*, and the person taking the principal at the expiration of the trust is known as the *remainderman*.

Living trusts are ordinarily irrevocable, unless the trustor expressly reserves the right to modify or revoke. Testamentary trusts cannot be changed or altered after the death of the testator by any of the remaining parties.

Trusts, except those established for charitable and for some types of pension plan purposes, cannot be made perpetual, and the time limit varies somewhat in different jurisdictions. The English rule that a trust may not be established for a term of years but only for the life of a person or persons named in the trust indenture generally prevails. For example, the law in the State of New York permits a trust to be established to exist for the lives of any number of persons named in the trust indenture at the time the trust is created, provided that the number is not so unreasonably great as to make it difficult to know when the last life is terminated. Following the English practice, the life of the trust is extended twenty-one years and nine months beyond the death of the last person named as one of the "lives" upon which the termination of the trust depends.

The trust applied to business. In organizing a business in the form of a Massachusetts Trust, or a business trust, therefore, the organizers draw up a deed or declaration of trust that names a board of trustees; places in the hands of the board the absolute legal title to all the property of the proposed business; specifies the terms and conditions under which the trust is to be managed and the business conducted; and makes themselves, together with others who may later become shareholders, the beneficiaries, who are to receive both the income during the life of the trust and the trust property at the expiration. The essential provisions in the organization of a business trust are:

1. The deed or declaration of trust drawn up to define the rights and powers of the trustees and holders of trust certificates.

2. Two or more trustees who are to hold in trust and manage the capital or property supplied by the shareholders.

3. Shareholders or certificate holders, who are the beneficiaries as well as the donors of the trust, and who will receive transferable certificates representing their respective interests in the profits and in the property on dissolution.

4. Provisions for the division of profits, the appointment of trustees to fill vacancies, meetings of shareholders, and dissolution at the termination of the trust.

5. Provisions that no liability is to attach to either trustees or shareholders, but only to the trust estate, and directions that such a statement be included in all contracts made by the trustees.

The board of trustees then proceeds to select officers for the company and otherwise to conduct the business just about as a board of directors would do in a corporation.

The ownership of the business is divided into shares, and the participants receive certificates (similar to certificates of stock of a corporation) called, by some, *certificates of stock* and, by others, *certificates of beneficial interest.* Among these shares, the board of trustees distributes available profits of the business as dividends.

Now, when a board of trustees is appointed at the beginning of a trust, that board is permanent during the life of the trust and cannot be changed either by the trustor or the beneficiary. If a trustee dies, resigns, or is legally removed for mismanagement or other good cause, a new trustee may be elected by the remaining trustees or by the stockholders, depending upon the provisions of the deed of trust. Beyond this, however, the personnel of the board is in no way under the control of the membership, and there are no periodical elections as in the joint-stock company and the corporation.

In business trusts organized in this manner, the stockholders are not personally liable for the debts of the organization, and creditors can look only to the trustees as such or, more usually, only to the property of the business for satisfaction.

Trust control by stockholders. The characteristic of a trust that places the members of the board of directors permanently in their respective positions, so that they cannot be ousted or changed periodically at the whim of the stockholders, is a very good feature in cases in which it is desirable to have the management remain constantly in the same hands. Many investors, however, have been found to be unwilling to place their money in the stock of a business in which they have no control whatsoever and no voice in saying who shall run the business as long as it exists, after the board of trustees is once chosen. This unwillingness has led to the organization of some Massachusetts Trusts, or business trusts, which are true to form in other respects, but in which the deed of trust provides that the stockholders may, by their vote, elect trustees each year or at other stated intervals, just as is done in the joint-stock company or in the corporation. Although such an organization is still generally *called* a trust, nevertheless this departure from one of the principal characteristics of the trust (the continuance of the same trustees) renders it absolutely not a *true trust.* The most important result is that the members or stockholders are no longer free from liability for the firms' debts, but are treated in this respect as partners having full personal liability.

Limitation of stockholder's liability. This gaining of control through the right to elect trustees periodically, at the cost of giving up freedom from liability and assuming full liability for the firm's debts, is, however, quite distasteful to the shareholders. Means must be found, if possible, to limit this liability and, at the same time, to retain the right to change trustees. Such limitations and rights are generally effected by inserting in the deeds of trust of organizations of this type, which have provided for the periodical election of their trustees, a special clause setting forth the fact that the stockholders shall not have such personal liability. Specimens of these clauses in actual use are as follows:

FROM THE DECLARATION OF TRUST OF THE MASSACHUSETTS ELECTRIC COMPANIES

The Trustees shall have no power to bind the shareholder personally, and the subscribers and their assigns and all persons or corporations extending credit to contracting with, or having any claim against the Trustees shall look only to the funds and property of the Trust for payment under such contract or claim, or for the payment of any debt, damage, judgment, or decree, or for any money that may otherwise become due or payable to them from the Trustee, so that neither the Trustees nor the shareholders, present or future, shall be personally liable therefor.

In every written order, contract, or obligation which the Trustees, shall give or enter into, it shall be the duty of the Trustees to stipulate that neither the Trustees nor the stockholders shall be held to any personal liability under or by reason of such order, contract, or obligation.

FROM THE DECLARATION OF TRUST OF THE BOSTON PERSONAL PROPERTY TRUST

Neither the trustees nor the *cestuis que trustent* (shareholders) shall ever be personally liable hereunder as partners or otherwise, but that for all debts the trustees shall be liable as such to the extent of the trust fund only. In all contracts or instruments creating liability, it shall be expressly stipulated by the trustees that the *cestuis que trustent* shall not be liable.

So long as these provisions are strictly observed, they serve their purpose and protect the shareholders from liability to all creditors who have been duly notified of the provisions and who have entered into contract or accepted credit upon these terms. If, however, the trustees have failed to insert the provision in the contract or to call the attention of the other party to its existence, then the liability of the shareholders still exists. Thus, we have a condition similar to that of the members of the joint-stock company described earlier in this chapter.

Advantages and disadvantages of the trust form. The advantages and disadvantages of the trust form of business organization may be set forth briefly as follows:

Advantages:

1. Its formation is simple and inexpensive.
2. It admits of the aggregation of large capital.
3. It insures freedom from personal liability on the part of the stockholders, unless they have a right to change trustees.
4. It insures stability during the period of its life.
5. It provides flexibility as to expansion, management, and movement.
6. It is practically free from government control; and it had, originally, freedom from heavy taxation.

Disadvantages:

1. It has no control over the personnel of the trustees if it be a true trust.

2. It is limited in duration.

3. Its securities may not be as easily marketed as are those of the corporation.

4. There is the possibility of unlimited liability for shareholders if they have the right to change trustees.

5. Credit is somewhat limited because of this uncertainty of liability and because of the time limitation on the life of a trust.

6. It is taxed by the Federal Government and by some states as though it were a corporation.

Questions for Study and Review

1. State eight factors that should be considered in choosing a suitable form of business organization.
2. What are the advantages and disadvantages of the individual proprietorship as a form of business organization?
3. What conditions must be present if a general partnership is to be implied in law?
4. What is the authority of a general partner in the conduct of the firm's business?
5. State six limitations upon the authority of general partners to act for the firm.
6. To what extent are partners liable for the firm's debts?
7. State seven ways in which a general partnership may be dissolved.
8. What is meant by *delectus personarum* in connection with a partnership contract?
9. State at least ten points that ought to be covered in a partnership form of agreement.
10. Summarize the advantages and disadvantages of a partnership form of organization.
11. Explain the organization of the limited partnership, and state the relationship of the limited partners to the business and their liability for loss through debts of the firm.
12. What is a joint venture? How is it formed? Why is it more or less stable than the partnership? What are the liabilities of participants for debts of the firm?
13. State the principal characteristics of a joint-stock company. Is there any way in which the personal liability of its shareholders can be avoided? Explain.
14. What is a Massachusetts Trust? By what other names is the same type of organization known?

Problems

1. A partnership with five partners finds it desirable to curtail the agency powers of the various partners by assigning certain duties and powers to each

and by limiting the power and authority of each partner to the specific duties assigned to him. How and to what extent can this be done?

2. Mr. Adams and Mr. Bryan are partners in a retail business which needs $8,000 additional capital. Mr. Bryan urges Mr. Cole to supply the new capital and become a partner. Under what conditions may Mr. Cole become a partner?

3. Anderson, Bagley & Caldwell is the firm name of a partnership having three partners with the names mentioned. At the start, Mr. Anderson invested in the business $60,000 in cash; Mr. Bagley, $30,000 in cash and property worth $10,000 and Mr. Caldwell invested property worth $20,000. The business started out very well. During the seventh month Mr. Anderson needed some cash and drew from the company $10,000 as an advance against expected profit. In the eighth month, Mr. Bagley similarly took out $6,000, and in the tenth month Mr. Caldwell, in like manner, took out $5,000. At the end of the first year, after allowing for cash already drawn by the partners, the firm has profits of $9,000 to be divided. What will each partner be entitled to out of this sum if (a) there is nothing in the partnership agreement as to the method of dividing profits, and (b) the partnership agreement provides that the partners shall participate in the profits in proportion to their respective investments in the business?

4. Messrs. Archer, Barclay, and Carpenter engage in business as the Acme Shoe Co., a partnership. The company starts out with a capital of $360,000, the partners investing, respectively, $180,000, $110,000 and $70,000. During the third month, it is found that the business needs additional funds to meet unforeseen expenses, and Mr. Barclay lends the firm $60,000. Before the end of the year, the partners see that they cannot make a success of the business and the firm is dissolved. At dissolution, it owes outside creditors $190,000, and the proceeds from the sale of all of its assets amount to $400,000. How shall these proceeds be divided among all interested parties?

5. The partnership of Anderson, Buckman & Cole was started on a capital of $300,000 which was contributed in equal shares by the partners. The business has not been prosperous, and the partners believe it would be better to dissolve and take their present losses. At a forced sale, the business will bring the full value of capital invested, namely, $300,000, but they owe the firm's creditors the sum of $390,000. Outside of the business, the three men own respectively, in cash and salable property free of all exemptions, $80,000, $60,000 and $40,000. However, Mr. Anderson has personal debts of $30,000, Mr. Buckman $20,000 and Mr. Cole $12,000. Estimate how their finances will stand if they dissolve at once.

6. The Empire Tailoring Co. is a limited partnership organized under the statutes of the State of New York. Mr. Ayers and Mr. Boyd, both residents of New York City, are the general partners, and Mr. Crump, who is the owner of valuable property and resides in Newark, N.J., is a limited partner. The business prospers and they wish to open a branch in Newark, N.J. What steps must be taken to protect the status of Mr. Crump as a limited partner?

7. Mr. Austin and Mr. Barrett are partners in a retail grocery business. They need additional capital and urge Mr. Campbell to invest $10,000 and become a partner of the firm. Mr. Campbell declines but agrees to let them have $10,000 for the business under the following conditions: that they discontinue their meat business and agree not to change the location of the business or to open any branches without his consent; that he be given ⅓ of the net profits annually; and, that he have the right to withdraw his money upon six months' notice. (a) If this is an oral agreement and the partnership fails, can Mr. Campbell be held as a partner? (b) Can the parties draw a limited partnership agreement to include these terms? (c) How can Mr. Campbell lend his friends $10,000, receive ⅛ of the profits, and still incur no liability beyond the loss of his investment?

8. Several gentlemen have purchased 40 acres of land immediately adjoining a growing town. They wish to develop it and sell it off as building lots at a considerable profit to themselves, but do not wish to form any permanent association, seeking merely the most convenient method of accomplishing this one deal. Advise them as to the form of organization to use and give your reason.

9. Mr. Wallace owns 20 shares of stock in a joint-stock company and sells them to Mr. Walker. What rights has Mr. Walker after the stock is transferred to him? How do Mr. Walker's rights differ from those of Mr. Cole in Problem 2 of Chapter III, and why?

Assigned Problem

Brown, White, and Grey are partners in a firm with capital of $800,000 which has been contributed by the partners as follows: Brown $400,000; White $300,000 and Grey $100,000. The partnership agreement provides that profits and losses are to be shared in proportion to the respective investments in the business. In addition, Brown has lent the firm $60,000. The partnership dissolves owing outside creditors $200,000. Outside of the business, three partners have available the following personal assets; Brown, $150,000 which includes the $60,000 owed to him by the firm; White, $80,000 and Grey $35,000. In the order named, they have personal debts of $50,000, $35,000 and $15,000. The proceeds from the sale of the partnership assets amount to $940,000. Explain the financial standing of each partner as a result of dissolution of the partnership.

CHAPTER IV

Corporate Organization

Wide use of the corporation. The corporation is without doubt the most important, as well as the most complicated, form of business organization used in the United States. So much so that practically all of the remainder of this text will be devoted to the financial activities of businesses organized in this form.

Although only about 20 per cent of all the firms in this country are corporations, these firms represent about 80 per cent of all the capital invested and, hence, greatly outweigh in importance all the other forms of business organization. The corporate form of organization is used for purposes other than business, such as social clubs, fraternities, churches, municipalities, educational and charitable institutions, and many others; but these are beyond the scope of *business finance* and hence will be only mentioned and classified in this text.

Attributes of the corporation. The corporation is a very old form of organization whose roots are lost in antiquity. In its earliest days it appears to have been used almost exclusively for organizations of a municipal and religious character; its wide use for business purposes dates from comparatively recent times. The main underlying idea is that of the *collective person,* a number of units grouped together as one entity, which means that regardless of the number of members, owners, or stockholders in a corporation, it is regarded by the law as a fictitious person entirely separate and distinct from all those who compose it. Thus, the organization is endowed with continuous life during the period of its charter regardless of the deaths or misfortunes of its members and regardless of any partial or entire changes, substitutions, or replacements among them. This continuous life, or continuous succession as it is called, makes the corporation the most stable of all business forms for, if incorporated in perpetuity, it may conceivably go on forever—an impossibility for any other form. Legislative enactments in the various states have given the corporation many additional attributes, such as limited liability of members, complete transferability of ownership, the right to have several classes of stock, the right to own and hold stock of other corporations, the right of members to delegate management to directors, the right to adopt various types of voting by members, and so on. Each of these will be discussed in its proper place.

Since the number of stockholders is unlimited and the corporation has the legal right to borrow funds, it may be seen that the form is ideally suited for businesses desiring very large capital, for its fund-raising ability is limited only by the amount of money it can induce innumerable investors to place in it, either through stock purchase or through loans.

The corporation defined. There have been, from time to time, many legal and economic concepts of the corporation, but the idea most widely accepted today is that it is legally a *fictitious person*. Upon this basis, an acceptable definition may be framed as follows:

A corporation is a voluntary association of persons (natural or legal) organized under and recognized by the law as a person, fictitious in character, having a corporate name and being entirely separate and distinct from the persons who compose it, for the accomplishment of some specified purpose or purposes. It has continuous succession during the period of life assigned by its charter and the right to perform as a natural person could, all the functions expressed in its charter, implied thereby or incidental thereto.

This definition brings out the fact that a corporation is not an organization *formed by the state,* as many say, but one formed voluntarily by *persons* in accordance with the provisions of the state law and then duly *recognized by the state* as a corporation. The persons forming the corporation may be either natural persons or legal persons, that is either individuals or several existing corporations forming a new one by means of consolidation. It also brings out that the *legal person* recognized by the state is *fictitious* in character and neither imaginary nor artificial, as stated in so many older definitions. When the legal entity is brought into being through incorporation, no court today imagines that a real person has been created, nor has it any idea that there is any artificial thing brought into existence in the shape of a person. In all cases the courts recognize that the corporate person is a legal fiction, a person who the courts know does not exist; yet, for purposes of convenience, they treat this "person" as if he did exist.

Other definitions. Definitions of corporations have been made by the thousands and the decisions in many cases at law have hinged upon the definition accepted or made by the particular court trying the case.

A careful analysis and comparison of a few of the most famous views is very interesting and profitable.

Probably the most widely quoted definition ever given in this country is that pronounced by Chief Justice John Marshall in the Dartmouth College case in 1819, as follows:

A corporation is an artificial being, invisible, intangible, and existing only in the contemplation of the law. Being a mere creature of law, it possesses only those properties which the charter of its creation confers upon it, either expressly or as incidental to its very existence. These are such as are supposed best calculated to effect the object for which it was created. Among the most important are immortality, and if the expression may be allowed, individuality, properties by which a perpetual succession of many persons are considered as the same, and may act as a single individual. They enable a corporation to manage its own affairs, and to hold property without the perplexing intricacies, the hazardous and endless necessity of perpetual conveyances for the purpose of transmitting it from hand to hand. It is chiefly for the purpose of clothing bodies of men in succession with these qualities and capacities that corporations were invented, and are in use. By these means, a perpetual succession of individuals are capable of acting for the promotion of the particular object, like one immortal thing. [*Dartmouth College v. Woodward,* 4 Wheat. (U.S.) 518, 636]

An old and famous English description is that given by Lord Coke (1552–1634):

A corporation aggregate of many is invisible, immortal, and rests only in intendment and consideration of the law. They cannot commit treason, nor be outlawed nor excommunicated, for they have no souls, neither can they appear in person, but by attorney. A corporation aggregate of many can't do fealty, for an invisible body can neither be in person nor swear; it is not subject to imbecilities or death of the natural body and divers other cases.

Blackstone (1723–1780), in commenting on the continuous life of the corporation, gives us a number of very excellent and clear expressions on the subject:

In order to facilitate business and to increase production of wealth, there have been created by acts of the public power, running back to remote antiquity, associations for business, religious, governmental, and charitable purposes known as corporations. These artificial persons are called bodies politic, bodies corporate, or corporations, of which there is a great variety, subsisting, for the advancement of rights and immunities, which if they were granted only to those individuals of which the body corporate is composed, would, upon their death, be utterly lost and extinct. To show the advantages of these incorporations, let us consider the case of a college in either of our universities, founded for encouragement and support of religious learning. If this were a mere voluntary assembly, the individuals which compose it might indeed, read, pray, study and perform scholastic exercises together, so long as they could agree to do so, but they could neither frame, nor receive any laws or rules of their conduct; none, at least, which would have any binding force for want of a coercive power to create a sufficient obligation. Neither could they be capable of retaining any privileges or immunities; for, if such privileges be attacked, which of all this unconnected assembly has the right, or ability, to defend them? And, when they are dispersed by death or otherwise, how shall they transfer these advantages to another set of students, equally unconnected as themselves? So also, with regard to holding estates or other property, if land be granted for the purpose of religious learning to twenty individuals, not incorporated, there is no legal way of continuing the property to any other persons for the same purpose, but by endless conveyance from one to the other, as often as the hands are changed. But when they are consolidated and united into a corporation, they and their successors are then considered as one person in law; as one person, they have one will, which is collected from the sense of the majority of the individuals; this one may establish rules and orders for the regulation of the whole, which are a sort of municipal laws of this little republic; or rules and statutes may be prescribed to it at its creation, which are then in the place of natural laws; the privileges and immunities, the estate and possessions, of the corporation, when once vested in them, will forever be vested, without any new conveyance to new successions; for all the individual members that have existed from the foundation to the present time, or that shall hereafter exist, are but one person in the law, a person that never dies; in like manner as the River Thames is still the same river, though the parts which compose it are changing every instant.

William A. Wood, in his *Modern Business Corporation*, defines the corporation quite carefully as follows:

According to contemporary practices a corporation is an association of natural persons, or of other legally constituted persons (other corporations) authorized by law to act as a unit, under a corporate name, for the accomplishment of certain definite and prescribed purposes. It is a 'person' constituted by law, separate and distinct from its stockholders, and, in a certain sense, is a citizen. Action at law may be maintained against it the same as against a natural person.

A mere reading of these definitions shows that the entire underlying idea is that of the *collective person* created under the law through the union of its members, bound together by the corporate charter.

Formation of a corporation. For long ages the granting of a charter of special rights or monopolies to a group of persons as a corporation was a crown prerogative in the European monarchies, though later on the parliaments took over the greater part of this power. When the American colonies were under English rule, charters in this country were granted by the King of England, by the British parliament, by the royal colonial governors, by the proprietary colonial governors, and by the colonial legislatures. This overlapping, and often conflicting, authority would doubtless have led to much confusion and trouble had not the colonies gained their independence and the new colonial governments declared that all corporations[1] in existence, regardless of their source, would be recognized as legal. Thereafter American incorporating power was vested in Congress and in the legislature of each of the respective states.

Procedure in forming a corporation. For many years after the establishment of the Republic, the incorporation of a company in any state

---

[1] Actually these were originally *joint-stock companies*, each granted special powers often with no similarity in form of management.

required the passage of a special act of the legislature. This often resulted in log rolling, political unfairness, and other abuses. Furthermore, the number of incorporations was increasing so rapidly that the legislatures bogged down under the mass of bills introduced and it rapidly became a physical impossibility to pass a special bill for each company. Therefore, one after another, the various states passed enabling acts. Such acts generally took the form of a *General Corporation Law*, or a Corporation Code, under which qualified groups could file a Certificate of Incorporation or Articles of Incorporation in prescribed form which, when approved, accepted, and filed by the secretary of the state, or other designated state officer, gave the company its corporate existence. Practically all corporations are now formed in this manner, although it is still possible in most states to organize under a special act when, in the judgment of the legislature, the objects desired by the incorporators cannot be obtained under the provisions of the general law. There is no general federal incorporation law. The power of the Federal Government to create corporations is limited to powers granted in the Federal constitution.

Classes of corporations. Corporations of the several states are governed almost entirely by statutory enactments and as these in the different states grew up independently of one another they gradually became quite divergent in detail, which made it necessary for the student of corporations to gain familiarity with the details of his own state laws and those of every other state with which his company might have to have legal association. Many felt the need of a Uniform Corporation Act along lines similar to the Uniform Partnership Act (p. 33). After long and arduous work, the Committee on Business Corporations of the American Bar Association has completed and published its "Model Act" and there is a tendency on the part of many state legislatures, in making new amendments or provisions to their laws, to be guided considerably by the provisions of this act. Many have hopes that in the not too distant future, the act will be adopted in its entirety by most of the states.

At the present time the states agree upon grouping corporations into three main classes, namely: municipal corporations, stock corporations, and non-stock corporations.

Municipal corporations include counties, towns, cities, school districts which through their incorporation attain their governmental character and the right of government, taxation, bond issue, and so on. They, of course, do not have any stock indicative of ownership and are the most important of the non-stock corporations.

A *stock corporation* is one having its ownership represented by shares of stock, among which it is authorized by law to distribute dividends or shares of the surplus profits of the corporation. A corporation is not a stock corporation simply because it has issued certificates of stock, which are in fact merely certificates of membership and which are not authorized by law to entitle the holders to dividends (such as golf clubs, fraternities, athletic associations, etc.). The stock corporations are comprised of moneyed corporations (banks, insurance companies, and so on), transportation companies, or other business corporations.

A *non-stock corporation* is one which has no stock or whose stock is not dividend-bearing; examples are religious, social, educational, and charitable organizations.

Since the New York law is fairly representative, it is used here to show how each type of corporation is formed under, and takes its name from, its appropriate law.

Our attention will principally be devoted to what are known as the *business corporations*, that is, those shown in the diagram (p. 61) to be formed directly under the Stock Corporation Law, other than banking, insurance, railroads, and transportation.

The incorporators. The persons who originally form a corporation are known as the *incorporators* and it is they who map out the plans for the company and file the certificate of incorporation, or who have the bill introduced into the legislature in case the incorporation is to be accomplished by a special act. Nearly all the states require that the number of incorporators be three or more, and some states have special age, citizenship and residential requirements. New York, for instance, requires three or more incorporators of whom at least two-thirds shall be residents of the United States and at least one a resident of the State of New York. Delaware, New Jersey, Virginia, Arizona, Maryland, Maine, California, and others have no such restrictions.

The certificate of incorporation. The certificate of incorporation (in some states known as the Articles of Incorporation) is the document through which the corporation obtains and possesses its legal existence. This document is presented by the incorporators to the secretary of the state, together with the proper organization tax and filing fees. When the certificate is approved, accepted, and filed by the secretary of the state in the state files, the incorporators then file a copy in the office of the County Clerk in the county in which the principal office of the corporation is located.[2]

The incorporators will then hold an organization meeting,[3] formally accepting by resolution the charter from the state, electing the regular board of directors to succeed the temporary board appointed in the certificate of incorporation, adopting a set of by-laws, and transacting any

---

[2] In New York, two copies are retained by the secretary of state, one of which is sent to the proper county office.

[3] In some states the formation is not complete until the "acceptance" at this meeting. In New York acceptance by the secretary of state completes the legal formation.

General Corporation Laws.

- **Municipal Corporation Law.**
  - County Law.
  - General City Law.
  - Second-Class City Law.
  - Town Law.

- **Stock Corporation Law.**
  - **Banking Law.** — Banks, trust cos., savings banks, investment cos., safe deposit cos., personal loan cos., savings & loan assns., and credit unions.
  - **Insurance Law.** — Life, health, and casualty corporations. Fire insurance corporations. Marine insurance corporations. Title and credit guaranty corporations. Life or casualty insurance corporations upon the cooperative or assessment plan. Fraternal and beneficiary societies, orders, or associations. Corporations for the insurance of domestic animals. Town and county cooperative insurance corporations.
  - **Railroad Law.** — Railroad corporations.
  - **Transportation Corporation Law.** — Ferry, navigation, stagecoach, and tramway corporations. Pipe-line, gas & electric light, and waterworks corporations. Telegraph and telephone corporations. Turnpike, plankroad, and bridge corporations. Freight terminal corporations.
  - Corporations for any lawful business not embraced in one of the above.

- **Religious Corporation Law.** — Church corporations of any denomination.

- **Membership Corporation.** — Cemetery corporations, hospitals. Boards of trade, and various other corporations of a similar nature.

- **Educational Corporation Law.** — Colleges, universities.

- **Cooperative Corporation Law.** — Marketing, etc. Mutuals.

other desired business. The newly elected directors will then meet and formally organize the board. The corporation is then legally formed and is entitled to operate under its charter.

Contents of the certificate of incorporation. The certificate of incorporation is entitled and endorsed as follows: "Certificate of Incorporation of . . . [*name of company*], pursuant to . . . [*article and title of state general law under which corporation was founded, e.g.*, in New York, 'pursuant to Article 2 of the Stock Corporation Law']"; and states (according to the New York provisions):

1. The name of the proposed corporation.

2. The purpose or purposes for which it is to be formed.

3. The amount of capital stock and the number and par value of the shares of which it is to consist; or, if there is to be stock without par value, the information concerning it required by law (see S. C. L., Sec. 12).

4. If the shares are to be classified, the number of shares to be included in each class and all of the designations, preferences, privileges, and voting powers, restrictions, or qualifications of the shares of each class.

5. The city, village or town, and the county in which the office of the corporation is to be located, and the address to which the secretary of the state shall mail a copy of process in any action or proceeding against the corporation, which may be served upon him.

6. Its duration.

7. The number of directors (not less than three).

8. The names and postoffice addresses of the directors until the first annual meeting of the stockholders, and, if such an address is in a city, the street and number and other particular description thereof. The number of directors so named must be the number stated pursuant to paragraph 7 above.

9. The name and postoffice address of each subscriber of the certificate of incorporation, and a statement of the number of shares of stock he agrees to take. If the address of any such subscriber is in a city, the street and number, or other particular description thereof.

10. The statement that all of the subscribers of the certificate are of full age, that at least two-thirds of them are citizens of the United States, that at least one of them is a resident of the State of New York, that at least one of the persons named as a director is a citizen of the United States and a resident of the State of New York.

11. The secretary of the state is hereby designated as the agent of the corporation upon whom process in any action or proceeding against it may be served.

12. If the meetings of the board of directors are to be held within the state only, the certificate or by-laws must so provide.

13. Any desired general provision for the regulation of the business and the conduct of the affairs of the corporation.

Most of the provisions of the certificate of incorporation are self-explanatory but a few words of detail may well be added concerning some of them.

The corporate name. In the first paragraph the name must be in the English language. This has been construed to mean that the name may be printed in any language, but must be composed in English letters or characters. The name chosen must not conflict with the name of any other domestic or foreign corporation doing business lawfully in the state. Ordinary business corporations are not permitted to use the words *trust, bank, banking, assurance, insurance, indemnity, guarantee, guaranty, title, casualty, surety, fidelity, bonding, savings, installment loan, benefit, co-operative* (See G.C.L., Sec. 9; Education Law, Sec. 66; Penal Law, Sec. 964). Moreover, every corporate name must have "such word or words, abbreviations, affix or prefix therein or thereto as will clearly indicate that it is a corporation as distinguished from a natural person, firm, or copartnership" (See G.C.L., Sec. 9). It is customary to use the word *corporation* or *incorporated,* or an abbreviation of either of them.

Corporate powers. Under paragraph 2 of the Certificate of Incorporation there are stated in detail the purposes for which the corporation is organized. These are usually made very broad and inclusive. The corporation is authorized to do any or all of the things specified in the certificate under this paragraph. Hence they are called the powers of the corporation. Those powers especially set forth in the certificate are known as the expressed *powers.* However, the corporation is in reality not limited to these. It has also what are known as the *implied* powers and *incidental powers* (see definition of the corporation, p. 56). If it is clear that certain additional powers are necessary in order to carry out effectively the powers expressed in the certificate, these additional powers are said to be *implied.* All corporations, for example, have the implied power to create a corporate seal and to maintain a bank account. Further, it may be that, in the process of operating or expanding its business, the corporation may discover that its profits could be increased, or its main business protected, if it engaged in activities that are in the nature of side lines, or related activities. Powers assumed to carry out such activities are known as *incidental* powers.

A familiar illustration may make this clear. Suppose that a company is incorporated with the express powers to buy, sell, deal in, tan, prepare, and manufacture leather and leather goods. Though the certificate of incorporation may explicitly so provide, it must be clearly implied that the company will have the right to own property, machinery, raw materials, raise funds, hire help, execute contracts and leases and to do many other things. If it uses tan bark in its processes, it would have the right to procure it in the most satisfactory manner. If difficult or expensive to procure in the market, the company would have the right to purchase oak forests and strip off its own bark. Having done this, the company could sell the resulting timber as a by-product. If difficult to dispose of in its natural state, the company could establish and operate mills for converting it into lumber. This, of course, is an incidental power and can be used only in disposing of the lumber to the extent to which it is produced in leather manufacturing—the expressed power or purpose.

These incidental powers are sometimes very important and the by-products sold under such powers may be very profitable. Within the limitation of its powers expressed, implied or incidental, the corporation is free to act. But is not permitted to exceed it powers to the least degree. Any act committed outside of its corporate powers is known as an *Ultra Vires act*, and is illegal. Acts within the corporate powers and thus permissible are known as *Intra Vires acts*.[4]

Duration of a corporation. The third, fourth, and fifth paragraphs need no explanation. As to the sixth, all that need be said is that the life of the corporation and of the certificate may be, and usually is, made perpetual, although any term of years may be named as the life period.

General provisions of the Certificate of Incorporation. The remaining paragraphs should be sufficiently clear. Attention should be directed, however, to several things which, although not required, are often used in the certificate. Subdivision 2 of Sec. 10 of the General Corporation Law of New York provides: "The certificate of incorporation of any corporation may contain any provision for the regulation of the business and the conduct of the affairs of the corporation, and any limitation upon its powers, or upon the powers of its directors and its stockholders, which does not exempt them from the performance of any obligation or the performance of any duty imposed by law." Other states have similar laws.

Experienced organizers utilize this provision for the purpose of giving stability to the corporation and protection to the stockholders by inserting therein rules for the internal management of the corporation. Provisions such as giving the corporation the right to hold and dispose of stock of other corporations; giving the corporation a lien on the stock of a member indebted to it; regulating the amount of working capital and the manner of declaring dividends; and providing for cumulative voting, for committees of directors, for classifications of directors, as well as other features that may be desirable.

Certificate of incorporation a contract. The certificate of incorporation is a contract, primarily between the state and the corporation, as definitely determined by the Dartmouth College Case (see citation, page

---

[4] The courts, today, seem to give very broad discretion to directors in the exercise of incidental powers by their corporations.

57) and cannot be altered, amended, or abrogated except by mutual consent. At present, however, the various states reserve, as one of the conditions of granting the certificate, the right to repeal, amend, alter, and change the charter by due process of law, although granting the corporation the right to present objections. The corporation has also the right to amend the certificate in any legal respect upon obtaining the favorable vote of stockholders holding a prescribed part of its stock at a special meeting called to consider this matter.[5]

The corporate charter. There is a widespread tendency to speak of the certificate of incorporation as the corporate charter. This is incorrect. A charter represents the complete grant of authority; hence the complete charter of a corporation consists not only of the certificate of incorporation but also of all the laws upon which the certificate itself rests. Thus the charter of a business corporation would be the certificate, resting upon the Stock Corporation Law, resting upon the General Corporation Law, resting upon the state constitution, resting upon the United States Constitution, and any provision of any of these underlying laws or constitutions that has any bearing whatever upon the corporation is a part of its charter, while anything in any one of them that violates any provision of an underlying one is, of course, void.

The corporate by-laws. Still another instrument for the government of the corporation is the by-laws. These are in reality simply a set of rules adopted by the stockholders, sometimes by the directors, to govern the internal operation of the corporation. By-laws usually cover such matters as management of property, calling of special meetings, establishment of quorums, prescription of special duties of directors, the titles of company officers and the duties of these officers, and methods of voting. In addition, it is usually provided that the by-laws can be amended at any time by a majority vote of the stockholders.

Other classifications of corporations. In a few paragraphs preceding this it was stated that corporations were legally classified as municipal, stock, and non-stock corporations. By popular usage, however, other descriptive names are employed to indicate their corporate character.

1. There is a division or classification based upon the relative extent to which state and private control are involved:

(a.) PUBLIC CORPORATIONS. Counties, cities, towns (Municipals), incorporated villages, turnpikes and others of a similar type.

(b.) QUASI-PUBLIC CORPORATIONS. Corporations having a franchise to use public property for private gain. Examples are Consolidated Edison Co. of New York and Detroit Edison Co.

---

[5] The legally required majority may be different for the amendment of one change of the certificate than for another.

c. PRIVATE CORPORATIONS. Those formed for private business and private gain, owned by private stockholders.

2. Again there is a grouping based upon the kind of business done, the product turned out:

a. RAILROAD CORPORATIONS

b. PUBLIC UTILITY CORPORATIONS

c. INDUSTRIAL CORPORATIONS

d. BANKING CORPORATIONS

and many others.

3. Finally, there is the grouping based upon the place of incorporation.

a. DOMESTIC CORPORATIONS. A corporation is domestic only in the state in which it is incorporated.

b. FOREIGN CORPORATIONS. A corporation is known as a foreign corporation in every state other than the one in which it is incorporated.

c. ALIEN CORPORATIONS. Alien corporation is the name given by many to a corporation doing business in a country other than its own. This latter, however, is not a legal designation. Legally all corporations whether chartered in another state or another country are known simply as *foreign* corporations.

Corporate organization taxes. Corporations are generally subject to two principal forms of taxation, the preliminary or organization tax by the state of the organization, the annual taxes called the *franchise taxes* by the state, as well as the federal income tax. Annual franchise and other taxes are part of this discussion. Here in this chapter on the corporate organization we are interested mainly in the taxes incident to the formation. All of the states levy an organization tax which has to be paid when the certificate of incorporation is filed. The amount varies widely in the several states and is calculated in various ways. New York imposed a tax of five cents on each $100 of authorized par value capital stock, and five cents for each share of no-par stock regardless of its selling price. It can be readily seen that the use of no-par stock with a low selling price would result in a large tax cost. One hundred dollars procured by a corporation through the sale of 5 shares of $20 par value stock would result in a tax of five cents. An equal amount procured through the sale of 5 shares of no-par stock sold at $20 per share would result in a tax of twenty-five cents, five times as much. This and similar laws in a number of other states have brought about a tendency to use par value stock with low par value, rather than no-par stock where a large number of shares is desired at a minimum tax.

The arrangement of this organization tax in several states may be interesting and useful in showing the great variation of method and the vastly different ways of treating the no-par stock.

Delaware

Shares with par value

Up to and including $2,000,000	1¢ per $100.
Over $2,000,000 up to and including $20,000,000	$200 plus ½¢ for each $100 over $20,000,000
Over $20,000,000	$1,100 plus 1/5¢ for each $100 over $20,000,000

Shares without par value

Up to and including 20,000 shares	½¢ per share
Over 20,000 shares up to and including 2,000,000 shares	$100 plus ¼¢ for each share over 20,000
Over 2,000,000 shares	$5,050 plus 1/5¢ for each share over 2,000,000
Minimum organization tax	$10

New Jersey

Shares with par value	20¢ per $1,000
Shares without par value	5¢ per share
Minimum organization tax	$25

California

$25,000 or less	$15 (minimum)
Over $25,000 but not over $75,000	25
Over $75,000 but not over $200,000	50
Over $200,000 but not over $500,000	75
Over $500,000 but not over $1,000,000	100
Over $1,000,000	100 plus $50 for every $500,-000 or fraction thereof over $1,000,000

Stock without par value—Same as above but computation based on assumed value of $10 per share ....

There are as many variations as there are states. In some states the tax is very low while in others it can involve payment of a large sum. Since, however, it is only paid one time in the entire life of the corporation, it is seldom the deciding factor in the determination of the state in which to incorporate.

There are also sundry filing fees, some of which are:

Delaware	....	$20
New York	....	40
New Jersey	....	15
California	....	20
Colorado	....	25
Arizona	Filing certificate	$10
	Appointing of agent	5
	Issuing certificate	10
	Filing with county	10
	Each certified copy	10

Difficulties in corporate formation. Many businessmen are deterred from organizing their firm into a corporation because of the alleged difficulty of so doing. As a matter of fact, corporate formation presents very few difficulties to those learned and experienced in the field. Of course, it should not be attempted by those who are not thoroughly conversant with the laws and practices. Many lawyers, as well as incorporating companies,[6] specialize in doing incorporating work and will attend to all the details for a very reasonable fee. The person who is inexperienced in matters of this sort had better utilize such expert assistance. This is advised not because he could not, in all probability, draw up a certificate of incorporation which would be accepted by the authorities, but rather because he ought to make sure that he has included all the provisions that he is entitled to and should include for his own protection and welfare.

Liability of corporate stockholders. One of the distinguishing features of the corporation is the limited liability of its members. It has already been seen that individual proprietors are fully liable personally for all the debts of their business, and that members of general partnerships, the general partners in a limited partnership, members of joint-stock companies, and members of certain types of business trusts are jointly and severally liable for the debts of their companies. Generally speaking, however, stockholders in corporations are not liable for any of the debts of the firm and the greatest loss they can suffer through disaster to the business is the loss of their investment.

There are minor exceptions to this general statement. A stockholder, possessing stock for which the issuing company has not been paid up to the full par value is directly liable to the firm's creditors for the amount of the unpaid portion on his shares for any debts contracted by the corporation in which he holds such shares. Some states provide that this liability ends when the holder disposes of his stock, others (like New York) provide that the liability stands for two (or a stated number of) years after the disposal of the stock, if suit is brought within that time. Since there is very little part-paid stock outstanding, it may be said that the actual liability of corporate stockholders is almost trivial. A few states, including New York, provide that all stockholders, both part paid and full paid, are jointly and severally liable for all debts due and owing by an insolvent corporation to any of its laborers, servants, or employees, other than contractors, for services performed by them for such corporation provided suit is brought in the prescribed manner (S.C.L., N.Y., Sec. 71).

The management is delegated. The authority and responsibility for the management of the corporation is, under the law, delegated entirely to a board of directors which is elected periodically by the stockholders'

---

[6] Incorporating companies are corporations and cannot practice law; their incorporating services are rendered to lawyers only.

votes. Beyond electing these directors and having the right to vote on certain questions concerning at one time all the corporation's property, such as sales, leases, mortgages, amendments of certificate, consolidation, merger, the stockholders take no active part in the management. The details of management, the part of both board and stockholders therein will be found in Chapter V.

The corporation has stability. The corporation has, to a very marked degree, the characteristic of stability so much desired in business forms. Having continuous succession, its life is unaffected by the transfer of shares or by anything that may happen to a shareholder or a director. War between nations represented by the stockholders does not affect the status of the corporation. There is no *delectus personarum* and new members may enter at any time simply by taking over stock of old holders. The corporation ends with the lapse of the period of life prescribed by the certificate of incorporation. It can also be dissolved by court order for non-use of franchise, or for fraudulent or illegal acts. The corporation may also be dissolved by a vote of holders of two-thirds of the stock at a special meeting, or without such meeting upon the written approval of 100 per cent of the stockholders. With these few normal exceptions, the corporation may be said to have perpetual as well as continuous life.

Flexibility. The corporation is extremely flexible in regard to the important features of expansion, management, and movement. Since it can readily appeal to the investment or speculative instinct of hundreds of thousands of individuals, it can almost invariably, if reasonably prosperous and sound, raise any reasonable amount of additional capital for expansion by simply offering its stocks and bonds to the public. It may thus enlarge to any reasonable extent along its present lines, or through broad charter powers can go into many related or incidental lines.

Its flexibility as to management is assured by the fact that it is managed under almost absolute powers by the board of directors, elected by the stockholders. This board can formulate and alter management policies almost at will. If its policies are not satisfactory to the stockholders, they have the power, if they choose to exercise it, to choose new and different directors at the next regular election.

All corporations have complete freedom of movement within their respective states. No state, however, has the power to grant a corporation authority to operate in another state. If a corporation desires to "do business" in a state other than its own, it must request of and receive from the other state a certificate of authority. This is obtained by making proper application, giving full information concerning all details of your corporation, submitting copy of the certificate of incorporation from its own state, paying the prescribed fees, pledging to observe all the laws and to pay the required taxes of the foreign state. A corporation may thus enter into and do business in any number of states in addition to its own. It must be understood that a corporation may sell, deliver, and collect for its products or services in and into other states, or do anything that may be construed as within interstate commerce, without being considered as "doing business" in that state, and without procuring the certificate of authority. The question of "what constitutes doing business" is one of the most difficult and complicated in the entire law of corporations, and each transaction across state lines should be studied with great care before being indulged in. Any corporation found actually doing business in a foreign state without the proper certificate of authority is considered as something of an outlaw and will be denied all rights and powers in that state, including the right to appear in its courts for any purpose whatever and in some states be subject to fines.

Some states are very favorable to foreign corporations and have few restrictions or special regulations, while others are considered "hostile," charging higher taxes than they charge to their domestic companies and not permitting them to engage in some kinds of business. Often a corporation wishing to do business in a foreign state will find it cheaper or otherwise more satisfactory to organize and operate a separate and distinct subsidiary company in the outside state.

Legal status of the corporation. The status of the corporation as a legal entity or fictitious being, with continuous existence, transferable ownership, delegated managerial authority, limited liability of members, only slightly restricted movement into the various states, is thoroughly established by the laws of all of the states, but despite this the statutes of the several commonwealths differ widely in detail, thus causing considerable trouble and uncertainty when a corporation may be concerned with more than one state.

Government control. Corporations are more subject to governmental control and supervision than are any other forms of business organization. They are closely watched by and subject to the visitorial powers of the state and, in many instances, of the national government. They are heavily taxed and have to render multitudinous reports. Some states are much more liberal in their treatment of corporations, especially in such matters as allowing broader powers, exacting lower taxes, and giving greater freedom in choice of accounting methods, than are others, and are profiting by becoming the great incorporating states, and the domiciles of many of our largest and richest corporations.

Advantages and disadvantages of the corporate form. The principal advantages and disadvantages of the corporate form may be tabulated as follows:

Advantages:

1. Possibility of aggregating large sums of capital.
2. Limited liability of stockholders.

3. Continuous succession.

4. Marketability of ownership.

5. Adaptability to efficient organization and flexibility of expansion and movement.

Disadvantages:

1. Formation is complicated and requires the services of an expert to be really efficient.

2. Stockholders usually have little voice in the conduct of the business.

3. Non-uniformity of the corporation laws of the various states causes difficulty.

4. Strict governmental control and heavy taxation are burdensome.

Questions for Study and Review

1. Explain in detail the terms: (a) private corporation; (b) public corporation; (c) quasi-public corporation.
2. Name and explain the three kinds of powers possessed by corporations.
3. Explain in detail and compare the certificate of incorporation and corporate by-laws.
4. Explain the reasons for making a complete study of selecting the state in which to incorporate.
5. Explain the limited liability of corporate stockholders.
6. Discuss the principal advantages and disadvantages of the corporation as a type of business organization.
7. Explain the stability of the corporate form.
8. Give a definition of a corporation; make your definition embody the modern concept of the term.
9. What information is generally required in a certificate of incorporation?
10. Explain the legal requirements as to the corporate name.

Problems

1. By means of a diagram, show the complete charter of (a) a trust company, (b) a manufacturing company.

2. Mr. Anderson buys 100 shares of Abbott Corporation common stock with a par value of $50 per share and pays the full amount to the corporation. If the corporation fails with no realizable assets, how much does he lose? If Mr. Anderson had sold the stock to Mr. Brown for $60 per share before the corporation had failed, how much would Mr. Brown lose under the same circumstances?

3. A corporation is organized with a capital of $1,000,000 divided into common stock with a par value of $1.00 per share. What corporation fees would have to be paid to the state? If the incorporators were to use no par value stock, what fees would be incurred?

4. (a) Suppose that all of the stockholders in a corporation died, and that the directors are not stockholders, not being required to be such in this company. What steps should the board of directors take?

(b) If the same thing happened in a joint-stock company and in a Massachusetts trust, what would the board of governors and the board of trustees do?

5. The Tastee Meat Corporation was incorporated two years ago as a butcher shop in a fast growing community. Most of the meat was purchased from a local packing house which enjoyed a good reputation in the county. The owners of the packing house now wish to retire and offer to sell out to the owners of the Tastee Meat Corporation. Can the Tastee Meat Corporation safely buy and operate the packing house under their present charter which does not specifically mention meat packing? Can the Tastee Meat Corporation purchase a ranch at a later date so that they may be assured of a supply of animals for the packing house? The Tastee Meat Corporation would also like to operate the ranch as a dude ranch with a swimming pool and a nine-hole golf course in addition to using it as a source of supply for the packing house. Suppose they also want to acquire the sporting goods store now located next door to the meat market. Can the present certificate of incorporation be amended to include the operation of a sporting goods store?

6. Prepare a statement of expressed powers used in a certificate of a corporation formed to manufacture shoes.

7. You plan to incorporate a manufacturing company with 10,000 shares of no par value common stock, and 10,000 shares of $100 par value preferred stock. What would be your organization tax (a) in New York, (b) in Delaware, (c) in New Jersey, (d) in California?

8. Discuss the contents of a certificate of incorporation of a manufacturing concern.

Written Assignment

Draw up a certificate of incorporation for _____.

NOTE: Forms of certificate of incorporation for New York State bearing full and complete directions for drawing up, may be obtained from the publishers of this text. Regular forms for other states (but without directions) may be obtained from commercial or legal stationers.

Managing a Corporation

Who owns the corporation. The stockholders are the actual owners of a corporation. But who are the stockholders? For many years it was assumed that they came from the wealthy families of the country. Times change and gradually it became apparent that the middle income group, too, are stockholders. Precise information was lacking until the Brookings Institute undertook to find out in 1952. Its study showed that 6,500,000 persons owned stock in public corporations. By the end of 1955 that number had increased by 33 per cent. At present it is increasing by about 500,000 persons per year. Added to the 8,630,000 or more persons who own stock in public corporations, an additional 1,400,000 persons own stock in private corporations. Obviously these 10,000,000 people cannot all be wealthy—there just are not that many rich people in America. Both the study of the Brookings Institute and the later study of the New York Stock Exchange disclosed that the greater number of stockholders are from the middle income group. Two-thirds of all stockholders, it was found, earn less than $7,500 a year. Some are in the lowest income groups and are buying shares in American industry through stock purchase plans of the corporation for which they work. Although women shareholders outnumber the men, the men hold more shares than the women. Stock ownership is not restricted to one state although New York, California, and Illinois have about 40 per cent of the stockholders of the nation.

Most companies prefer that their stock be widely held, for many reasons. For one thing, the stockholders form a loyal group of customers. General Motors has almost 600,000 stockholders to whom they quite naturally hope to sell cars. General Foods Corporation has a special order department for stockholders who may buy gift packages at cost. These stockholders throughout the country are a potent advertising group for the company. Second, management is not unaware that it is more difficult to wage a successful proxy fight against them if the stock is widely scattered throughout the country, with each stockholder holding a rela-

tively few shares. Stock in public utilities, because they are local industries, is less widely held than that of the industrials.

Although there are many more people employed in the United States
than there are stockholders, a great many of the large corporations have
more stockholders than employees. This is not surprising when it is
realized how much capital equipment is required in a large firm. Sinclair
Oil Corporation, to take only one example, has about $50,000 invested
for each employee. It takes quite a few shareholders to amass that
amount. There are five and one-half stockholders to each employee in
that company. Other large corporations, on the other hand, have more
employees than stockholders.

Stockholders in management. Just what does stock ownership in a
corporation signify? Does it mean ownership of the profits and power to
control operations, or is it something less than this? The individual proprietor of a business has the complete control of the business in his hands.
The responsibility is his and the profits or losses are his to spend or reinvest as he chooses. Does ownership of stock carry the same responsibility and the same power as ownership of the individual proprietor or
the general partner? Although the stockholders are the true owners of
the corporation, their share in the management is generally small. Their
franchise is felt primarily in their right to elect directors although they
must consent to changes in the name of the corporation, to increases in
the number of shares, to combine with other corporations, and to perform certain other acts. Stockholders form a body entirely separate from
the board of directors, although directors individually are sometimes
holders of large blocks of shares. In small companies, all of the stock
may be owned by members of the board of directors, and every stockholder may be on the board. Where the stockholders are also directors
the duties and powers of these persons assembled as stockholders are
quite different from those they have as directors. All the rules and laws
promulgated for each body must be observed just as carefully as though
the stockholders and directors were different persons in fact.

In large corporations, it is virtually impossible to unite control with
ownership. The physical impossibility of communicating with stockholders to poll them on company action is appreciated when it is remembered that American Telephone and Telegraph Co. has over a million
and a half stockholders virtually all over the globe. Then, too, it is almost literally true today that as business has become larger and larger it
has become more and more complicated, so that no one man in a large
firm knows what is going on in all phases of the operation. Stockholders,
even if they could be consulted, would not be generally competent to
vote intelligently on matters concerning the law of labor or finance.

However, to deny stockholders entirely the right to control the enterprise in which they have invested their savings would be to invite

manipulation on the part of unscrupulous management. To protect investors, many of whom have little understanding of their company's operations, Congress enacted a series of laws which were designed to make
available to the stockholder information which he should have in order
to invest intelligently and to follow the operation of his company. Perhaps the best known of these laws is the Securities Act of 1933. The objectives of this act were to require a complete disclosure of all pertinent
facts to the prospective security purchaser and to make it easier for a
person misled by the underwriters (and the management of the company) to secure redress in a law suit. The Securities and Exchange Act of
1934, among other things, provides the stockholder with a voice at the
meetings of the corporation through the proxy regulations promulgated by
the Securities and Exchange Commission which administers these laws.

Although the number and the composition of the stockholder family
in the United States is interesting, the mere number of stockholders is
not in itself of much significance. Almost universally each share of common stock carries one vote per share. It is necessary to know, therefore,
not only how many stockholders there are but also how many shares
are owned by each. Equitable Gas Co., a public utility, has 11,310 stockholders living in all states of the union. Of these, 91 per cent own 44
per cent of the stock, with average holdings of slightly less than 90
shares. The other 9 per cent of the stockholders, consisting for the most
part of banks, brokers, corporations, and fiduciaries, account for 56 per
cent of the shares, or an average of about 1,150 shares per holder.

The stockholders generally delegate to the directors all the rights of
management, except those few that the laws provide can be exercised
only by consent of a certain portion of the stockholders. If directors do
not manage the affairs of the company to suit the wishes of the stockholders, the latter can show their superior power of control by electing
new directors in their places at the expiration of their terms. In the
meantime, however, the stockholders are powerless to control the actions
of any members of the board unless they can be shown to have acted
in bad faith or incompetently, or in an illegal manner. In such cases they
may be removed by court order and the vacancies filled by electing new
directors. However, the rather common practice on the part of stockholders of giving their voting proxies at election to the proxy committee of
the board of directors tends to make the board practically self-perpetuating. In any case, however, if rights of minority stockholders are in-
fringed, the courts can be called upon to compel the management to
accord to such minority its legal rights.

Stockholders' meetings. The *regular meetings* of stockholders for the
election of directors and the transaction of other business are usually held
annually, but *special meetings* for special purposes may be called at
other times. The rules governing such meetings are embraced in the by-

laws of the organization. Any business may be transacted at regular meetings, except such matters as the law provides can be taken care of only at special meetings called for the purpose. Actions requiring specially called meetings are generally:

(a) Such as require an amendment of the certificate of incorporation, namely: (1) change of corporate name, (2) changes in the purposes or powers of the corporation, (3) changes in respect to the capital stock or capital, such as increasing or reducing the amount of authorized stock, increasing or reducing the par value of the shares, increasing or reducing the number of shares of stock, changing certain shares from par value to no-par value or vice versa, (4) changes in the number of directors (5) changes in the location of the home office, and so on, or:

(b) Actions which at one time affect the interests of all of the stockholders, such as: (1) selling all the assets of the company, (2) placing a mortgage on the property, (3) entering into a consolidation with other companies, (4) determining upon a dissolution, and so on. It is well to remember that special meetings can transact only that business for which they are called (S.C.L. of New York, Secs. 35, 36, 37, 38, 45).

The by-laws provide what number of shares shall constitute a quorum for the transaction of business at regular stockholders' meetings, while the law frequently sets the quorum for various special meetings. As a rule, no quorum is necessary at special or adjourned meetings held to elect directors who, for some reason, could not be chosen at the appropriate regular meeting. For this purpose, the laws of most states provide that those present at such meeting, regardless of number, may elect.

Voting. All common stocks of corporations listed on the New York Stock Exchange (with one or two exceptions) and the American Exchange have voting power. However, in non-listed corporations, particularly the smaller and closely held concerns, there may be a restriction on the voting power of the stockholder amounting almost to complete disfranchisement. A corporation acting through its board of directors does not have the right to deprive a stockholder of the voting right, but it does have the power in most states to offer a non-voting stock. However, the stockholders themselves may consent to become disenfranchised, though it is not common. Unlike common stock, the holders of preferred stock have often a restricted voting power. Often the preferred has a vote only if six quarterly dividends are passed. In that event, they may have a vote equal with the common, or they may elect some or all of the board of directors until the dividends are resumed. Usually the preferred stock has a vote on questions which vitally affect their position such as merger, consolidation, recapitalization, sale of mortgage bonds, and the like. The New York Stock Exchange does not admit preferred stock to listing unless it has at least a minimum of voting privilege.

In the early days of American corporations, the stockholders voted under the common law since there were no state laws pertaining to corporations. Common law provided one vote for each shareholder regardless of the number of shares he owned. Hence, under the common law, two stockholders owning 1 share of stock each could outvote one stockholder holding 1,000 shares. As time went on, it became recognized that a corporation was essentially an aggregation of capital rather than an association of individuals. It followed, therefore, that a more equitable distribution of power would result if each shareholder was given voting power in proportion to the amount of money invested by him. Laws were enacted by the several states which made the vote depend upon the share rather than the owner and automatically made voting power proportionate to the capital investment. In some states, another method of voting, called cumulative voting, is permissible. Under this system of voting, limited to election of directors, each stockholder is entitled to cast the number of votes which is equal to the number of shares of stock owned by him multiplied by the number of directors to be elected. He may cast all such votes for a single director, may distribute them among the total number of directors to be voted upon, or vote for any one or more of them as he sees fit. An understanding of the cumulative method of voting and of its operation is important in the control of the corporation whose charter provides for this method of electing directors. Some states, Illinois for example, require that cumulative voting be used in electing directors.

Cumulative voting. Mr. Madison, who owns 20 shares of stock in Corporation A, which is to elect five directors, is entitled to 100 votes (obtained by multiplying 20, the number of shares owned, by 5, the number of directors to be chosen). There may be any number of nominees from whom Mr. Madison may select the five he prefers and gives 20 votes to each of them. If he prefers, however, he can give 25 votes to each of four candidates, 50 votes to each of two, or the entire 100 votes to any one, thus strengthening the chances of the election of his choice. He is not limited, of course, by these divisions of his votes, but can apportion them in any manner whatever.

A stockholder or group of stockholders may be desirous of electing a certain number of directors of their own choice, and it is of value to them to know in advance how many directors can be assured of election by the votes from the stock they have, or how many additional shares will be necessary to elect the group they wish. A number of convenient formulas have been derived to determine this, of which the following may be taken as an example:

$$X = \frac{ac}{b+1} + 1$$

1. Need to know how many are going to vote.

In this formula, a represents the total number of voting shares of stock participating in the election; b, the total number of directors to be elected; c, the number that the particular group wishes to elect; and X, the number of shares it is necessary to hold to elect c out of b directors.

Let us suppose that the M Corporation has 1,500 shares of voting stock outstanding, that 1,000 of these shares are represented at the meeting in person or by proxy, and that there are nine directors to be elected. Mr. Weston, a stockholder, wishes to be certain of the election of five of them. How many shares of stock must he control? Substituting in the above formula, we have:

$$X = \frac{1000 \times 5}{9 + 1} + 1 = \frac{5000}{10} + 1 = 500 + 1 = 501 \text{ shares}$$

Thus, if he controls the votes of 501 shares, he can be certain of electing five out of the nine directors, provided he distributes all of his votes as evenly as possible among five candidates he desires. Similarly, we may find that, in order to elect four directors, he would need 401 shares; to elect three, he would need 301 shares; and so on. Thus, if he has set his mind on the election of any particular number of directors, he knows just how many shares he may be short of the required number, and he can set about acquiring the necessary remainder.

On the other hand, he may not wish to acquire any additional stock. He may simply want to know how many directors he can be sure of electing with the stock he has, and thus know among how many of the candidates he may safely divide his votes. Presume, for example, that in this same company he owns 425 shares. Then, in the formula, the *425* takes the place of the X, and the number he can elect, represented by *c*, becomes the unknown quantity. The equation, then, takes the form and solution indicated below:

$$425 = \frac{1000c}{9 + 1} + 1$$
$$425 = 100c + 1$$
$$424 = 100c$$
$$c = 4.24$$

Thus Mr. Weston, with 425 shares, could mathematically elect almost four and one-quarter directors, but, of course, since there is no such thing as a fraction of a director, and Mr. Weston has not enough votes (501) to elect five directors, he can elect only four, and could not be prevented from so doing, provided he divided all of his votes properly among them.

As a matter of fact, it would require only 401 shares to elect the four directors, and if these were all he wished to elect he would be able to dispose of 24 shares of his stock and still not weaken his chances at the election, or he might be able to get control of 76 additional shares bringing his total number up to the 501 shares necessary to elect five.

Protection through cumulative voting. Cumulative voting assures to holders of comparatively small amounts of stock at least some representation on the board of directors. They are assured this representation through no other voting method. Let us consider again the M Corporation, mentioned under *cumulative voting*. In this corporation, there are 1,000 shares of stock voting at an election of directors. Suppose that one group of stockholders holds 501 of these shares and another group holds 499 of them. Under the statutory method of voting, the larger group could cast the votes of 501 shares for the first candidate put up, against the votes of 499 that the smaller group could cast for its choice. They could do the same with the second, and the third, and so on, until they had elected the entire nine directors, thus leaving the large minority with no representation whatever on the board. Under the cumulative plan of voting, however, the smaller group could elect (see p. 77) four of the directors, while the larger group could elect five. This is, of course, a fair representation. If there were a stockholder or group of stockholders holding as few as 101 shares, they could, by concentrating their votes on one candidate, elect him to the board and thus get representation.

Voting by proxy. If a stockholder cannot be present at a stockholders' meeting, he is permitted to have someone attend for him and vote his stock. This is termed voting by proxy, and the person who acts for the stockholder is called the proxy. Proxy is also the term generally applied to the written authorization the stockholder gives to another person to represent him, and to vote his stock. Legally a proxy is a power of attorney, transferring the right to vote without transferring the share. These proxies must be executed by the stockholder himself, or his personal representative. A proxy can be revoked at any time by the person who executed it except in those states which permit irrevocable proxies. Generally they are executed for one meeting, but proxies can be executed to constitute some person a proxy for all meetings that may occur within a given time, usually not more than a year.

A stockholder may give his proxy to anyone he pleases, and in many cases friends, relatives, attorneys, or accountants act as proxies. By far the most general practice, however, is for the stockholder who does not wish to attend a meeting to conform to the request of the board of directors and send his proxy to the proxy committee of the board. Prior to 1934, the stockholder was frequently asked to sign a proxy which constituted a blank check to management. The proxy form, signed by the stockholder, authorized one or two men, whom he seldom knew, to vote in his place and stead at the meeting as they saw fit. The stockholder had no way of knowing what proposals were coming up for consideration at the regular annual meeting, nor in what manner the proxies would vote on these motions. Nor was there any way in which a stockholder could raise questions or make motions on his own without actually attending in person or giving his proxy to someone with written instructions as to what he wished done. In the Federal Securities Act of 1934, an attempt was made to make the stockholders' meetings more democratic by providing, to some extent at least, a forum for the stockholders. Now if the stockholder does not appear in person he can at least have his motion transmitted to all the stockholders and the question put to a vote by means of a proxy marked so that each stockholder can vote on the proposal in advance of the meeting. As the stockholder indicates his choice by marking the appropriate square, so must the proxies vote.[1]

Suffrage of the corporate stockholder was recognized to be an important right. But to exercise the right of suffrage intelligently any voter, whether it be at the village election or the corporate election, should have as much information as possible. To make this possible in the corporate meeting, the proxy regulations of the Securities and Exchange Commission provide that before any solicitation for the proxy may be made by the management, the stockholder must be given an annual financial report. This report may precede or accompany the proxy solicitation. The proxy must state that the solicitation of the proxy is made on behalf of the management, if that is so. In addition, it must state clearly and impartially each matter to be acted upon by the meeting whether proposed by the management or by one of the stockholders, insofar as the management has advance notice of a stockholder's proposal.

This does not limit the right of a stockholder to make a motion at the meeting without previous notice. Any proposal a stockholder has notified the corporation that he wishes to make must be included in the proxy statement along with a statement of up to one hundred words prepared by the stockholder in support of his motion. On the proxy itself, there must be a space provided for the stockholder to register his vote, and those persons designated by him as his proxies must vote according to the stockholder's directions as signified by what amounts to a marked ballot. Thus, in a recent notice of an annual meeting of the Sinclair Oil Corporation, the stockholders were notified that the annual meeting would consider:

1. The number of directors for the ensuing year.
2. The election of four directors for the term of three years.
3. Also act upon a resolution proposed by a stockholder relating to the Retirement Allowance Plan.
4. Also act upon a resolution proposed by another stockholder relating to cumulative voting.

[1] See Regulation X 14, Securities and Exchange Commission. It may be found in *Financial Handbook* page 427, Ronald Press, N.Y., 1949.

5. Other business properly brought before the meeting.

The proxy statement which accompanied the notice of meeting was part of the same seven-page pamphlet. It stated that the proxies would vote to continue the number of directors at twelve unless the stockholders directed otherwise by marking the proxy in the space provided. In other words, the stockholder had one method of voting to increase the number of directors—mark the appropriate box labeled "yes." He had two methods of voting against the proposition—either mark the ballot space marked "no," or leave both spaces blank. If the latter, the proxies would automatically vote against the proposal. Management had nominated four men to be directors and the stockholders' proxies would vote for the election of the nominees unless specifically directed otherwise.

As a practical matter, short of an organized proxy fight, there is little way in which an outside candidate could be elected a director. The men named in this particular notice were already directors and this constituted a re-election. Nevertheless, the company furnished a brief résumé of their connections. Two of the nominees were officers of the corporation and two were from outside the company. In addition, the names of all of the directors and their connections was also set forth for the information of the stockholders. The twelve directors together owned or controlled 60,775 shares of common stock. At the time of the proxy, there were 15,487,555 shares outstanding. The directors, therefore, owned or controlled only .0039 per cent of the voting stock.

Resolutions numbered three and four were proposed by individual stockholders and not the management. The first sought to limit executive pensions to $25,000 annually. The woman who introduced the resolution owned 10 shares of the company stock. Her statement, printed immediately following the statement of the resolution, contained ninety-three words in support. The proxy statement also advised the stockholders that another stockholder who owned 935 shares requested that he be listed as co-sponsor. Resolution number four was offered by a stockholder holding 5 shares of common stock. He proposed that cumulative voting be employed in the election of the directors.

The rules for proxies promulgated by the Securities and Exchange Commission also require that the remuneration paid to members of the board of directors and certain financial transactions of the board members with the corporation be set forth for the information of the stockholders in order to prevent abuses by the management in paying excessive compensation to themselves and to the officers. Motions by stockholders to decrease salaries and inquiries from stockholders on the floor at corporate meetings as to high salaries paid to officers are fairly frequent.

Corporations in recent years have made great efforts to attract stockholders to their meetings and have taken pride in the turnout. Organizations such as Newport News Shipbuilding Corporation attract large numbers of stockholders by offering them a free lunch and delightful trip around the Chesapeake Bay in an excursion boat, immediately following the meeting. Standard Oil Co. of New Jersey for some years has been giving an elaborate luncheon to the stockholders present, and sending a verbatim report of the meeting to all stockholders who were unable to be present.

So successful have these meetings become in recent years and so verbose are those attending that an edited summary of the meeting has had to take the place of the verbatim report which would be expensive to prepare and circulate. At stockholders' meetings, the officers of the corporation are usually present and available to the stockholders. Many corporations include a tour around the plant so that stockholders can see what is going on and talk to employees. Where a good many of the stockholders are also employees, it has a double barreled interest. Some, like Southern Co., have the legal meetings in the place appointed in the by-laws, and then have regional meetings throughout the United States. Some companies have televised their meetings over a closed circuit to the various cities.

Directors. It is well established in corporate law that the corporation can act only through its board of directors, except in the unusual situation where the stockholders act by unanimous vote at a meeting and the board of directors subsequently ratifies the action. In small, closely held business corporations it is not uncommon to find that all of the stockholders are both officers and directors in addition and therefore little attention is in fact paid to the legal distinction between those who direct and those who own. However, when it comes to performing legal acts such as opening a bank account, buying or selling land or other property, lawyers will insist that the formalities be rigidly adhered to so that the transaction may be given full legal effect.

The number of directors may be fixed for each corporation in the certificate of incorporation or in its by-laws. Subject to the rather general limits placed on the number of directors by the law of the various states, each corporation may fix for itself the number of directors it wishes. New York, for example, requires three directors as a minimum number, but makes no provision about a maximum number. Allied Chemical and Dye Corporation has sixteen directors, General Motors Corporation has thirty-three. Small corporations would naturally tend to have fewer directors than large corporations.

The board of directors elects from its own membership its Chairman and its important committees, such as the executive committee, the finance committee, and the proxy committee. General Motors, whose size and complex business activity make it difficult for the board at large to keep abreast of all phases of operation, has set up five committees. The financial policy committee has eleven members, the operations policy committee twelve members, the administrative committee twenty-two members, the audit committee four members and the bonus and salary committee five members. The executive committee is usually composed of very capable members of the board and it devotes considerable time to the day-to-day management of the company's business. This committee meets more frequently than the entire board and transacts a great deal of routine business between the meetings of the entire body. In many of the large corporations, the members of this executive committee are at the offices of the corporation at all times and, of course, are paid regular salaries.

The finance committee is the name given by some corporations to what is really an executive committee. However, the complexity of the financial operations of a firm can easily justify a separate committee whose attention is devoted to financial operations alone. Frequently the budget director of the company reports to this committee. It is certainly necessary that the treasurer, comptroller, and financial vice-president be in constant liaison with the workings of the committee.

Favorable labor relations, along with good stockholder relations, have become of major importance to the continued health of the corporation. General Motors Corporation has 599,000 employees working in all types of jobs and scattered all over the United States and several foreign countries. Some of these employees are members of labor unions, some are not. To retain their good will means not only freedom from costly work stoppages but an enthusiastic work force. In a recent study of employees at Swift Co. it was found that while the employees were loyal to the union, this loyalty did not preclude a loyalty to the plant which, if it was not downright enthusiasm, at least showed that employees thought this the best meat packing plant in which to work. To formulate policy with respect to employees, a special committee of the board of directors is often deemed a necessity.

The proxy committee is usually composed of members of the board of directors although it need not be. Its function is to receive the proxies of the stockholders on behalf of the management. In a large corporation, the combined stock holdings of the members of the board will usually be less than 1 per cent of the total, as it is in Sinclair Oil Co., already mentioned. Unless there were some method of collecting the votes of the stockholders, corporate management would not be in a position to stay in power nor to carry out its program. It might be added, also, that unless proxies were sent to someone there would seldom be a quorum authorized to transact business and that therefore there would be no meeting. In receiving the proxies or voting power of a large number of stockholders, this committee exercises a tremendous power in the stockholders' meetings. It is not unusual to find that this committee votes 90 per cent of all votes cast at a meeting. Many stockholders automatically sign the proxy sent to them by management. Others are pleased with the operation of the company and are quite willing to give the management the proxy as a vote of confidence. Others, it must be admitted, do not know what it is all about but, receiving a satisfactory dividend, are content to go along. A group seeking to oust the management by means of a proxy fight usually finds it both difficult and expensive.

Meetings of the board of directors. The board of directors, as we have seen, formulates the broad policy of the corporation, directs the general business operations, and supervises the work of the officers. It does not attempt to carry on the details of the business operation. That is the function of the officers, such as the president, vice-president, treasurer, and others whom the board has appointed. The board may exercise all the powers granted to it by the certificate of incorporation and the by-laws, and may transact, ordinarily, all matters pertaining to the welfare of the company. The laws of most states, however, provide that certain matters of more lasting and vital interest to all stockholders can be accomplished only with the consent of the stockholders and usually upon a vote of a greater number than a bare majority—often two-thirds or even three-quarters. Such matters are changing the number of directors, mortgaging, selling or leasing all property or at least a substantial portion of the property, changing the place of business, changing the capitalization of the corporation, changing the classification of the stock or adding newly authorized stock, entering into a combination, dissolution of the business, amending the certificate of incorporation, and other matters of similar importance. Other than these matters, the operation of the business is in the hands of the directors to the same extent that it would be in the hands of an individual proprietor.

All actions of the directors in the management of the corporation must, to be valid, have their origin in a meeting of the board after due notice has been given in accordance with the by-laws. That is to say, no director or group of directors can transact any company business except at a regular or special meeting of the board at which a quorum is present. Unlike stockholders' meetings, a member of the board must be physically present to vote. Voting by proxy is not permitted.

The by-laws of the company provide the rules under which the board of directors meet and operate. Meetings are, like stockholders' meetings, either general meetings or special meetings. Usually the time and place of the directors' general meetings are provided in the by-laws. Some state laws require that such meetings be held within the limits of the state of incorporation. Other and more liberal state laws provide that the meetings may be held wherever it is most convenient for the directors. Delaware is such a state. Meetings which must be called from time to time and which are not specified in the by-laws are called special meetings. It is generally easier to call a special meeting of the board of directors than it is to call a special meeting of the stockholders. For one thing there are fewer directors and it is easier to notify them of the meeting. The by-laws, again, provide just who can call a special meeting, for what business, and the place.

Notice of either a general or special meeting should be in writing, but notice of the time and place of the meeting may be waived by the directors. Thus a meeting, particularly where the directors are also employees of the company, can often be called on very short notice.

Directors, as a rule, do not receive a salary for their work. They serve for the prestige the office carries, or for some collateral advantage that might be gained, or purely for the enjoyment that men derive from working. Nevertheless, in more and more of the larger corporations, when the directors are required to spend a great deal of time in preparation for the meeting and to read through anywhere from a few hundred up to a thousand pages of material covering all phases of the business on which they must come to decisions, salaries are paid to directors. In other corporations, like Standard Oil Co. of New Jersey, where the directors are also employees and officers, the regular salaries paid would undoubtedly reflect the time devoted to their functions as corporate directors. The remuneration of directors should not be determined by the directors themselves, but should be provided for in the by-laws, or fixed by vote of the stockholders assembled in meeting.

Qualifications of directors. There are no special qualifications which a director must possess. It is usually only necessary that the person chosen be old enough to enter into contracts. This age varies from state to state, and even within a state, depending upon the nature of the contract. The by-laws or state law usually require that the director be a stockholder, though this is not universally so. General Douglas MacArthur was Chairman of the Board of Remington Rand, Inc. for some time before he owned a share of stock in that corporation.

The reason for requiring a director to own stock in the corporation of which he is a director is simple. It is commonly felt that a man with a financial interest at stake will devote more attention to the business. However valid this reason was in years gone by, it has lost much of its persuasiveness. Today management is chosen for its professional competence rather than its financial contribution. In any event the financial contribution of management usually is so small that it is hardly an incentive to the individual director to be more careful, or a deterrent to carelessness. To require of a director that he invest substantially all of his fortune in the company of which he is a director would mean losing many valuable men.

In some states, the directors of banks or insurance companies are held by the courts to a higher standard of competence and a higher degree of care than are the directors of ordinary business corporations. Certain qualifications indicative of competence should be possessed by the person who accepts the directorship of a bank or insurance company to avoid embarrassment and liability on his part. A director is not responsible for a loss suffered by the corporation as a result of his, or the board's, poor judgment if all members acted honestly in good faith and within their powers as directors. This would suggest that the stockholders give close attention to the choosing of the members who will represent them on the board and in whom they entrust the business operations. Moreover, in most states, no provision is made either in the corporate statutes or in the by-laws for the removal of directors. There is an exception made, however, for the removal by the state of a director for cause. Theft of corporate property would certainly be grounds for removal by the state. Refusal to carry on the duties of a director for a protracted period might be another.

Directors must direct. They cannot agree among themselves or with the stockholders to be mere "dummies." They must be present at the meetings of the board, though an occasional absence with or without cause is not usually sufficient reason for holding a director liable for loss to the business. Although a director must conduct the business affairs of the company with all reasonable prudence, there is no standard of prudence set up. If a director is elected who is utterly lacking in business experience and is, in fact, a real "dummy," then the stockholders cannot expect much from him. If the company should lose through his actions, it is not unreasonable to expect them to bear the loss without complaint so long as the director acted in good faith. Their only redress would be to elect another, better qualified man at the next election.

Directors are liable for wilful negligence, for causing a loss to the company by neglecting to take action where such action is required, or for doing a wrongful act. Where it is possible to spell out a standard for directors, it is the standard of what a reasonable man would do in the conduct of his own business. It is hardly safe to generalize, however, when discussing the conduct of directors. What might be wrongful at a given time and under special circumstances might be perfectly proper at another time. Stockholders individually cannot sue directors for a personal loss suffered because the corporation has lost money. Nor can the stockholder sue collectively to recover corporate losses. The theory is that the stockholders, being separate and distinct from the corporation, suffered no individual loss. The loss was sustained by the corporation. Therefore, the corporation must sue the directors. However, since the directors manage the corporation and are understandably reluctant to sue themselves, the stockholders are permitted to sue on behalf of the corporation and any judgment won is for the benefit of the corporation and not the stockholders.

Corporate officers. The *chairman* of the board of directors is not an officer of the corporation. However, he may be the chief executive officer either because he combines the job of president with his position as chairman of the board, or because of his influence and dynamic personality. The chairman of the board not only acts as the presiding officer of the board when it is in session, but usually exercises very important control over the affairs of the company in general. He is usually a more influential man than the president and may give instructions to him. He may not only interest himself in a general way in the internal workings of the business, but also devote a large part of his energies to maintaining proper relations between the corporation and those with whom it comes in contact on the outside.

The *president* is the chief executive of the company and is responsible for its proper internal management and operations. All departments, through their respective heads, are responsible to him. The laws of some states require that he be selected from the membership of the board of directors, a fact which, of course, enables him to keep the board in close touch with the workings of the business. He usually presides over stock-holders' meetings.

The *vice president* in smaller companies is intended to be a substitute for the president in his absence or incapacity and is usually given minor duties in assisting the president. In larger corporations, however, there are frequently a great many vice presidents, each of whom has definite and important duties. They are usually the responsible department heads. We often see such titles as "Vice-President in Charge of Production," "Vice-President in Charge of Purchasing," "Vice-President in Charge of Sales," "Vice-President in Charge of Personnel," and so on.

The *treasurer* has custody and charge of the funds and securities of the company. He has the right to sign checks for payment of obligations and, also, to endorse for the company its checks, notes, and other obligations. He is responsible to the finance committee of the board of directors. The credit and collection departments are generally under the supervision of the treasurer. In the larger corporations, there are both comptroller and auditor, as described below, but in the smaller companies the duties of both of these officers are often performed by the treasurer or his clerks.

The *comptroller* is the principal officer in charge of the accounts of the company. He has supervision of the bookkeeping, accounting, auditing, and reporting procedure. All reports concerning financial conditions should be approved by him. He is generally counted upon by the finance committee to do a large part of the financial planning and budgeting for the company.

The *auditor* examines the books and records of the business to see how the funds have been used and to determine the financial status of the business, which is to be shown in a balance sheet, and the result of operations to be brought out in the profit and loss statement. He should keep the directors informed as to the financial condition of the company. In addition to the work of the company's auditor, periodic audits are made by outside, independent auditors.

The *secretary* keeps the minutes of all meetings, including those of the directors, the stockholders, and the various committees, and has charge of the records. He is generally authorized to sign, with the president, all contracts, leases, mortgages, bonds, stock certificates, and other such documents, and to affix the corporate seal. He has charge of the certificate books, transfer books, and stock ledger. He is usually provided with one or more assistants to aid him in his work.

Power and protection of the minority. The maxim "the majority rules" is true in a corporation only if we define pretty carefully what we mean by the term *majority*. When one speaks of the controlling interest in a corporation, one is likely to think of a 51 per cent control. From a practical standpoint, however, it is rare in a corporation of any size to find any person or group owning that much stock. In American Telephone and Telegraph, no one person owns even 1 per cent of the stock. A 1 per cent interest in the common stock of General Motors is worth about $112,000,-000 on the market. However, it is not necessary to own a large percentage of the stock in order to control the company. Far less than 51 per cent of the stock will generally assure control for one or more of the following reasons:

1. Stock may be divided into voting and non-voting classes. These classes may occur in varying proportions in different companies. The most common method is to make the commonstock voting and the preferred stock non-voting. If in a corporation 50 per cent of the stock is voting and 50 per cent is non-voting, it is evident that, whatever the circumstances, a majority of the voting stock—that is, 26 per cent of the total stock—would exercise control.

2. Regardless of what portion of the stock may have the voting power, a considerable minority of the voting stockholders may be closely organized and in agreement to vote together on certain questions, or at an election. The remainder may be unorganized and their votes divided in several ways. Presume that about 30 per cent of the votes are banded together and that the other 70 per cent have no organization. If the 70 per cent are divided in several ways, the minority will very likely carry their points. Of course, the larger the minority and the more they can divide up the votes of the majority, the better is their chance of prevailing.

3. A minority of the stock may constitute a majority of the stock actually voting. In the previous two paragraphs, it was assumed that all of the voting stock was cast at stockholders' meetings. This would be most unusual. As a matter of fact, it is unusual, except in a fairly small organi-

zation, to have more than 80 per cent of the stock represented at a meeting, and frequently much less is in evidence. In such a case, a minority consisting of 41 per cent of the voting stock would control the meeting even though all of the remaining shares were united against it.

4. Sometimes stock votes by classes, and a minority class may be given the privilege of choosing a majority of the board of directors. The preferred stockholders of the Public Service Electric and Gas Co. elect a majority of the board of directors if dividends upon any of the three classes of preferred stock are in arrears in an amount equal to one year's dividend.

5. Stock with a strict vetoing power exerts a strong negative control over various affairs of a company. A certain class of stock (presume it to consist of about 20 per cent of the total) may be classified as nonvoting for ordinary purposes, and yet the certificate of incorporation may provide that certain things may not be done without the consent of the majority of this class of stock. In such a case, the holders of the majority of this stock, which would be only about 11 per cent of the entire stock, can absolutely block any action on the part of all the remainder.

6. By far the most common example of a minority of stock controlling is found in the meeting of any large corporation, where no individual or group owns more than, at most, 1 per cent of the stock outstanding. The directors who, as explained previously, seldom own much of the voting stock, often gain control by procuring proxies for themselves through the proxy committee. Influential groups of stockholders other than the directors frequently use the same system—with one big difference. The law provides that the expense of the directors procuring the proxies is an expense of the company, as otherwise no meeting would be possible. Any other group must pay its own expenses, which would not be low. In smaller corporations, the secretary is often the one who seeks and obtains the proxies of the stockholders, casting the votes, of course, according to the desires of his immediate employers, the directors.[2]

Controlling through voting trusts. It is sometimes desired to place the control of all or part of the stock in the hands of one person or of a few persons. This may be done through a *voting trust* agreement. Under this agreement, any number of stockholders transfer their stock to *voting trustees*, by whom the stock is held and voted at the stockholders' meetings. The old certificates are canceled and new ones issued in the names of the voting trustees. The real owners of the stock are given voting trust certificates to show that they are, in reality, the owners of the shares held by the voting trustees. They are thus enabled to claim their dividends when they are collected by the trustees and to recover their stock at the expiration of the trust.

---

[2] When a dissident group is successful in waging a proxy battle for control, the expenses of their solicitation of proxies may be recovered from the corporation.

These certificates, sometimes called *certificates of beneficial interest,* are negotiable when endorsed in blank, and are frequently listed and dealt in on stock exchanges. One of the principal prerequisites for the information of a voting trust is that it must be open to all stockholders of the company who desire to participate. Conditions relative to the trust differ slightly in the several states. In New York and New Jersey, for example, it cannot exceed a period of ten years. Since 1925, it is no longer legal in New York State for stockholders of banking corporations to form voting trusts.

This form of control is often resorted to when a business is in financial difficulties. If a corporation is unable to pay certain obligations, such as interest on its bonds, or perhaps principal, the bondholders may forego the foreclosure and extend the time for payment, provided the business can be put under the control of themselves or their representatives. In such a case, a voting trust could well be formed, the voting trustees being named by the creditors. If, under the management of the trustees, the business is made to prosper and pay off its debts, the trust will be dissolved and the control given back to the stockholders.

At the very start of a business, in order to keep the control and management in the hands of the originators until the business has had a chance to become established, a voting trust is sometimes used by a corporation, instead of turning the control over to a large number of stockholders.

Controlling through holding companies. The stock of a corporation may, in most jurisdictions, be owned and held by another company instead of by individuals as stockholders. Such a company, holding the stock of another corporation (and generally the stock of several other corporations at the same time) for control purposes, is known as a *holding company.* It draws dividends upon and votes the stock it holds, just as an individual stockholder would do. This arrangement places the control of the subsidiary company indefinitely in the hands of a small group (the directors of the holding company), whereas the device of the voting trust does so only during the limited life of the trust. Holding companies will be discussed more fully later.

Corporate books and records. The management of a corporation must maintain two classes of books or records, known respectively as the *corporate books* and the *financial books.*

Corporate books consist of the minute books for all meetings: directors', stockholders', and committees'; the stock book, a detailed record of all stock transactions; and the transfer book, usually consisting of stubs of the issued certificates bound in the certificate book. The stock book should contain the names of all persons who are stockholders in the corporation, showing their place of residence, the number of shares held by each of them, the time when they respectively became owners thereof, and the amount paid in thereon.

The *financial books* are the ordinary books of account used in recording the financial transactions of the corporation. They are similar to those used in any other business.

Statutes usually provide that the *corporate* books must be open for the inspection of stockholders, with certain regulations, and they provide a penalty for refusal to allow such examination. The *financial* books, however, are not open to the inspection of the stockholders. Corporations usually issue an annual or semiannual financial statement showing their condition, and, from these statements, stockholders can generally get desired information concerning the finances of the corporation. Under most statutes, however, holders of a certain percentage of the stock may demand at stated intervals a special sworn statement from the treasurer, in addition to the regular statements.

Questions for Study and Review

1. What are the functions and duties of the board of directors of a corporation?
2. Name the principal committees of a board of directors, and tell the functions of each.
3. What are usually the principal officers of a corporation, and what are their respective duties?
4. Name and describe three methods of voting for directors used by stockholders in corporations.
5. Describe in detail the right of proxy.
6. Mention at least five ways by which ownership of less than 51 per cent of the stock may give control of a corporation.
7. How does the system of cumulative voting assure the minority a representation on the board of directors?
8. Describe a voting trust, and tell what purposes it serves.
9. Describe a holding company.
10. What books must be kept by a corporation? How are they classified? Do stockholders have free access to them?

Problems

1. A corporation of which you are a stockholder has sent you a notice of the annual meeting and a proxy form. Describe the usual contents of the notice and the proxy form. Explain what you would do with the proxy form in the event that (a) you plan to attend the meeting in person, and (b) you will not be able to attend the meeting in person.

2. The by-laws of the Jackson Manufacturing Corporation provide that "at any meeting of the stockholders, a majority of the capital stock of the company, present in person or represented by proxy, shall constitute a quorum for all purposes, unless the representation of a larger number shall be required by law, and, in that case, the representation of the number so required shall con-

stitute a quorum." The company has outstanding 125,624 shares of voting stock. How many shares will be required to constitute a quorum at (a) a regular meeting, and (b) a special meeting?

3. You have been invited to become a member of the board of directors of a corporation. (a) How is your compensation determined? (b) How long is your term of office? (c) If you as a member of the board of directors know in advance that you will not be able to attend the next meeting of the board, how can you arrange to have your vote cast on questions which may arise at the meeting?

4. The Jamestown Manufacturing Corporation has outstanding $300,000 of $50 par value voting common stock. A meeting of the stockholders is to be held to elect by the cumulative method of voting the nine directors who constitute the board. It is expected that 5,000 shares of the outstanding voting stock will be represented at the meeting in person or by proxy. You own 1,801 shares of the common stock. (a) How many shares of the stock will you need to own to be able to elect five of the directors? (b) How many directors could you safely attempt to elect with the stock you already own?

5. You are one of the creditors of a corporation that has just become insolvent. You and the other creditors are convinced that, if foreclosure is not made and the company is placed under efficient management provided by the creditors, it will recover financially and will pay the creditors in full. It cannot do this if foreclosure is resorted to at once. Suggest a method by which the creditors can procure control for a definite period.

Written Assignment

A corporation has outstanding $500,000 of $25 par value voting common stock. A meeting of the stockholders is held to elect by the cumulative method of voting the seven directors who constitute the board of directors. At the meeting there are 7,150 shares of the common stock represented in person and 8,850 shares represented by proxy. You own 4,800 shares of the common stock and attend the meeting. (a) What percentage of the outstanding common stock is eligible to vote at the meeting? (b) How many shares of the stock will you need to own to be able to elect four of the directors? (c) How many directors could you safely attempt to elect with the stock you already own?

CHAPTER VI

Financing by Means of Stock

The owned capital of a business. The owned capital of a business, as distinguished from borrowed capital, is that part of its capital actually and permanently invested in it by its proprietors, whether they be partners, proprietors, trustors, stockholders, or what not, and in many cases, in addition to this, certain parts of the earnings which have been, from time to time reinvested, or "ploughed back" into the business. This part of the capital in a corporation is in reality permanently owned by the business and the directors are under no obligation to return it to or distribute among the owners of the business at any time except pro-rata, or as otherwise provided by contract, in case of dissolution. When, however, a corporation sells stock to produce such owned capital it is presumed to obligate the company to pay to the investors from time to time, usually at stated intervals, their proportionate shares of any profit believed available for such distribution. It does not, however, involve the corporation in any fixed or compulsory obligation to the investor in case such profits are not available or in case the Board of Directors does not, for any equitable reason, see fit to declare such a dividend.

Almost all of the original capital of corporations, and a very large part of that later acquired, is obtained by the sale of stock and it is the purpose of this chapter to discuss at some length the various types of stock and its use as an instrument of financing.

Capital stock, capital, capitalization. Before entering any discussion of financing it is necessary to clarify the meaning of the terms *authorized stock, capital stock, capital,* and *capitalization.*

Authorized stock means the total amount of stock of all classes authorized by the certificate of incorporation, whether it be issued in whole or in part or, as yet, entirely unissued.

Capital Stock represents the actual amount of stock of all classes which is issued and outstanding at any time, and not necessarily the total amount of authorized stock, a large part of which may be unissued.

Capital, as explained in Chapter I, consists, from the point of view of the business man, of all the property of every kind employed in the business. The accountant and investor consider capital the total ownership. It is expressed in dollars by adding to the amount invested in ownership, the surplus, and the undivided profits. In the case of a corporation it is generally spoken of as the sum of the capital stock and the surplus, and is its *net worth.*

Capitalization is a very freely used word, and everyone accepts it as having to do with the capital, or securities, or value, or size of a corporation. But if we should try to pin almost anyone down to a real definition, we would find out then how vague is the impression that the word conveys. The legal profession uses capitalization to indicate the total amount of authorized capital stock of a corporation, but this is far from the concept of the financier and accountant. Capitalization in the general business, financial, and accounting sense does not pertain to the actual amount of money, funds, or capital on hand but to the par or face value of the financial instruments used to procure it. This can usually be best expressed as the sum of face or par value of all outstanding stock and bonds. Many accountants believe that under certain conditions there should be added to this the face value of other specific long term obligations, but to determine this in any case requires judgement of a high degree and such an addition is seldom found in a balance sheet except with elaborate footnotes of explanation. For purposes of simple definition, therefore, the sum of outstanding bonds and stock is probably more satisfactory. If no par stock is issued the value at which it is carried on the balance sheet will ordinarily be used,

A simple illustrative case with figures will probably bring this out more clearly:

The certificate of incorporation of Company A authorizes 500 shares of preferred stock and 1,000 shares of common stock, each of $100 par value. The company has sold at par and issued 450 shares of preferred and 800 shares of common. It has sold and issued at face value ($1,000 each) 50 twenty year 6% first mortgage bonds; and has borrowed from the president of the company $2,000 on a two year note to take advantage of a quick buy in raw materials. It has procured from its local bank $6,000 on 50 day notes to pay current bills and take advantage of cash discounts. Its books at the present time show surplus and undivided profit of $22,000. What are the company's authorized stock, capital stock, capital, and capitalization?

While accountants might view this differently, in all probability the most common opinion may be represented as follows:

Authorized Stock

500 shares Preferred stock at $100	$ 50,000
1,000 common stock at $100	100,000
Authorized	$150,000

Capital Stock

450 shares Preferred stock at $100		$ 45,000
800 shares common stock at $100		80,000
	Capital stock	$125,000

Capital

Capital Stock		$125,000
Surplus and Undivided Profit		22,000
	Capital	$147,000

Capitalization

Capital Stock		$125,000
50 bonds at $1,000		50,000
	Capitalization	$175,000

Since the loans from the president and from the bank cannot be classified as long term obligations they would in no circumstances be shown as part of the capitalization.

Here it may be noted that while these four definitions seem rather similar and somewhat confusing, yet when shown in actual figures they display very positive differences.

The act of capitalizing. All of the above discussion refers to the term *capitalization* when used as a noun meaning the amount of long standing obligations. But there is another sense, somewhat verbal, which indicates certain activity on the part of the company organizers or managers, and its definition can be stated as follows:

Capitalization is the act or process of fixing the value of an enterprise, for the purpose of determining the capital liabilities that the company may assume in exchange for the property.

Basis of stock financing. Financing by means of stock is simply arranging to operate a corporation on permanently owned capital invested by interested parties, who, by virtue of their investments become owners or *stockholders* of the company. *Stock, in the financial sense, is merely the name for the aggregate ownership of a corporation.* There are, however, in most corporations, a large number of investor-owners, and hence the ownership or stock is divided into a number of units or *shares,* of which each investor or stockholder may own one or many.

A share of stock then is one of the units of ownership. This stock or ownership is tangibly represented by *certificates of stock.* These are engraved certificates bearing the name of the corporation, a description of the kind and type of stock represented, and the statement that Mr. Blank is the owner of so many shares. It bears the signatures of the corporate president and treasurer, and those of the registrar and transfer agent. While the printed description of the stock on the face of the certificate is convenient, it must not be accepted as absolutely complete and, to be absolutely certain, one must get the description from the certificate of incorporation.

On the back of the certificate, there is printed the form to be used in case the stock is to be transferred to a new owner. This is a very convenient and practical method of representing the ownership, because the ownership can be transferred by the transfer of the certificate itself. The owner wishing to sell his stock fills in the transfer form on the back of the stock certificate by listing the name of the transferee and affixing his own signature (certified) and handing the document to the buyer, who sends it to the corporation's transfer agent who will cancel and file the old certificate and supply a new one to the new owner. Most frequently, however, the seller will dispose of his holdings through a broker. He will fill out the transfer authorization to the broker, but since he does not know to whom the broker will sell he cannot fill in the name of the new buyer (transferee), thus "endorsing in blank." The broker will fill in the proper name when the sale is made. In this process the seller assumes a certain risk, for under the provisions of the Uniform Stock Transfer Law the certificate endorsed in blank becomes *negotiable* and, if lost or stolen, he may lose its entire value. (See paragraph on negotiability of stock certificates on page 106.)

If the seller's certificate represents 60 shares and the holder desires to sell only 25 of them, he will so indicate on the authorization for transfer, and the transfer agent will cancel the old certificate and send a new one for 35 shares to the seller and one for 25 to the buyer.

The transfer agent and the registrar. Every corporation must appoint a transfer agent and a registrar who are responsible for all transfers and recordings of the stock. In larger companies they are usually trust companies, but in quite small corporations a company officer is used as the transfer agent. The transfer agent maintains, among other records, a *shareholders' ledger* showing the names and addresses of all shareholders, the number and classes of shares held by each, the date of acquisition, the serial numbers of their certificates, and the amount paid in on each share.

The registrar maintains, among other records, the *share register* recording the total number of authorized shares of every kind, the number outstanding, the number unissued, and the number in the treasury. It is his responsibility to see that there are no erroneous issues, fraudulent issues, or overissues of any kind, and he must authenticate by his signature every certificate which is issued.

The names and addresses of shareholders as they appear on the *shareholders' ledger,* maintained by the transfer agent, is the official list of *shareholders of record,* sometimes called *registered holders.* The names and addresses of each holder of record as they appear on the *stockholders' ledger* are conclusive evidence as to the shareholders entitled to receive notice of meetings, to vote at such meetings, to examine corporate books, to receive dividends, and to own, enjoy, and exercise any other property or rights deriving from such shares.

Features of stock financing. It must be understood that while every corporation must have stock and must do its fundamental financing by means of the owned funds contributed by the stockholders, there are few corporations that are financed by stock exclusively. Almost every business finds it necessary to borrow occasionally for short-term periods, and many companies find it profitable to use long-term borrowed funds represented by bonded indebtedness. (For borrowed capital and bonds, see Chapters VII and VIII.) Financing by stock has many important features, affecting both the corporation and the individual stockholder, which must be understood by the financier.

As for the investor, stock gives him a permanent investment—not one that will be repaid to him at a future time, thus necessitating the trouble of reinvesting. If, however, the stockholder does not wish to retain his funds permanently in any one particular company, the stock is fully transferable and he has the right to dispose of it at any time and to place the proceeds elsewhere. Concerning the income from the investment in stock, the stockholder shares the fortunes of his company; large earnings ordinarily produce large dividends, whereas small earnings bring small dividends or perhaps none at all. Stock ownership, through its voting power, usually gives the holder a certain amount of control in the business (see Chapter V) which is greatly desired by many investors.

Dividends. Owners of stock in a corporation participate in the prosperity of the company by receiving their proportionate shares of any profits that the board of directors from time to time sees fit to distribute among them. This distribution of surplus is generally made annually, semi-annually, or quarterly, and all money or other property so divided among the stockholders as profit on their investment is known as *dividends*.

Classes of stock. Financing by stock requires more than a mere determination to issue and sell stock in a certain amount. It involves making a choice among a large number of classes and kinds of stock that have been developed.

From the standpoint of the issuing company, stock must be looked upon as a commodity which it wishes to sell to the public. Like all other commodities, it must be made as attractive as possible to the prospective buyers in order that it may be disposed of easily and at an advantageous price.

Stocks are issued, therefore, in several classes, providing numerous combinations of the three elements *income, control,* and *risk.* The average buyer of securities wants as large and as steady an income as possible with the smallest risk, and takes comparatively little interest in control. The cautious investor will take a smaller income if there be less risk attached, whereas the speculatively inclined will assume a greater risk if there seems to be a possibility of greater income or value appreciation. Instances occur when the control of the company is the chief end sought by the stock buyer, and he will practically ignore present risk and income in order to get the control.

All stocks may be divided into two great classes, *common stock* and *preferred stock* and these two main classes are subdivided into many types with various characteristics.

Common stock. Common stock is simple ownership in a corporation with certain fundamental legal rights and no others; it has no special preferences or privileges whatever. These fundamental legal rights of *all stockholders* both common and preferred are:

(1) To have proportionate ownership in the undivided assets of the corporation and to hold a certificate stating this ownership in shares.

(2) To transfer the ownership of his shares.

(3) To receive dividends when earned and declared by the board of directors.

(4) To inspect the corporate books (this does not include the financial books).

(5) To subscribe, in proportion to holdings, to any new issue of stock (stockholders' privileged subscription right).

(6) To have proportionate control through voting power.

(7) To vote on other questions affecting the corporate property as a whole.

(8) To protect the corporation against wrongful acts of a majority.

(9) To restrain *ultra vires* acts of the corporation.

(10) To share in the proceeds of dissolution.

It must be understood that while these are the basic rights of all stock, still every class may not have them all. It is quite common for a corporation to issue preferred stock, and even special classes of common stock, without the voting power by making such specification in the certificate of incorporation. By such specification, either preferred or common stock can be deprived of some of these ten fundamental rights, except that at least one class must be left with the voting power. No additional right can be conferred upon common stock for such would constitute it a preferred stock.

Preferred stock. Preferred stock is stock that, while it possesses the same rights and privileges as common stock (unless otherwise specified in the certificate of incorporation), has in addition certain more or less valuable and desirable preferences. It may be preferred as to dividends or preferred as to assets, or preferred as to both. In popular usage, the term preferred stock means preferred as to dividends.

Being *preferred as to dividends* means that this stock is entitled to receive a specified rate of dividend out of the earnings before any dividend is given to the stock not so preferred. It does not mean that a certain dividend is guaranteed, but merely that if any part of the surplus be declared as a dividend, the amount necessary to pay the specified rate of dividend on the preferred stock must be used for this purpose before any is allocated to pay a dividend on the stock not so preferred. If the entire amount declared as a dividend is required to pay the dividend on the preferred stock, it means simply that the non-preferred or common stock gets nothing. In prosperous companies, however, it is usually possible to pay the stipulated rate on the preferred stock and still have sufficient moneys left to pay an equal, or even greater rate to the common. It seems ordinarily fair that the common stock should get more than the preferred since the preferred cuts down its risk by taking out its share of dividend first.

Being *preferred as to assets* means that in a case of the dissolution of the corporation and the distribution of the assets among the stockholders, the holders of stock preferred as to assets will receive their portion of the proceeds of dissolution before other stock not so preferred. The rate of preferential return of capital is fixed in the certificate of incorporation and is usually the par value of the stock, sometimes slightly better. This preference is, of course, no service to the stockholder as long as the company is prosperous and there is no danger of dissolution and distribution of capital. Where the company is weak, however, with some danger of dissolution, with insufficient assets to return to everyone his full par value, then this preference is something of a safeguard. Under other circumstances it may be a detriment. If a company dissolves under prosperous conditions and no stock is preferred as to assets, there may be enough assets to pay every share considerably more than par. If, however, there had been some stock preferred as to assets up to par value, it would get only the par value and any larger distribution would go to the common stockholders.

These two great classes of stock, common and preferred, in their simple forms, have not by any means satisfied the wants of investors and speculators. Hence, a large number of variations have grown up, particularly in preferred stock, affecting the income, control and risk of the stockholders in various manners. The more important of these various classes will be explained.

Nonparticipating and participating. *Nonparticipating preferred* stock is stock which, through the terms of its issue and sale, is to receive a preferential dividend at a stipulated rate and nothing whatever beyond that. All other dividends in this case, regardless of amount, go to the common stock.

Participating preferred stock is that which first receives its preferential dividend at the prescribed rate, and after that participates or shares with the common stock in the remainder of the funds declared as a dividend. This participating or sharing may be done in any one of a number of ways as may be prescribed by various certificates of incorporation. Regardless, however, of the method of participation if the preferred stock shares in any way in the dividend over and above its basic stipulated rate, it is participating stock.

Types of participation. The most usual type of participation is known as _simple participation_, which means that in the allocation of the dividend, first the participating preferred stock receives payment up to and including its regular stipulated rate; next (if there be any remaining dividend) payment is made to the common stock up to and including the same rate as that which was paid to the preferred; third, if there still remains any dividend undistributed, it is divided among all of the shares regardless of class, or just as though they were all one class.

Assume that we have a corporation with 5,000 shares of 5% $100 par, simply participating, preferred stock and 5,000 shares of $100 par common stock, and it declares a dividend of $60,000. The distribution will be:

1st 5% to the preferred	$25,000
2nd 5% to the common	25,000
3rd The remaining $10,000 of the dividend will go at the rate of $1 per share to every share, both preferred and common	10,000
Total Dividend	$60,000

If the amount of the dividend had been $40,000, it would have been divided as follows:

1st 5% to the preferred	$25,000
2nd $15,000 (3%) to the common	15,000
Total Dividend	$40,000

Similar easy calculations can be made for any amount of dividend.

In the above example, it was assumed that the total amount in par value of the preferred stock equaled that of the common. More often, the amount of common exceeds that of the preferred. In this situation, when step three is reached with funds still to be distributed as dividends, each class will share in the remaining amount in the same proportion that it bears to the total stock outstanding. For example, if the amount of preferred was 25 per cent of the total stock it would now be allocated one-fourth of the remainder. In this way, each class is treated alike and each share would receive the same rate of dividend.

Other types of participation, when used, may be termed _special_ participation because of lack of any common pattern. For example, it may be arranged that _immediately_ after being allocated its regular preferential share at the stipulated rate, the preferred would participate proportionately with the common stock in any additional distribution. Perhaps it might be stipulated in another issue that after the preferred has been paid its regular rate of dividend and the common stock has received some amount, say $3.00 per share, the preferred will receive an additional $1.00 per share or an additional 2 per cent or some such arrangement.

The use of no-par stock and low par stock which began to be very common in the 1920s, made it difficult to compute a fair participation on the theretofore usual simple participation basis. This resulted in placing in the certificate of incorporation definite instructions governing such special participations as those just described.

Should the certificate of incorporation merely stipulate that the preferred stock is to be participating without detailing the methods to be used, it will be considered to participate *simply* on the basis that all stock must be treated alike unless it can be clearly shown that a different arrangement was intended. According to the weight of authority as evidenced by many court decisions, in the absence of specific provisions relative to participation, preferred stock will be non-participating. The only state, apparently, where the opposite rule prevails is Pennsylvania.[1]

Many of the original issues of preferred stock were found in railroad corporations where such stock was given to bondholders in exchange for their bond in time of financial reorganization brought about by financial difficulties. For many years there have been no issues of participating preferred stock by any well-known corporations. Instead it would appear that preferred stock buyers are given speculative advantages through the widely used practice of making the preferred stock convertible at the holder's option into common stock. This practice will be subsequently discussed in this text.

Non-cumulative and cumulative stock. The dividends on preferred stock may be *cumulative* or *non-cumulative*.

Provision is often made in the certificate of incorporation that if sufficient dividends are not declared in any one year to pay the full dividend on the preferred stock, there is no obligation on the part of the corporation to make up the deficiency in any future year. This means that dividends or parts of dividends not paid to preferred stockholders in any given year are lost to them forever. Stock governed by this provision is known as *non-cumulative stock*.

Cumulative preferred stock, on the other hand, is stock the stipulated dividend of which, if not paid in full in one or more years, carries over or accumulates from year to year until fully paid. When dividends have not been declared, or have been declared in amounts insufficient to pay the full specified rate on this cumulative preferred stock, they are said to be *in arrears*. As long as these arrears are not paid up, they constitute a claim on future earnings that has precedence over any dividend claim of the common stock. In other words, common stockholders are not entitled to receive any dividend whatever as long as the cumulative preferred dividends are in arrears.

---

[1] *Sternbergh, Appellant v. Brock*, 225 Pa. 279 (1909), also *Englander, Executor v. Oshorne et. al.*, 261 Pa. 366 (1918).

In case the certificate of incorporation makes no provision as to whether preferred stock shall be or shall not be cumulative, the courts have held, that by virtue of an implied contract, they shall be cumulative. That is to say, in order for the preferred stock to be non-cumulative as to dividends, the certificate of incorporation must specifically so provide.

A company sometimes provides that its preferred stock shall be non-cumulative for several years, after which it shall become cumulative. This provision relieves the company of the necessity of paying full dividends on the preferred stock during early years when earnings are expected to be small or of having the dividends accumulate as a charge against the dividends of future years. Yet this method assures that the stock will have almost as good selling power as if it had been fully cumulative from the first and certainly gives the common stock more appeal.

There have been some court decisions to the effect that should there be earnings available for dividends on the non-cumulative preferred stock and the directors in their discretion did not pay them, that such stock will be cumulative to the extent that the dividend was earned in the years of non-payment. The most famous of these was the New Jersey case cited below in footnote 2 but it appears that the decision was the result of a New Jersey statute (since amended) and some ambiguity in the statements made in the certificate of incorporation relative to the particular issue of stock.[2] Nevertheless there is a question of equity involved where the evidence would show that the directors deliberately passed the payment of the non-cumulative preferred dividend in order to have funds available to pay a common dividend in a subsequent year. Where, however, the directors have refrained from paying the dividend in order to put the money into needed capital improvements, the decision of the U.S. Supreme Court cited below has clearly stated that such a dividend not paid is forever lost to the holders of the stock.[3]

Redeemable or callable stock. Preferred stock, or certain classes of preferred stock, are sometimes made redeemable or callable. This means that the corporation has the option, under the conditions and on the terms specified in the certificate of incorporation, of redeeming or buying back the stock from the stockholders. This redemption right rests, of course, entirely with the company and the stockholders can neither compel nor refuse the redemption of their stock.

Some advance notice of intended redemption is usually provided for,

---

[2] Moran v. United States Cast Iron Pipe and Foundry Company, 95 N.J. Eq. 389 (1924), aff'd, 96 N.J. Eq. 698 (1924) for a federal case arriving at a similar decision see Collins v. Portland Electric Power Co. 7 F. (2nd) 221 (1925), aff'd, 12 F. (2nd) 671 (1926).

[3] Wabash Railway Co. et al. v. Barclay et al., 280 U.S. 197 (1930).

and a redemption price is generally set at a small premium above par so as to compensate the holder for the loss of his investment and give him an opportunity to seek a reinvestment of his money without suffering loss of income in the interim. Redemption at a premium is not universal, however; some companies have the redemption price set at par. If the redeemable stock has the voting power, its redemption may have considerable effect on the control of the corporation because of the elimination of all votes represented by it.[4]

Redeemability may have a material effect upon the market price of stock, the tendency being to keep the market price lower than it otherwise might be. If the stock is redeemable at 110 and has an investment value of 140, a prospective buyer would in all probability decline to pay this much for it, fearing that the corporation might exercise its redemption power and deprive him of his stock at 110. Such action would entail considerable loss to him. If on the other hand the investment value is below the redemption price, the redemption feature would ordinarily have no effect on the market, unless it were to make the stock slightly less attractive because of the fact that there is an upper limit to the possible price rise.

Convertible stock. One or more classes of stock may be made *convertible*, that is exchangeable at the option of the holder into some other specified security of the company. Conversion, unlike redemption, is at the option of the holder. The certificate of incorporation may make certain stipulations or set a certain time limit for conversion, but within these restrictions the stockholder may demand conversion at his pleasure. The most usual conversion permitted is from preferred stock to common stock. Convertible stock of this type is rather popular, especially in new or young companies because it enables the holder to receive preference as to dividends when the earnings are small and there is little left for the common dividends, and yet he can trade his stock in for common in case the earnings become large and the common is receiving handsome dividends. Having once converted, of course, he cannot reconvert to what he had before.

Companies with outstanding convertible stock are required to keep on hand, unissued, at all times sufficient of the stock into which it is convertible to meet all demands for conversion, thus they cannot put out its full amount of authorized stock, and should make allowance for this in drawing up their certificates.

The matter of control, also, enters into consideration as non-voting preferred is often converted into voting common stock. This feature will sometimes induce stockholders to convert even at a financial loss.

---

[4] An example is the fight between Harriman and Hill for control of the Northern Pacific Railroad. See J. Gilpin Pyles, *The Life of James J. Hill,* New York: Doubleday, Page & Co., and George Kennan's *E. H. Harriman,* Boston: Houghton Mifflin Co.

Occasionally stock is issued that is convertible into bonds. This is very rare, however, and is hedged about with various protective stipulations to prevent improper use of the privilege. If this were not the case, holders of such stock in a weak or insolvent company could convert their stocks into bonds and thus share in the proceeds of dissolution ahead of many creditors and on an equal footing with other bondholders of the company who acquired their bonds through bona fide purchase.

Such a practice would be manifestly unfair. The money that stockholders pay into a company for their ownership is a part of the owned capital of the company and it is upon the strength of this owned capital and the security afforded by it that the company is enabled to obtain its borrowed capital through the sale of bonds. If, therefore, a large number of stockholders are permitted to convert their stock into bonds, thus becoming creditors of the company instead of part owners, it naturally means an increase of bonded debt, with no increase whatever of assets, and lessens the value of all other bonds.

Even should such conversion be permitted only at the option of the company, it is rightly permissible only to the extent of the surplus and undivided profits, in order that the amount paid in by the stockholders may remain intact.

Protected preferred stock. Among features formerly occasionally given to preferred stock to enhance its attractiveness to investors was a provision requiring the corporation, in addition to paying the current dividend on the preferred stock, to put aside a reserve fund to cover one or two years' future preferred dividends before anything could be paid to the common stockholders. The practice has gone into complete disuse. Instead we may encounter a requirement of a protective fund for a different purpose, that of retiring a certain amount of the preferred stock each year or to be accumulated for the eventual retirement of all of it.[5]

Prior preference stock. A stock which is issued subsequently in time to other stock but which by agreement of the old stockholders takes precedence over their stock in dividend rights is known as *prior preference stock.* The fact that a certain stock has a dividend preference over other stocks does not in itself constitute it a prior preference stock. This name must be used only when a newer stock has displaced one or other issues in priority of claims for dividends.

Deferred stock. This is a stock the dividends on which are not to be paid until after the expiration of some given time, or until the happening of some particular event, or sometimes until after the dividends on some other stock have reached a certain size. It was formerly used in

---

[5] The Sherwin-Williams Company's 4 per cent preferred stock has a sinking fund provision requiring an annual deposit sufficient to redeem, at the call price of 105, 3 per cent of the highest amount of preferred stock at any time outstanding.

financial reorganizations and also for bonus payments to corporate executives. It is seldom encountered today.

Guaranteed stock. Guaranteed stock is any stock whose dividend is guaranteed at a certain rate by some company other than the issuer. Such dividends are usually guaranteed and paid by one corporation which is using property of another under a lease in which it is provided the regular dividend on the lessor corporation's stock will be paid as part of the rent. A corporation cannot guarantee a dividend on its own stock for under the law a dividend cannot be paid except out of a surplus and of course no company can possibly guarantee that it will have a surplus at any year in the future.

Voting and non-voting stock. All stockholders have the inherent right to participate in the control of the corporation through voting for the directors, but through certificate of incorporation provision many companies do issue some non-voting stock. It is generally customary to give the vote to the common stock and to withhold it from the preferred. The vote may be apportioned among the several classes of stock in any manner desired, provided that at least one class is vested with voting power. If stock is originally issued as voting stock it cannot thereafter be deprived of the vote without the consent of the holder.

Vetoing stock. Vetoing is the name given to stock which does not have the general voting power but which is entitled through provision of the certificate of incorporation to vote on certain questions or under certain conditions. Thus a certain issue of preferred stock may be voteless except on the question of authorizing additional preferred stock, and on this it may have the vote.

It is quite common to give non-voting preferred stock the right to vote after its dividends have not been paid for a certain number of quarters and to continue this voting power as long as the dividends are unpaid or, in the case of cumulative stock, as long as the dividends are in arrears. In such cases, this stock is sometimes given the right to vote along with the common, sometimes the exclusive voting right and sometimes the right to elect a specified number, or the majority, of the directors.

Par value and no-par value stock. For many years the certificates of incorporations used to attach to each share of stock a par or face value. This par was most commonly $100 but could be any amount. This did not represent that the $100 par share was really worth $100. It may have had a market value of $80, a book value of $90, and an investment value of $85, all changeable from day to day as economic and financial conditions changed, but the $100 par value established in the certificate of incorporation did not change except when the certificate was amended in the manner provided by law.

It served, however, as a legal minimum which the corporation must charge for the stock upon issue and was supposed to assure every stockholder, and creditors too, regardless of the current value of the stock, that the share had yielded to the company assets worth the par of the share. Many financiers, investors, and financial writers claimed that use of an arbitrary par value for the stock, especially printing this on the face of the certificate, was a deception which led many to believe this to be the actual value, whereas it might not have any relation to any of the several values of the stock.

It may be seen that there could not be any assurance that the original par value had been received in cash because stock can be issued for property and for services. Furthermore, it could be immediately lost through poor investment.

No-par stock, having no valuation of any kind printed upon it, is free from this objection. It was felt that the absence of a printed par value upon the stockholder's certificate should make him realize that his share did not represent any specific amount but rather a proportionate equity in the assets of his corporation. After a great deal of argument, New York in 1912 authorized the use of no-par or non-par value stock, or shares without par value, and its use has spread to all the other states.

Sometimes the certificate of incorporation provides that the no-par stock shall have a stated issue price, representing the minimum that may be accepted by the company in payment for this stock. Other certificates often provide that such stock may be issued at a price fixed by the by-laws (alterable from time to time), or by resolution of the board of directors, or even at the current market price.

The ability thus to make the issue price flexible is often of great advantage in disposing of unissued stock. All no-par value shares issued in accordance with the statutes of the state and the provisions of the certificate of incorporation are deemed fully paid and non-assessable and the holder of such shares is not liable to the corporation or its creditors in respect thereto.

Every certificate of stock without par value must show the total number of such shares authorized, as well as the number represented by the certificate, and also the authorized number of par value shares, if any, and their par value. This information makes it possible to determine the proportionate interest in the net assets of a corporation which a given no-par stock certificate represents at the time of issuance. Having no par value or base upon which to estimate a percentage dividend, it follows that the total dividend allotted to no-par shares is simply divided equally among all the no-par shares outstanding and declared as so many dollars and cents per share.

Negotiability of certificates of stock. Ownership in corporations, as evidenced by certificates of stock, is made more liquid, more easily transferable, and hence more generally desirable, by reason of the fact that modern legislation makes a certificate negotiable by endorsement. That is, by endorsement of the certificate by the owner, it can be transferred from one person to another. The transferee, if an innocent purchaser for value, will have absolute and sound title to the stock represented by the certificate, regardless of whether the title of the transferor was good or not. He does not purchase merely as good a title as the previous holder had, as would be the case with non-negotiable property. Thus title to these negotiable certificates (when endorsed) may pass through the hands of a finder or a thief on to an innocent purchaser for value.

If a certificate is lost or stolen, the owner should immediately notify the transfer agent of his company and ask for a new certificate. If the missing certificate is not found, the company will issue the owner a duplicate upon his putting up a bond to indemnify the company in case the original later shows up in the hands of a legitimate holder, that is, an innocent purchaser for value.

In each state the negotiability of stock certificates dates from the passage of the law under which such certificates are made negotiable. The law in question is the Uniform Stock Transfer law. This was enacted in New York September 1, 1913, and in New Jersey March 8, 1916. Any certificates dated prior to passage of this act in their respective states are still non-negotiable.

Names defining stock status. Each of the descriptive stock titles we have been discussing is intended to set forth the specific character and attributes of a class of stock. There is, however, another group of names which does not in any way indicate the characteristics of the stock or the rights and privileges it carries to its owners. Each of these designations can apply to stock of any class and is intended to show the status of the ownership of the stock under consideration.

These designations may be shown and diagrammed as follows:

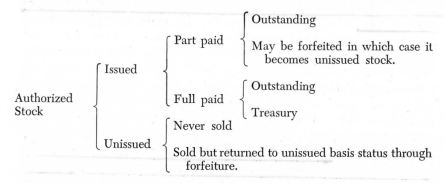

A brief explanation of each of these terms may be helpful.

Authorized stock. *Authorized stock* is the total stock of all classes that the corporation is authorized to issue according to its certificate of incorporation. Regardless of what stock is sold and what is unsold, and regardless of the price charged for it or the amount received for it, the total quantity of authorized stock remains the same. The amount of authorized stock can be neither increased nor diminished except through an amendment to the certificate of incorporation.

Issued stock. *Issued stock* is that part of the authorized stock which is issued or sold by the company. It may be issued or sold for cash, property, or services, and may at a given time be held by an outside individual, or by another company, or may be in the treasury of the issuing company. In any case, it constitutes issued stock.

Unissued stock. A corporation is not required to issue all of its authorized stock and often does not do so. The excess, therefore, of the authorized stock over the issued stock constitutes the *unissued stock.*

Full paid stock. *Full paid stock* is stock that has been issued by the company and paid for either in cash, property or services up to its full par value. Or in the case of stock without par value, it is stock that has been paid up to the full amount set by lawful methods as the selling price of the stock. Full paid stock carries no liability to the creditors, except that in a few states all stockholders (full paid and part paid alike) are liable for unpaid wages to servants of an insolvent corporation. Full paid stock may at a particular time be outstanding stock or treasury stock, two terms discussed below.

Part paid stock. Corporations are not permitted by the statutes of most states to issue or sell their stock at less than its par value. They may, however, sell it on a part payment or installment plan by which the purchaser pays a stipulated sum at the time of purchase and obligates himself to pay the balance at specified times or as the directors of the company may call for installments. Stock thus purchased but not as yet paid up to full par value is known as *part paid stock.* Such stock makes the holder liable to corporation creditors for the amount by which the par value exceeds the amount which has been paid into the company thereon. When stock is sold on the part paid plan, it is quite common for the company to keep possession of the certificate until complete payment is made though some follow the practice of delivering the certificate at once and marking it "part paid."

Outstanding stock. *Outstanding stock* is the issued stock, either full paid or part paid, owned or held by any parties outside of the issuing company itself. It is, in fact, all of the issued stock except that which may be held by the company as treasury stock.

Treasury stock. *Treasury stock* is a corporation's own stock which has been issued and reacquired by purchase, donation, or otherwise. It must in every case be full paid stock, otherwise it cannot be accepted and held as treasury stock. While held as treasury stock, it does not vote or draw dividends. It can be sold by the company below par if desired or given as a free bonus because the company has already received the full par value for it before it could go into the treasury. In case of sale or reissue it again becomes, of course, outstanding stock and regains whatever dividend and voting rights it originally had. While held in the treasury, it constitutes an asset of the company and on the balance sheet may appear on the asset side, but it is generally considered preferable to show it as a deduction from stock issued and outstanding. Many persons speak of unissued stock as treasury stock, which is entirely erroneous. Treasury stock has been sold, has produced capital, and is an asset of the company, whereas unissued stock is unsold, has produced no capital, is not an asset, in fact is nothing but unassigned potential ownership represented by a stack of unsigned, unauthenticated, unissued certificates.

Creation of treasury stock. The most common transaction resulting in the creation of treasury stock is through outright purchase by the corporation of some of its outstanding stock. There are many legitimate reasons for so doing. In a privately owned company, there is no market for the stock and an owner wishing to retire may sell his stock to the corporation if it has a surplus and cash available to pay for it. A corporation may buy up some of its preferred stock with a view to retiring it. It may buy in its stock below par or stated value (if no par) to create a capital surplus for some proper purpose (see Chapter XIV).

Stock may be donated by a large stockholder in order to eliminate a deficit resulting from a disaster such as the extremely rapid and drastic decline in inventory values which occurred in 1920.

When it was very uncommon to authorize stock at less than $100 par value and before the advent of no-par stock, a new corporation might anticipate great difficulty in selling its stock at $100. Part paid stock cannot be used in a public offering and the following expedient was sometimes used. The promoters or organizers were paid for organization services, and for property turned over to the corporation in stock instead of cash. By prearrangement, part of the stock would be donated back to the corporation to become treasury stock. Having been initially fully paid for in property or services, it could now be sold below par if necessary to meet market conditions. This practice is no longer necessary because today there is no particular virtue attached to the $100 par value. For example, the present par value of General Motors stock is $1.67 per share. Also if deemed desirable, no-par stock could be sold at any price determined by the board of directors.

Forfeited stock. When a person holding part paid stock, on which the installments of unpaid portions up to the par value are callable, fail to meet any specific call of the directors, his stock is forfeited to the corporation and reverts to the status of unissued stock.

There are several ways in which the company may handle forfeited stock. It may resell it to the highest bidder as part paid stock. If the selling price is no greater than the amount of the delinquent installments, then the original purchaser loses by forfeiture his entire deposit; but if it is in excess of the amount of the delinquent installments, the original depositor is given the excess up to the amount of his deposit, less, of course, the expenses of the resale. It may be sold as full paid stock. In this case, the portion of the selling price necessary to bring the total already received by the company up to par is retained by the company, and the balance, if any, less the expenses of the sale, is turned over to the original holder. The law of New York and of some other states provides that in default of payment of a call upon part paid stock, the board of directors may, after sixty days' notice to the defaulting stockholder, declare forfeited not only the stock but all previous payments made thereon. (S.C.L., Sec. 68 and Sec. 74.) The corporation may, if it wishes, resell or reissue the forfeited stock without payment of any kind to the defaulting holder.

Questions for Study and Review

1. Define and explain the terms *Capital Stock* and *Capital*.
2. Discuss in detail the term *Capitalization*.
3. Differentiate between *Owned Capital* and *Borrowed Capital*.
4. What are the fundamental rights of a stockholder in a corporation?
5. What is the difference between the terms *Preferred as to Dividends* and *Preferred as to Assets?*
6. What is *Cumulative Stock* and what is meant when one says that the dividends are in arrears? Explain.
7. Explain the meaning of *Participating Stock*.
8. What is *Convertible Stock?* Is *Convertibility* a desirable feature for the stockholder?
9. What is meant by *Redeemability* of stock? May it ever have any effect upon *Control?*
10. Distinguish between *Treasury* Stock and *Unissued Stock*. Between *Treasury Stock* and *Outstanding Stock*.
11. In what ways may a corporation handle *Forfeited Stock* and previous payments made thereof?
12. What may a corporation accept in payment for its stock?
13. What is *No-Par-Value* stock?
14. How are dividends declared on no-par-value stock? Why are they declared in this manner?
15. What is meant by *Negotiability?*
16. Are *Certificates of Stock* negotiable? What law governs this matter?

Problems

1. The balance sheet of the Hampton Corporation as at the end of the last fiscal year is as follows:

Assets		Liabilities	
Current Assets	$ 817,874	Current Liabilities	$ 378,349
Fixed Assets	1,147,973	Funded Debt	175,460
Miscellaneous Assets	194,974	Reserves	36,614
		Preferred Stock (1)	110,300
		Common Stock (2)	555,400
		Surplus	904,698
Total	$2,160,821	Total	$2,160,821

(1) Par value $100; authorized 5,000 shares; outstanding 1,103 shares
(2) Par value $25; authorized 50,000 shares; outstanding 22,216 shares

Determine the corporation's (a) capital stock, (b) capital, and (c) capitalization.

2. The Modern Printing Corporation has outstanding 20,000 shares of $5 no par value cumulative preferred stock and $3,000,000 of $25 par value common stock. Last year the corporation paid a total dividend of $80,000, and this year proposes to pay a total dividend of $480,000. How much would each class of stock receive in each year on a per share basis?

3. The Ralston Corporation has outstanding $2,000,000 of 5 per cent $50 par value preferred stock. The preferred stock is callable at $60 a share and is convertible into common stock at the ratio of two shares of common stock for each share of preferred stock. The corporation has 300,000 authorized shares of common stock of which 200,000 shares are outstanding. (a) If the corporation elects to retire all the outstanding preferred stock by calling it for redemption, how much cash will it need to have on hand for this purpose? (b) If all the preferred stockholders elect to convert the preferred stock into common stock, how many shares of the common stock will then be authorized but unissued and how many shares will be outstanding?

4. A corporation has outstanding 100,000 shares of preferred stock and 400,-000 shares of common stock. The preferred stock has four votes per share and the common stock one vote per share. There are 1,250 preferred stockholders and 16,000 common stockholders. Comment on the effective voting power of the respective classes of stock.

5. The following statements represent successive steps in the raising of capital for a corporation:
(1) The National Hat Manufacturing Corporation is organized with authorization for $500,000 of common stock with a par value of $10 per share.
(2) The corporation sells and issues $300,000 of its stock at par in the market through underwriters.
(3) Mr. Foster sells a patent to the company for $40,000 and takes payment in stock.
(4) The market price of the stock declines and the corporation buys 5,000 shares in the open market.
(5) The corporation buys out the Whylie Corporation and gives 21,000 shares of its stock in payment.
Prepare a chart indicating the changes in the authorized, issued, unissued, outstanding and treasury stock caused by each of the above transactions.

6. Mr. Alton was the owner of a certificate for 50 shares of stock in the Eastern Shipping Co., a New York corporation. If he loses the certificate, what steps may he take to obtain a duplicate?

7. The Whiteside Corporation has outstanding 300,000 shares of $5 preferred stock which is convertible into common stock at the ratio of 3 shares of common for 1 share of preferred. The common stock, with a par value of $60, consists of 6,000,000 shares of authorized stock of which 4,200,000 are outstanding. Subsequently the corporation reduces the par value of the common stock to $20 a share and exchanges 3 shares of the new $20 par value stock for each $60 par value old stock. Discuss the effect of this change in the common stock upon the value of the conversion privilege of the preferred stock.

Written Assignment

Part I:

A corporation has outstanding $1,000,000 in 5 per cent $50 par value preferred stock and $3,000,000 of $50 par value common stock. The preferred stock is cumulative and simple participating. The corporation plans to distribute

$350,000 to the stockholders as a dividend. How would this $350,000 be distributed on a per share basis to each class of stock if (a) the preferred stock is not in arrears, and (b) the preferred is in arrears to the extent of $1.50 a share?

Part II:

A corporation is organized with authorization for $800,000 of $40 par value common stock. It issues and sells at par 8,000 shares of the stock. Later, it buys certain property for a price of $16,000 which it pays in stock. Subsequently, it buys 500 shares of the stock in the market at $25 a share. Before the end of the year, it sells 2,000 shares of the stock to Mr. Gray at par, and distributes as a bonus to employees 300 shares of the stock previously purchased in the market. State the amount of authorized, issued, unissued, outstanding and treasury stock in terms of number of shares at the end of the year.

CHAPTER VII

Financing with Borrowed Capital

The use of borrowed capital. While some business concerns, large and small, have not made use or at least rarely have made use of borrowed funds, the practice of borrowing money to use in business operations is general. Such borrowing may be only for short terms to finance seasonal peaks in operations or may be for a hundred years and for hundreds of millions of dollars. Funds obtained through long-term borrowing are used in the same manner and for the same purposes as are capital investments by the owners.

Trading on the equity. When part of the funds employed in a business is borrowed, the business is said to "trade on the equity." The expression is just another way of saying that when a business obtains part of its capital through borrowing, the owners have only an interest or equity in it. In electric utilities, for example, long-term borrowed capital may account for 50 or 60 per cent of the total funds invested in the business. The equity or owners' interest represented by stock and surplus is only 40 or 50 per cent.

Effects of trading on the equity. There is always more risk in using borrowed capital than capital represented by owners' investment. Lenders are creditors and have claims on the business prior to those of any owner. Failure to pay creditors their claims when due, including failure to pay interest on borrowed capital, could and frequently does result in bankruptcy or reorganization, often resulting in complete loss of owners' equity in the business. Obviously, then, the management of a business would not use borrowed funds, if it were not advantageous and believed safe. The assumption of a few figures will illustrate both the advantages and possible disadvantages of using borrowed capital. We shall suppose that in a business with an owner's investment of $400,000, a return of 10 per cent or $40,000 is earned.

The management believes that if the concern could expand facilities to $600,000, the same rate of return of 10 per cent would be maintained.

Arrangements are made to borrow $200,000 at 5 per cent. If the management is correct in its estimate of a continued rate of earnings of 10 per cent, the result of the first year's operations appear as follows:

Net earnings on $600,000 capital	$60,000
Less interest at 5% on $200,000	10,000
Earnings available to stockholders	$50,000
Rate of earnings	12½%

It may be seen that through the use of the borrowed capital, the owner's rate of return has been increased from 10 per cent to 12 per cent.

Assume that because of adverse business conditions, earnings on total capital drop to 4 per cent:

Net earnings on $600,000 capital	$24,000
Less interest on $200,000 at 5%	10,000
Earnings available to stockholders	$14,000
Rate of earnings	3½%

The result here from the standpoint of the owners is not a happy one. Had the business been operating on the owners' investment only, the return would have been $16,000 or 4 per cent. Interest paid on the borrowed capital reduced stockholders' return to 3½ per cent. Let us now assume that in a poor year the business lost $10,000. This would have been a loss of 2½ per cent on the owner's investment if borrowed money had not been used. If $200,000 has been borrowed, the fixed charges of $10,000 interest must be paid whether business is good or bad and the loss to the owner would have been not $10,000 but $20,000 or 5 per cent. This gives rise to an easily remembered expression, "Trading on the equity magnifies profits and losses." The above discussion should make it clear that any concern intending to use long-term borrowed funds as part of its capital should enjoy a high degree of earnings stability. At least the management should have good reason to believe that even in years of poor business, there will be enough income to cover the interest charges.

One other factor in connection with the use of borrowed capital which is of great importance to the business management is that the advantage gained from the comparatively low cost of borrowed funds as against funds obtained through the sale of stock is greatly increased by the fact that interest is an expense which may be deducted in computing earnings for federal income tax purposes. If a corporation is paying taxes at the rate of 52 per cent on earnings, this has the effect of reducing the cost of borrowed capital to approximately one-half the interest paid.

Secured and unsecured loans. Many loans are made merely in return for the borrower's promise to repay. The borrower's promise is usually in writing and specifies a definite maturity date when the loan must be paid. There is usually in all but short-term bank loans[1] a promise to pay interest regularly and a stipulation that if this is not done the loan becomes immediately due and payable, regardless of its maturity. A simple illustration of a secured loan would be one obtained from a pawn broker where as security for the promise to repay, some article of personal property is left as security for the loan. Short-term bank loans made to businessmen frequently are unsecured but banks also make many secured loans, requiring the borrower to leave with the bank for security stocks, corporate and government bonds or documents giving title to specific chattels such as order bills of lading and warehouse receipts. Sometimes, even bank loans are secured by mortgages upon chattels or real estate. The latter type of security will be discussed later in this chapter.

Unsecured loans, however, are not limited to short-term bank loans but are common today in long-term debt financing by corporations in almost any type of business. For example, the long-term borrowings of the American Telephone and Telegraph Co. are in excess of $2 billion, none of which is secured by more than the corporation's promise to pay.

Liens as security. At common law a *lien* merely gave a right to hold possession of property as security for a debt; for example, the right of a warehouseman to hold possession of goods for the payment of storage charges upon them. In many types of liens used in business today, statutes permit a borrower to retain possession of property, while at the same time an agreement may be made with a lender giving him a lien upon the property. In case of non-payment of the debt or other breach of agreement the sale of the property, in a manner prescribed by law, is permitted for payment of the debt. Such a procedure is usually known as a *foreclosure*. Any excess remaining from the proceeds of sale over and above the costs of the foreclosure and the debt, of course, goes to the borrower. For the protection of the holder of the lien against other creditors or claimants against the borrower, it is usually required by law that the lien be recorded in some public office.

Some large long-term corporate loans are secured like the short-term loans mentioned above by the pledge of specific security such as stock and bonds of other corporations left not with the lender, for a single large corporate loan may be obtained from many lenders, but with a trustee who holds possession for the security of all the lenders. Such pledged security is called *collateral* and the loans secured by it are known as collateral loans. This type of loan will be discussed more fully in the next chapter. The pledging of collateral as security for a loan is a transaction, the basic elements of which are familiar to all. There is, however, another type of secured loan, much more common to long-term borrow-

---

[1] Short-term bank loans are usually obtained by discounting the borrower's notes at a bank. Interest is, in effect, paid in advance.

ing. Most secured loans for a term of years are protected not by the lender being given physical custody or possession of property, but by giving him a mortgage or lien against the property of the borrower.

If the property has sufficient value, it is possible to obtain several successive loans upon it which give rise to *first, second, third, fourth,* and so on, *liens.* These successive liens take precedence one over another, in the order of their making. The terms *senior* and *junior lien* are frequently used. The lien having first claim on a property is senior to all others, and the one having the last claim is junior to all others. Any intermediate lien is junior to all having claim ahead of it and senior to all having claim subsequent to it. *Prior lien* means a lien placed upon property and taking precedence over one or more liens already upon it. It may be, and usually is, prior to all other liens, but it may by arrangement be made prior only to the second and subsequent liens, the third and subsequent liens; or, in fact, it may be inserted at any place in the line of liens. Of course, a prior lien can be placed upon the property only with the consent of all the creditors whose claims it is to precede.

Security and equity. The security back of a first lien is the actual property upon which the lien is placed, but in dollars and cents it is the actual price that this property brings, over and above the costs of selling when it is sold to satisfy the lien. This amount, of course, is only an estimate at the time the loan is made and the lien placed. A very substantial equity should, therefore, be demanded by the lender to protect against probable depreciation in the value of the mortgaged property.

The security back of a second lien is what is left of the selling price after the selling expenses and the full claim of the first lien have been paid. Likewise, the security back of each junior lien is what is left of the selling price after the selling expenses have been paid and all senior liens satisfied.

Any amount remaining after the selling expenses and all the liens have been paid belongs to the borrower, the former owner of the property, and is known as the *owner's equity.* While the loans and liens are actually standing upon the property, the owner possesses his equity in it, but its amount and value are only an estimation, as the property may sell for either more or less than contemplated.

The owner's equity, after the first lien, becomes the security for the second lien, and so on, since the equity after each lien becomes the security for the succeeding one. Thus:

$100,000 Value of property, security of 1st lien.
  50,000 Amount of loan secured by 1st lien.

$ 50,000 Owner's equity, and security of 2nd lien.
  15,000 Amount of loan secured by 2nd lien.

$ 35,000 Owner's equity after 1st and 2nd liens.

When property securing several successive liens is sold to satisfy them, the senior lien foreclosing is (after the payment of the taxes and the expenses of foreclosure and sale) entitled to complete satisfaction before a junior lien receives anything. Likewise, each lien in succession must be satisfied in full before the next participates. Since sales to satisfy liens are generally brought about by insolvency of the debtor, there is often not enough left to satisfy more than the first or second lien. The question of precedence and participation of liens will be discussed in more detail in the following study of mortgages.

The mortgage. When real property is to be pledged as security for a loan, the practice is for the borrower to mortgage it to the lender for the life of the loan. The mortgage itself is not the promise to pay. The promise to pay is found in a note or bond, a separate document which is mentioned in the mortgage as consideration for the agreement. The promise to pay is a binding contract without the mortgage, which is merely security for the promise. A simple illustration of the use of a real estate mortgage is found in the quite common method used in purchasing a home. The buyer makes a down payment so as to provide an equity in the property, establishing his own interest and providing a margin of safety for a lender. To finance the balance, the buyer signs two instruments, a bond or promise to pay and a mortgage, which pledges the property purchased as security for the promise. The buyer, now a borrower, is known as the *mortgagor.* He may retain possession of the property as long as he meets the conditions of the bond and mortgage, such as paying interest and meeting installment payments on the debt if required. The lender who makes the loan and accepts the mortgage as security for the bond is known as the *mortgagee.* Both bond and mortgage may be transferred by the mortgagee. The lender might be a private person or an institution such as a savings bank. It is possible that instead of an actual loan of money by a third party, the seller may accept the bond and mortgage and the down payment in exchange for a deed to the property.

Formerly, the mortgage was considered to transfer title to the property to the lender, subject to being defeated by payment of the bond and the observing of any other promises made by the borrower as part of the mortgage contract. In other words, the borrower possessed an equity or right of redemption which could be exercised when conditions of the loan contract had been fulfilled. This right was expressed in a clause in the mortgage known as the defeasance clause. In the common law form of mortgage, the wording of the mortgage down to the defeasance clause is similar to an ordinary deed, apparently on its face transferring title to the property to the lender. It is so interpreted in some states and it must therefore be provided, either by statute or the contract, that possession of the property remains with the mortgagor until default. In quite a number of states, the mortgage is considered a mere lien and title does not pass until legal steps are taken after default to foreclose the lien. At such a foreclosure proceeding, it is customary for the property to be sold to the highest bidder and the proceeds applied to pay the costs of the foreclosure and the amount of debt for which the foreclosure has been effected. Any balance left over will be paid the mortgagor. Should the proceeds of sale be insufficient to pay the mortgage in full, the mortgagee will ask the court for a deficiency judgement against the mortgagor for the difference between the amount realized from the sale and the full amount of the debt as evidenced by the bond.

Statutory form of mortgage. The wording of the common law form of mortgage is rather long and cumbersome. Lawyers were reluctant to change it because the meaning of the terms and expressions used had been established by the courts and there was no certainty as to what interpretation might be placed upon new statements. The legislatures of some states have, therefore, authorized a shorter form of mortgage giving it by statutory definition the desired legal effect. A specimen of the statutory form used in New York follows:

THIS MORTGAGE, made on the *first* day of *September* nineteen hundred and *fifty-one*,

Between *Joseph H. Williams, of New York, N.Y.,* the mortgagor, and *William A. Johnson, of New York, N.Y.,* the mortgagee.

WITNESSETH, that to secure the payment of an indebtedness in the sum of *ten thousand* dollars, lawful money of the United States, to be paid on the *thirty-first* day of *August* nineteen hundred and *fifty-six* with interest thereon to be computed from *September 1, 1951* at the rate of *four* per centum per annum, and to be paid *annually on the thirty-first day of August each year, beginning with the thirty-first day of August 1952,* according to a certain bond or obligation bearing even date herewith, the mortgagor hereby mortgages to the mortgagee the lands, premises, and property situated in the City of New Rochelle, County of Westchester, State of New York, with the buildings and all other improvements thereon, bounded and described as follows, to wit:

[Here follows complete description and location of property.]

And the mortgagor covenants with the mortgagee as follows:
1. That the mortgagor will pay the indebtedness as hereinbefore provided.
2, 3, 4, 5, and so on follow the usual covenants as to insurance, repairs, taxes, inspection, etc.

The covenants referred to in the short form of mortgage above are also commonly found in most long form mortgages, where they follow the defeasance clause. The parties by these several covenants agree that the principal amount will become due and payable if interest or installments on the principal are not paid as agreed, that the borrower will keep the property in good repair and keep it insured against fire (insurance policy is expected to show the mortgagee's interest). The mortgagor promises that the taxes will be paid and, if not paid, the maturity of the debt will be accelerated or if the mortgagee should pay them, the amount may be added to the debt. The mortgagee is given the right to enter for inspection or for protection of the mortgagee's interest upon default and a number of other items. Naturally, the above will vary depending upon the law of the state in which the property is located and the nature of the property itself.

Operation of foreclosure claims. If the principal of a mortgage debt is not paid at maturity, or if any default is made, an accelerated maturity is thus brought about. The mortgagee will then start proceedings of *foreclosure and sale* to procure a court order for the selling of the mortgaged property and the satisfying of his debt from the proceeds of the sale.

If there is only one mortgage on the property, the first of the proceeds, after the expenses of foreclosure and sale have been paid, go to the creditor, and anything remaining goes to the debtor. If the property does not bring enough to satisfy the mortgage lien, the purchaser, nevertheless, receives a clear title; the creditor receives all of the proceeds and has a personal claim against the debtor for any balance of the loan not satisfied by the sale.

There is a rather widespread impression that if the proceeds from the sale of a piece of mortgaged property are not sufficient to satisfy the mortgage, the mortgagee loses the shortage; that he is, in other words, entitled to no more than the proceeds from the property that he accepted as security for his loan. This impression, of course, is not correct. The law looks upon the debt as the principal thing and the mortgage as an incident. If A owes B $10,000, and B collects by sale of A's property only $7,000, then A certainly still owes him $3,000. In other words, if B, through either his goodness of heart or ignorance of values, had advanced A money in an amount larger than A's security warranted, he should not be penalized for it. When there are several successive mortgages, however, the procedure is not quite so simple as when there is but one. The foreclosure on any one mortgage brings about the settlement of itself and all mortgages junior to it, but does not affect in any way the status of mortgages senior to it.

Thus, if foreclosure is made on the first mortgage, the buyer gets the property clear of all incumbrances, and the purchase price (after the cost of foreclosure and sale has been deducted) will be applied to paying off all the mortgages in sequence. Any mortgagee or mortgagees concerned who find the proceeds exhausted before they are satisfied have a personal claim against the mortgagor for the amounts still due them.

When foreclosure is made, let us say, on the second mortgage (and there are several successive mortgages on the property), the standing of the first mortgage is not affected. The purchaser acquires the property subject to the first mortgage, taking care, of course, not to pay more for the property than the difference between its real value and the claim of the first mortgage. The first clear money from the sale goes to pay the second mortgage and each in succession down the line. Any unsatisfied mortgagee, as above, has a personal claim against the mortgagor but not against the specific property just sold. The effects of the foreclosure of any mortgage in the series can be analyzed in the same manner.

Suppose a piece of property is security for four successive mortgages: the first for $50,000; the second for $30,000; the third for $20,000; the fourth for $10,000. To see the result of foreclosure and sale by any one of the mortgages, at various net prices, study the table below.

TABLE OF MORTGAGE LIEN CLAIMS ON PROCEEDS OF SALE

Foreclosed By	Purchaser Receives	1st Mtg. of $50,000 Receives	2nd Mtg. of $30,000 Receives	3rd Mtg. of $20,000 Receives	4th Mtg. of $10,000 Receives	Mortgagor Receives
1st Mtg. Net Proceeds $100,000	Clear title.	$50,000	$30,000	$20,000	Personal claim on mortgagor in the sum of $10,000	Nothing.
2nd Mtg. Net Proceeds $55,000	Title subject to the 1st mtg.	Holds mortgage as before.	$30,000	$20,000	$5,000 and personal claim on mortgagor of $5,000.	Nothing.
3rd Mtg. Net Proceeds $30,000	Title subject to 1st and 2nd mtgs.	Holds mortgage as before.	Holds mortgage as before.	$20,000	$10,000	Nothing.
4th Mtg. Net Proceeds $15,000	Title subject to 1st, 2nd, and 3rd mtgs.	Holds mortgage as before.	Holds mortgage as before.	Holds mortgage as before.	$10,000	$5,000

The Corporate Mortgage

The corporate mortgage. The corporate mortgage follows the general lines of the real estate mortgage, but there are a number of additional features that must be taken into account.

Corporations will, as a rule, mortgage not merely their real estate, but even the business itself, including the ground, buildings, machinery, stock, raw materials, trade names, trademarks, patents, goodwill, cash, accounts receivable, securities owned—in fact, their every asset. Thus, the corporate mortgage is much broader in its scope and requires much more detail in the description of the mortgaged property than does the real estate mortgage. Furthermore, since the bonds issued under the corporate mortgage are almost always very large in number and are often paid off in varying manners and at various times, the instrument becomes especially complicated in this respect.

A corporation may, of course, secure a loan through a regular real estate mortgage upon a certain piece of its property, or several loans by different mortgages on respective pieces of property. The general practice, however, which happens to be also the best financing, is to avoid a number of small mortgages and to consolidate all loans as much as possible.

Other distinct features of the corporate mortgage follow in the succeeding paragraphs.

Mortgage bonds. Borrowing corporations include, usually, our big businesses, and when they borrow, they do so in large amounts. While it is possible for a corporation to obtain a loan of even millions of dollars from a single institution such as a life insurance company using a mortgage made out to the institution as security for the loan, such large loans are usually participated in by a large number of persons and each must be given an evidence of the indebtedness of the company to him, as well as be provided with security through a mortgage. To supply the evidence of indebtedness, the corporation issues its bonds to the persons lending the money.

A *corporate bond* is a written promise, under seal, to pay a specific sum of money (usually $1,000) at a fixed time in the future (usually more than ten years after the promise is made). It is generally one of a series of similar bonds, all of which usually carry interest at a fixed rate, and if mortgage bonds, are covered by a so-called deed of trust, or mortgage, in which the corporation's property is mortgaged to a trustee for the benefit of all the bondholders. Although many bond issues are not secured by mortgages, an agreement is nevertheless made with a trustee to protect the rights of the bondholders.

The trustee. Although it is perfectly feasible to evidence the debt of the corporation to each of the lenders by issuing to him bonds in the amount of his contribution, it is manifestly impracticable to execute a mortgage to each one in order to secure his individual loan. The matter of mortgage security is provided for by executing only one mortgage, which secures all the bonds issued under it and is made out not to the bondholders direct, but to a trustee who holds it for the benefit of all the bondholders.

Under the Trust Indenture Act of 1939, a trustee must be "a corporation organized to do business under the laws of the United States or of any state or territory . . . which is authorized under such laws to exercise corporate trust powers, and is subject to supervision or examination by federal, state, or territorial authority." The act further provides that the trustee shall have a combined capital and surplus of not less than $150,-000.

The above law undoubtedly contemplates a continuation of the usual practice of appointing a national bank or trust company as trustee. This has been the practice for many years and is desirable because a corporation has continuous life and is more likely than a natural person to be impartial, independent, and capable. In addition, banking corporations are subject to governmental supervision.

A corporation acting as a trustee in a corporate mortgage sometimes finds it difficult or impracticable to perform its functions in states outside the one in which it is organized. For this reason, many modern mortgages provide for a natural person (usually an officer of the corporate trustee) as a co-trustee with the corporation, so that he may, under his constitutional rights, act freely in any state where the corporate trustee may find it impracticable to operate.[2]

In such a case, the corporation is known as the *corporate trustee* and the natural person as the *individual trustee*.

Parties to the corporate mortgage. From the foregoing, it is clear that one of the essential differences between the real estate mortgage and the corporate mortgage is that the latter is an instrument of three parties, and the former is of only two.

The three parties to the corporate mortgage are the corporation, the bondholders, and the trustee.

The corporation gives the mortgage in order that it may keep possession and control of its property and at the same time assure the bondholders the greatest possible security. It, therefore, procures the loan at the lowest possible rate of interest.

The bondholders demand the mortgage in order that they may obtain and hold the earliest and the strongest possible lien on property to assure the repayment of their loan.

The trustee is served by the mortgage through obtaining hereby the legal right to protect the bondholders without assuming any correlative obligations.

The duties of the trustee are:

1. To authenticate the issue of bonds. That is, to sign a statement on each bond affirming that it is in reality one of the bonds issued pursuant to the terms of the mortgage. This authentication is a warranty on the part of the trustee that its issuance does not exceed the amount of bonds authorized under the mortgage.

---

[2] The Trust Indenture Act of 1939 contains a provision permitting the appointment of co-trustees.

2. To represent the bondholders in the protection of their rights.

3. To enforce the lien in case of default.

4. To comply with the provisions of the Federal Trust Indenture Act. Since the corporation mortgage is made out to the trustee and not to the real lenders of the money, the question is frequently asked as to who is the mortgagee. This is answered by stating that both trustee and bond-holders are mortgagees, the former being designated as the *legal mort-gagee*, and the latter as the *beneficial mortgagee*.

The opening clause of the corporate mortgage will, therefore, usually appear approximately as follows:

THIS INDENTURE, dated the fifteenth day of October, one thousand nine hundred and fifty-one, between the Upton Manufacturing Co., a corporation organized and existing under the laws of the State of New York, hereinafter called the "Company," party of the first part, and The Newton Bank and Trust Co., a corporation organized and existing under the laws of the State of New York, herein called the "Corporate Trustee," and William C. Maple, herein called the "Individual Trustee," parties of the second part, WITNESSETH:

It will be seen, then, that the lenders or bondholders, who are really a party in the agreement and who are the beneficial mortgagees, do not appear as a party in the mortgage. That document merely gives to the trustees a lien upon the property for the benefit of the bondholders. The rights and privileges of the bondholders are, however, fully set forth in the body of the mortgage.

Form of the bond. The mortgage gives the *security* to the bondholders by giving a lien to the trustee on the property of the corporation to guarantee the repayment of the debt and the payment of the interest. The bond is the document naming some specific amount (usually $1,000), to the extent of which the bondholder participates in the entire loan and in the protection of the mortgage. In other words, the bond is the cor-poration's *evidence of debt* to him.

The bond should be worded carefully so as to set forth its purpose in a clearly understandable manner.

To every bond of the coupon type there is attached a series of coupons, each of which is worth the interest for a period of six months. The coupon usually reads about as follows:

No. $25.00

On the fifteenth day of . . . ., 19. . . ., the Upton Manufacturing Co. will pay to the bearer at the agency of the Company in the Borough of Manhattan, in the City of New York, or at the office of The Newton Bank and Trust Co., in the City of New York, as the bearer may elect, twenty-five dollars in United States currency, being six months' interest then to become due on its First Mortgage Thirty-Year, Five Per Cent Bond No. . . . . unless said bond shall have been called for previous redemption. . . . .

Treasurer.

Then, there will also be the *certification of the trustee*, which authenticates the bond and which generally reads as follows:

This bond is one of the bonds described in the within-mentioned mortgage and deed of trust.

The Newton Bank & Trust Co.

By . . . .

Trust Officer.

Types of mortgages. After a corporation has decided to borrow money through mortgage bonds, it has to determine upon the manner in which the bond issue shall be carried out. This procedure is, of course, provided for in the mortgage. But three distinct types of mortgages have been developed and are in current use. These are the *closed end mortgage,* the *open end mortgage,* and the *limited open end mortgage.* Each will be explained separately.

The closed end mortgage. The *closed end mortgage* is one under the terms of which the corporation may issue bonds in a certain designated amount and all of the same issue.

As far as the buyer of these bonds is concerned, the name means that he knows exactly how many bonds are secured by his mortgage at the time of its making. He knows, further, that at no future time can additional bonds be issued under it, thus reducing his proportionate security. To the corporation the name means that if, prior to the repayment of these bonds, it needs to sell other bonds and use the same property for security, it can do so only by making another mortgage, which will be junior to the one in question. The bonds of the junior mortgage will probably have to carry a higher rate of interest or else be sold at a discount in order to counterbalance the lesser degree of security. Since a corporation is never, by any means, sure that it will not desire to sell more bonds within a few years, the closed end mortgages are not universally desirable. However, suppose a corporation requires funds, say, for the erection of a factory building and equipping it with machinery; with no further expansion contemplated, it might well obtain part of the capital through this type of mortgage. Were the corporation engaged in a rapidly expanding industry and regular growth requiring future financing with borrowed capital anticipated, this type of mortgage would probably not be suitable and one of the mortgages described below would be chosen. It should be observed that, in recent years, industrial corporations requiring borrowed funds for purposes of expansion have frequently been able to avoid giving mortgages when borrowing through the use of unsecured bonds known as debentures.

The open end mortgage. The *open end mortgage* is just the opposite of the closed end mortgage. It simply authorizes the issuance of bonds without setting forth the number to be issued. Under such a mortgage, a corporation may issue bonds in whatever number it sees fit; later it may put out another issue, and still later another, and so on as long as it can find purchasers. The various issues of bonds, though some may be dated years ahead of others, have no priority one over another; all are issued under the same mortgage, and, in case of foreclosure, all holders will share *pari passu* in the proceeds.

It may appear that a bondholder who possesses bonds of one of the earlier series under such a mortgage faces the possibility of watching the equity grow thinner and thinner as the corporation continues to issue more bonds against the same property. In actual practice, such a thing is usually avoided by placing in the mortgage certain restrictions, or *escrow provisions*, which protect the bondholder against the carrying too far of such future bond issuing. These restrictions will be taken up later.

Public utilities are large users of open end mortgages. They are in an industry which is constantly expanding and there is a steady need for new capital. Open end mortgages give to the public utility a flexible as well as simplified capital structure; the different issues of bonds called *series* under such a mortgage bear interest rates current at the time of issue and, because most series are redeemable, the corporation may put out a new issue at lower interest when such an opportunity occurs and use the proceeds to redeem an earlier issue bearing higher interest. When a series contains provisions not covered in the basic open end mortgage, these are covered by a supplemental indenture filed with the trustee. For example, Kansas Power and Light Co. has an open end mortgage with a number of series outstanding. In 1949, a new series due 1984, bearing interest at the rate of 2¾ per cent, was issued and the proceeds applied in part to the redemption of an earlier series carrying an interest rate of 3½ per cent with a maturity date of 1969.

Railroads have also made extensive use of open end mortgage bonds. These have been issued not only to finance new construction but, in recent years, series have been used to refund or redeem earlier issues under other mortgages with a view to consolidating the various issues under one mortgage, thus simplifying the lien structure of the railroad as well as taking advantage of any possible saving in interest rates.

Limited open end mortgage. This type of mortgage is similar to the open end mortgage except that a limit is placed on the maximum amount which may be outstanding under it. When this point is reached, the mortgage becomes a closed end mortgage. If used by an industrial corporation, the limit is likely to be fairly low and subject to restrictions. An example is provided by the B. F. Goodrich Co. open end issue, limited to $45,000,000. Bonds under this mortgage may be issued only up to 66⅔ per cent of the value of the new property and then only if the previous two years' earnings have been at least twice all bond interest charges including those of the proposed new issue. In addition, the mortgage contains a number of other restrictions relating property values to outstanding bonds. Public utilities are likely to set a much higher limitation. For example, Pacific Gas and Electric Co.'s basic mortgage is $1,000,000,000, of which there are at present sixteen series outstanding.

It should be made clear that a corporation not only finances but refinances within the limits of the mortgage and may redeem and refund issues made under it as expedient. For example, the Pacific Gas and Electric Co., which identifies its series by letters of the alphabet, has no series now outstanding earlier than that bearing the letter *I*, issued in 1936 but has completely gone through the alphabet and just recently sold a series designated *AA*. This corporation follows the practice of making all series redeemable and all provide for sinking funds for retirement. The result is that within the billion dollar limit established in the mortgage, the amount of bonds outstanding is never static and even the number of series outstanding changes from time to time.

A common practice is to make it possible to raise the limit of bonds which may be issued, provided the consent of holders of two-thirds or three-quarters of the outstanding bonds is first obtained. Because maximum limits have been reached so many times resulting in more costly junior mortgage financing, the present tendency is toward the use of unlimited open end mortgages by public utility corporations.

Restrictions or escrow provisions. From a general description of an open end mortgage, it would appear that a corporation might persist in issuing bonds from time to time until the amount of bonds outstanding under the mortgage would be much greater than the entire value of the mortgaged property. Such a procedure would thus wipe out all equity and give only partial security. Of course, most bond buyers are accustomed to investigate the issues offered to them and would decline to buy weak late issues under open end mortgages. The terms of the mortgage itself, however, do not prevent such offerings, and so there is nothing to protect the equity of the buyers of the early issues, except the probable market resistance against the sale of the later offerings. In order to make open end mortgage and limited open end mortgage bonds more marketable, therefore, most such mortgages contain certain restrictions or escrow provisions to guard against this very thing and so protect the bondholder to a considerable extent.

These restrictions vary considerably in intent and in wording, but the usual ones are as follows:

1. Restricted to a percentage of the cost or fair value of new property acquired. *The percentages usually vary between 60 per cent and 75 per cent.*

2. Restrictions based upon the relationship of earnings to interest on funded debt. *For example, the earnings for a previous period of 24 or 36 months must have been some multiple of the total interest charges, in-*

cluding the proposed new issue. A commonly used limitation is that the earnings should be twice the interest charges.

3. No additional bonds shall at any time be issued if their issuance would cause the total fixed charges to exceed a certain proportion of the net quick assets.

4. Total funded debt must not exceed a certain percentage of the total capitalization.

The after-acquired clause. Corporate mortgages may contain a clause annexed to the section containing the description of the property which states that any property acquired in the future will become subject to the lien of the mortgage. This clause is, of course, quite proper for, and is usually found in, open end mortgages. When added to closed end mortgages, it would make it necessary to finance the acquisition of new property through the issuance of bonds junior in claim to the after-acquired clause mortgage. Because investors often measure the risk of a bond investment in terms of the security of the lien provided by the mortgage, junior mortgage bonds are likely to carry a higher interest rate, thus increasing the cost of capital to the issuing corporation.

Avoidance of the after-acquired clause. Because of the higher cost of junior mortgages financing, a corporation with an after-acquired clause mortgage may wish to avoid its consequences. Various methods and types of financing will accomplish this, some of which follow:

1. *By a refunding mortgage.* The procedure followed in refunding bond issues will be discussed in detail in Chapter IX. It is sufficient to say here that, in the refunding process, a new mortgage is issued and the bonds secured by it are offered to holders of bonds secured by the after-acquired clause mortgage, or are sold and the proceeds used to pay off these holders of the original issue who prefer the cash. When this operation is completed, the refunding mortgage replaces the mortgage containing the after-acquired clause. The sale of additional bonds secured by the refunding issue will provide the funds necessary for the acquisition of new property.

2. *By using a purchase money mortgage and a financing company.* The mortgages thus far considered have been those given for the purpose of securing the repayment of borrowed money. There is in common usage also the *purchase money mortgage,* one given by the purchaser of property to the seller to secure to the latter payment of all or a part of the purchase price. Thus, Mr. A may sell a certain property to Mr. B for $30,000, receiving $10,000 in cash and retaining a purchase money mortgage on the property for $20,000. Mr. B gets, not the actual clear title to the property bought, but in reality a $10,000 equity in it. A purchase money mortgage on property takes precedence over any other lien that may be placed upon it by the mortgagor. Hence, an after-acquired clause mortgage will have a superior lien not on the new property, but only

upon the equity the purchaser has in it. There may be instances when the owner of the property will not accept a purchase money mortgage, or the property may consist of several parcels divided among many owners. In such a case, use has been made of an intermediary financing company or syndicate (or a construction company may be utilized), which put up the cash to pay for the property. The purchase money mortgage was then executed to a trustee, bonds are issued against it, and the proceeds from the sale were used to pay the intermediary company which, having served its purpose, was now completely out of the transaction. (See page 133.)

3. *By leasing the property.* Instead of acquiring the title at once, arrangements may be made to lease the property for a period of years and to pay a regular rental sufficient to cover the purchase price and a return to the owners of the property. At the expiration of the lease, title is transferred to the lessee corporation. In some cases, the property, usually equipment, may be purchased on a conditional sale agreement under which the title may revert to the vendor or his assignee if there is a default in payments required by the contract of purchase. This latter type of arrangement is similar to that used in the sale of automobiles and other chattels on an installment payment plan. In the lease arrangement, the mortgage with the after-acquired clause will not become a lien until title passes to the lessee corporation and, if the conditional sale plan is used, any title possessed by the buyer is subject to the conditions under which the property was acquired. While the lease plan can be used to acquire title to land and buildings, it is chiefly used as a method of acquiring machinery and equipment. Most of the railroads' rolling stock is acquired through a lease plan, the lease extending for ten to fifteen years. At the termination of the lease, title is passed to the railroad. This practice is fully described in the next chapter. Once title passes to the railroad, an after-acquired clause in the railroad corporation's mortgage will take effect, but by that time the acquisition of the equipment has been completely financed at low rates. [3]

4. *By means of a subsidiary company.* In this plan, title to the new property sought to be acquired is taken by a subsidiary corporation. Since, legally, such a corporation has an identity separate from that of the parent holding corporation, it may issue a mortgage and bonds in its own name for the purpose of acquiring the property. These will not be subject to the after-acquired clause mortgage of the parent company. The

---

[3] See Equitable Life Assurance Co. plan, described in the chapter following. Because title does not pass in this plan, the rent paid is a deduction from gross income for federal income tax purposes. Should the lease provide for transfer of title at the time of final rental payment, the rent paid is treated for tax purposes, not as an expense, but merely as part of the purchase price.

parent company may lend marketability to the bonds of the subsidiary company through a guarantee of the interest and principal.

5. *By means of consolidation.* A corporation with an after-acquired clause in its mortgage may *consolidate* with one or more other corporations, absolutely giving up its individual corporate being and becoming only a part of an entirely different corporate entity. In such a case, additional property acquired by the consolidated company cannot be considered as newly-acquired property of a constituent company. This fact effectively protects the new property from the action of the after-acquired clause of the old mortgage.

Questions for Study and Review

1. What is meant by the expression *trading on the equity?* Would a concern operating entirely on borrowed money meet your definition?
2. Explain why it is said that "trading on the equity magnifies profits and losses?"
3. Would it be correct to assume that because a concern had a high average income that it might, with safety, obtain a high proportion of its capital through borrowing?
4. When is a loan said to be unsecured? Secured? Are unsecured loans limited to short-term bank loans?
5. If a borrower has given a lien as security for the payment of a debt, what is likely to happen if the debt is not paid?
6. By the assumption of appropriate figures, illustrate the difference between security and equity in connection with a lien on property.
7. Has a mortgagee who is foreclosing his mortgage any further claim if the property brings less than the amount due at the foreclosure sale? Explain.
8. Mortgage financing requires two instruments to be signed; what are they and what is the relationship between them?
9. What happens to a second mortgage if the first mortgage is foreclosed? Suppose it is the second mortgage that is foreclosed? What happens to the first mortgage?
10. Define a corporate bond.
11. What is the purpose of having a trustee in a mortgage bond issue? What are the duties of a trustee?
12. What federal law governs indentures in connection with a public sale of bonds?
13. Explain the difference between closed end, open end and limited open end mortgages.
14. What is the meaning of the word *series* used in connection with open end mortgages?
15. Give an illustration of an escrow provision or restriction used with open end mortgage bond issues. What is the usual purpose of such restrictions?
16. What is the after-acquired clause? Why would it handicap future debt financing of a corporation if present in a closed end mortgage? Suppose the mortgage was of the open end variety, would the same handicap be present?

17. Why would the lease method of acquiring property avoid an after-acquired clause?

18. How does the purchase of property under an open end mortgage avoid the after-acquired clause?

Problems

1. A corporation with capital of $1,000,000 has average annual earnings of $100,000. If it had an additional $500,000 of capital, it could increase its annual earnings by $50,000. Describe the available means of raising the additional $500,000 of capital. (Assume that the cost of borrowing is 4 per cent per annum.)

2. The Mohawk Electric Utility has the following capital structure in the first year:

Bonds 3½%	$340,000,000
Preferred stock 4%	100,000,000
Common Stock	165,000,000
Capital surplus	75,000,000
	$680,000,000

If the corporation earns $30,000,000, what is the rate of return on the common stock? What is the advantage, percentagewise, to the common stockholder through trading on the equity?

3. Mr. Appleby had invested $25,000 in a small manufacturing business on which he has been able to earn 15 per cent, or $3,750, a year. He believes that if he can obtain additional capital, he can continue to earn the same rate of return on the larger volume of business. He, therefore, borrows $10,000 at an interest rate of 5 per cent per annum giving as security a mortgage on his factory. In the next year Mr. Appleby's expectations are realized and he earns 15 per cent on the total investment. In the following year Mr. Appleby earns only $1,000, due to a general business recession. Show how the above facts illustrate the principle that "trading on the equity magnifies profits and losses."

4. The Elwood Power Co. is expanding rapidly and wishes to provide for present and future capital needs through the use of a mortgage bond. The mortgage drawn by counsel contains an after-acquired clause. What should be the attitude of the Elwood Power Co. toward this clause with respect to its effects on (a) current financing, and (b) future financing?

5. Prepare a schedule of mortgage lien claims, under various foreclosures, upon the proceeds of sale (similar to that shown in the text of this chapter), using the following figures:

Amount of 1st mortgage	$20,000
Amount of 2nd mortgage	8,000
Amount of 3rd mortgage	15,000
Sale under 1st mortgage foreclosure brings net	$50,480
Sale under 2nd mortgage foreclosure brings net	26,925
Sale under 3rd mortgage foreclosure brings net	19,000

Written Assignment

Do for Oct 24th

Part I:

What type of mortgage would be particularly suitable in each of the following cases? State the reasons for your choice.

  a. A new manufacturing corporation wishes to raise one-half the cost of its land, factory and equipment by borrowing through the sale of mortgage bonds to the public.

  b. A public utility corporation is expanding rapidly and foresees a continuance of the present rate for a long time in the future.

  c. The expansion program of a corporation is expected to take ten years at a total cost of $35,000,000.

Part II:

The "X" Corporation has a total capital of $8,000,000 of which $6,000,000 is common stock and $2,000,000 is 5 per cent mortgage bonds. What is the effect of "trading on the equity" in each of the following cases?

  a. The earnings are at the rate of 10 per cent on the invested capital.

  b. The company earns $100,000.

  c. The company has a loss after taxes, but before interest, of $400,000.

CHAPTER VIII

Classification and Types of Bonds

Corporate bonds. The bonds issued by corporations are promises to pay a specified amount of money to lenders at a specified date. There are in existence certificates of debt which do not provide for payment at a definite time or even at a time which is subject to present determination. The Canadian Pacific Railway perpetual 4 per cent convertible debenture stock is an example of such an issue. These issues are often erroneously called perpetual bonds but, lacking a fixed or determinable maturity date, they do not meet the definition of a bond. A more accurate term might be perpetual annuities. Bonds take many forms and even where an individual issue seems in major respects to conform to one of the major classifications set forth below, there may be many minor differences, disclosed by a study of indenture provisions. For example, the manner and amount of sinking fund payments provided for in two otherwise similar debenture bond issues may vary greatly. To a high degree, bond issues differ one from another because an issuing corporation must conform to the desires of investors for security and income. The nature of the corporation's business, however, the type of assets which predominate and the traditional borrowing pattern of the industry all influence investors' demands.

Rights of individual bondholders. As pointed out in the preceding chapter, a trustee is appointed whenever corporate bond issues are marketed to the public; he not only holds any lien upon property or assets pledged as security for the bonds, but is empowered to enforce against the corporation any indenture provisions on behalf of the bondholders. Direct action on the part of individual bondholders other than their right to approve or disapprove any special proposition, such as an amendment of the indenture, is almost impossible. Indentures often state that a trustee may do or must do certain things when ordered by holders of a specified proportion, say 75 per cent of the outstanding bonds, but such concerted action is far different than individual action.

Classification of bonds. It has been shown in the discussion in Chapter VI that there are many types of stock with which the corporate organizer must be familiar so as to make a wise selection for his company. Similarly, the corporation that contemplates financing by means of bonds has many kinds from which to choose. The names of these are often confusing, owing to the fact that the name applied to a bond is not always truly descriptive of the character of the security. It is advisable, in all cases, for a prospective investor not to rely upon the name appearing on the face of a bond, but rather to go back to the mortgage and therein read carefully all the characteristics of the security in question.

It is recognized that bond indentures, whether covering mortgage bonds, collateral trusts, or debentures, are usually long and, for the average investor, difficult to understand. This presents no real obstacle to learning the important facts about a bond before purchasing it. The well-known publications of Fitch Investors Service, Moody's Investors Service and Standard and Poors Corporation present the essential facts about bond issues of most corporations in summary form and in easily understandable terms. If the issue is new, the prospectus offered to investors at the time of the initial offering to the public by investment bankers will also contain the essential information.

For the purpose of study, corporate bonds may be classified on the basis of the:

1. Purpose to be accomplished.
2. Security of the principal.
3. Amount of income the bondholders are to receive.
4. Manner of payment of the interest.
5. Manner of payment of the principal.

Under each of these main headings may be grouped certain classes of bonds, aggregating practically all the important types, in accordance with the scheme on the next page.

With the above outlines clearly in mind, we may proceed to a detailed discussion and study of each of the subordinate classifications.

Purchase money and similar bonds. Purchase money bonds are issued under a mortgage given as part of the purchase price of property. In the days of railroad construction, a temporary corporation or sometimes merely an unincorporated syndicate was formed to finance construction of an extension or railroad division after acquiring the property for the purpose. The property, with construction completed, was then sold to the railroad. The construction organization was paid in purchase money mortgage bonds and sometimes in stock in the railroad. These securities the construction company hoped to sell to the public at a profit. Extension improvement or construction bonds may be names used for these issues. Today they are usually junior bonds, unless the words first mortgage or first lien are found in the title. As far as railroad financial struc-

SCHEME OF BOND CLASSIFICATION

Grouping of Corporate Bonds.

On Basis of Purpose to Be Accomplished.
1. Purchase money, construction, extension, or improvement bonds.
2. Consolidated or unified bonds.
3. Adjustment or reorganization bonds.
4. Funding or refunding bonds.

On Basis of Security of Principal.
1. Prior lien bonds.
2. First, second, third, etc., mortgage bonds.
3. Bridge, terminal, dock, divisional, etc., bonds.
4. First and consolidated, first and refunding, general mortgage, etc., bonds.
5. Debenture bonds.
6. Subordinated Debenture bonds.
7. Receiver's certificates.
8. Collateral trust bonds.
9. Car or equipment trust bonds.
10. Assumed, guaranteed, indorsed, and stamped bonds.

On Basis of Amount of Income Bondholder Is to Receive.
1. Bonds of stipulated interest rate.
2. Income bonds.
3. Profit-sharing bonds.
4. Participating bonds.
5. Tax-exempt bonds.

On Basis of Manner of Payment of Interest.
1. Registered bonds.
2. Coupon bonds.
3. Coupon bonds registered as to principal.
4. Interchangeable bonds.

On Basis of Manner of Payment of Principal.
1. Gold, silver, and legal tender bonds.
2. Redeemable or callable bonds.
3. Convertible bonds.
4. Serial bonds.
5. Sinking fund bonds.

tures are concerned, these titles have largely disappeared. Many such issues were replaced by income bonds during the 1930s, when so many railroads were reorganized; others have been refunded into larger consolidated issues in moves to simplify the capital structure.

In present-day practice, it is possible for a corporation too small readily to market a bond issue to acquire real estate, including buildings, by making a down payment in cash and giving a purchase money mortgage for the balance. Large companies are likely to finance such purchases through a bond issue, secured by a mortgage upon all of the issuing concern's assets or by an issue of debenture bonds. The latter are discussed in a subsequent paragraph in this chapter.

Consolidated or unified bonds. Corporations, especially railroads, sometimes have several issues of bonds of varying dates of issue, various times of maturity, and probably various rates of interest. These have been issued from time to time in a way that may be described as *hand-to-mouth financing*, In such instances, it is desirable and quite customary to combine, consolidate, or unify these several issues into one single large issue supported by a single blanket, general, unifying, or consolidated mortgage, under which the new bonds take the appropriate name.

In issuing such unifying mortgage bonds, a sufficient amount is generally authorized, not only to take care of the total amount of outstanding issues, but also to provide for future issues for a considerable time. Such unification greatly simplifies the company's finances and gives the bonds the desirable quality of marketability, in a much greater degree than ever possessed by the superseded issues.

Occasionally, the issue of consolidated bonds is not large enough to consolidate all bonds outstanding, and, later, another consolidated issue is put out to consolidate other old issues. In such cases, those first issued are known as *first consolidated mortgage bonds*, and the later ones as *second consolidated mortgage bonds*, and so on. This does not mean that they have first and second lien on the property, but merely that they are the first and second consolidated issues from the standpoint of date of issue (see discussion of *first and consolidated bonds* further on in this chapter).

Adjustment or reorganization bonds. Bonds bearing these names are used and issued at the reorganization of a company to adjust claims against the old property, usually in an attempt to cut down the bonded indebtedness and reduce fixed charges. Though they are sometimes unsecured, they are generally issued under junior mortgages and receive their interest only if it be earned. They are, in fact, usually income bonds, which will be described later in this chapter.

Funding or refunding bonds. *Funding bonds* are those issued for the purpose of converting floating indebtedness into a bonded indebtedness. *Refunding bonds* are those issued for the purpose of raising funds to retire previously issued bonds. Occasionally an issue of refunding bonds is not sold on the market at all, but is simply taken over by old bondholders in exchange for bonds of the old issue turned in. When an earlier issue of bonds is refunded in whole or in part into a later issue, the later issue obtains for the benefit of all of its holders the proportionate claim of the refunded bonds in the earlier lien. Funding and refunding will be treated in detail in the next chapter.

Prior lien bonds. *Prior lien bonds* are issued under a mortgage that, with the consent of old bondholders, takes precedence over one or more mortgages already on the property.

First, second, third, etc., mortgage bonds. These terms are used to indicate the order in which the mortgages back of the respective bond issues are placed upon the property. The first mortgage is first in point of time and is the senior lien upon the property. The others follow in consecutive order.

The use of the word "first" in the descriptive title of a bond issue is frowned upon by investment bankers as well as by government regulatory agencies, such as the Securities and Exchange Commission and the Interstate Commerce Commission, unless they are secured by a first lien on part of the property.

Bridge, terminal, dock, and divisional bonds. *Bridge, terminal, and dock bonds* are usually those of a bridge, terminal, or dock company secured by a mortgage on the specific property of the company. Such a company is often owned by, or else leases its property to, one or several railroads jointly. The roads that use the property generally guarantee the interest on such bonds to guard against the possibility of loss of use through foreclosure of the mortgage.

Of course, one railway company alone may construct its own terminals, bridges, and so forth, and issue bonds against them. But it is both cheaper and more convenient to use joint freight yards, union stations, common bridges, and the like, and a separate company is usually formed to take charge of these. An example is found in the bond issue of the Terminal Railroad Association of St. Louis and the St. Louis Bridge Co., which is owned by fifteen railroads entering St. Louis, who are under a perpetual contract to use its terminal facilities and required to pay fees to cover all interest and costs of operation.

Divisional bonds are quite often senior mortgage bonds having as security the property of a railroad division. Because they have a superior lien to other general mortgage issues covering the same property, they are often referred to as *underlying* issues. In most instances, these bonds were issued at the time the division was first constructed. Gradually they are disappearing through being refunded at maturity into other issues.

First and consolidated, first and refunding, etc., bonds. Bonds bearing names *first and consolidated, first and refunding,* and *first and general mortgage* are confusing because of their titles. In the first place, they are not first mortgage bonds in the sense that they represent a first lien on all the property of the issuing company. They are secured by a first mortgage on a portion of the company's property, but on the remainder they may be only second, third, fourth, fifth, or lesser liens, owing to various existing underlying mortgages on different parts of the property. They become first mortgages on other parts of the property as they replace older bonds either by consolidation, refunding, or purchase. It is the usual intent that these bonds shall eventually replace those of all existing mortgages and, thus, in reality, become a first lien on the entire property.

The term *general mortgage bonds* means bonds secured by a general or blanket mortgage on all the company's property, already subject in whole or in part to prior mortgages.

Debenture bonds. The title merely indicates debt (from *debere*, to owe) but, in the United States, has come to mean a bond which is not secured by a specific lien and is therefore issued against the general credit of the debtor corporation only. In England, the same type of security is referred to as *debenture stock,* but there in the event of default, a lien attaches to the corporation's assets in favor of the bondholders. Here the holders of ordinary debenture bonds share their claims with other unsecured creditors of the issuer.

There has been, for several decades, a steady increase in the number of debenture issues. During the last decade debentures, publicly and privately sold, have exceeded both in number of issues and amount the total of mortgage bonds sold. This is probably due in part to the excellent bond market and also to the general over-all prosperity of American industry prevailing since 1940. Today, few large corporations are liquidated in bankruptcy; they are reorganized under one of the sections of the Federal Bankruptcy Act applicable. Bondholders do not exercise their foreclosure rights even when protected by mortgages. Instead, bondholders vote to accept some sort of adjustment, perhaps to accept a different kind of security in place of their original holdings. (See Chapter XVII.)

The chief security to the bondholders lies in the earning power of the debtor corporation. The mortgage is mostly of value as a means of giving preference if a liquidation or adjustment becomes necessary. If buyers of bonds believe that the possibility of failure is extremely unlikely, they are not greatly concerned about whether a mortgage exists or not.

Debentures frequently contain a clause sometimes referred to as "the covenant of equal coverage," which makes it mandatory for the corporation to permit the debentures to share ratably in a lien or mortgage subsequently placed upon the property. Debenture bond agreements usually provide for gradual retirement through the application of a sinking fund for this purpose. To facilitate retirement, the indenture must also carry a redemption clause making the bonds callable. To take advantage of speculative stock markets in recent years, many issues are made convertible into common stock of the issuer.

Corporations whose chief assets are in inventories, accounts receivable, installment accounts and the like, naturally have to use debentures for .public debt financing. There are no fixed assets to pledge. Corporations which do a great deal of short-term financing, such as through bank loans or commercial paper (see Chapter XII), are likely to use debentures, because having mortgage creditors with a priority of claim might contract the amount of short-term loans obtainable. Corporations with a long-established record of earnings in basic or essential industries sell debentures simply because investors regard the corporation so highly that it does not have to offer a mortgage as security.

Subordinated debentures. Of increasing importance, at the present time, is a new type of debenture bond which, by the terms of the indenture under which it is issued, is subordinated to other unsecured debt of the corporation, often including bank loans. This security originally was used by finance companies who were desirous of maintaining their credit with banks and in the commercial paper market (the latter are sources of short-term funds which are vital to the finance business). Its use spread to other fields and such issues are now common. Without doubt another motivation is often that of saving on income taxes realized by the payment of interest which is deductible, while the dividends paid on stock which might otherwise have been issued are not. To make the issues as much like stock as possible, many of the subordinated debentures are income bonds (which are discussed later on) and obligate the corporation to pay interest only if earned. The corporation marketing subordinated income bonds has increased contingent but not fixed charges.

Within the last few years, corporations, chiefly railroads, have offered subordinated income debentures to their preferred stockholders in exchange for preferred stock. This offer is usually accepted because the bond is a higher grade security having a creditor's claim against the issuer. Sometimes the interest on the new debenture is a slightly lower rate than the dividend on the preferred stock. Substantial savings in taxes have resulted. Whether or not this type of debenture is a permanent method of financing remains to be seen but the present popularity deserves the above discussion.

Trustee or receiver's certificates. When a concern is unable to meet its obligations, an application for the appointment of a trustee under provisions of the Federal Bankruptcy Act may be made by the debtor corporation or its creditors. If the application be granted, the court will appoint a trustee to take charge of the property and operate it, while a plan of reorganization or other adjustment for the benefit of the creditors is worked out. In come cases, it becomes the duty of the trustee to liquidate the business if, after examination, there seems to be no prospect of successful reorganization. Prior to 1932, there was no provision in the Federal Bankruptcy Law providing for such procedure and recourse was had to the equity courts who appointed a receiver to take over and operate the property, just as the trustee does today. (See Chapter XVII.)

In order to operate the business and often to restore neglected assets to productive state, the trustee may require funds. In such cases, the court may authorize the issuance of trustee's certificates which, because of the old and now obsolete equity receivership procedure, are often still erroneously called by the old name *receiver's certificates.* These certificates are usually sold to investing institutions who bid competitively for them. They bear no definite maturity date but are to be paid at the time the reorganization is completed. For security, the court gives them priority of claim over other indebtedness of the corporation; at least, they are placed ahead of indebtedness upon which there has been a default. The court having jurisdiction over the reorganization proceeding will hold a hearing on the trustee's application for authority to sell trustee's certificates where creditors, if they wish, may state their objections or voice their approval.

Collateral trust bonds. A concern owning securities, bonds, or stocks of other companies—either separate companies or subsidiaries—may deposit them in trust as security for an issue of its own bonds. Bonds secured thus rather than by real property, are known as *collateral trust bonds.* Holders of such bonds are protected by the general credit of the issuing company, the market value of the pledged securities, and the value of the property of the companies whose securities are put up as collateral. This type of secured bond has been principally used by holding companies which deposit the stock of subsidiaries. The power to vote the stock remains with the holding company unless there is a default. Voting power would then pass to the trustee. Some issues of open end or limited open mortgage bonds are also collateral trust bonds. As the proceeds from the sale of the mortgage bonds are sold and the proceeds used to refund or call other issues, the bonds so acquired may be deposited with the trustee as additional security. This is especially true where only part of an issue having a prior claim to that of the open mortgage issue has been redeemed. The practice is observed in railroad financing where an attempt is being made to consolidate a number of small issues into one open end mortgage issue.

Equipment trust notes. These notes are issued in connection with the financing of equipment acquired under the so-called *Philadelphia* or lease plan. The notes are issued to mature in equal amounts, usually over a fifteen-year period. Title to the equipment remains with a trustee until the last of the notes are retired. The security is therefore the ownership of the equipment held in trust for the note holders plus a guarantee or endorsement of liability for payment at maturity and for the payment of interest by the lessee corporation, most of the time a railroad. The same plan has been used to a limited extent as a method of acquiring airplanes and busses. The notes are retired much more rapidly than the equipment depreciates so that the security actually increases as the notes are retired. These securities have a record of so few defaults that they are considered among the highest grade investments.

A car building company, or other equipment manufacturing concern, agrees that it will, upon the receipt of a down payment (usually 20 to 25 per cent of the price), build the equipment and turn over the title and ownership to a trustee named in the agreement. The trustee makes the property available to the road under the terms of a lease. The railroad gives over to the trustee interest-bearing equipment, trust notes or equipment trust bonds representing the full purchase price, minus the amount of the original down payment made the car manufacturing company. These notes or bonds are in ten, frequently fifteen annual series, an equal part maturing each year. One series is redeemed each year and, when the last series has been redeemed, the equipment has been completely paid for and title passes to the railroad. The trustee sells the notes or bonds to investors and immediately remits the proceeds to the car building company to cover the balance due on the purchase price. The notes bearing different maturities issued under the above plan are known as *serial* notes.

It might be possible to obtain the same result through the use of a conditional sale on an installment basis, much the same as automobiles are sold on an installment payment plan. Title to the railroad cars would then revert to the trustee upon default by the railroad on any installment. However, the laws of the various states differ as to the protection given to a vendor under conditional sales contracts, so it is not used in public financing. Following the close of World War II, when demands for railroad equipment exceeded the output of manufacturers, and only piecemeal deliveries were made, some railroads financed equipment by buying it from the manufacturer on an installment plan conditional sale basis. The manufacturer sold these contracts to banks, thus obtaining their money immediately; the railroad paid the installments to the bank holding the contract. This method is usually used where a single institution such as a bank or insurance company agrees to finance the purchase of equipment.

The lease method, as it is called, is the method by which the railroads acquire most of their equipment. The conditional sales plan, or *New York plan*, is a method now used for private, not public financing.

One of our large life insurance companies, the Equitable Life Assurance Co., has a plan whereby ownership of the equipment remains with the insurance company, which buys it from the manufacturer and then leases it to the railroad. The lease contains provisions for renewal at the end of the initial term, which is for thirty years, but no purchase clause, whereby the railroad could eventually obtain title. The absence of a clause containing a purchase option is obviously intended to permit the railroad to deduct the rent paid as an operating expense for income tax purposes.

Assumed, guaranteed, indorsed, and stamped bonds. When one corporation acquires another by purchase or merger, or gets control through lease or ownership of majority of the stock, it assumes the latter company's debt, including its bonds. These bonds are then known as *assumed bonds*. Assumed bonds are not necessarily guaranteed bonds, though they are sometimes erroneously given that designation. The assuming company may guarantee them, but unless it specifically does so, they are not guaranteed bonds. Of course, the assuming company is responsible for the payment of interest and principal without the specific guarantee.

When a company other than the issuing company guarantees the payment of interest or principal, or both, on certain bonds, they are known as *guaranteed bonds*. Such guarantee is intended to strengthen the market value and the loan value of the bonds. When the bonds are guaranteed at their issue, the terms of the guarantee are usually recited on the face of the bonds. Often, however, they are guaranteed after issue, and the guarantee appears on a separate instrument.

One corporation may simply indorse the bonds of another, thus implying a guarantee of payment and assuming liability, just as does the endorser of a note. This practice gives rise to *indorsed bonds*.

It is sometimes desired, subsequent to original issue date, to make some changes in the tenor of bonds, such as to add a new condition to which they are subject, or to insert some new privilege to which they shall be entitled. Such addenda may be stamped on the bonds, which thereupon are known as *stamped bonds*.

Bonds of stipulated interest rate. The great majority of all bonds are issued to bear a *specified or stipulated rate of interest*. This is paid to the bondholder annually or semiannually, always at the same rate. The income is not affected in any manner by fluctuations in the company's earnings or by any action on the part of directors or officers in the company. This interest constitutes a fixed charge on the company. A *fixed charge* has been defined as a charge whose nonpayment will cause the company to lose possession or control of its property. That is what happens in the case of nonpayment of the fixed or stipulated bond interest. Immediately upon default in any payment, the bondholder may foreclose through the trustee and proceed to collect both interest and principal.

Income bonds. Bonds are sometimes issued with the condition that interest at a certain rate will be paid upon them only if it is earned in excess of other fixed charges. Such bonds are known as *income bonds*. Their interest does not constitute a fixed charge, and failure to pay it, except when earned, does not give the bondholders the right to sue. If the earnings available for income bond interest are not sufficient to pay the full amount, then such portion as is earned is usually paid.

Income bonds often rise out of reorganization, when holders of defaulted bonds accept, in their stead, income bonds. They may be secured by a junior mortgage, they may be collateral trust bonds, or they may be simply debentures. They may be either cumulative or noncumulative.

Profit-sharing bonds. *Profit-sharing bonds* have a fixed minimum rate of interest, enforceable as is the interest on any other bond with a fixed interest rate. In addition to this, they share in excess earnings of the issuing company. Any method of profit-sharing may be arranged. This type has practically disappeared.

Participating bonds. Like the profit-sharing bonds discussed above, the use of the participating feature has almost disappeared in present practice. It was originally used to lower fixed interest charges in a reorganization, the lower interest-bearing bonds replacing bonds with a higher interest rate. The present practice is to issue income bonds in such a situation. The same speculative advantage gained through the use of the participating feature may, if desired, in connection with any bond issue, be gained by the present practice of making the bonds convertible.

Tax-exempt bonds. The United States Government exempts from all Federal income taxes all government bonds issued prior to World War I; the First Liberty 3½s; state bonds; bonds of insular possessions; bonds of municipalities, districts, or political subdivisions of a state; Federal Land Bank Bonds; and Joint-Stock Land Bank Bonds. The various states similarly exempt from state income taxes the same government bonds, their own state bonds, and bonds of their own municipalities and subdivisions. All such bonds are known as *tax-exempt bonds*. The term *tax-free bonds* is applied almost indiscriminately to the same bonds. The latter term, however, might be applied more properly to taxable bonds issued with a tax-free covenant clause. This is an agreement that the issuing corporation will itself pay the normal income tax on such bonds, without deducting it from the interest payments to the holder. Under the present revenue law, the issuing company can pay this normal tax only to the extent of 2 per cent. There is much agitation at the present time to have the income from government, state, and other public bonds made fully taxable. It may be noted that the new defense bonds and others issued in connection with World War II are taxable.

Registered bonds. *Registered bonds* have the owner's name written on the face and are registered on the records of the issuing corporation. They can be negotiated only by indorsement and transfer on the books of the company. They have no interest coupons, but the company sends the interest at each period to the person recorded on its books as the owner. A bank or trust company is usually appointed as registrar for bonds of this class and keeps complete records of all issuances and transfers. The complete history and ownership of each bond can thus be traced.

Coupon bonds. A *coupon bond* is not registered in the name of the owner and, at maturity, is payable to the bearer, the title passing by delivery without indorsement.

To a coupon bond is attached a series of coupons. Each coupon entitles its holder to the interest for the period represented by it. The coupons themselves are negotiable promises to pay the interest for certain periods, just as the bond itself is a promise to pay the principal when due. To collect the interest for a stated period on a coupon bond, the holder simply clips off the appropriate coupon and presents it for payment to the issuing company or its fiscal agent. As a matter of fact, the holder usually simply deposits it in his bank for collection.

Registered coupon bonds. Some bonds bear negotiable coupons to take care of interest payments but have the body of the bond, representing the principal, registered. This combination is known as a *registered coupon bond,* or a coupon bond registered as to principal.

Interchangeable bonds. Some bond issues consist of both coupon and registered bonds. A buyer may take his choice, and then, if he so desires after purchase, he may exchange his bond for the other types. Such are called *interchangeable bonds.*

Gold, silver, and legal tender bonds. Some bonds state the medium in which their payment is to be made and take their names accordingly. *Gold bonds* usually specify that they are payable in "gold coin of the present standard of weight and fineness." Under the 1935 "Gold Decision,"[1] the Gold Clause in bonds was abrogated and holders of gold bonds must now accept any legal money. Whether or not this will remain a permanent condition cannot be foretold. *Silver bonds* are not used in the United States.

Callable bonds. Bonds that by the terms of their issue, may be called for redemption by the issuing company before the date of their maturity are known as *callable* or *redeemable bonds.* It is quite common to issue callable bonds redeemable at certain specified times, or within certain time limits, or upon certain notice. To compensate the holder for the loss of his investment, a redemption price somewhat above par value is usually set.

Convertible bonds. *Convertible bonds* are convertible at the option of the holder into other securities of the issuing corporation. The conversion privilege usually means the right to convert into preferred or common stock and is set at a certain ratio: sometimes par for par; sometimes at a given figure, as at 110, or 120, and so forth. When a company issues bonds convertible into stock, it must have authorized and available sufficient stock to make the conversion if required.

Serial bonds. Bonds of a single issue, but made up of various groups with varying dates of maturity, are known as *serial bonds.* It is customary to divide the entire issue into a number of groups, all issued at the same time but with the groups maturing successively at equally distant periods.

---

[1] 55 Supreme Court Reporter 307 (1935).

The periods between maturities of the various groups are sometimes as small as six months and sometimes as long as several years. The system provides for methodical and gradual reduction of the issue. The entire issue bears equal interest; if the bonds are sold at a uniform price below par and redeemed at par, the yield on the shorter-term ones will be larger than that on those of longer terms. The yield is sometimes made uniform by arranging a varying scale of prices, which constantly diminish as the terms of the bonds increase, thus helping to make all the bonds equally desirable and salable.

Sinking fund bonds. *Sinking fund bonds* are bonds issued under an agreement by which the issuing corporation is required to set aside regularly out of earnings such sums as, with interest, are calculated to be sufficient to redeem the bonds at maturity. This agreement gives the bondholders assurance of a systematic provision for repayment of the loan. The sinking fund payments are obligatory: failure to make them constitutes a default on the mortgage and gives the bondholder foreclosure rights, as would a default in an interest payment. In present-day practice most sinking fund bonds contemplate an annual retirement of a stated amount of the bonds, or where the sinking fund is not a fixed amount but allowed to vary with earnings, the amount of the annual sinking fund must be used for retiring the bonds. For this purpose the bonds are callable. The corporation may call the bonds or purchase them in the market. Occasionally the corporation may request tenders (offers) of bonds from holders to fulfill sinking fund requirements.

Questions for Study and Review

1. What would the management of a corporation expect to gain by consolidating its bond issues?
2. What is the purpose of replacing a fixed charge bond issue with an income bond issue in a financial reorganization?
3. Explain the difference between a funding and a refunding issue.
4. The words "first and consolidated" appear in the title of a bond issue. Explain their probable meaning.
5. What is a debenture bond? What would the investor look for to insure safety of his investment before purchasing a debenture bond?
6. What type of business is most likely to use collateral trust bonds? What is the security back of such an issue?
7. What is a subordinated debenture bond? Why have finance companies made frequent use of them?
8. Railroads have used subordinated *income* debentures to retire preferred stock issues. Explain the purposes behind such action.
9. What are trustee's (formerly known as receiver's) certificates? To what use are the proceeds of such issues usually put? When do they mature?
10. What type of security arises in the purchase of railroad equipment under the lease (Philadelphia) plan? Who owns the railroad equipment while any part of such issues are outstanding?

11. Why can it be said that the security behind an issue under the lease (Philadelphia) plan increases as the maturities are reached?

12. Why might an investor prefer a registered bond?

13. How is interest paid on coupon bonds?

14. The words *series* and *serial* are used in connection with bond issues. What is the difference in meaning of the two as so used?

15. What is a sinking fund bond? Must the sinking fund usually be held to maturity of the bonds before being used?

Problems

1. The Ravenswood Electric Light & Power Corporation has acquired four smaller utility companies each of which had several mortgages on various plants. These bonds mature on different dates and bear different rates of interest. Suggest how the company can simplify its capital structure and at the same time improve the rating of the bonds.

2. Trustees have been appointed by a court to take over the operation of a railroad corporation's property. Because of heavy losses, the railroad is being financially reorganized under a Federal Bankruptcy Act proceeding. The trustee finds the property so rundown that continued operation is impossible without immediate funds.

(a) What type of security may the court authorize for sale in such a situation?

(b) What assurance does the purchaser receive as to payment?

(c) Will these securities carry a definite maturity date?

(d) How and to whom are such securities sold?

3. A finance company which relies heavily on bank loans and the sale of commercial paper as a means of financing feels the need of additional long-term financing. It does not wish to sell stock but prefers to sell bonds to gain the benefits of trading on the equity and because bond interest is deductible from income for tax purposes. However, the sale of ordinary debentures will have the effect of reducing its line of credit with banks.

(a) What type of debenture bond could be sold that would not affect the company's bank credit?

(b) If the finance company wished to avoid creating a fixed interest debt, could any other feature be added that would make the interest only a contingent charge?

(c) How would the addition of these features be likely to affect the interest the company would have to pay on the bonds?

(d) If the interest rate on the proposed issue seemed too high, what feature might be added to the bond issue which might make it possible to market the bonds at a lower rate?

4. (a) The Atlantic & Western Railroad is in need of $20,000,000 worth of rolling stock. All of its present property is mortgaged, and the mortgage contains an after-acquired clause. The road has only $4,000,000 available toward purchasing the needed equipment. Explain how it can finance the purchase of the equipment.

(b) Suppose that the equipment obtained by the railroad depreciates to a junk value of $200,000 by the end of twenty years. Explain how the equity back of the equipment trust notes will constantly increase if the entire issue is matured by the end of the tenth year.

5. Corporation A has 15,000,000 shares of common stock outstanding; Corporation B, 6,000,000 shares of common and 3,000,000 shares of non-voting preferred, and Corporation C, 9,000,000 shares of common. The market price of the stock is as follows: A, $25 per share; B, $42 common and $63 preferred, and C, $40 common. A syndicate wishes to gain control of the three corporations.

(a) Suggest a method of financing this project.

(b) What capital structure would be practical?

Written Assignment

What type of bond issue would be most suitable under the following conditions?

a. A holding company plans the acquisition of the control of a number of other corporations. Two-thirds of the cost of acquiring control is to be financed through the sale of secured bonds.

b. Because of financial difficulties, a corporation is being reorganized. It is necessary to reduce fixed charges. Bondholders object strongly to accepting stock in exchange for their 5 per cent bonds. As the law requires that the approval of two-thirds in amount of each class of creditors is necessary to put a plan of reorganization into effect, a new plan must be proposed. What other security may be offered and still accomplish the desired reduction in fixed charges?

c. A corporation operating a chain of retail stores follows a policy of renting rather than owning the premises. It has an excellent record of successful operations and enjoys a high credit standing. It needs $2,000,000 for expansion which it wishes to obtain through a bond issue.

d. Assume that the corporation in (c) hopes to retire the bonds rapidly. What clause or provision should be placed in the indenture to facilitate retirement?

e. In negotiations with an investment banker with a view to marketing an issue of debenture bonds, the banker insists that the corporation include a provision in the bond indenture to protect the debenture bondholders against the possibility that the corporation may subsequently issue mortgage bonds to which the claim of the debentures would be subordinated. What would be the nature of such a covenant?

CHAPTER IX

Conversion, Refunding, and Redemption

Extinction of bonded indebtedness. A bond represents a debt of the issuing company, and the bondholder is a creditor of the company. The bond, in addition to being an evidence of indebtedness, is also a written promise to repay this indebtedness at some definite time in the future. Thus, when a corporation issues bonds, it is its expressed intention and compulsory duty to make, in so far as may be possible, a satisfactory settlement with the bondholders at or before the maturity of the bonds; and the bondholders purchase the bonds because they are assured of this definite settlement. A plan of bond financing, therefore, is not complete unless it takes into consideration the method for extinguishing the bonds.

The normal procedure in a bond issue is that the instruments, having a certain maturity date, seldom less than ten and usually not less than twenty years, be sold to the public; that regular interest be paid on them either annually, semiannually, or quarterly during their entire life; and that upon the maturity date, the issuing company call in the bonds and pay each holder in cash, the face value of his certificate, which payment constitutes the redemption of the bonds.

Economic conditions, however, seldom remain static for any length of time. The outlook of business conditions changes constantly, and types of bonds that may be in popular demand as a security one year may be less in demand in another. Interest rates fluctuate with monetary conditions and with these changes, of course, the prices of outstanding bonds change. The character of bond investors changes and those who have funds one year to invest in debt securities may switch in another year to stock, or to a different type of bond. The relative popularity of the income bond and the subordinated bond following World War II is illustrative of this changing scene. In the years following World War II the huge sums of money invested in insurance policies and pensions by the people of the United States has led to a tremendous demand on the part of these institutions for bonds. These exigencies of business, fluctuations in interest rates, demand of investors for additional features in bonds, and many other factors bring about conditions under which many bonds do not run the normal course of being paid in cash at maturity, but are settled for with various mediums either at maturity or at some prior date.

A bond of a corporation may, therefore, be extinguished either at or before maturity. There are three methods of so doing, known respectively as converting, refunding, and redeeming; each will receive consideration.

Extinction by conversion. Conversion means simply the exchanging of one security for another and, as used here, consists in the exchange of bonds for stock. The conversion privilege is exercised wholly at the option of the bondholder, but such privilege is limited entirely to bonds which, by the terms of their issue, are made convertible. Although any type of bond issue may be made convertible, these bonds in present practice are typically debenture bonds. Although convertible bonds may sometimes be convertible into preferred stock, the usual convertible bond gives the holder the privilege of converting into common stock of the company at a ratio provided in the bond indenture at the time of its issue. In recent years, some corporations have financed by means of long-term notes containing a provision that the notes may be converted into bonds at the option of the institution holding the notes at some subsequent date. However, this must not be confused with the conversion being discussed here.

Reasons for having convertible bonds. The usual reason for making bonds convertible is that this feature adds a speculative element, *i.e.*, a possibility of value appreciation to the bonds, which very often will enable the issuing corporation to sell the bonds at a lower interest rate or accomplish what may amount to the same thing, sell them at a higher price. Obviously this is more likely to be true in times of a rising stock market when such an issue would attract not only the usual investor in bonds but those interested in speculating in stock. In setting the conversion ratio, that is, in stipulating the number of shares of stock the bondholders will receive when converting a bond, the corporation will seldom provide that the bond may be converted into the number of shares of stock which would exactly equal or exceed the price at which the bond was sold at the time it was issued. Rather a ratio will be established which would give to the bondholder, were he to convert immediately, shares of stock whose present market value would be less than the initial selling price of the bond. There are occasional exceptions to this practice, the most outstanding being that of the American Telephone and Telegraph Co., which has sold convertible bond issues to its own stockholders which were convertible at par (10 shares of $100 par value of stock for one $1,000 bond) plus the payment of an additional premium. For example, in 1955 this company offered to its stockholders the right to buy a convertible debenture bond bearing interest at 3⅝%, convertible at $148 per share. Which meant that for every $100 of debentures plus $48, the bondholder could obtain 1 share of common stock. This issue was dated Oct. 13, 1955 and was convertible from Dec. 13, 1955 to Oct. 13, 1965 inclusive. The price range of the common in 1955 was 127¾ to 187¾. Considering the price of the stock at the time the bonds became convertible there was an immediate advantage to conversion. The corporation, however, received a higher price for its stock than the $100 at which it has traditionally made new issues to its stockholders, a practice that the company apparently does not wish to stop.

Strange as it may appear, poor stock market conditions may also prompt a corporation to attach the conversion provision to a bond issue. After World War II, we had a period during which convertible bonds were extremely popular. Many believed that a depression would follow after a few years of postwar prosperity, and therefore were hesitant about purchasing common stock. Others were not sure what was going to happen—past history suggested the possibility that a depression was coming, but all the signs around them belied the historical precedent. To both groups, the convertible bond seemed to offer the ideal solution. Corporations sold these bonds with the knowledge that they would be converted in the near future, in all probability; the bondholder bought with the double feature of safety and potential appreciation, as times remained good and the stock continued to rise. As far as the corporation was concerned, the conversion of the bonds into stock furnishes a convenient and relatively easy way of getting rid of bonded indebtedness and the fixed interest charges incident to bonds. It was accomplished simply by a further division of the ownership and without any cash payment.

Offsetting the advantages to the corporation in using convertible bonds are the disadvantages that must be considered. The corporation must retain at all times sufficient stock, authorized and unissued, to meet the demand of those who wish to convert. As the state imposes an organization tax on the amount of the stock authorized whether issued or not, the existence of convertible bonds means that the corporation must incur the incorporation tax on authorized stock which may never be issued. There is a danger, too, that if substantial amounts of the bonds are converted, the earnings per share of the stock will be less, as there will be more shares outstanding with no increase in earnings, for conversion seldom brings in new capital. Not only will existing stockholders be unhappy at such prospects, but the result may depress the market price of the company's stock and make future sale of additional stock difficult. Offsetting this, however, is the fact that bonds are usually converted by the holders in a rising market and the price of the stock rises in spite of the conversions. The principle, nevertheless, is true, though its effect may not be measured. Of more concern to the management probably is the fact that its control might be seriously affected through the issuance of additional stock; indeed, it may be that an opposition group would gain sufficient stock through conversion to wrest control from the present management.

A further disadvantage accrues to the company upon the conversion of bonds into stock. Interest on bonds is an expense of operating the business which may be deducted before computing the income tax. Dividends, on the other hand, are not considered an expense of operation and therefore the income tax must be computed on profits before taxes, Suppose a company has a profit of $200,000 before interest of $50,000, and that the tax rate is 50 per cent. The income tax would be computed as follows: $200,000 less $50,000 multiplied by .50. The tax is $75,000. The stockholders would have $75,000 left. If the corporation had the same income, but paid out the $50,000 in preferred dividends, then the tax would be $200,000 x .50 or $100,000. The $50,000 dividend to the preferred would leave the common with only $50,000.

Finally, the shift from debt to equity reduces the advantages of trading on the equity discussed in Chapter VII.

Rates of conversion. Convertible bonds are made convertible into stock at a ratio which must be set forth in the bond indenture. For example, it may be provided that for each $1,000 bond the holder may receive 40 shares of common stock. Or the conversion basis may be indicated by stating that the bonds are convertible into common stock at $25 per share. Bonds are said to be at their conversion point when the conversion will result in neither profit nor loss. Thus, if the $1,000 bond is, by contract, exchangeable into 40 shares of stock, the conversion point price of the stock may be found by dividing the price of the bond ($1,000) by the number of shares to be received, in this case 40. If the price of the stock is given, the conversion price of the bond may be found by multiplying the price of the stock by the number of shares. To illustrate: assume a bond which is selling at 120 is convertible into 20 shares of stock, what is the conversion point? Divide $1,200 (the price of the bond) by 20 (the number of shares of stock received upon conversion) and the result is $60. If a share of stock is selling at $50 and the conversion ratio is 20 shares, then the conversion of a bond selling at $1,200 would result in a loss of $200 to the bondholder.

The rate of conversion is not always constant over the life of the bond. Usually the price at which the stock will be exchanged increases over the period during which the bond is convertible. Conversely stated, fewer shares will be given upon conversion the longer the conversion is put off. The scale, nevertheless, is fixed and is part of the original contract between the corporation and the bondholder. That the rate of conversion should vary is only fair. One of the reasons for the increase in the value of the stock on the market is the progressive increase in earnings per share resulting from the retention in the business of the profits. Thus the stockholder is forced to increase his investment in the company each year as part of the earnings are retained in the business and not paid to him in the form of dividends. It would be unfair to permit the bondholder to become a stockholder after this had been going on for a number of years and share both in this added stockholder investment (since the bondholder now becomes a stockholder) and also in the increased profits. To be equitable, therefore, the bondholder usually receives fewer shares of stock upon the conversion as the years go by.

Aside from the above consideration of the fairness of the offer, a corporation may wish to establish conditions which will accelerate the rate of conversion. It is possible that financing was accomplished with convertible bonds only because at the time it was uneconomical to sell stock. This may have been the result of security market conditions or the income tax rates may have been very high, presenting a saving through the tax deductions for interest costs which could not be ignored. Making the conversion ratio less advantageous to the bondholder the longer he delays the exercise of the option, may result in extinguishing the debt more quickly.

In an actual conversion, an adjustment is made on account of the accrued dividends on the stock and the accrued interest on the bonds; the corporation charges the converter with the former and credits him with the latter. The difference is paid in cash by the party with the smaller credit.

Prices of convertible bonds. Market prices of convertible bonds will behave differently from bonds which are not convertible. When the security of the corporation into which the bond is convertible is rising, the value of the bond will rise above its true investment value. Thus a bond with a par value of $1,000 which is convertible into 40 shares of the company's common stock will sell at approximately $1,200 if the common stock goes to thirty. However, if the price of the stock declines, the price of the bond will decline only until it reaches its true investment value and will not go below this point. The true investment value of a bond depends upon its safety, the rate of interest, and other features. This value will be the same as for any other bond possessing similar characteristics whether or not it has the conversion feature.

Extinction by refunding. Refunding is the exchange of bonds of one issue for those of another. It differs from conversion in this way: conversion is a special privilege accorded to the bondholder by the terms of his bond and usually means the converting of bonds into stock; refunding is not an enforceable right of either the company or the bondholder, but is a matter of mutual agreement between them, and means always an exchange of bond for bond.

An issue of bonds may be refunded at its maturity, or it may be refunded prior to maturity. In either case, both holder and issuer must agree; and at no time can the company compel the bondholder to accept a new bond to succeed his old one, nor can the bondholder compel the company to issue him a new one to succeed his old one. At maturity, the holder can demand cash and the company can insist on paying in cash. As a matter of fact, refunding at maturity is seldom accomplished by an actual exchange of securities unless the company is embarrassed. In most cases, the new securities are sold in the open market in the regular way and the old ones taken up. Prior to maturity, both the holder and the company can decline to make a change of any kind, unless the bond be specifically either convertible or redeemable.

Refunding being an issuance of one set of bonds to replace old bonds outstanding does not, of course, do away with the bonded debt, but merely substitutes one set of bonds for another. It is not, therefore, in a strict sense, an extinction of the debt, but often extends it in point of time or reëstablishes it on a new basis. The actual old bonds are taken in and canceled, and to that extent we may consider the debt to be extinguished and a new one made in its place.

Refunding at maturity. When a series of bonds reaches its maturity, the holders may reasonably expect to receive in cash the face value of the bonds. Often, however, it is not convenient or possible for the issuing company to pay off this debt. Or it may be that the company is perfectly able to pay off the bonds, but it can still continue to use the money profitably in the business. For one of these or for other reasons, it may wish to extend the loan. An issue of refunding bonds is then authorized; all the old bondholders will be invited to accept the new bonds in place of the expiring bonds, and thus extend the loan over the life of the refunding issue. Bondholders who demand cash instead of accepting new bonds are paid in cash through the selling of the necessary number of bonds to other investors.

Refunding before maturity. Often bonds are refunded into a new issue before they have matured. This is usually done by the company either for the purpose of consolidating several outstanding issues, all refundable into one new issue, or in order to get the debt into a more desirable form as to term, interest rates, redemption price, or other features.

The refunding of several old issues into one new issue places all bondholders on the same footing; it makes the entire funded debt easier to handle; it gives the bonds greater marketability on account of the large size of the issue; and when the new issue is greater in amount than the combined old issues, thus making what are usually called *first and refunding bonds,* it enables its company to borrow additional moneys on this security, which it probably could not borrow on a separate bond issue junior to the old outstanding ones.

When bonds are refunded at maturity, the old issue always entirely disappears, either through being traded in for new bonds, or through being redeemed by cash obtained through the sale of the refunding bonds. When, however, an attempt is made to refund one or more old issues before maturity, a number of bonds of each of the old issues may still remain out, owing to the refusal of the holders to give them up for either new bonds or cash. The success or failure of the refunding proposition depends upon the number of old bondholders who can be induced to trade in old issues for the new bonds. To persuade bondholders to refund, various inducements are frequently offered them in connection with the new bonds, such as: a higher rate of interest, better security, better marketability, a cash bonus, promise of a sinking fund, and others. If outstanding bonds are *redeemable* a complete refunding operation is greatly facilitated, for the bondholders realize that if they do not accept the refunding offer, then their bonds may be called by the issuing company.

Refunding with aid of bankers. When a corporation has made all its plans and arrangements to carry out further financing through refunding, it would be disastrous if the refunding plan failed. Arrangements are, therefore, often made with investment banker groups, to assure the taking of the entire refunding issue. By this arrangement, the investment bankers usually agree to put up cash for any old bonds for which the old bondholders will not accept new bonds in exchange. For all cash thus advanced, the banking group take new bonds and sell them to reimburse itself. The bankers are paid by means of a straight commission or by being privileged to buy its necessary bonds at a discount.

Old bondholders, knowing that the successful completion of the refunding plan is guaranteed, are naturally more willing to enter into it, so that the securing of bankers' aid not only furnishes cash for the redemption of bonds whose owners demand it, but also causes a greater number to be actually refunded.

Refunding by short-term notes. It sometimes happens that, at the maturity of a bond issue, there may be good reasons for refunding into short-term notes. It may be that short-term notes are popular and command an excellent market, a condition often prevailing when interest rates are abnormally low. It may also be expedient when interest rates are very high and, rather than issue long-term bonds at the prevailing high rate, short term-notes will be sold in the hope that by the time they mature, the level of interest rates will have declined and the corporation will be able to refund the short-term issue with long-term bonds bearing a low rate. Occasionally the long-term issue is authorized at the same time the short-term notes are issued and deposited with a trustee as security for the short-term notes.

Characteristics of the short-term corporate note. All notes are written promises of the makers to pay a sum of money to the payee (or holder, or bearer) at some future time, and in this respect are similar in purpose and character to bonds. As a matter of fact, no exact line can be drawn between notes and bonds. Bonds bear the corporate seal; notes may or may not do so. The usual distinction made between notes and bonds is in length of life. Short-term promises to pay—those having maturities up to five years—are generally called notes; long-term promises to pay, usually for ten years or more—are commonly called bonds. Yet, there are occasional issues of ten-year notes and five-year bonds. In other words, while the general rule that notes are issued for less than five years and bonds for more than ten years is usually true, the name that a promise to pay will bear depends principally upon what the issuing company sees fit to denominate it at the time of issue.

In recent years short-term notes have usually been privately sold by being directly placed with large investment institutions such as insurance companies.

Like bonds, corporate notes may be either *secured* or *unsecured*. Unsecured notes are often called debenture notes and are frequently of very short life. Many issues of corporate notes, and especially those of considerable duration, are secured. The security is almost invariably of the collateral variety, consisting of stocks and bonds of other corporations held by the issuing corporation.

Notes are also issued in both *registered* and *coupon* forms.

Notes are sometimes made redeemable in order to permit a corporation to redeem them before maturity, if desirable; and to make them attractive to investors, they are sometimes made convertible into some other security of the corporation.

Some issues have a provision that a sinking fund must be established and maintained better to assure their repayment either at or before maturity: such are called *sinking fund notes.*

It is not uncommon in large note issues to have them mature in series, usually a specified number or proportion each year.

Occasionally there have been notes actually secured by a mortgage on property, or by the company's own bonds and it is not unusual to protect them by a provision to the effect that during their life the company shall not issue any other obligation which might take precedence over them.

Thus it may be seen that notes may possess practically all the attributes and characteristics of bonds.

Disadvantages of short-term notes. The use of corporate notes has several disadvantages which must be carefully weighed against the advantages.

The immediate cost in interest rate may be higher than that of bank borrowing, bond borrowing, or raising capital by stock selling. When notes are used as a temporary expedient in the place of bonds during an expectedly short period of high interest rates, it is impossible to predict just when, if ever, the rate will fall. If it does not fall soon, one or more renewals of the notes may be necessary; such action will, thus, not only carry on the high rate of interest for a longer period, but will also involve the cost of several resales of the refunding or extending issues.

Notes sometimes fall due in the midst of an unexpected financial slump; such conditions make it almost impossible to meet the notes and very difficult to renew them. With long-term bond obligations, there is ample time to prepare for the maturity; but with the short-term notes, a single error in judgment, a single improper forecast, or a single unlooked-for setback brings on the maturity unprovided for.

Extinction by redemption. Redemption is the actual paying off of the loan or debt represented by the bond. All bonds are redeemable at maturity and some, which are known as *redeemable* or *callable* bonds, are redeemable at the option of the issuing corporation at some time prior to maturity.

Redemption actually extinguishes the bonded debt absolutely, and severs all relations between the bondholders and the company; conversion changes the status of a bondholder to that of a stockholder; refunding simply gives the bondholder new bonds for old.

While bondholders may at maturity of their bonds accept bonds of a refunding issue, or may agree to any other settlement that the issuing company may offer, they usually have the right to demand payment in cash. If this is not made, they may foreclose upon the company and collect through the trustee of the mortgage.

Redeeming before maturity. By the terms of the indenture the issuing companies are sometimes given the option of retiring or redeeming the bonds before maturity. Times for redemption vary in different indentures; sometimes redemption is permitted at any time; sometimes, at any time before a given date, after a given date, or between two given dates; and sometimes, on any interest date or on certain specified interest dates. In fact, the time or occasion of redemption may be fixed in any manner by the indenture. It must not be understood that an entire issue need be redeemed all at one time before maturity. Such redemption, in fact, is very unusual. It is customary to redeem the issue in installments, either as the issuing company finds convenient or desirable, or as may be specified in the indenture.

Redemption prior to maturity is at the option of the company, and no bondholder has the right to demand such redemption of his security. Of course, some indentures provide that the company must redeem a certain number of bonds each year, and to this extent the company's option is abrogated.

Mandatory and solicited redemption. Bonds may be called for redemption either *mandatorily* or *by solicitation.* Bonds may be mandatorily called only when the indenture under which they were issued provides that the bonds may be redeemed or called by the corporation. Under this method, the bonds to be redeemed are selected by lot and the holders notified by publication. They, thereupon, turn in their bonds at the redemption price. If for any reason whatever the holder of a called bond fails, or declines, to have it redeemed, the interest on it stops at the date set for redemption; the principal, however, is held indefinitely by the trustee for the bondholder. Some indentures provide that if a bondholder does not demand his principal within a given number of years, the trustee shall return it to the company.

Under the solicitation method, the company can merely offer the redemption of a certain number of bonds, and request holders to turn them in. If an insufficient number is turned in, nothing can be done about the matter, except possibly to purchase bonds on the open market, provided they can be obtained at or below the redemption price established by the corporation.

Very frequently indentures provide for a combination of mandatory and solicitation methods. The usual arrangement is that the company shall call for a certain number of bonds for redemption. If this solicitation does not get the required number, the remainder of the quota for redemption may be mandatorily called by lot.

Redemption price. The indenture itself fixes the price which the company shall pay the bondholder for a bond called for redemption before maturity. This *redemption price* is almost invariably greater than the face value of the bond. The actual price is usually fixed at par, plus a reasonable premium. The total thus determined makes a great number of bonds redeemable at 105 and 110. It is believed that this bonus will serve to enable the person whose bond has been redeemed to take time to find another investment for his money without suffering any actual loss in interest. When a bond is redeemed at a high figure very shortly after its issue, it, of course, means a high rate of yield for the time the money was invested.

Sources of funds for bond redemption. When bonds are redeemed for cash and are not merely converted or refunded, there are two methods of providing the cash to take them up:

1. There is a voluntary setting aside of moneys received from earnings, or any other sources, in such amounts as make it possible to meet the bonds when they are to be paid either at or before maturity. This is done by the management as a matter of business and financial policy but not on account of any agreement or understanding with the bondholders.

2. There is the putting aside of a sinking fund to pay off the bonds. This sinking fund is made obligatory by the terms of the mortgage, and

failure on the part of the company to make the prescribed payments gives the bondholders the right to foreclose.

A sinking fund may be provided to accumulate the cash for the redemption of any bonds; but it is used particularly in cases where there is danger of the shrinkage in value of the protecting assets, or in the case of extractive businesses the assets of which are actually used up in the operation.

Building of the sinking fund. Payments into a sinking fund are provided for in a number of ways, but practically all can be classified under two general headings:

1. Periodical payments to be a _proportionate_ or _fractional part_ of some unit basis, such as a certain percentage of the gross earnings, of the net earnings, of the surplus, or of the amount of depletion of assets. The principal weak point in methods of this type is that if the company becomes inoperative or unproductive, the sinking fund does not grow, while the bonds still race toward maturity.

2. Periodical payments to be a _fixed_ or _stipulated sum._ This method assures the regular growth of the sinking fund, but places upon the company a fixed obligation which it may not be able to meet in times of business depression or non-operation.

Many modern indentures provide for the building of their sinking funds by a judicious combination of these two basic methods.

Serial redemption. An issue of bonds is frequently put out as serials, that is, all issued at once but having various groups maturing in succession at regular intervals. This type of issue spreads the actual payment of the bonds over a long period, starting usually one year after the issue. Sometimes the entire issue is put out at the same time, and sometimes a few of the series are retained for future use.

The spreading out of the repayment can be accomplished without having the bonds in series, by using a sinking fund and redeeming certain numbers of bonds from time to time. In the case of non-serial sinking fund bonds, however, the purchaser never knows when his bond may be called for redemption and hence is always uncertain as to the life of his investment. In the serial bond issue, however, each bondholder knows at the start just when the series of which his bond is a part will be redeemed, and can arrange all his financial plans accordingly.

Serial bonds may be protected by a sinking fund as well as non-serial bonds, but the practice is not so common.

In arranging the series under a serial issue, two methods are used: first, each series may consist of the same number of bonds; and second, each series may consist of a greater number of bonds than its predecessor.

Under the first method, the reduction in interest each year due to the retirement of bonds accrues to the issuing company to be used for any desired purpose.

Under the second method, it is customary to make each successive series of such size as can be redeemed by the amount available for the redemption of the previous series plus the interest saved through its redemption. Thus, by utilizing the saved interest each period to redeem an increased number of bonds, they can be redeemed quite rapidly with a uniform outlay. This method is particularly adapted to public financing where the money to repay the bonds is obtained through taxation and remains constant in amount from year to year.

When bonds are redeemable at a premium, or when they are sold under par but are redeemable at par, those redeemed shortly after issuance will, of course, produce a considerably higher yield than those running a long time before redemption. In the case of serial bonds sold below par, therefore, an adjusted scale of prices is sometimes arranged (the highest prices are for those bonds maturing first, and the lowest for those maturing last) so that the actual yield will be practically the same on all the series of the entire bond issue.

Questions for Study and Review

1. Explain and compare the three methods of extinguishing bonded indebtedness.
2. Which usually sells higher, convertible bonds or the stock into which they are convertible? Why? Show how their respective prices may rise and fall comparatively.
3. Explain the difference between refunding and conversion. Contrast refunding at maturity with refunding before maturity as to purposed effect.
4. You hold bonds of two corporations, each of which is asking you to refund your bonds into a new refunding issue. Company A is refunding with the aid of a banker, and Company B is refunding without the aid of a banker. In each case, what questions would you determine before deciding whether or not to refund?
5. How can you distinguish between bonds and notes?
6. Describe the two principal conditions under which short-term corporate notes are issued.
7. What are the disadvantages of short-term notes?
8. Explain your opinion of the practice of financing long-term requirements by means of short-term obligations.
9. *a.* Suppose that you neglect or decline to send in for redemption a bond that has been properly called. What will happen to it?
   b. Explain what is meant by mandatory and solicated redemption.
   c. What are the disadvantages to an investor of redeemable bonds and what offsetting advantage does the issuing company usually offer?
10. Name several methods of making payments into a sinking fund and tell the advantages and disadvantages of each.
11. Explain two methods and the advantages of serial redemption.

Problems

1. A corporation has outstanding $10,000,000 of 4 per cent bonds which are convertible into the common stock at the ratio of 5 shares of common for

each $1,000 bond and are callable at 104. The authorized common stock is 200,000 shares, of which 120,000 shares are outstanding. What would be the effect upon (a) the amount of funded debt outstanding, (b) the annual fixed charges, (c) the cash position of the corporation, (d) the number of shares of stock outstanding, and (e) the corporate taxable income, if all the bonds are (1) converted, and (2) called for redemption?

2. Mr. Ammons holds 40 bonds of the X Company which are convertible into stock at 125. The bonds are quoted on the market today at 107, and the stock at 105. (a) If Mr. Ammons converts today, will he do so at a profit or at a loss, and what will be the extent of his profit or loss? (b) With the stock still quoted at 105, what would have to be the quotation on the bond in order that he might convert without profit or loss? (c) If the bonds remained at 107, what would have to be the quotation on the stock in order that he might convert without profit or loss?

3. The Wilston Corporation has outstanding a $2,000,000 issue of 5½ per cent bonds which are callable at 105½. A proposition is made to call the bonds for redemption and to refund them out of the proceeds of a new issue of 4 per cent bonds which will be callable at 104 and which will run for the same length of time as the unexpired term of the old bonds, namely, twenty years. It is estimated that the new bonds may be sold to an underwriting syndicate at par. The proposition includes a provision that the bonds required to be issued in excess of $2,000,000 are to be retired at 104 in equal annual amounts during the life of the issue. How much will the company save by the refunding (without discounting future savings down to present values)?

4. A corporation issued $637,000,000 of 3⅞ per cent debentures which were convertible into 1 share of common stock on payment of $48 in cash with each $100 of debentures surrendered for conversion. At the end of the first year, $319,000,000 of the bonds had been converted. Explain the effect of the conversion upon (a) the remaining debt outstanding, (b) the fixed charges on the debt, (c) the number of shares of common stock outstanding, and (d) the cash funds of the company.

5. (a) A corporation has outstanding an issue of $1,000,000 5 per cent preferred stock and 10,000 shares of no-par value common stock. The net earnings before federal income taxes are $300,000. How much is available in dollars per share of common stock, if the income tax rate is 52 per cent? (b) Assume that instead of the issue of preferred stock, the corporation has $1,000,000 of 5 per cent bonds outstanding, other facts being the same. How much is available in dollars per share of common stock?

Written Assignment

Some time ago a corporation found that it needed to procure $10,000,000 of borrowed funds for a period of twenty years. Let us assume (though, of course, these rates may not be currently correct at any particular time) that the current interest rate on bonds was 4½ per cent per annum. This was higher than usual because of a poor securities market. The corporate officers and directors had good reason to believe that within six years the bond interest rate would be down to approximately 3½ per cent.

Which of the following plans would probably be most advantageous to the company?

a. Issue straight, non-callable, 4½ per cent, twenty-year bonds.

b. Issue 4½ per cent, twenty-year bonds, callable at 102, with the idea of calling at the end of six years and refunding through the issuance of new 3½ per cent bonds for the remaining fourteen years of the loan period. Issue three-year notes, extended by a second set of three-year notes (assuming for the sake of the problem that the interest rate on these short-term capital notes will be 5 per cent), and then, at the end of six years, take up the notes through the issuance of 3½ per cent bonds for the remaining fourteen years of the loan period.

In each case let us assume that bankers will charge 1 per cent commission for selling any type of note or bond herein considered.

CHAPTER X

Capitalizing the Corporation

Concepts of capital. Like many other financial terms, *capital* has been given a number of meanings depending upon how it is to be used and who is using it.

1. Economists speak of capital as "wealth used in the production of further wealth."

2. Businessmen frequently use "capital" to refer to the total assets employed by the business (usage in this text).

3. In the accountant's usage, capital usually means the net assets or stockholder's interest as shown by the balance sheet.

4. At law, as used in statutes and charters, capital usually means capital stock.

Capitalization in popular usage generally refers to the balance sheet value of stocks and bonds outstanding, or used in another way, the act or process of determining the dollar value of all types of corporate securities to be issued by a corporation. *Capital structure* usually refers to all sources of long-term capital used by the corporation, whether evidenced by outstanding securities or not. Since reinvested earnings often represent a steady stream of involuntary capital contributions made by the stockholders, it is appropriate to consider surplus as part of the capital structure.

The meaning of financial plan. The financial plan of a corporation has many aspects. The term quite often means capital structure, although it also may be used to refer to some type of budget, such as a capital budget or working capital budget. The authors prefer to use the term interchangeably with that of capital structure. This chapter will be chiefly concerned with the problem of determining the amount of capital to be raised and the form it should take.

Long term capital planning. The rapid rate of expansion of many businesses often makes it imperative that a long-term forecast of capital requirement be made. Some large industrial plants and public utilities work out plans from five to ten years ahead. Naturally, such plans are not accurate as to detail, but they do attempt to forecast expansion possibilities in such a way that the financial plan may be so shaped as to provide for financing the projects and, also, to avoid haphazard growth. As each year passes, the forecasts are revised and a new year added to the plan. The plans for the coming year are gone over very carefully and worked out in detail. The financial requirement is carefully estimated, and a budget established. The budget is broken down into months and shows in detail the projected capital expenditures, so that adequate provision can be made for funds. The advantages of having planned so far ahead become apparent when current budgets are considered.

When a company knows in advance approximately what is required in the way of materials and funds, bids can be obtained, cost estimates prepared, and perhaps tentative contracts awarded. It is also possible to acquire raw material or sources from which these may be obtained. For example, a telephone company needs thousands of poles every year. This demand may mean that timberlands must be leased or acquired to insure the supply. As far as finances are concerned, reserves can be set up to provide for expansion and plans be made to enter the capital markets at the most propitious time.

Purposes in raising capital. No business can be established without at least some outlay of capital. In financing a business, funds must be provided for the following purposes:

1. To defray the costs of organizing.
2. To finance the acquisition of fixed assets.
3. To supply current assets.
4. To cover the cost of establishing the business.

The cost of organizing the business. By the *cost of organizing the business* is meant the cost of promotion, including the compensation of the promoters, legal fees, investigation costs, organization taxes, and all expenses of like nature, sometimes referred to as *cost of intangibles.* These expenses, prior to the financing of the business, are borne by the promoters or investment bankers organizing the business. It is only fair that this cost should be passed on to the ultimate owners or stockholders, since it is as much a cost of the building of a business as is the cost of the bricks for the walls. True, when the business is finally organized, there will be no tangible asset in the balance sheet to represent these expenditures. As will be seen, however, capitalization is not determined by tangible assets alone.

The cost of fixed assets. In most businesses, certain tangible assets, such as furniture and fixtures, buildings and equipment, must be purchased before the businesses are opened for trade. Estimates of such costs are usually made during the promotion stage, but the actual acquisition of such assets does not take place until financing is either completed or well under way, though as part of the assembling stage in promotion, contracts may be let providing for such assets.

Current assets requirement. In addition to the funds necessary for investment in the plant and equipment, or so-called *fixed assets*, it is necessary to provide a certain amount for investment in the *liquid* or *current assets* of the concern. Some cash must be kept on hand, since not all customers pay cash, and inventories of finished goods and raw materials must be financed. Total current asset investment in the business may be partially obtained from temporary sources, but the greater part of it should be permanently provided for through the sale of stock or long-term bonds.

The costs of establishing the business. In many lines, a large part of the *costs* of doing business are more or less *fixed*, and the costs do not vary directly with the volume. The business, therefore, must be built up to a certain point before these fixed costs can be absorbed in the selling price of the product and profits realized. Prices at the outset usually cannot be fixed at a point high enough to absorb the high unit costs attendant upon low volume. A simple illustration will make this clear. Suppose the fixed costs of the business amounted to $16,000 a month and the variable costs, that is, the cost of material and labor, were $20 per unit. Also assume that the product could be sold at a price not greater than $40 each, providing a margin of $20 above the variable costs. If 400 units only were sold the first month at this price, the fixed costs to be borne by each produce unit would be $40; this would entail a loss per unit of $20, on account of fixed costs alone. If, in the second month, 800 units are sold, all the fixed costs are absorbed and the *break-even point* has been reached. The business is now operating without profit or loss from this account. Thereafter, as volume increases, profits will likewise increase. Of course, it must be understood that there are limiting factors. The so-called fixed costs will eventually rise to some extent, and the selling prices may have to be lowered to bring in a larger number of purchasers.

It may be several months before production reaches a profitable volume. In fact, after a business is actually started, a month or several months may elapse before the product is ready for the market or, in the words of the production manager, "until the factory is tooled up and into production." The losses during this period due to lack of momentum are the *costs of establishing the business* and must be considered in computing the amount of capital required.

Determining the amount of capital to be raised. Obviously the amount of capital necessary is determined by the sum of the organization costs, the costs of tangible assets, the current assets requirements, and the costs of establishing the business. However, the *capitalization* of the business, that is, the determination of the amount of the securities to be issued, is not arrived at in this manner. Capitalization should be based on earning power, In other words, the process of capitalization begins with an estimate of the future net income of the business. No one puts money into a business without expecting a return upon it in the shape of dividends or interest. The value of a business is determined by its ability to earn a return upon capital invested. The higher the rate and regularity of its earnings, the greater the value of the business and the greater the amount of capital that may be safely invested in it. Another way of stating the same thing is to say that a business is worth that amount upon which an adequate return may be realized. An adequate return contemplates compensation for the use of capital and for the assumption on the part of the investor of the risks pertinent to the business.

Suppose, for instance, in the promotion of a manufacturing business, it is determined that $60,000 a year can be earned with regularity and that earnings in this type of business are ordinarily 10 per cent on invested capital. The business may be capitalized at 10 per cent or $600,-000 ($60,000 ÷ .10 = $600,000), which would represent the total par value of the capital securities to be issued. In other words, we have assumed here that this business is worth ten times its earnings.

If it be desired to use stock without par value, the price at which it is desired to market the stock is the deciding factor. Should it be desired to sell the stock at $40 a share, the earnings per share, if the stock is to sell ten times the earnings, must be $4. Dividing $60,000 by $4 we have 15,000 shares as the number to be issued.

If the capitalization arrived at in this manner is not sufficient to pay all of the costs of starting the business, including the costs of the tangible assets, the proposition should be reconsidered, for the assets must be capable of paying a satisfactory rate of return on the amount to be invested in them.

Estimating the earnings. When the promotion is that of a consolidation or when it represents the public offering of stock in a closed corporation, the past earnings of the concern often offer the best basis upon which to estimate future earnings. But in an entirely new company, the problem is difficult. Earnings depend not only upon the assets, but also upon the skill of the management. The latter is an intangible factor and difficult to appraise. When management is a very important factor, considerable conservatism should be shown in making estimates of earnings. Probably the best basis in a new enterprise is to study the earnings of concerns similarly situated in similar businesses. Such information can be obtained from the published reports of such concerns and from various statistical agencies. Conservative estimates should be the rule, for if earnings are overestimated, overcapitalization will in all probability result.

As will be pointed out later in this chapter, the stability or regularity of earnings is almost as important a factor as the expected average amount of those earnings. The regularity of earnings has an important effect on the choice of securities.

Determining the capitalization rate. One of the most difficult steps in arriving at the capitalization of a corporation is the determination of the *capitalization rate*. The rate at which a concern should be capitalized should always equal that return on the invested capital that would adequately compensate the investor for the use of his funds and the risk he undertakes. No set rules can be established, for the investors' desires in the matter change with the times. When business is good, the public is optimistic and thinks lightly of the risks involved. At such times, capitalization will more than likely be at a low rate and will give a higher value to the enterprise. But in times of business depression or uncertainty, the public takes a very pessimistic view of the value of securities and is likely to exaggerate the risks to be run. A business that might be capitalized at 10 per cent in a period of prosperity would have to be capitalized at perhaps as high a rate as 20 or 25 per cent to attract purchasers to its securities in a period of poor or uncertain business.

At any one time, the capitalization rate can best be determined by noting the price at which securities of similar businesses sell and by observing the earnings of those companies. If the common stock is selling at an average of 8 times the earnings, the capitalization rate is 12½ per cent. This rate will indicate the basis of capitalization that, at the moment, will best facilitate the marketing of the securities. Of course, a new concern will not, as a rule, be able to capitalize at as low a rate as the stock prices and earnings of more established concerns might indicate. Although there are some exceptions, even in prosperous times the buyers of securities will place a higher value on the stock of a well-known concern than on that of a new one with no earnings record.

However, despite the rate established on the basis of the values assigned to similar businesses by security buyers, those responsible for the financial plan of a corporation may well have a mind to the future in times when they might be tempted to capitalize at too low a rate. A low rate of capitalization results in a large issue of securities. They may command a good price during prosperous times when such a low rate is possible, but they are bound to fall in price as the first note of pessimism strikes the ear of the security buyer. The market decline may seriously injure the credit of the corporation and make future financing difficult.

It is axiomatic that the greater the risk, the higher must be the capitalization rate. The rate will be higher in those enterprises in which skill in management is a more important factor than advantage of location or excellence of assets.

When no-par value stock is used, the same procedure is followed, and the number of shares may be ascertained by dividing the value (ascertained by capitalizing the earnings) by the price at which it is desired to sell the stock.

Choosing the type of securities to be issued. Once a value has been placed upon the business, the problem arises as to the best type of securities to issue and the proportionate amounts of each. There are certain fundamental rules for the choice of securities, which may be accepted as established principles:

1. Bonds should be issued only when future earnings are expected to be reasonably stable and well above the interest and sinking fund requirements.

2. Preferred stock may be issued when the average earnings over a period of years are expected to be well above the preferred dividend requirements.

3. When earnings cannot be predicted with reasonable certainty, common stock should be used.

It may be seen that as far as the choice of bonds to form part of the capital structure is concerned, the stability of earnings, is the principal factor to be considered. This is demonstrated by the fact that the electric utilities are able safely to use a capital structure consisting of 50 per cent and, in some companies, 60 per cent in bonds. Earnings should be not only sufficient to cover interest and sinking fund requirements, but should be large enough to provide, even for the most stable business, an ample margin of safety. Stability is merely relative. All industries are affected by business cycle changes to some degree. Even in the electric utility industry, it is generally considered that the margin of safety should be at least 100 per cent; in other words, interest should be earned at least two times.

Conditions may change with time, so that an industry once considered highly stable may find its earnings fluctuate sharply with the business cycle. At one time, railroads were considered so stable that earnings of 50 per cent above the bond interest were accepted as a sufficient margin of safety. Now because of competition and other factors, such as high operating costs, railroads, with some exceptions, find their earnings follow closely general cyclical changes affecting most industrial businesses.

An electric utility corporation, because of the known stability of such an enterprise, could use bonds in its initial financing. Most other types of companies should avoid the use of bonds until earning power has been proved through some years of experience.

Preferred stock may be used if earnings average sufficiently high to provide a good margin, probably at least 100%, above the annual dividend requirements. Most preferred stock now issued is cumulative and earnings, therefore, should be fairly stable. If arrears accumulate, the price of the preferred stock and especially the common stock will decline.

New financing would be difficult and the general credit of the corporation would suffer.

Other factors affecting choice of securities. The principles outlined in the last paragraph should be adhered to as far as possible in making up the financial plan, but there are other factors that exercise a very important influence on the choice of securities and upon the proportion of the various kinds of securities to be used. Some of these factors may at times be so important as to limit the choice to a given type, or types, of securities, regardless of the fact that it may be more prudent or desirable to finance through the use of another medium. Some of the more important of these factors are:

1. The traditions and present style of the security market.
2. The desire for control on the part of the promoters or present management.
3. Plans for future expansion.
4. The cost of financing.

1. *The traditions and present style of the security market.* The vagaries of the security buyer's demands are not surpassed by the patrons of a millinery shop. There are times when not only an entirely different kind of security is demanded by the buyer but when the general type must be modified and given special features to make it attractive. There are times, also, when it is easier to sell common stock than any other class of security. The period from January, 1928, to October, 1929, furnishes an example of such times. Almost any type of common stock was popular; but in order to sell bonds and preferred stocks, special features had to be annexed to such securities. Such features were the privilege of converting into common stock, or the practice of giving option warrants with the bonds or preferred stock (the warrant being a right to buy common stock at a certain price). To sell bonds alone, in many cases, would have necessitated offering them at low prices or high interest rates; such a practice made this type of financing too expensive. During the period, common stocks were in such demand by a speculatively minded public as to command good prices for the poorest and most speculative securities. In periods of depression, bonds are more desired by security buyers, because (1) low money rates and low corporate earnings make these lower-yield securities more attractive and (2) the investor is afraid to risk his money in stocks, which are more or less speculative. A table on page 168 indicates at five-year intervals the amount of bonds, stock and notes issued in corporate financing in the United States.

In marketing securities, the desires of the security buyers must be met or they cannot be sold. The buyer and not the seller usually establishes market conditions. As in marketing other products where the prestige of an important dealer may lead buyers into following his suggestions, the prestige of large investment banking houses employed to sell the securities may make it possible to market a type not popular at the moment. This is a risk, however, that few investment bankers would care to run. The chances are the corporation needing immediate financing will have to follow the current market pattern.

2. *The desire for control on the part of the promoters or present management.* The common stock of a corporation is usually voting stock. A practice did arise in the middle twenties of issuing non-voting common, but the rules of the New York Stock Exchange, as well as governmental regulation, oppose the issuance of non-voting stock without at least some contingent voting rights. The use of a non-voting preferred stock, carrying the right to vote if dividends are not declared, may offer a means of raising capital without jeopardizing control. Bonds do not carry the voting privilege and may be used by an established concern to avoid loss of control. In either case, investors are given some advantages to offset the foregoing of the voting right.

NEW CORPORATE SECURITY ISSUES (in millions of dollars)
(for all purposes, publicly and privately offered)*

Year	Bonds and notes	Preferred stock	Common stock	Total
1939	1,979	98	87	2,164
1945	4,855	758	397	6,010
1950	4,920	631	811	5,362
1955	7,420	635	2,185	10,240
1957	10,035	408	2,497	12,940

*Securities and Exchange Commission Estimates.

The necessity of making preferred stock and bonds convertible may also create a control problem that involves the privilege of converting into voting stock. The necessity arises, as indicated above, in meeting the demands of investors during the marketing of securities. When the earnings become attractive, holders of bonds or preferred stock bearing this privilege will convert into voting stock and thereby endanger control. This danger can be overcome by issuing warrants to those in control that give options to purchase sufficient voting stock at set prices, to insure, if exercised, the possession by the present management of a controlling interest. Even though the options evidenced by the warrants are never exercised, the possibility of the warrants being so utilized would probably keep control in the hands of the original voting stockholders.

The voting trust has been utilized as a device to insure the retention of control in a certain group. The Pennroad Corporation was organized for the purpose of investing in railroad securities for the furtherance of plans of the Pennsylvania Railroad. The Pennsylvania Railroad itself was unable to hold these securities without the express permission of the Interstate Commerce Commission. In order to finance the Pennroad Corporation and still keep control in the hands of the Pennsylvania Railroad, without direct stock ownership on the part of the latter, the Pennroad stock was deposited, upon issuance, with voting trustees who were directors of the Pennsylvania Railroad, and only the voting trust certificates were sold to raise capital.

The danger lies in the obligations assumed by the present management in exchange for the privilege of retaining control. Preferred stock is usually cumulative, and failure to pay dividends could seriously handicap the corporation as arrears continue to accumulate. The contingent voting rights that are now so commonly found in preferred stock contracts may result in a sharing with, or loss of control to a minority group. Failure to pay bond interest may result in the appointment of a trustee in a reorganization proceeding in which serious sacrifice will be expected of the common stockholder.

3. *Plans for future expansion.* Every business must grow; it cannot stand still. It is not to be implied that the business must grow larger in terms of total assets and that it must spread out into many divisions and branches, but it must keep up with the times and the natural trends in its own community. Plants must be modernized to keep up with the progress of science and inventions and with the demands of customers, who need new products. If a business does not keep pace with the times, it favors competition and may irretrievably lose its markets. Public service corporations must expand with the growth of population and industry in the territory served, or they fail to give the service demanded by their franchises. Nor is it desired to indicate that all concerns expand only because circumstances have forced such action. The natural pride and desire for gain and prestige on the part of the owners and managers usually provide sufficient stimulus for expansion.

Expansion, in many cases, may be entirely financed through the plowing back of earnings into the business. Certainly this method is followed to some degree by all business. The possible exceptions are the public utilities, in which the rates charged are supposed merely to represent a fair return in existing property. Hence, earnings on capital invested may be inadequate to allow as large a margin above reasonable dividends as might be the case with industrials.

However, extensive expansion is likely to require new capital. If the business has already burdened itself with a mortgage that has heavy fixed charges, or if the mortgage contains an after-acquired clause, future financing may be difficult. The same difficulty will be experienced if the business has an excessive amount of high-dividend preferred stock outstanding. The possibility of growth should always be kept in mind when any financing is undertaken, and care should be taken not to handicap progress in future years with heavy expenses in the earlier ones.

4. *The cost of financing.* The cost of financing and its effect on the financial plan have already been touched upon in the discussion of the

varying demands of the security buyers at different times. It is desired here merely to emphasize further that, however desirable it may be to finance with a certain type of security, the high interest or dividend rates and the low prices at which that type of security might have to be sold make it too expensive to use. To some extent, a corporation may overcome this handicap by making bonds or preferred stock (when the market dictates that these be used) redeemable or, perhaps, convertible into common stock. This will allow the corporation to redeem at a time when common stock meets with favor and can be sold. Or, if the corporation becomes prosperous, the holders of securities that bear the conversion privilege may convert them to enjoy the higher returns offered by common stock ownership. ✓

Typical capital structures. To summarize the foregoing, it may be well to comment briefly on capital structure employed in a few industries.

Railroad corporations no longer use bonds to the degree formerly used. Since 1932, there has been a wholesale reduction in the proportion of bonds in railroad capital structures. Even if equipment issues are included, the average falls below 40 per cent. The reduction in fixed interest charges is even greater. This was brought about by the substitution of income bonds for fixed interest bonds in the reorganizations that began in the 1930s. Refunding of existing issues into lower interest-bearing bonds is another factor in this connection. Many railroads applied high earnings of war years to the reduction of debt securities and new issues today must carry some sort of sinking fund provision for debt reduction if they are to meet with Interstate Commerce Commission approval.

Preferred stock in railroad capital structures has declined also. Some of it has been replaced by subordinated income debentures, thus increasing the debt but not the fixed charges. In railroad finance, many of the preferred stock issues originated not as new financing but were issued to replace bonds in the many reorganizations taking place in the depression of 1893-1896. Preferred stocks no longer form an important part of most railroad capital structures. A study of present-day capitalization indicates about 6 per cent for all American railroads.

The electric utilities show the use of debt securities to approximately 50 per cent of the capital structure. The larger part of the debt financing consists of open end mortgage bonds, either unrestricted or with a large limit. There has been some debenture bond financing of medium maturity, seldom exceeding thirty years, to take advantage of the lower interest rate recently obtainable on shorter term issues. Preferred stock financing averaged somewhat less than 15 per cent for the industry.

The preferred stock is usually non-voting and seldom convertible. These utilities apparently want their preferred to be highly considered by the investors' market for the dividend requirement when added to the bond interest has a margin of safety in most companies of 100 per cent of earnings. In other words, the average earnings appear to be at least twice the preferred dividends plus prior charges. Common stock equity comprises the balance. Even though utility rates are strictly regulated, the savings in the cost of capital provided by use of bonds and preferred stock usually result in a respectable return on the common stock.

The greatest variation in capital structures is found in the so-called industrial field, where we find extractive industries, manufacturers of durable goods, such as steel, textiles and consumers' articles ranging from automobiles to soap. A complete discussion of these is, of course, far beyond the brief summary attempted here. Many of the largest and a high proportion of the small industrial concerns use no debt financing other than short-term seasonal loans. Where bonds are issued, they seldom exceed twenty-five years in maturity and some provide for serial redemption. Few industrial corporations obtain as much as one-third of their capital through the sale of bonds. Because the investor is deeply conscious of the vulnerability of most industrial concerns to business cycle changes and because of the great importance of managerial skill in competitive industries, it is not unusual to find bond indentures containing special protective provisions. Dividends may be restricted if net current assets decline below a stated amount.

Sinking funds to be applied to a steady reduction in the amount of the issue are also common to industrial borrowing. In form, about 80 per cent of the issues are debentures. Because of the commonly used sinking fund provisions, most industrial issues are callable, so that the sinking fund as accumulated can be applied to retirement of the debt.

The use of preferred stock by industrial corporations further emphasizes the lack of uniformity in industrial capital structures even among concerns following the same line of business. There seems to be an effort to keep the amount of preferred stock issued well within the standards usually expected by investors. The amount of preferred stock should not exceed the net tangible assets of the corporation and the dividend requirement should have been earned at least twice over in a representative period, especially three to five years. Most preferred issues of recent years have been made callable and convertible.

Industrial corporations in this country have relied in their financing largely upon common stock and retained earnings. Where market conditions dictate and offer exceptional opportunities for debt financing, bonds have been used. They have usually been in modest amounts and with sinking fund and retirement provisions calculated to pay off the debt rapidly.

Overcapitalization. When a business is unable to earn a fair rate of return on its outstanding securities, it is *overcapitalized*. Overcapitalization may be the result of overestimating earnings at the time of promotion, or it may be due to subsequent developments that reduce the earning power.

An illustration of the latter situation is found in the plight of many American railroads. Built in anticipation of a virtual monopoly of freight and passenger transportation, it was thought that volume would increase in direct proportion to the development of industry and increases in population. The private automobile, the truck, and now the airplane have destroyed the monopoly. So serious is the situation that railroad after railroad has passed through costly financial reorganization and, in the opinion of some financial authorities, further drastic reductions in debt structures of many such carriers will be necessary before they may be said to be properly capitalized. The trend in fashions that affects a basic product, such as the decline in the use of woolens for women's apparel, is another illustration of what may happen to the market. Indeed, we are constantly overwhelmed with proof that

> "The best laid schemes o' mice an' men
> Gang aft agley."

Whether overcapitalization is the result of errors in the original plan, or whether it is due to developments during the succeeding years, it may result in the following disadvantages:

(1) When a large part of the capitalization consists of bonds, there may be a failure to pay the fixed charges; such a failure results in foreclosure or reorganization.

(2) The credit of the concern is injured; and financing of any kind becomes very difficult.

(3) Dividends are reduced or omitted; securities decline in price; and holders grow dissatisfied.

(4) The business loses to its competitors through inability to obtain funds for expansion.

(5) The management is tempted to reduce depreciation and maintenance charges in order to keep up dividends.

(6) When reorganization takes place, the resulting publicity may injure the goodwill of the business.

Remedies for overcapitalization. Overcapitalization presents a situation that is extremely difficult to remedy. The problem may involve one or more of the following steps.

1. Reduction of the amount of bonded indebtedness.
2. Reduction of the rate of interest paid on bonds.
3. Redemption of high-dividend preferred issues.
4. Reduction of the par value of the stocks.
5. Reduction in the amount of common stock outstanding.

Although the first four methods listed above offer theoretical solutions to the problem of overcapitalization, they are actually of little practical value.

Without going through an outright reorganization, the procedure for which is discussed in a subsequent chapter, it is practically impossible to reduce the amount of bonded indebtedness in such a way as to remedy overcapitalization. Funds for redemption of bonds would have to come from reinvested earnings or from sale of stock. Since profits may be extremely small, or perhaps nonexistent, it would be necessary to sell additional stock. But the stock would undoubtedly be selling at low prices, because of the inability of the overcapitalized company to earn a satisfactory rate of return. Therefore, the amount of stock to be sold to raise the money would necessarily be large, and instead of remedying the situation, it might be aggravated.

Because of the poor credit standing of the company and the high degree of risk implicit in its securities, it is more than likely that the outstanding bonds are already selling at a substantial discount from their face value. Under these conditions, how can an overcapitalized company hope to market a new issue of bonds bearing a rate of interest that is lower than those already outstanding?

It is often desirable, from the point of view of the common stockholder, to redeem high-dividend preferred stock. This is particularly true when such dividend requirements substantially reduce the amount of earnings available for distribution to the common stock. As a practical matter, however, the attempts of an overcapitalized company to redeem high-dividend preferred stock would meet with no more success than an attempt to redeem bonded indebtedness. The poor credit standing of the company, together with the high cost of security capital with which to redeem the preferred stock, would ordinarily doom such a proposal to failure.

Often, it is suggested that an overcapitalized company can correct the condition by reducing the par value of outstanding stock. This recommendation corrects nothing; it merely succeeds in obscuring the condition through the simple expedient of "window dressing" the balance sheet. For the sake of simplicity, let us assume that a corporation is capitalized exclusively with 1,000 shares of $100 par value common stock and that total earnings average $1,000 a year. The company earns $1 per share, or 1 per cent on the outstanding $100 par shares. Now if the corporation were to reduce the par value of its shares from $100 to $10 and credit the difference to surplus, the $1 per share of earnings would represent a 10 per cent return on the new stock. But why stop there? Why not reduce the par value from $100 to $1 and thus increase the rate of return to 100 per cent? Thus, through the simple expedient of accounting, it would be possible to convert a condition of overcapitalization to one of undercapitalization.

As a practical matter, however, the stockholder does not like, as a rule, to accept a lower par value stock in exchange, share for share. A *split-up* of a higher par into several shares of lower par, of course, leaves the aggregate amount of stock capitalization the same. It is true that the par value of the shares held by the stockholder has nothing to do with the real value of his shares and that the acceptance of a share at lower par value does not diminish his proportionate share of ownership in the corporation or affect the market value of his stock, but the average stockholder is inclined to believe otherwise; and it would be difficult to try to convince him to the contrary.

Although reduction of the amount of common stock outstanding may also be difficult to accomplish because it is hard to persuade the stockholder to turn in several old shares in exchange for one new share, this method does correct some of the outward symptoms of overcapitalization. As the result of a *split-down*, the market price and earnings per share of new stock are greater, thus helping to restore the credit position of the corporation and the investment quality of its stock. Again it is to be noted that, while this would not decrease his proportionate ownership, the average stockholder may not be convinced that his position would not be damaged by the procedure. However, the tendency of stockholders to follow the lead of the management and to send in proxies giving the management full authority makes it possible to reduce a common stock capitalization in some instances. The reduction, in a ratio of one new share for four old, accomplished by the Standard Brands corporation in September, 1943, is an illustration of common stock recapitalization. This corporation received the approval of its stockholders for a change from approximately 12,700,000 no-par common shares, to 3,175,000 shares without par value. Illustrations of *split-downs* in recent years have been few. Just as *split-ups* are normally associated with high earnings and high stock market prices, *split-downs* are a feature of periods of depressed stock market levels.

Undercapitalization. When a corporation is earning an extraordinarily large return upon the amount of stock outstanding, it is said to be *undercapitalized*. Undercapitalization is not to be confused with a condition implying lack of funds; it refers merely to the amount of stock outstanding. Undercapitalization is not an economic problem, but a problem in adjusting the capital structure. The situation is recognizable through the very high prices its stock consistently commands on the stock exchange and is due, also, to the fact that the earnings of the corporation are regularly very high. The condition is not as serious as a state of overcapitalization, though the following disadvantages do exist:

1. The limited market and the unusually small supply of stock cause large fluctuations in the market price.

(2) The stock usually does not command as high a price as warranted by its earnings, because of the limited number of purchasers.

(3) The high rate of return may stimulate competition.

(4) In the case of large combinations, there may be governmental action under anti-trust statutes.

(5) It may be easier for an outside group to acquire control.

It might seem that the corporation need not concern itself about the price at which its outstanding stock is sold on the exchange nor with its fluctuations. Nevertheless, it may find that the rumors and the publicity accompanying wide fluctuations in the price of its securities may react unfavorably upon the corporation and affect its credit and its business. When the amount of stock outstanding is small, any substantial buying and selling of its shares causes wide fluctuations in the price and much unfavorable publicity may result.

As to the disadvantage from the standpoint of competition, this is more theoretical than real. Competition will recognize a good thing without waiting to see the earnings statement of the corporation.

Probably many governmental investigations and legal actions brought against corporations for violations of the laws against monopoly and restraint of trade originate in the publicity given to large earnings per share of stock. Many times the reason for large earnings per share lies not in the taking of extraordinary profits on the product, but in the dividend policy of the corporation. If a large part of the earnings each year is retained and reinvested in the business, the reinvestment per share of stock outstanding may constantly be built up until it reaches large proportions and the earnings per share reflect the earnings of an investment far in excess of even the high market value of the stock. Whether or not the condition of undercapitalization will make it easier for outside interests to gain control depends on whether the amount of stock outstanding is really small, which may not be the case. Undercapitalization merely implies that the amount of stock is small relative to the corporation's earnings. This could be true even though a large amount of shares are outstanding. Also the high price of shares of an undercapitalized company tends to discourage those who would like to buy in.

It must not be implied from the foregoing discussion that undercapitalization is to be associated with comparatively small corporations only. Large corporations may have exceedingly high earnings per share, causing the stock to sell at very high prices or at prices which exceed the popular level for similar enterprises. Most corporation managements desire to increase the number of stockholders and may correct the apparent undercapitalization through the application of one of the remedies discussed below. General Motors Corporation has split its stock a number of times; the result in each case was to proportionately reduce the market price and probably, in due course, increase the number of individual shareholders. Naturally some of the shares produced as a result of the split fall into the hands of new owners.

Remedies for undercapitalization. The remedies for undercapitalization are comparatively simple. If the surplus is large, stock dividends may be declared to increase the stock outstanding. Stock with a par value may be split up into a number of shares of lower par value, or they may be exchanged for a number of shares without par value. If the corporation already has stock without par value, a *split* can be arranged, which will give two or more shares for one. Any of these methods will increase the number of shares outstanding and thus distribute the earnings over a greater number of shares.

To declare a stock dividend, a corporation must have a surplus, part of which is transferred from surplus to the capital stock account to exactly offset in dollar value the amount of dividend declared. If the stock has a par value, the amount so transferred must equal the par value of the stock dividend. If the stock is of the no-par value variety, dollar value of each share for stock dividend purposes must be arbitrarily fixed by the board of directors. Should the no-par stock have a stated value established in the certificate of incorporation, the arbitrary figure chosen will not be below this stated value. In either case, the stockholder will not object to this procedure; he will, in fact, welcome it because it still seems to him that through it he is getting something for nothing, although it should be apparent that his proportionate ownership in the corporation has not been changed in the least.

Questions for Study and Review

1. Name and briefly explain four purposes for which a business raises capital.
2. Distinguish between the cost of organizing a business and the cost of establishing a business.
3. Upon what basis should the capitalization of a corporation be determined?
4. What factors may determine the rate at which the earnings in a given business should be capitalized for the purpose of determining the amount of securities which should be issued?
5. *a.* State three fundamental rules for the choice of the type of security used in a financial plan.
   b. Name four other factors that may act as limitations regarding the choice.
6. Discuss the importance of current styles in the security market as a factor in determining the financial plan.
7. Give six disadvantages of overcapitalization.
8. Give five remedies for overcapitalization.
9. *a.* Name four disadvantages of undercapitalization.
   b. How may undercapitalization be corrected?
10. Is undercapitalization peculiar to small business? Explain.

Problems

1. A careful study of prospects of a new enterprise seems to indicate that the average annual earnings will be $250,000 and that a return of 25 per cent

will be required by investors. What should be the capitalization of the new concern? If the capitalization is to consist exclusively of common stock, determine the number of shares if (a) the stock has a par value of $50, and (b) the stock has no par value.

2. A corporation is operating with the following capitalization:

4½% Debenture bonds	$100,000
6% Preferred stock	200,000
Common stock	700,000

Average annual earnings of the corporation are $100,000. Assuming that the entire amount is available for interest and dividends, and that holders of common stock should receive a 10 per cent return on par value, how would you appraise the adequacy of these earnings? Would you consider the business overcapitalized? Undercapitalized? Why?

3. Comment on the capitalization of each of the following corporations which are in an industry in which a rate of return of 20 per cent is required to attract capital:

	Company A	*Company B*
Average annual earnings	$ 800,000	$2,400,000
Capitalization	10,000,000	8,000,000
Shares ($100 par)	100,000	80,000

4. A corporation has 1,000,000 shares of $50 par value common stock outstanding and is earning at the rate of $15 per share. The stock is currently selling at $250 a share. The management is considering a proposal to split the stock on a five-for-one basis. Discuss the purpose and the effect of making this adjustment in the stock.

5. A corporation has 2,000,000 shares of $25 par value common stock outstanding and is earning at the rate of $0.50 a share. The stock is currently selling at $5 a share. A proposal is made to split-down the stock on a one-for-five basis. Discuss the purpose and the effect of making this adjustment in the stock.

Written Assignment

A corporation has outstanding 200,000 shares of $10 par value common stock. It has an earned surplus of $1,000,000. Average annual earnings are $200,000, and are expected to remain so. A dividend of $1 per share is being paid and no change in total dividend is contemplated. The stock is split two-for-one. What would be the dollar amounts of each of the following?

a. par value per share
b. number of shares outstanding
c. total par value of outstanding shares
d. earnings per share

e. dividends per share
f. earned surplus
g. total dividend

CHAPTER XI

Raising Long-Term Capital

The problem of raising long-term funds for business financing. A business requires funds not only for initial establishment but for the financing of normal growth, modernization of plant and equipment and for expansion of operations. There are few concerns which can remain the same size for any protracted period. Population growth and the concern's own success in rendering valuable services or manufacturing reliable products bring additional business to its doors, which must be accepted or result in encouraging competition. In most lines of business, continuous success requires that trends in public demand be carefully followed. Manufacturers who do not keep an up-to-date plant may have difficulty retaining labor. Technical improvements in machinery or equipment require replacement of obsolete facilities if a concern is to meet competition. An alert management often sees opportunities for profits in expanding operations far different from those originally contemplated when the business was started.

In a business subject to seasonal influences diversification of products may be necessary to stabilize operations and income. All of the above usually require additional capital. In some firms a policy of leaving a portion of the profits in the business may be sufficient. Henry Ford's automobile business was built to large size by this method. In other situations, outside financing is necessary, and new owners must be sought through the admission of additional partners or sale of stock. Corporations entering a highly stable business such as electric utilities may obtain part of their initial funds from the sale of bonds and going businesses of proved earning power may also obtain funds in this manner.

Methods of providing funds for long-term capital. While there may be a degree of uniformity as to the choice of methods of raising funds in a particular industry, there is no common pattern followed by all. In some cases the difference will be only in the relative importance of one method as compared to others. For example, one concern may rely heavily on bonds and less on the issue of preferred and common stock. Another may also use the same three types of securities but rely more on equity, *i.e.*, preferred and common stock financing, than upon bond financing. Great differences may exist even in corporations in the same field. The New York Telephone Co. relies on bonds for more than 40 per cent of its capital while the Ohio Bell Telephone Co. uses common stock only. Both of the above are subsidiaries of the American Telephone and Telegraph Co. A fairly high degree of uniformity as to relative use of stock and bonds in financing is found in the electric utility companies whose debt securities, as previously stated, comprise about 50 per cent of the capitalization. The funded debt of the Norfolk and Western Railway Co., comprises about 17 per cent of the capitalization, while that of the Pennsylvania Railroad Co., exclusive of equipment trust issues, is approximately 58 per cent.

Financing through reinvestment of earnings. Small businesses, including both partnerships and corporations whose stock has not been distributed to the general public, usually referred to as "closed" or "close" corporations, are, like the individual proprietorship, largely dependent for growth upon the extent to which the owners leave profits in the business. Profits retained in a partnership are usually made part of the firm's permanent capital by crediting each partner's capital account with his share of the retained profits. In a corporation, the retained earnings may be left in the surplus account or made a permanent part of the owners' contribution by declaring a stock dividend for the amount retained. Many initially small concerns have grown to large size in this way. Quite often, when the original owners seek to retire, the concern becomes publicly owned, through a recapitalization and sale of stock to the public.

The practice of retaining earnings for investment in the business is not limited to small concerns, however. With the exception of corporations subject to public rate regulation, the practice of retaining a substantial amount of earnings is common. United States Steel Corporation has always followed a practice of retaining a considerable amount of earnings and in recent years augmented the amount through charging off a high depreciation rate on assets when the plants are operated in excess of 70 per cent of capacity. The company refers to the additional depreciation so charged as "accelerated depreciation." Many others, such as Standard Oil of New Jersey, General Electric Corporation, General Motors Corporation, in fact most well-known American industrial corporations, have seldom disbursed all that has been earned, preferring to reinvest 30 per cent to 40 per cent of annual earnings. Some corporations periodically capitalize retained earnings through stock dividends. Others, General Motors Corporations, for example, merely split up their shares so that the book value and equity per share in future earnings is reduced. Either method may be undertaken as a means of keeping stockholders from being discontented with a corporation's dividend policy, increasing the number of shareholders and perhaps keeping the market price of the stock down to popular levels.

While the interpretation of Sections 531-537 of the Internal Revenue Code of 1954 (Section 102, 1939 code) is somewhat obscure, a management retaining earnings in excess of 30 per cent of annual net income should be able to show that the amount is retained or justified by the needs of the business. A penalty tax can be assessed on earnings retained without justification. A corporation's management should, of course, only retain earnings when they may be profitably employed; otherwise, injustice is done to the stockholders. A business with fluctuating earnings in prosperous years, to avoid financial difficulty in poor years, may properly retain earnings for that purpose. Financing with retained earnings is not subject to the same critical examination on the part of the public as the raising of funds through the sale of securities. Therefore, a management free from the restraint of general public appraisal of the purposes for which the funds are to be utilized may engage in highly speculative ventures or fail to exercise proper control over expenditures.

Financing through the sale of bonds. The sale of bonds is a method of raising long-term capital which may be used for any proper business purpose. To use bonds with safety, earnings should be stable and the company's business, even in poor years, should produce earnings with a substantial margin of safety over the bond interest. This margin should be at a minimum, probably at least 100 per cent in excess of fixed charges or, putting it in another way, earnings should be at least twice the amount of bond interest. When these conditions exist, borrowed capital may usually be obtained at relatively low cost and substantial gain made through trading on the equity. Public utilities, particularly, in the electric light and power business as we have seen, have been able to finance at least 50 per cent, probably more, of their growth through the use of bonds. In the American Telephone and Telegraph Co. about 35 per cent of expansion has been financed through the use of bonds. Railroads made excessive use of bonds in financing, probably in their original belief in a monopolistic position with respect to freight and passenger transportation and a further belief that the demand for their services and resulting profits would parallel the growth of the country.

Railroads, with some exceptions, found that their expectations were not realized and have gone through two painful reorganization periods. One was in the 1890s and another in the 1930s. The result has been a substantial reduction in the amount of bonds in railroad financial structures, which has largely been achieved through outright sacrifice of bondholders in the process of reorganization. Thus, legal proceedings and aggressive debt reduction programs since World War II on the part of management have resulted in the reduction in the amount of bonds. Investing institutions such as insurance companies now place a higher estimate on the risks of railroad bonds and set higher standards with respect to the relationship of earnings to bond interest.

Financing with term loans. Considerable financing has taken place since 1936 through the use of installment type loans, chiefly obtained from banks and insurance companies. This source has been used by large and relatively small concerns. These loans have been used for practically all business purposes. They are of short maturity, ranging chiefly from three to five years and occasionally ten years from the date made until the last installment. In making use of this type of loan, anticipated earnings must be well in excess of the annual installment paid on the principal as well as the interest due. Because of the extremely low interest rates which have prevailed until recently, there has been real economy in financing with these shorter maturity loans for the rate of interest paid has been lower than would have been required for longer maturities.

Financing with stock. Stock financing is conservative financing in that the capital so obtained represents investment by owners. It is sometimes referred to as equity financing. Where risks of widely fluctuating earnings are high, stock will naturally form the principal type of external financing. Failure to earn enough to pay dividends, while resulting in a decline in the market price of the stock and injury to the investment credit of the corporation, will not of itself bring about failure as the owners must assume these risks as incidental to their ownership.

The sale of new stock divides the ownership of the company into more parts or shares than formerly existed. If the stock is sold to outsiders, the proportionate interest of the old stockholders is reduced, as is, also, their proportionate sharing in dividends. As long as the expanded company is struggling to produce earnings sufficient to pay dividends on the enlarged capital at a rate equal to those formerly paid on its old or smaller capital, this works a hardship on the old stockholders. But when the company has once reached the point where it can equal its old or former dividend rate, this hardship no longer exists. As a matter of fact, the justification for expansion by stock sales is the hope and belief that the company will, through the economies of size, soon be able to surpass its former dividend rate and thus repay the old stockholders for their temporary lessening of income, not only by the increased dividends, but also by the increased market value of their stock.

If, as is often the case, the new stock is bought by the old stockholders in proportion to their respective holdings, then each one still has the same proportionate ownership as before, though he has more funds invested and more shares. This is compensated for, however, as soon as the earnings are sufficient to pay at good rates dividends on the increased stock and thus give all the stock a fair value.

If the additional stock possesses the voting right, the control will be readjusted if the sale is made to outsiders. Of course, it will remain pro-

portionately unchanged if the old stockholders buy the new stock in proportion to their old holdings.

Privileged stock subscriptions. It is a well-established principle of corporation law that, before a new issue of stock may be sold to the general
public, the present stockholders must first be permitted to subscribe to
the shares in proportion to their holdings. This right does not apply to
unissued stock of the original authorization of which the outstanding
shares are a part, but to stock subsequently authorized. For example, if
a corporation had originally been authorized to issue 100,000 shares of
stock, but had issued only 50,000 of them, the subsequent issue of the
remaining 50,000, or any part of them would not give rise to a right on
the part of the holders of the first issue of 50,000 to subscribe before the
stock was offered to the public.[1] If, however, after the original 100,000
shares have been sold, an additional 50,000 shares are authorized and
offered for sale, the new stock must first be offered to old stockholders
in the proportion of one new share for every two of the old held. This
privilege is sometimes voluntarily surrendered by stockholders through a
clause to that effect included in the certificate of incorporation.

The legal basis for the right of each old stockholder to subscribe in proportion to his holdings to new issues of stock may be summarized as
follows:

1. Each stockholder has a right to maintain his proportionate control
in the corporation.

2. Each stockholder is entitled to keep his equity in the existing surplus intact.

Numerous court decisions have established the above principles at
law.[2] The general rule is that the sale of treasury stock does not give rise
to the subscription privilege,[3] and the company is not usually required to
offer new shares to old holders of nonvoting, nonparticipating, preferred
stock, since these have no voting power and no control over the surplus
in the first place. The corporation may, also, under certain circumstances,
buy property and pay for it by issuing new stock that has not first been
offered to the stockholders.

Although the company is not required to place any particular price

---

[1] In New York, new issues of stock are not subject to the preemptive subscription
right of old stockholders when such stock is issued in a merger, for a consideration
other than cash, to satisfy conversion or option rights previously granted, treasury
stock, stock issued pursuant to a plan of reorganization under Federal Bankruptcy
statutes and stock originally authorized in the certificate and sold within two years
from date of filing such certificate; see New York Stock Corporation Law, Section 39.

[2] See Stokes *v.* Continental Trust Co., 186 N.Y. 285 (1906).

[3] When stock has remained in the treasury for such a long period that the control
and equities of the outstanding stock may be said to have crystallized, it may be
argued that such stock should first be offered to old stockholders before public sale.
The general rule, however, does not support this position, but see Glenn *v.* Kittan-
ning Brewery Co., 259 Pa. 510 (1918).

upon the new stock offered to old stockholders, it must not, at some later time, offer the same stock to outsiders at a lower price. If the corporation refuses to give a stockholder an opportunity to buy the stock before selling it to others, the stockholder can demand of the corporation that he be permitted to buy and then recover damages. The latter will be measured by the difference between the price at which the stock was sold to others and its market price at the time the company refused to let him buy it.

The corporation laws of some states permit the inclusion in the certificate of incorporation of a clause denying the holders of the corporation's stock the preemptive right to subscribe to new issues. This does away with possible legal questions which might arise should the corporation issue stock as a bonus to employees and under other circumstances where it might seem expedient to issue stock without first offering it to all stockholders. Nevertheless where a large amount of stock is to be sold, the corporation may, and usually does voluntarily offer it first to all stockholders, not only to preserve their good will, but because they represent the best market.

Although a corporation may offer to bondholders the right of subscribing to stock upon special terms or before offering it to outsiders, bondholders may not claim the subscription privilege as a matter of right, and have no right to a first offering of bonds. Occasionally, bondholders may be given the privilege of converting their bonds into stock on a favorable basis, although the bonds, when issued, carried no conversion privilege.

Stockholders' rights. The right of a stockholder to subscribe to his proportionate part of any new issues of stock is known as his *privileged subscription right;* since his subscription under this right would preclude any other person from procuring the stock, it is known as a *pre-emptive right.* Since it arises from and rests in the old stock that he actually owns, it is known also as an *inherent* right.

When an occasion arises involving privileged subscription, the corporation sends to the stockholders certificates or warrants evidencing their right to subscribe. A warrant may be issued for one right or for any number of rights, just as a stock certificate may be issued for one share or any number of shares. This brings us to the necessity of actually defining *a right,* as the term is used in finance.

A *right* is the purchasing privilege inherent in, belonging to, or given by, *one share of the old stock.* A stockholder always receives *one right* for *each* share of old stock owned by him. This right may entitle him to buy varying amounts of the new stock, the amount depending upon the proportionate increase of stock. For example, if the company is increasing its capital stock by 20 per cent, then it must give to every old share a right to subscribe to one-fifth of a new share, or the privilege of subscribing to one new share for every five old shares, or every five rights,

held. Similarly, a 50 per cent increase would entitle an old stockholder
to subscribe to one-half share for every old share or right held, or one
new share for every two old shares or rights. Thus, while rights may and
do vary in purchasing power, they never vary from the principle that
one right always represents one old share.

When it becomes known through the announcement of the board of
directors of a corporation whose securities are sufficiently distributed to
be bought and sold by the public that new stock is to be issued, *trading
in* the right may begin on a "when, as, and if issued basis." The rights
are declared to stockholders of record of a certain date, and until that
date, trading must be carried on as indicated above, for no warrants evidencing the rights have been delivered to the stockholders, and the market price of the stock will include the value of the rights. Further, the
announcement of the directors is subject to the decision of the stockholders, who must vote on the increase of authorized stock. On or about
the record date, the price of the stock is quoted less the value of the
right, or, as it is usually stated, the stock sells *ex-rights.* The rights are
now traded in separately under the same rules for delivery of the warrants as exist for stock certificates. At the time of announcing the issuing
of rights, a date for their expiration is set.

Disposition of stockholders' rights. With respect to stocks listed on the
New York Stock Exchange, the time within which rights may be exercised is usually limited to about fourteen days. A stockholder may *exercise* his *rights* by using them to procure new stock. That is, for every
share of new stock he desires, he turns in the required number of rights
and the selling price set by the issuing company. If the stock is increased
20 per cent, the stockholder will have the privilege of subscribing to one
new share for each five old shares held by him. He will be given one right
for each old share held; this right is good for one-fifth of a new share.
Thus, if the *offering price* is $110 per share, he will turn in five rights
and $110, and will receive one new share; or ten rights and $220 and
will receive two new shares; and so on. Since fractions of new shares are
not issued, he cannot exercise any odd rights he may receive less than
the number required to procure one new share; but he may sell them to
another person to make up a unit, or he may buy enough odd ones to
make up another unit for himself. It often happens that the old stockholder does not wish, or is unable, to exercise his rights by purchasing
new stock. In that case, he may *sell* his *rights,* as they are transferable
and entitle any holders to exercise them. The proposition of selling his
rights brings us naturally to a consideration of their value.

The value of a right. If a stockholder sells his rights, he will theoretically receive for them an amount equivalent to the loss in value of the
old stock held by him. That there will be a loss in value of the
old stock will be seen when it is remembered that each share added to

the outstanding capital stock of the corporation will add to the assets of the corporation an amount which is less than the value of a share of the old stock before the sale of the new. If this were not true, the right would, as stated above, be worthless.

This theoretical value of the right attached to an old share of stock can be determined by simple arithmetical analysis, or, more readily, by the application of one of a number of simple formulas which have been deduced for the purpose. A formula which is accurate and also easy to apply is the following:

$$P = \frac{M - S}{n + 1}$$

in which P is the value of the right, M the market price of the old stock, S the subscription price of the new stock, and n the number of old shares required to obtain one new share.

To illustrate, let us assume that a company whose stock is worth $125 a share increases its stock by 25 per cent and gives its stockholders the right to subscribe for new stock at the rate of $100 a share. Each share held by a stockholder would give him the right to subscribe to one-fourth of a new share, and the theoretical value of this right could be found as follows:

$$\frac{\$125 - \$100}{4 + 1} = \frac{\$25}{5} = \$5$$

Since for each 4 shares of old stock outstanding (the price of which is $125 a share) there is sold one new share at $100, the difference between the price of the old stock and that received for the new ($125 less $100, or $25) is spread over 5 shares, and creates a loss of $5 in the value of each share. Thus it is seen that <u>the value of the right attached to the old share is equal to the loss in value of the old share.</u>

This may be shown in another manner as follows:

Market value of old stock (4 shares @ 125) $500
Offered price new issue (one share)   100

                                            $600

Average value after new issue $600 ÷ 5 = $120
$125 — $120 = $5 loss in value each share, i.e.,
the value of the right.

<u>When the stock sells _ex-rights_ after the record date, its value is, of course, less by the value of one right than when it sold _rights-on_, or, as expressed by traders, _cum-rights_, before this date.</u> This requires a change in the formula used above:

$$P = \frac{M - S}{n}$$

Assuming the same figures as above, with the stock quoted $120 ex-rights, the result will be:

$$\frac{\$120 - \$100}{4} = \frac{\$20}{4} = \$5$$

There is a tendency on the part of the stockholder to look upon rights as being in the nature of a dividend, which is evidenced by the usual advance in the market price of the stock in anticipation of rights. As a matter of fact, an issue of new stock accompanied by an offer of rights really offers the stockholder a compulsory choice, either to increase his investment in the corporation or to reduce his proportionate ownership in the corporation through the sale of his rights.

The actual value of the rights. It is stated above that the theoretical value of the stock after the new stock is issued will be its old price ($125) less $5, the value of a right, or $120. As a matter of fact, however, there are several reasons why the stock and the rights may have a value which is different from the theoretical one. If, for example, people decide that the company will be able to maintain the old dividend rate on the increased outstanding capital stock or, possibly, to increase it, the price of the stock after the operation may be as high as it was before, or higher. On the other hand, some stockholders, seeing the natural adjustment downward (which was explained above) may become alarmed, throw their stock on the market, and thus depress the price considerably below its theoretical value.

1. *Stockholders.* Because of the preemptive right to subscribe, most corporations are legally obligated to offer new issues of stock to old stockholders. The offer of the new shares is usually at a price somewhat below the market and if the corporation is successful, particularly in a time of prosperity and a rising stock market, the entire issue may be absorbed by the old stockholders. Not only may stock be sold in this manner, but the American Telephone & Telegraph Co. has demonstrated, through the successful sale of a number of issues, that convertible bonds may be sold in this way. A sale of a corporation's stock by means of preemptive rights to old stockholders is more likely to be successful if the following conditions are present:

(a) A large number of stockholders with the stock well-scattered among them.

(b) A rising stock market, at least a good stock market record for the company's stock.

(c) A good earnings record on the part of the corporation.

(d) An attractive offering price below the present market price of the corporation's stock.

Because there is always the possibility of a stock market decline taking place during the relatively short period the rights are open for exercise, which might make stockholders unwilling to exercise their rights, most concerns protect themselves by making a *standby* underwriting contract with investment bankers to insure that the stock, if not taken by the stockholders, will be taken at an agreed-upon price by the underwriting investment bankers. (See page 195.)

2. *Bondholders.* A corporation seldom makes a direct offer of new stock to bondholders as the buyers of bonds are not usually interested in stock and have no preemptive right to subscribe to such issues. Direct offer of a new issue of bonds may be made in the case of a refunding issue where the old issue is maturing or may be called for redemption. Bonds, most of the time, are marketed through investment bankers who are quite likely to approach bondholders of the corporation as lively prospects for sale of the new issue on the premise that existing bondholders are well acquainted with and have faith in the issuer.

Sources of funds for investment in corporate securities. The billions of dollars invested in the securities of private business corporations in the United States have come from many sources: private individuals, various investing institutions and even lending agencies of the government itself. A large part of these securities can be purchased by anyone interested by merely placing an order to buy in the securities markets of the country. Even though the securities may not be listed on or traded in on one of the country's stock exchanges, they may be bought and sold outside the exchanges in the active so-called over-the-counter market which is maintained between investment bankers and dealers who buy such securities from one another by telephone for the benefit of their customers. Reliable statistics which might present a complete and accurate picture of where the funds come from that are daily invested in new as well as established business corporations are lacking. Some which are available and which are reasonably reliable will be included in the discussion below.

1) *Friends of the management.* Small corporations seeking additional capital investment normally do not have the assistance of investment bankers but must seek funds from those who may be directly approached by the management, and induced to buy the stock or bonds of the enterprise. For lack of a better term, the expression "friends of the management" is used to include such persons as local businessmen who are interested in the corporation's growth and success because of the benefits it may bring to the community in employment, utilization of locally produced raw material, etc. Sometimes local community organizations such as Chambers of Commerce and employee organizations will help in obtaining investment in the concern. In order to induce a concern to locate in a city, some have actually received gifts of buildings and land from the city government. It should be pointed out that many smaller cities, not large enough to support an organized securities market, will have investment dealers among their businessmen. Occasionally these dealers may act as underwriters for an issue of securities of a local company, too

small to warrant interest of investment banking concerns in the larger cities. In such cases, the local dealers will usually not buy the securities for resale but merely undertake to sell them for a commission.

2. *Creditors.* Creditors sometimes find it to their advantage to finance a concern which they believe is well managed and which offers a good market for the creditors' products. This, however, is of such infrequent occurrence as to make it of little general importance as a means of financing.

3. *Customers.* Sale of securities, especially preferred stock, to customers was at one time a common practice by public utilities but is seldom heard of today. Financing of subcontracting concerns by primary contractors enjoying large government contracts has been frequent, but has not usually been accompanied by the issuance of securities. Purchase of stock by a large corporation to increase productive facilities of a small company furnishing important parts or material used by the larger company is not at all uncommon. Generally speaking, it is probably not good business for a concern to receive substantial financing from a vendee, if it wishes to keep its independence in matters of pricing and production.

4. *Employees.* As a general rule, a corporation cannot to any great extent supply its needs for money through the sale of securities to its employees. The practice is frequently found, however, as a profit-sharing scheme in connection with a management policy.

5. *The general public.* After all, most of the investment capital for large enterprises, both new and old, comes from the general public. The general public may be divided into classes according to the kinds of securities they buy. They may be grouped as follows:

a. *Buyers of investment securities.* This type of buyer is primarily interested in safety of principal and, of course, an income commensurate with the safety of the issue. The degree of safety is not dependent upon the type of security, that is, whether it is a common stock, preferred stock, mortgage bond or debenture bond, but upon many factors such as the type of industry, stability of earnings and the past record of earnings. For many investors, the factor of federal income tax is important, with the result that securities of private corporations must be sold in competition with those of state and municipalities, the income of which is exempt.

The largest buyers of bonds and the buyers of some high grade stocks are so-called institutional investors. Some of these are not entirely free agents in the choice of securities but are governed by state regulations established by law and administered by state authority. These are the so-called "legal investments." Savings banks and trustees, both private and institutional, are subject to these regulations. Life insurance companies are also subject to investment restrictions. The state laws or regulations of a state governmental department usually lay down certain limitations on the type of industry in which investment may be made and standards which are expected to be followed in selecting the securities of the type authorized. Lists of approved securities are published by some of these state government departments. In recent years, there has been a tendency to liberalize the rules to permit investors such as life insurance companies and savings banks to include a limited amount of stock in their portfolios of securities held for investment. Because of the difficulty in reducing the selection of common stocks to a simple statement of standards, the investing institution is expected to use a high standard of prudence in making its choice. Preferred stock investment, however, is likely to be subject to prescribed standards.

Life insurance companies, the largest institutional investors, at the end of the year 1957, owned $15,252,000,000 of public utility bonds, $878,-000,000 preferred stock and $464,000,000 common stock of this industry, $3,863,000,000 American railroad bonds and $99,000,000 railroad preferred and common stock. Other investments in bonds of industrial and miscellaneous corporations totaled $21,717,000,000 and preferred and common stocks totaled $3,391,000,000.[4]

Savings banks in the United States at the end of the year 1954 held $845,000,000 of railroad bonds, $1,332,000,000 of public utility bonds and $349,000,000 of industrial bonds and, as of June 30, 1955, the investment in stocks totaled $622,400,000, of which bank stocks comprised $327,-000,000. On the basis of the figures stated and as of the dates mentioned, the investment in these bonds comprised 8.5 per cent and the investment in stocks 2.1 per cent of savings banks assets.[5]

Fire and casualty companies are not bound by the strict regulations applicable to life insurance companies and therefore are investors in stocks to a much greater extent than in bonds. These companies are a very important source of investment capital. As of 1957 they owned approximately $6,400,000,000 of common stocks, $800,000,000 of preferred stocks and $1,200,000,000 of corporate bonds.[6]

Investment trusts or investment companies invest heavily in stocks of American companies. Aside from income, these companies usually make their investments with a view to value appreciation. However, selections are carefully made and highly speculative securities are avoided. Some of these organizations sell their own shares against a fixed and definite portfolio of selected stocks which is changed infrequently and only in accordance with rules established at the time the trust was established. Such companies are referred to as closed end investment companies.

[4] Life Insurance Fact Book 1958, Institute of Life Insurance.
[5] Savings Bank Fact Book 1956, Savings Bank Trust Co., N.Y.
[6] Best's Fire and Casualty, *Aggregates and Averages* (New York: Alfred M. Best Co., Inc., 1957.)

Others maintain an actively managed portfolio making frequent investments in line with current developments.

The latter are so-called open end investment trusts, actively selling their own shares and investing the proceeds. Their funds come largely from private investors who, by the purchase of trust shares, hope to benefit by the skilled management of the investment trust and achieve a high degree of safety through the diversification of the portfolio of securities held by the trust. These companies are subject to regulation of the Securities and Exchange Commission, which is charged with the administration of the Investment Companies Act of 1940.

Some idea of the importance of the investment companies may be seen in a report covering 144 open end companies made by the National Association of Investment Companies at the end of the first quarter of 1958. At that time, the 144 member companies had net assets of $9,462,830,000. An earlier study indicated that 82 per cent of the assets of twenty of the largest of these companies consisted of common stock, 7.5 per cent bonds and 6.7 per cent preferred stock. The balance represented the current cash position. While these proportions may vary slightly from time to time due to market conditions, they appear to be typical. Twenty-four closed end companies as of the same date as above had $1,281,373,000 in net assets. Referring to the same earlier study, five of the largest closed end companies had invested 86.77 per cent of their net assets in common stocks, 5.37 per cent in bonds and 4.04 per cent in preferred stock.[7]

Pension funds. In the last two decades, there has been a great growth in various types of pension plans for employees. Some of these have been placed with insurance companies and the resulting investment of the funds are included in the insurance investment data shown above. Others are privately administered and are often referred to as self-insured. They have become an important source of investment capital. At the close of 1954, over $10 billion was invested in various types of corporate securities, making this source of capital next in importance to the life insurance companies in this respect. The portfolios show that the above total was divided into approximately $6 billion of corporate bonds and notes, $3 billion of common stock and $500,000,000 of preferred stock. In the one year of 1954, over $588,000,000 of common stock was purchased, of which $550,000,000 represented stock in the corporations other than that of the employer concern.[8]

Unlike the life insurance companies, their funds are not regulated by law but only by the self-imposed terms under which the pension plan was established.

---

[7] Staff Report to the Committee on Banking and Currency of the U.S. Senate, dated Dec. 28, 1956.

[8] Figures based upon Survey of Corporate Pension Funds, 1951-1954, Securities and Exchange Commission.

Foundations, universities and colleges. Numerous foundations created for various purposes usually try to keep their funds invested in a diversified portfolio which will produce income to be used by the trustees of the foundation in furthering their objectives. Colleges and universities also have endowment funds which must be invested. The terms under which foundations and endowment funds are established usually give full discretion to those placed in charge as to the manner of investment. Because the income of these nonprofit organizations is tax-free, there is a tendency to invest chiefly in private industries and to avoid tax-free bonds which sell on a low yield basis. These institutions are therefore another source of capital for American industry.

b. Buyers of speculative securities. There is a large segment of security buyers who purchase largely for value appreciation rather than primarily for income. They are willing to assume greater risks than the buyers of investment securities for the possibility of greater gain. The securities classed as speculative are not necessarily confined to new companies or to comparatively new industries but comprise the securities, both bonds and stocks, of corporations whose business is likely to be affected considerably by the cyclical fluctuations, natural phenomena such as weather and political considerations, domestic and foreign, which have to be studied and weighed by the buyer. Most stock of competitive business is speculative because so much depends upon the skill of management in developing and retaining the market for their products. Some are more speculative than others. A new business, a new consolidation of existing companies, an old concern branching out into new fields or risking capital in new developments all offer higher degrees of risk to the buyers of their stocks than those marketing well-established products with long records of successful management. The average speculative buyer maintains a great deal of flexibility in his purchases and holdings. He is ready to sell to take a profit or avoid a loss and to buy other securities which he believes will rise in value. Some purchase with a view to holding for long-term developments, others may be looking for quick profits because of some immediate situation. All are an essential part of the security market. Without those willing to speculate, there would be no market for most stock and few new enterprises could obtain the capital to begin, or finance, later expansion of their operations.

State regulation of security sales. Prior to 1933, the only regulation of security sales was that imposed by the various state governments. State laws regulating security sales are commonly known as Blue Sky Laws and regulations made by state authorities in carrying out such regulations, as Blue Sky requirements. All of the states, except Nevada, have some legislation designed to protect security buyers. The laws vary considerably in the different states as do the types of securities or conditions under which certain securities are exempt from regulation. In forty-three states, non-exempt securities must be registered with a state commission before the securities can be sold in the state. In forty-four states, security dealers and brokers must be licensed and in some, dealers must purchase a prescribed bond as security for proper conduct of business. In thirty-two states, fraud in the sale of securities is a statutory offense and subject to injunction proceedings, even criminal prosecution by the attorney general. In four states (New York, New Jersey, Maryland and Delaware) the only legislation is of the latter type. Some of the states which include in their laws the regulating of the securities before sale, have set up rather strict standards for qualification of securities before they may be sold within the state.

Exemptions of securities from the operation of the state laws vary so much from state to state that any listing here would be impracticable. Some states exempt securities listed on the important stock exchanges, securities issued in accordance with regulations of the Interstate Commerce Commission and state public service commissions.

State regulations have not been very effective. It is easy to cross state lines in the sale of securities. The acts have not always had proper and competent administration. Meeting the regulations in the several states in the case of an issue distributed nationally has been troublesome to investment bankers and expensive to the issuing corporation which must bear the costs of qualifying their securities before sale.

Public service commissions in many states have jurisdiction over the issuance of public utilities' securities and generally over the purpose for which they are used. Like Blue Sky Laws discussed above, there is little uniformity either in the laws of the several states or in the extent of the jurisdiction exercised by the several Commissions.

Federal regulation of security sales. Federal regulation of security sales began with the Federal Securities Act of 1933. The administration of this legislation was first given to the Federal Trade Commission but, in the following year with the adoption of the Securities and Exchange Act of 1934, establishing the Securities and Exchange Commission, this agency was charged with the duty. The commission consists of five members appointed by the President to hold office for ten years. The main office is in Washington, D.C., but the country is divided into eight zones with a regional office and administrator in each.

The basic purpose of the Act is not to set up a federal commission to approve or disapprove an issue of securities *but to require the issuer to give complete information regarding the issue.* If this is done, the Securities and Exchange Commission has no power to disapprove the issue, no matter how speculative. On the other hand, when the issuer has complied with all registration requirements so that the issue may be sold, the Securities and Exchange Commission has not approved it on the basis of merit. All that the Commission has done is to signify that, as far as it is able to ascertain, all material information required in the registration has been given and appears to be correct and that the law has been complied with.

The act of registration requires the supplying of complete answers to a questionnaire which is filed with the Securities and Exchange Commission. Twenty days must normally elapse between the date of filing and the effective date of the registration when the securities may be sold. This period is provided to give the Commission an opportunity to check the registration statement to see if the Act and regulations have been met. The Securities and Exchange Commission has the power to shorten this period in a situation where they believe the longer period is unnecessary. Public sale of securities in excess of $300,000 must be registered. However, if a *public* offering of a smaller amount is being made, information to that effect, with some details as to the issue, must be filed five days previous to the sale.

Because the filing of a registration statement, even if copies are obtainable for a small fee, would not be likely to place pertinent information in the hands of the security buyer, the issuer must prepare a prospectus based upon the registration statement but not as detailed. Sales of securities may be made by prospectus only. All investment bankers or dealers concerned with the sale at the time of initial distribution must have copies of the prospectus on hand to offer to prospective buyers. They may be obtained also from the issuer. While the registration fee charged by the Securities and Exchange Commission is but 1/100 of 1 per cent of the aggregate price of the issue, the cost of printing so many copies of the prospectus plus the expense of preparing the registration statement, including attorneys' fees, may be considerable. This adds to the expense of financing and is one reason why some issues are privately sold by direct placement with a few buyers. This practice will be discussed later under "Direct Placement."

The Securities and Exchange Commission has the power to issue a "stop order" where it is not satisfied with the information contained in the registration statement. In other words, should the Commission, upon examination of the registration statement, believe that it contains false or misleading information or omission of a material fact, it may immediately suspend registration. Because such a "stop order" is a very drastic step and would adversely affect the subsequent marketing of the securities, even if the defect were corrected, the issuer will usually be permitted to amend the statement informally without the actual issuance of the stop order. However, if the amendment is not promptly forthcoming or information presented which will clear up any possible misunderstanding, the stop order will be put into effect. Of course, if it appears that there was a *wilful* attempt to falsify or conceal material facts, a stop order may be expected, as well as criminal prosecution, as provided in the Act.

Various remedies are provided in case a purchaser of the securities finds false statements or material omissions in the prospectus after he purchased the securities, consisting of return of the purchase price of the security or damages if he has sold it. These damages run only in favor of the original purchaser and cannot be had if the purchaser had knowledge of the false statement or omission when the purchase was made. Should the *registration statement* be false or contain material omissions, liability for damages arising from loss on the sale of the securities may be had not only by the original purchaser but by any subsequent purchaser.

This liability extends for three years from the time the securities were sold. Liability under the act is joint and several and extends to the issuer, the directors (at the time of registration), accountants, engineers and experts named in the registration statements as having prepared some of the data, every underwriter and, of course, every signer of the statement. In suits to recover because of decline in the value of the security, there will be no liability if it can be shown that the decline in value was not due to the false statement or material omission. Also all but the issuer may avoid liability if it can be shown that the person sued, after a proper investigation, had reasonable grounds to believe all statements made were true and that the registration statement was complete. Reasonable standards are those expected of a prudent man acting with respect to his own property.

The act also provides penalties up to $5,000 and prison terms up to five years upon conviction for wilful violation of the provisions relative to untrue statements or material omissions of the Act.

In addition to the administration of the Federal Securities Act of 1933, the Commission, which has the duty of administering the Public Utility Holding Company Act of 1935, has direct control over the issuance of securities by registered holding companies and their subsidiaries in the electric and gas industry. An illustration of the exercise of this power will be discussed under competitive bidding.

Methods of financing through public sale of securities. The average business concern is ill equipped to market its own securities. Small corporations may have no alternative as it is difficult to interest any outside agency in undertaking such a sale. As it would cost almost as much as a large issue, the cost would be prohibitive.

In the usual course, large issues of securities are sold by specialized agencies known as investment bankers. Such organizations exist for one purpose, to handle securities and to render to the corporation all necessary services in connection with the sale of securities. They are merchants who buy securities from the corporation for resale, or sometimes guarantee the success of an offering made by a corporation to someone else, as will be discussed under Standby Underwriting later. On rare occasions, they may undertake the sale of securities for the issuer on a fee or commission basis without purchasing them. Investment bankers may purchase securities from corporations through private negotiations or acquire them by bidding for them in competition with other bankers. While it is customary for only one banking firm to conduct negotiations, the actual purchase contract is participated in by several firms ranging from half a dozen to twenty-five or more.

Advantages of selling through an investment banker. The complex nature of a public sale of securities and the nature of the securities market in general have made investment banking organizations absolutely essential in marketing securities through public sale. Some of the advantages of employing their services in the floating of an issue are:

(1) The corporation receives the advice of the banker regarding the best way to finance.

(2) The company is relieved of the necessity of organizing a selling campaign.

(3) It is usually cheaper to sell through the banker.

(4) It assures to the corporation a successful sale within a certain period.

(5) The corporation receives the assistance of the investment banker's legal counsel in meeting the requirements of the Securities and Exchange Commission and in other legal matters concerning security issues.

Standby underwriting. Investment bankers are often called upon to protect a corporation by guaranteeing the successful sale of securities which are first offered to someone else. This is what takes place when a corporation issuing stock, offers the stock to its own stockholders who have preemptive rights to subscribe to it. Naturally, at the time the stock is so offered, there is every expectation that it will be absorbed by the old stockholders. However, market conditions may deteriorate and the subscription period may end with stock still left unsubscribed. As a precaution or insurance against just such an eventuality, the corporation may make a contract with an investment banker who, for a fee, agrees to take up, at a stipulated price, any securities left unsold.

The same situation exists with respect to the refunding before maturity or at maturity of an issue of bonds. Refunding before maturity is usually undertaken to reduce interest payments and there always is a strong possibility that some investors will insist upon being paid in cash so that they may reinvest elsewhere. Conditions existing when a bond issue matures and is to be refunded are quite likely to result in a similar situation. Here, too, a contract may be made with investment bankers whereby the bankers agree to take up, at an agreed-upon price, the new bonds refused by the old stockholders and in that manner provide the cash to redeem the latter's bonds.

This type of underwriting contract is known as a *standby* agreement or the procedure is termed *standby* underwriting to distinguish it from or-

dinary underwriting, which has come to mean the purchase by investment bankers of securities of an issue for sale to the public.

The purchase group. Officers of a corporation desiring to sell an issue
of securities through direct negotiation with investment bankers normally begin discussions with the representatives of a single investment
banking house. If the house is a large one, it may have a buying department composed of a number of specialists, each of whom is an expert
in one or more industries. It is upon the recommendations of its specialists that the members of the concern will rely in making their decisions
as to whether or not to underwrite the issue. The investment bankers
will advise as to the type of security to issue in view of current market
conditions and the price to the public and to the bankers. The bankers'
attorneys will check the issue for legality, prepare the trust indenture, if
the issue is a bond issue, and, in many cases, the registration statement
and prospectus, frequently working with the issuer's attorneys on all
legal matters concerned with the issue.

Having made at least a preliminary agreement as to the terms under
which the issue is to be underwritten, the originating banking house now
asks other houses to participate in the purchase. The houses which agree
to participate in the initial purchase and sale of the securities are now
commonly referred to as the *Purchase Group.* In most corporate stock
issues and bond issues of a single maturity, it is customary for each house
to contract to purchase a definite amount of the securities, thus limiting
its liability therein.

Actually, there are two agreements: one is the so-called purchase
agreement made with the corporation in which each purchase group
member signs for the amount of his participation; the other is an agreement among the group members and the manager or group representative, which is usually the originating house. Both contracts are carefully
drawn, especially with a view to limiting each member to his agreed-
upon participation. Where each member's liability is limited this way,
the agreement is known as a divided account or limited liability account.
This type of agreement is not always used. For some issues, the agreement provides for additional liability on the part of each underwriter to
take up, in proportion to his holdings, securities remaining unsold at the
termination of the initial period as provided in the underwriting contract
or as extended by subsequent agreement. This so-called undivided account type is often used in underwriting bonds or note issues bearing
serial maturities. This is because some maturities, in recent years those of
shorter term, sell better than others. With the prospect of having to take
down securities left unsold, a banking house is not likely to satisfy its
participation by selling only those maturities which are in great demand.
Unlimited liability or undivided account syndicate agreements were generally used prior to 1933.

During the period allotted for marketing of the issue, the purchase group manager is ordinarily authorized to support the market, for it would be disastrous to the selling operations were the market to decline because of offerings being made below the established group price. Securities so purchased may be resold in the market if opportunity develops to do so at the group price or better. They may also be charged back against the house or dealer originally selling them. The agreement usually provides that the expenses of acquisition may also be charged against the house originally marketing the securities. The prospectus must indicate that market support is contemplated and careful records kept of all such activities so that complete reports may be made to the Securities and Exchange Commission.

The selling group. Large issues which require broad distribution make it necessary to form a selling group. This may be composed of underwriting houses not participating in the purchase group and smaller dealers. Such a group may cover the entire country. Each member of the purchase group receives or takes down the amount it desires for its own retail needs and the purchase group manager endeavors to distribute the remainder to dealers. The dealers buy on terms established in the offer made by the purchase group. Dealers receive preliminary prospectuses, sometimes called "red herring" prospectuses because of the statement printed in red ink that it is not the final prospectus which appears on its pages.

Because no offer of sale, even to a dealer, may be made until the release date, usually only after the twenty-day registration period is over, about the only information which can be given is that it is probable that a selling group will be formed and that it is expected that the securities will be released for sale on a certain date. Because the price is usually not determined until the last day of registration, the preliminary prospectus will not contain this information. The final offer, if firm, will state the amount the dealer may buy; otherwise it may merely invite the dealer to subscribe. Practice has been so perfected, however, that, in a matter of a few minutes after release of the issue, telegraph offices all over the country are in position to deliver the final offer. Definitive copies of the prospectus are delivered at the same time, thus complying with the regulations. When the issue is largely distributed to institutional purchasers, there is usually no need of a selling group. Indeed, the disposal of an entire issue of many millions meeting institutional investment requirements may be accomplished in a few hours.

Marketing of securities through competitive bidding. In contrast to the sale of securities by direct negotiation with investment bankers, is the practice of awarding the issue to the highest bidder. This method has long been followed in the marketing of state and municipal issues, where it is required by law. In the field of private finance, Massachusetts has required this method to be used for issues of both stocks and bonds of public utilities for over eighty years and the Interstate Commerce Commission has required that equipment trust securities be sold by competitive bidding since 1926. In 1941, the Securities and Exchange Commission acting under the powers conferred upon it by the Public Utility Holding Co. Act of 1935, adopted Rule U 50 which required all issues of electric and gas utility holding company securities and those of their subsidiaries to be sold through competitive bidding unless specifically exempted by the Commission. The Interstate Commerce Commission, in 1944, required that all debt securities of railroads in excess of $1,000,- 000 or more be sold competitively and in 1950 made the rule generally applicable to all interstate railroad securities, unless specifically exempted.

In 1950, the Federal Power Commission, which has jurisdiction over public utility securities of companies operating in two or more states and which are not subject to regulation of the Securities and Exchange Commission under the Holding Company Act, required that issues of securities of such companies be subject to competitive bidding. The advocates of competitive bidding maintain that it prevents a few banking houses or a house with which the issuer has had previous connections from gaining what amounts to a monopoly in handling all issues of a corporation. All bankers under this system have an equal opportunity to bid on the new issue. Furthermore, such advocates believe that the arm's length relationship between the corporation and the investment bankers and the competition among them for the issue, will result in a higher price to the issuer. Those opposed point to the low spread or profit to the bankers and claim that this has a tendency to restrict bidding to larger houses capable of disposing of the issue quickly and able to do so with a minimum of sales effort and expense. Because investment bankers have no part in advising the corporation or in preparing the new issue, critics of competitive bidding feel that as the issue is prepared by the corporation's own legal counsel, provisions which a banker might insist upon for the protection of the security buyer are likely to be absent. Only the test of time and the experience gained through both good and poor security markets will show whether competitive bidding represents the best way to market securities in the railroad and public utility industries.

Once an investment banker group has been awarded an issue on its bid, the procedure described above in connection with negotiated sale to investment bankers will follow. Because of the small spread and the fact that issues sold by competitive bidding are chiefly marketed to institutional investors, there are fewer instances where a selling group is formed. There is not enough profit to give the small dealer a concession which would interest him in the issue and the market provided by institutional investors is largely in the hands of the large underwriting houses.

Direct or private placement. In recent years, a practice has grown up of corporations selling their securities directly to large institutional investors, chiefly insurance companies. These direct placements are sometimes made with a single investor, and never with many, for it is desired to make the transaction a private and not a public sale, thus avoiding registration and prospectus expenses. The Union Carbide and Carbon Corporation debt financing, in recent years, provides an excellent example of private placement. In 1947, this corporation borrowed $150,000,000 at 2.70 per cent interest from three life insurance companies, distributed as follows: Metropolitan Life Insurance Co., $77,000,000, Prudential Life Insurance, $68,000,000, and Sun Life Insurance Co. of Canada, $5,000,000. These loans are to be retired at the rate of $10,000,000 per year with a final maturity of 1967. They may be prepaid if the issuer desires. In 1951, this company again privately placed $300,000,000 in 100-year 3¼ per cent notes in equal amounts with Metropolitan Life Insurance Co. and the Prudential Life Insurance Co. These notes also carry a prepayment option and may be converted at the option of lenders or borrowers into 25-year, 3½ per cent sinking fund notes on 30 days' notice any time after November, 1959.

Private placement now accounts for about 50 per cent of debt financing. As pointed out, there is considerable saving through not having to register the issue. Other savings are made in not having to employ a corporate trustee or to maintain registrar and transfer facilities, as is necessary in connection with public sale of bond or note issues. There is no expense for listing on a stock exchange. On the other hand, because there is no public market for privately placed notes or bonds, there are no opportunities for the corporation to retire the debt by buying up the securities when opportunity offers. Retirement must be accomplished strictly in accordance with the provisions in the loan agreement and usually at face value.

Bankers' commissions involved in public marketing are avoided. However, some investment bankers have developed a business of acting as "finders" of opportunities for private placement and may assist the corporation in negotiating such contracts. Fees paid for this service depend upon the size and nature of the issue. They are much less than the spread expected by bankers in a publicly sold issue, probably seldom in excess of 1 per cent and as low as 1/10 of 1 per cent. These fees are a private matter and competitive and therefore are not made public.

The securities exchanges. Closely related and essential to the successful marketing of large security issues on the scale required in this country where security purchases by private investors provide most of the funds needed by industry, are the stock exchanges. It is through the public auction which is taking place every minute during the day (while the exchange is open), that an investor in securities listed on an exchange may sell them if he wishes at any time, or if he desires to invest in a corporation's securities, buy through his broker. Not all securities are listed on the stock exchanges. Bank stocks, federal and state bonds, securities of small corporations whose stock is held only by a few persons are not listed. Persons wishing to sell or buy such securities must do so in the "over-the-counter" market which will be briefly described later, or by private negotiation.

Of the exchanges in this country, the New York Stock Exchange is by far the most important. Measured in terms of dollar value of stocks bought and sold, it accounts for 85 per cent of the business. Next in importance is the American Stock Exchange, formerly known as the New York Curb Exchange, whose business is restricted to securities not listed on the New York Stock Exchange. This exchange accounts for about 8 per cent of the national volume. Next in size is the Midwest Exchange, a combination of exchanges originally divided among the cities of Chicago, Cleveland, St. Louis and Minneapolis. The Midwest Exchange, however, handles only 2 per cent to 3 per cent of the business. The remainder is scattered among small regional exchanges existing in other large cities. Differences in time often makes some of the far western exchanges important to an eastern speculator who may wish to act upon events which he learns about after the eastern exchanges are closed. All of the exchanges outside of New York trade in securities listed on the New York Stock Exchange in addition to listing local issues.

Some corporations list their securities on one or more of these exchanges in addition to listing on the New York Stock Exchange. Others are traded in without formal listing, provided approval is obtained from the Securities and Exchange Commission. There are also exchanges in Canada, the one in Toronto being of great importance. The volume in number of shares of stock traded in on this exchange is at least one-third greater than that of the New York Exchange. But because so much of it is in low-priced oil and mining shares, the dollar value probably seldom exceeds 10 per cent of the volume.

A corporation must take the initiative in listing its securities by filing an application for listing. Each exchange has its own requirements which have to be met. For example, a corporation wishing to list its securities on the New York Stock Exchange, on which approximately 1,500 stock issues and about 1,000 bond issues are listed at present, must have net tangible assets of not less than $7,000,000 and annual earnings of at least $1,000,000. The corporation should have over 1,500 shareholders well distributed throughout the country and at least 300,000 shares in addition to any large number held by the principal owners. The corporation must agree to maintain a register and a transfer office in Manhattan. The corporation must pay an initial listing fee of not less than $2,000 and usually more, as the fee depends upon the amount of stock, and an annual fee for fifteen years after listing, which also depends upon the number of shares and is set at a minimum of $500. There are other rules and requirements covering the listing of additional securities by the same corporation and rules concerning removal from listing, the rendering of financial reports by the corporation and the like. Information submitted by the corporation in connection with its application for listing is printed by the exchange and available to members.

Listing of securities is a desirable feature with most investors and, therefore, the intention to list the securities will usually be stated at the time of issuance to help in marketing. Initial issues are not sold by the corporation on exchanges but through investment houses to the purchaser. Trading in securities does not begin until an initial purchaser decides to sell.

The advantages of listing do not all accrue to the holders of securities. By listing its securities, a corporation obtains a wider distribution. The fact that more people have a fundamental interest in the corporation facilitates new financing. It makes new stock financing by means of preemptive rights more likely to succeed. There is also a certain amount of advertising value and prestige associated with having the company on the list of an important exchange (especially the New York Exchange).[9]

Under the Securities and Exchange Act of 1934, all exchanges are under the jurisdiction of the Securities and Exchange Commission which has the duty of enforcing the Act and making such regulations as are necessary to carry out the intent of the Act. It requires exchanges to register and to adopt regulations for their members and establish trading rules to comply with the Act and the Commission's regulations. Each exchange must have the power to discipline its own members so as to insure that rules are observed. The purpose of the Act and regulations is to see that a free public market honestly conducted is available to those who wish to buy or sell securities. No attempt is made to prevent speculation but every possible means is used to eliminate manipulation and unfair trading practices.

The over-the-counter market. This term is applied to the sale of securities outside the stock exchange. It does not normally apply to those which are listed. Perhaps it might be termed a telephone market, as most transactions are handled by telephone between brokers buying and selling the securities. The securities handled in this market may be purchased outright by the house offering them for sale or may be handled on a commission basis for the owner. The market is especially important in bonds, where volume and number of issues dealt in exceed that han-

---

[9] The authors feel that detailed discussion of how securities are bought and sold on the exchanges is not appropriate in this text. An excellent short book on this subject written in nontechnical language is Louis Engel's *How to Buy Stocks* (Boston: Little, Brown & Company, 1953) and Bantam Books.

dled by the New York Stock Exchange. Though more difficult to regulate, the Securities and Exchange Commission has some control through the National Association of Security Dealers, an organization to which most over-the-counter dealers belong and which makes rules to enforce standards of conduct among its members.

Devices used as an aid in marketing bonds and preferred stock. When the stock market rises and the public is interested more in the speculative opportunities for value appreciation in their purchase of securities it is quite often difficult to sell fixed income types of securities, *i.e.*, pre ferred stock and bonds, except at prices below that which the issuers consider to be their real value. If, however, some speculative element can be added, the inducement may be sufficient to create a demand for the issue. Sometimes such an inducement may make it possible to sell preferred stock at lower dividend rates or bonds at lower interest rates. Three methods used as such marketing aids are discussed below:

1. *Stock as a bonus.* In recent years, the use of stock as a bonus to promote the marketing of preferred stock or bonds has not been common practice in floating such issues. It is used occasionally in the marketing of stock of small corporations whose stock is sold locally by the corporation itself or by local security dealers acting as investment bankers or as agents for the corporation. It has also been used by the real estate corporations as a means of financing the erection of large buildings. Where used, it has been customary to market securities in units, consisting, for example, of 2 shares of preferred stock with 1 share of bonus common stock. The device gives to the purchaser the security provided by a senior class of stock with the possible speculative advantages of the common.

2. *Conversion.* Convertible preferred stock and convertible bonds have been discussed in other chapters. The inclusion with a sale of bonds or preferred stock of a right to convert to common stock adds a speculative element which serves to help the sale in a speculative market when there may not be an active demand for fixed income type of securities such as preferred stock and bonds. Conversion ratios may vary, dependent upon the time of conversion. Where made variable, the usual effect is to make it more advantageous to the holder in terms of the amount of common stock he may obtain if conversion is accomplished earlier, frequently during the first five years after the issuance of the convertible security. Sometimes the conversion privilege has no time limit and remains until exercised. While conversion often contemplates an exchange of one security for those into which conversion is provided, with adjustments merely for accrued interest or accrued dividends, it may be provided that, in order to convert, the holder must present not only his convertible security, but a certain amount of cash. The various issues of American Telephone and Telegraph convertible debentures previously referred to in Chapter IX, which were made convertible at the rate of 10 shares of stock for one

bond have required a payment of cash in addition to surrender of the bond at the time of the conversion. The addition of a redemption provision at a low call premium gives the corporation some control over the exercise of the convertible option.[10] Calling the bond or preferred stock for redemption when the market value of stock obtainable through conversion is higher than the call price will ordinarily bring about conversion of substantially all of the outstanding convertible securities.

3. *Stock purchase warrants.* A stock purchase warrant is an option given by a corporation to the warrant holder to purchase under specified conditions of time, price and amount, some security of the corporation, usually common stock. Their use as a means of facilitating the sale of preferred stock and bonds was very common in the speculative markets of the late 1920s but not nearly as frequent today. In 1951, Plywood Inc. sold a limited open end debenture issue carrying with it detachable warrants with an expiration date of March 31, 1958, entitling the holder to purchase common stock in the ratio of 100 shares per $1,000 bond. The option prices started at $4.00 per share and increased $1.00 per share each year to 1958, the year of expiration.

It will be seen from the above example that the option price may vary according to the time of exercise. Occasionally, the variation is based upon priority of exercise. For example, the first ten thousand warrants exercised might obtain stock at $5.00 per share, the next ten thousand at $6.00 per share, etc.

When initially issued with other securities, the warrants may be known as *detachable* when they may be sold by the holder separately from the security to which they were issued and exercised by any subsequent owner. This type of warrant may be listed on stock exchanges and traded in regularly. In fact, they are often quite popular with speculators. The Plywood Inc. warrants in the example above were of this type.

Warrants may also be made *non-detachable* and are exercisable only by the owner of the security to which they were initially attached. To exercise them, the holder must present his bond or stock certificate to the corporation or its agent.

While a definite expiration date is usually fixed, warrants have been made perpetual. This may have the effect of keeping the corporation's capital stock outstanding continuously in a state of flux, as it must have on hand sufficient authorized stock to issue in exchange for warrants which may be presented from time to time, depending upon the whim of the holder.

Today, warrants are used in reorganization proceedings as a method of obtaining consent of creditors to sacrifices or for stockholders who,

---

[10] This practice was followed by the American Telephone and Telegraph Co. in its convertible debenture issues.

reluctant to abandon completely their corporation when their stock becomes worthless because of insolvency, may be willing to purchase warrants if offered to them at a low price.

More frequently in recent years, warrants have been issued as bonus incentives to excutives of corporations. Direct common stock bonuses have become less popular because they are taxable as income under the federal income tax laws, as of the value when given. The Internal Revenue Code provides advantages in the use of warrants for this purpose. If regulations are strictly followed, the tax, if any, will be computed on a capital gains basis at lower rates than the tax upon income, which is at a high rate for a highly paid executive.

Sale- and lease-back financing. This type of arrangement, while not giving rise to an issue of securities, should be considered as a method of financing the real estate required in the operation of a business. Essentially it consists of a sale of the real estate assets with an agreement to lease the premises back from the purchaser, who as the landlord will be paid a fixed annual rental sufficient not only to provide a good return on the price paid for the property but to amortize it during the life of the lease, which may extend for twenty years or more.

Under the terms of the lease, the business concern, now the tenant, usually agrees to pay all operating expenses concerned with the proper maintenance of the property, keeping it insured and paying the taxes. Sometimes instead of a fixed rental, the rent may gradually decline in steps over the period. Options to repurchase at the end of the lease are rare because in that case the Internal Revenue Bureau might not allow the rent to be deducted as an expense in computing federal income taxes. Instead there is usually an option to renew the lease. Other terms of the lease provide for possible necessary alterations or improvements to the property. Purchasers of property under sale- and lease-back arrangements are usually colleges or other tax-free institutions which are seeking to invest endowment funds at a higher yield than that obtainable from bonds. Yields on the investment over and above amortization may be as high as 4 per cent.

Financing the small company. Strange though it may seem, the small company is usually much more difficult to finance than the large one. The very small enterprise is usually an individual proprietorship financed only by the personal wealth of the owner and by what loans he is able to procure on his personal credit. Most small proprietors have small wealth and little credit, and their businesses often suffer for lack of sufficient capital.

Partnerships, both general and limited, are in a better position to finance themselves, because if sound, they can continue to take in additional partners with cash and credit.

Small stock companies and corporations that depend for capital upon the sale of their securities to the public are, as a rule, particularly difficult to finance. They cannot obtain the services of investment bankers, because the total of their issues is too small to be handled profitably by these houses. Very few banking houses can be induced to handle any issue of less than a million dollars. The small issues cost practically as much to investigate, advertise, and market as do the larger ones, and the rate of commission is so low that on small issues all margins are eaten up by costs. The issuing company, therefore, has to attempt to sell its own securities. The organizers generally work among their relatives, friends, and business acquaintances; frequently employ independent salesmen; and often seek assistance through newspaper and magazine advertisements and through direct mail solicitation. If the proposition is thoroughly sound, the securities can generally be disposed of, but only with great difficulty and at a large expense, as compared with the easy disposal of large issues through the channels of the investment banks. Recent federal legislation has provided for the establishment of investment companies to advance funds to small companies. At this writing, there still remains need for further clarifying legislation before actual operations are likely to begin.

Questions for Study and Review

1. Aside from the sale of stocks and bonds, what other source of funds for long-term financing is very important?
2. As between financing with stock and with bonds, what additional advantages has borrowing other than that interest is usually lower than dividends?
3. Upon what legal bases is a corporation required to first offer new stock to old stockholders?
4. Most preemptive rights provide that the new stock may be purchased at less than market value during the period of the offering. Is this a legal requirement? If not, why does the corporation do it?
5. Suppose *rights* to subscribe to new stock were offered providing for purchase of new stock at the same market price as that of the outstanding shares. Would there ordinarily be any value to the right? Why?
6. In what two ways may a stockholder realize upon *rights?*
7. State and explain the formula for the value of preemptive rights on a *cum rights* basis?
8. State four conditions which will help to insure the success of an offering of stock by means of *rights.*
9. Name three purchasers of securities which may be classed as institutional investors. Which of the institutional investors is of the greatest importance in terms of dollar value of its investments?
10. Is the term *speculative securities* restricted to those of those new ventures? Explain.
11. What are Blue Sky Laws? Why may these laws be of concern to issuers of securities?
12. Does the fact that an issue of stock or bonds has met the registration requirements of the Securities and Exchange Commission insure that it is of good quality? Explain.

13. What does it mean to say that the sale of registered securities is to be by *prospectus only?*
14. What is the principal function of an investment banking house? What are the advantages to a corporation of employing the services of an investment banker in connection with the issuance of securities?
15. What does the term *standby underwriting* mean? Give an illustration and description of its use.
16. How does the purchase group function in handling a negotiated contract for the sale of securities? What is the difference between this group and the selling group?
17. Briefly describe competitive bidding for security issues.
18. What is direct or private placement? Why may it be advantageous to the issuing corporation?
19. How may listing of a corporation's securities on a stock exchange prove of advantage to the issuing corporation?
20. What is a stock purchase warrant? What do the terms *detachable* and *non-detachable* used in describing warrants refer to?
21. May stock purchase warrants be used for other purposes than to aid the sale of securities? Illustrate.
22. Why may it prove more difficult for a small corporation to market securities than for a large corporation selling an issue amounting to several millions of dollars?

Problems

1. Mr. Thomas owns 10,000 shares of the common stock of a corporation whose balance sheet shows the following accounts:

Capital Stock
      Common $50 par value, 100,000 shares authorized, 60,000
         shares issued $300,000
      Surplus $1,000,000

   (a) Calculate Mr. Thomas' interest in the corporation and the book value per share of his stock.
   (b) The corporation now proposes to issue an additional 30,000 shares of the common stock for sale directly to the public. Calculate his interest in the corporation and the book value per share of his stock after the issuance of the new stock.

2. A corporation has authorized common stock of 1,200,000 shares, all of which is outstanding. It proposes to increase the authorized stock by 300,000 shares and to offer these shares to the present stockholders through a privileged subscription at $90 a share.
   (a) Calculate the theoretical value of a right with the old stock selling at $97½ a share.
   (b) What disposition may a stockholder make of his rights?

3. In each of the following cases, determine how many rights are required to procure 1 share of the new stock and the value of a right:

	Number of Old Shares	Number of New Shares	Market Value of Old Share	Offering Value of New Shares
(a) Company A	1,000	200	$110	$103
(b) Company B	3,000	1,000	109	100
(c) Company C	4,000	2,000	120	110
(d) Company D	6,000	1,000	115	115

4. A corporation plans to offer $10,000,000 of debenture bonds for sale to the public, and at the same time 1,000,000 shares of common stock to the stockholders through "rights." Explain the part played by investment bankers in the sale of each security.

5. The Andrews Woolen Mills, Incorporated, has outstanding 7,000 shares of its 10,000 authorized shares of $100 par value stock. It is prosperous, having average annual net earnings of $150,000. It has no bonded indebtedness. The directors are anxious to enlarge and expand, but desire to issue bonds and to trade on the equity rather than simply to sell the remainder of the authorized stock. Bonds are not readily salable because of a current bull market in stocks. Devise a plan which might enable the company to dispose successfully of $500,000 of bonds.

Written Assignment

1. A corporation whose stock is selling at $77 per share announces that it is going to increase its stock from 1,000,000 to 1,250,000 shares and offer the new stock to old stockholders at $67 per share.

(a) What is the value of the preemptive right on the day of the announcement?

(b) The day the stock sells ex-rights, the market price is $76. What was the value of the right at that time?

(c) Why is the value of the right 25 cents higher?

CHAPTER **XII**

Financing Working Capital
Requirements

Fixed and current assets. The balance sheet of most business concerns will show two types of assets, known as *fixed* and *current*. Reading down on the asset side in the usual balance sheet presentation, the current assets are listed first, beginning with cash, the most liquid, down through inventories, which are usually the least liquid items. The fixed assets follow, listing plant, machinery and real estate.

The distinction between the two classes of assets is elementary. The fixed assets remain in the business as long as useful. As far as plant and machinery are concerned, this usually means until the asset has deteriorated to a point where efficient operation is no longer possible, or until it becomes so obsolete as to place the concern at a disadvantage in competition.

Current assets are distinguished by constant movement or change in a going business. Some authors, for this reason, have encouraged the use of the term *circulating assets* or *circulating capital* as more clearly defining the nature of such assets.[1] The cash of a new business, not in-

---

1 John Stuart Mill, in *Principles of Political Economy* (New York: Longmans, Green & Co., 1923), wrote:

"Of the capital engaged in the production of any commodity, there is a part which, after being once used, exists no longer as capital: is no longer capable of rendering service to production, or at least not the same service, nor to the same sort of production. Such, for example, is the portion of capital which consists of materials. The tallow and alkali of which soap is made, once used in the manufacture, are destroyed as alkali and tallow; and cannot be employed any further in the soap manufacture, though in their altered condition, as soap, they are capable of being used as a material or an instrument in other branches of manufacture. In the same division must be placed the portion of capital which is paid as the wages, or consumed as the subsistence, of laborers. The part of the capital of a cotton-spinner which he pays away to his work-people, once so paid, exists no longer as his capital, or as a cotton-spinner's capital; such portion of it as the workmen consume, no longer exists as capital at all; even

vested in fixed assets, is almost immediately, at least in part, used to acquire inventories, and later to pay labor and other costs connected with inventories. As the inventories are sold, the investment may be expressed as accounts receivable and finally, when the latter are collected, they become cash again and the cycle is repeated. As we shall later see, the problem of keeping this movement as rapid as possible, is one of constant concern to those responsible for managing the business.

Fixed and current liabilities. The fixed liabilities usually consist of amounts due the lenders on debts having more than a year to run and the proprietor's investment in a corporation, the outstanding stock. Here, too, we find the surplus which, if unimpaired in the process of liquidation, must all be paid to the owners should the business cease operations and dispose of its assets.

Current liabilities are usually stated at the outset on the liability side of a balance sheet. All debts to be paid during the year, such as short-term loans, trade debts such as notes and accounts payable, accrued payroll, accrued taxes and the like, are to be found listed as current liabilities.

The exact nature of the various items found listed as current liabilities, as well as the current assets described above, will vary somewhat depending upon the type of business and even in one concern usually change from season to season within a year. A better understanding of the usual balance sheet presentation may be obtained by study of the simplified balance sheet seen below.

The current ratio. The ratio of the current assets to the current liabilities is known as the *current ratio.* This ratio is often used to test the adequacy of working capital. In fact, it is often erroneously stated that

---

if they save any part, it may now be more properly regarded as a fresh capital, the result of a second act of accumulation.

"Capital which, in this manner, fulfills the whole of its office in the production in which it is engaged by a single use, is called *Circulating Capital.* The term, which is not very appropriate, is derived from the circumstance that this portion of capital requires to be constantly renewed by the sale of the finished product, and when renewed is perpetually parted with in buying materials and paying wages; so that it does its work, not by being kept, but by changing hands.

"Another large portion of capital, however, consists in instruments of production, of a more or less permanent character; which produce their effect not by being parted with, but by being kept; and the efficacy of which is not exhausted by a single use. To this class belong buildings, machinery, and all or most things known by the name of implements or tools. The durability of some of these is considerable, and their function as productive instruments is prolonged through many repetitions of the productive operation. In this class must likewise be included capital sunk (as the expression is) in permanent improvements of land. So, also, the capital expended once and for all, in the commencement of an undertaking, to prepare the way for subsequent operations: the expense of opening a mine, for example; of cutting canals; of making roads or docks. Other examples might be added, but these are sufficient. Capital which exists in any of these durable shapes, and the return to which is spread over a period of corresponding duration, is called *Fixed Capital.*"

JOHN DOE MANUFACTURING CO.
Balance Sheet, December 31, 19—

Cash		$20,000	Notes Payable	$ 8,000
Notes Receivable		1,000	Accounts Payable	10,500
Accounts Receivable $ 5,000			Accrued Payroll	2,000
Less Res. for				
Bad Debts	150	4,850		
Inventories:				
Raw Materials ... $ 9,000				
Work in Process .. 3,000				
Finished Goods .. 8,000		20,000		
Total Current Assets		$45,850	Total Current Liabilities ...	$20,500
Land		8,000	First Mortgage	14,000
Buildings $10,000			Common Stock	20,000
Less Res. for Deprec. 3,000		7,000	Surplus	12,350
Machinery and				
Equipment $10,000				
Less Res. for Deprec. 4,000		6,000		
		$66,850		$66,850

the adequate current ratio should be two to one; that is, that the current assets should be at least twice the current liabilities. No such standard can be established. The current ratio is not a test of the adequacy of working capital. It merely indicates the extent to which the current assets may decline and still be sufficient to take care of the current liabilities. It will vary according to the type of business. <u>A concern that has a rapid turnover of its current assets will usually require a smaller excess of current assets over current liabilities than one with a slower turnover.</u> But, in practice, the current ratio shows a wide variation, as illustrated by the following examples:

	American Can Co.	Sears Roebuck & Co.	du Pont de Nemours & Co.	Swift & Co.	General Motors Corporation	United States Steel Co.	Detroit Edison Co.
1948	2.11	2.55	4.73	2.79	2.35	1.93	2.69
1949	2.00	2.54	5.17	3.76	3.60	2.06	1.92
1950	1.66	3.12	4.56	3.45	2.95	1.69	1.53
1951	2.19	2.38	4.77	2.92	2.84	1.38	2.66
1952	3.18	3.13	4.91	2.51	2.25	1.48	1.40
1953	3.82	3.12	5.26	2.76	2.21	1.42	1.43
1954	2.92	3.48	5.56	3.55	2.26	2.31	1.25
1955	2.77	3.61	5.21	2.57	2.54	2.07	1.08
1956	2.68	3.58	5.40	2.23	2.44	1.84	1.10
1957	2.53	2.98	5.49	2.41	2.61	1.90	1.44
10 yr. Average	2.59	3.05	5.11	2.90	2.61	1.81	1.65

In comparing similar businesses or in contrasting present conditions with those in the past, the ratio has value; but it should not be assumed that a standard can be established that is applicable to all types of business. In determining the amount of working capital a concern should have, many factors must be given consideration. These same factors, rather than the current ratio, are to be weighed when testing the adequacy of working capital in a going concern.

The cash position. Many persons use the term *cash position* to mean the same thing as working capital. The terms are not synonymous. The *cash position* of a business is expressed by the ratio of cash on hand and in banks to bank loans. There is no standard, although the usual requirement of the banks that bank balances equal about 20 per cent of the bank loans suggests that the ratio should at least approximate this figure.

The quick ratio. Another ratio used in testing the current position of a business is the ratio of cash plus receivables to current liabilities. This ratio is known as the *quick ratio.* Inventories are omitted from the current assets in computing this ratio because of the probable time lag in converting them to cash. Should sales decline the delay might be serious, making it impossible for a concern to pay its short-term debts when due. This ratio is sometimes called the *acid test*. As in the case of the current ratio, there is no standard generally applicable.

Working capital. The term *working capital* is not always defined in the same way. Businessmen are more than likely to use it to mean the *total of the current assets*. Members of the accounting profession usually disagree with this definition and state that working capital is the *excess of current assets over the current liabilities*. The difficulty arises through the use of the word *capital,* a word which is given many meanings. To be consistent, the accountant must deduct the current liabilities from the current assets to arrive at the working capital, for does he not define "capital" as "net worth" (the assets less the debts of the business)? In our discussion, we shall consider working capital to be the total current assets of the business and shall refer to the excess of current assets over current liabilities as the *net working capital.* Standard and Poor's Corporation, in classifying accounts in its various financial services, uses the term "net working capital" as defined above. Moody's Investors Service avoids the word "capital" by using in its financial manuals, the term *net current assets.*

It is important that the following discussion be based on a definite definition of working capital or otherwise one must abandon the term entirely which, in view of its widespread use, we are reluctant to do. We prefer to use it as synonymous with current assets for we may then, as most businessmen do, treat both short- and long-term financing as sources of working capital.

Regular working capital. No concern may safely operate without at least a part, and usually the largest part, of its working capital obtained from permanent or long-term sources so that it represents an integral part of the investment in the business. Such working capital is usually contributed by the owners, either as part of the original investment or through profits retained in the business. Semi-permanent sources of regular working capital are usually represented by funds obtained through the sale of bonds. How much of a concern's assets should be represented by regular working capital is not subject to exact or even approximate computation by mathematical formula. It depends upon many factors, some tangible and some intangible. Experience in a certain type of business, or studies of certain types of business, may show relationships between the amount of fixed and current assets. Such a ratio, however, will apply to the business under study and may or may not apply to a business of a different nature. Certainly, (one rule capable of general application would be that the amount so invested should be limited to that which can be profitably employed and which is necessary for the ordinary operation and plans of the business, including a reasonable margin of safety for emergencies.)

Seasonal working capital. In many lines of business, operations are highly seasonal and, as a result, working capital requirements vary greatly during the year. Were the management to maintain at all times sufficient working capital to finance peak seasonal needs, there would be times when the amount of idle cash on hand would be uneconomical, and the return on the business investment would suffer. Sometimes a business can offset the seasonal variations in one line of business by diversification; in other words, through carrying on more than one kind of business, a company can offset one seasonal peak with another. This, for many concerns, is not possible. In order to finance the additional working capital needs for peak seasons, short-term sources such as bank loans may be relied on; accounts receivable may be pledged for loans, or sold to a factor.[2] Various means of financing such as these will be discussed in detail later on in this chapter.

Factors affecting working capital requirements. No definite rule can be established for determining the working capital requirements of a business. A business should always have enough of a margin of current assets over current liabilities to make sure that it can pay its bills as they come due. How large this margin should be depends on many factors. It has been shown that the requirements of a business in this respect are not always the same. They vary not only from year to year, but also from

---

[2] While sources of working capital may usually be found to finance an unexpected increase in volume of business, a shortage of working capital caused by a decline in business may not be so easy to remedy, especially through the use of short-term borrowed money because lenders are reluctant to advance funds under such circumstances.

month to month. The requirements vary, also, depending on the type of business. In order to determine the proper amount of working capital a concern should have, careful consideration should be given to the following factors:

1. General type of business.
2. Turnover of receivables.
3. Turnover of inventories.
4. Relation of the terms of purchase and sale.
5. Seasonal variations in the industry.
6. Normal rate of expansion in the volume of business.
7. Banking connections.

A brief discussion of these factors may help to show their importance.

1. *The general type of business.* If the business is one dealing in such staple products as the necessities of life, demand is likely to be uniformly steady in periods of general business depression, as well as in periods of general prosperity. The inflow of cash at all times will probably be sufficient to take care of current liabilities, and there will be required a smaller margin of working capital over the amount of current liabilities. The same is true of most public utilities, largely for the same reason. Their services are always in demand and, also, are usually on a cash basis. Their income generally has sufficient regularity to meet the current liabilities as they become due. Thus, such businesses do not require a large reserve of net working capital.

2. *Turnover of accounts receivable.* The turnover of accounts receivable, or the average time during which accounts are unpaid, depends almost entirely upon the terms of sale. In periods of business depression, turnover of accounts receivable often is slowed up because of difficulties in collecting bills. Terms of sale in different lines are often dictated by hard to break customs. If terms are long, it means that a large part of the current assets may be tied up in customers' accounts. Accounts-receivable turnover, therefore, becomes an important factor in estimating the amount of working capital a concern should have. The turnover of accounts-receivable outstanding may be ascertained through the use of two simple formulas:

$$\text{Accounts-receivable turnover} = \frac{\text{Credit sales for period}}{\text{Average accounts-receivable outstanding}}$$

$$\text{Average length of period of accounts-receivable outstanding} = \frac{360 \text{ days}}{\text{Accounts-receivable turnover}}$$

3. *Turnover of inventories.* Inventories in a retail, jobbing, or wholesale establishment usually are of one kind: finished goods in a marketable state. In the case of a manufacturing establishment, however, inventories are of three kinds: first, inventories of the raw material to be consumed in the manufacture of the product; second, the goods or work in

process, the value of which is made up of the cost of raw material used plus the labor and expenses incurred up to the date of taking inventory; third, the finished goods, which represent the amount of completed products on hand. Inventories should be carried on the books at cost or market price, whichever happens to be lower.

In a manufacturing concern, turnover must be computed on each of these inventories; and in so doing, the following formulas are helpful:

$$\text{Raw material turnover} = \frac{\text{Amount of goods going into process during the period}}{\text{Average raw materials inventory during the period}}$$

$$\text{Work in process turnover} = \frac{\text{Amount of work in process transferred to finished product}}{\text{Average work in process inventory during period}}$$

$$\text{Finished goods turnover} = \frac{\text{Cost of goods sold}}{\text{Average finished goods inventory at cost}}$$

Probably no factor is so important in most cases from a working capital standpoint as the turnover of inventories. Inventories are usually the least liquid of current assets, and they are subject to price depreciation, deterioration, and other hazards. A concern that has a large inventory and that is going into a period of business decline, accompanied by a falling of prices, faces a serious working capital problem. Almost every business depression begins with a period in which declining sales are accompanied by price cutting or efforts are made to liquidate inventories. Severe losses of working capital result, causing failures of concerns which do not have sufficient reserves to meet current bills.

Sometimes the very nature of the business is such that inventories are large and turnover is slow. This is true, for instance, of the leather manufacturing business, where the process period is very long. Businesses having slow inventory turnover are likely to have a relatively larger amount of their capital tied up in inventories. Since this item is large, more working capital is required in the form of cash and accounts receivable in order to meet the current liabilities as they come due.

4. *Relation of the terms of purchase and sale.* If the terms on which goods are purchased on credit correspond closely to the terms of sale, receivables are liquidated as bills come due. This is of particular significance in a business in which purchases of raw materials constitute the main cost of doing business. When this is the situation and goods are purchased on credit, those from whom the goods are purchased are financing the carrying of the accounts receivable. Trade credit, although not increasing the amount of net working capital, delays the conversion of cash into inventories and makes possible the carrying on of a larger volume of business without additions to a concern's net working capital. The granting of credit to customers delays the turnover of current assets

and thus may require a larger amount of working capital to carry on business.

5. *Seasonal nature of the business.* Concerns that experience wide variations of activity from season to season usually have to augment working capital with bank loans, or other means of current financing, so as to carry over peak seasons. In preparing for such seasons, it is usually necessary to build up high inventories, and it is not economical, in view of the practice of rewarding prompt cash payments with substantial discounts, to finance inventories with trade credit. However, to keep enough net working capital to handle peak needs may also be uneconomical, for it means that there may be many months when capital will be idle. A compromise is to have enough net working capital to keep good bank credit, and finance inventories, in part, through short term bank loans.

6. *Normal rate of expansion in the nature of business.* An expanding business will require increases in working capital proportionate to the rate of expansion. Especially should the management avoid the temptation to utilize cash needed for working capital to acquire fixed assets or to borrow on short term for this purpose. No increase in volume of operations should be planned unless working capital to finance the expansion is available.

7. *Banking connections.* A concern that has established substantially good banking connections and enjoys the confidence of commercial bankers may rely on financing temporary expansion of current assets with bank loans. As long as the amount of working capital is adequate for average needs, the use of bank loans as a means of financing current assets is proper and has much to commend it. The fact that a high proportion of ordinary, unsecured, commercial bank loans are made for this purpose is indicative of the soundness of the practice.

Sources of working capital. The various sources of working capital require some explanation as to sheer suitability and the problems they involve. A list of the most important sources follows:

A. Sources of long-term working capital financing.
    1. Capital invested by owners (sale of stock, etc.).
    2. Long-term borrowing (sale of bonds, etc.).
    3. Accumulated profits invested in current assets.
    4. Sale of fixed assets no longer needed in the business.
    5. Depreciation allowances on fixed assets.
B. Sources of intermediate working capital financing.
    1. Term loans.
    2. Loans made by U. S. Government agencies (Small Business Administration).
    3. Federal Reserve Bank direct loans to business.
C. Sources of short-term working capital financing.
    1. Trade credit in the form of:
        a. accounts payable

    b. notes payable
    c. trade acceptances
  2. Bank loans
    a. unsecured
    b. secured by collateral
  3. Bankers' acceptances.
  4. Sale of commercial paper in the open market.

Working capital financing from long-term sources. The process of financing through the sale of stocks and bonds has been discussed in Chapter XI. A new business is usually restricted to the sale of stock until a record of successful operations has established credit acceptable to the bond market. Some businesses, such as utilities, which may be expected to enjoy stable or increasing earnings from the outset and where there is a substantial investment in productive assets may include bonds in their initial public financing.

American concerns regularly retain substantial amounts of annual earnings in the business. In fact, for many of this country's growing industries, large and small, retained earnings form a steady source of new capital, a portion of which may, if needed, be kept in the form of current assets.

Through the practice of providing for depreciation of plant, equipment or other fixed assets, and through depletion reserved out of earnings in extractive industries (see Chapter XIV), there is what amounts to an annual flow of investment from fixed to current asset status. The immediate result as shown by a concern's asset accounts is a decline in the amount of the fixed, and a corresponding increased investment in current, assets. Of course, there is no assurance that the amount contributed to current assets by depreciation or depletion will long remain there. The former may be used to replace old or increase the amount of fixed assets and the latter expanded in development of additional extractive properties. This is a matter determined by the management.

Intermediate term sources of working capital. This term is used to refer to sources of borrowed funds having more than one year and usually not more than five years to maturity. Term loans to be described in the following paragraph represent this type of financing. More broadly, short-term bonds of serial nature with the longest maturity ten years or less· should also be thought of as intermediate term financing. In use they· represent an addition to net working capital which is decreased each year by the current installment due and paid on the debt. It is contemplated that the earnings each year will be sufficient to pay the installment. If this is the plan, then the use of this source is equivalent to a present commitment of future earnings for net working capital purposes.

Term loans. Technically a term loan is for a period in excess of one year. In practice, three to five years is most common. A universal characteristic is a contractual obligation of the borrower to repay the loan in regular installments which may be quarterly, semiannual, or annual. The usual sources are banks and insurance companies. They may be secured or unsecured; however, some security, except to large concerns of unquestioned credit standing, is usually demanded. Other conditions, such as restrictions on dividends, use of the borrowed funds, salary limitations, etc., are often stipulated. Borrowers and lenders negotiate contracts, sometimes through a third party who acts for the borrower, and the terms may be varied to suit the particular situation. Occasionally the term may be as long as ten years. As commercial banks are usually reluctant to enter into loan contracts for so long a term, part of the loan, that to be paid during the last five years, may be shared with an insurance company.

The Federal Government made many such loans during the business depression and later in financing concerns engaged in defense contracts through the Reconstruction Finance Corporation. After this governmental agency discontinued operations, the Small Defense Plants Administration, another government agency lending to small manufacturers to finance government defense contracts, was reorganized into the Small Business Administration and continued lending to business on a term loan basis. The ostensible purpose of government lending, at the present time, is to provide financing to small and medium sized business concerns which do not have ready access to the capital markets or other sources of funds enjoyed by larger units. Much emphasis, in recent years, has been placed upon the desirability of assisting small business to participate in government defense contracts. During the depression years of the nineteen thirties, government loans through the Reconstruction Finance Corporation were extended to private business to spur business activity and reduce unemployment. Like the term loan contracts made with banks and insurance companies, the government attempts to safeguard each loan by suiting the terms of the contract to the particular circumstances in each case. Frequently, such loans are secured by mortgages in addition to provisions and restrictions similar to those of private lenders.

Because term loans are repayable in installments, the installment due during the current year represents a current liability and serves to reduce net working capital by the amount of the current installment and, of course, when it is paid, the working capital also.

Trade credit. Business in this country makes extensive use of trade credit, chiefly in the form of accounts receivable. Notes payable and trade acceptances are not often used by most concerns. From the point of view of the purchaser of goods on an open book credit basis, it is usually an expensive source of working capital. Terms usually provide that a discount may be taken if the goods are paid for within a prescribed discount period. A common arrangement is that of permitting the purchaser to take a discount if the goods are paid for within ten days following the date of the invoice. Sometimes other arrangements are made where many transactions take place each month. For example, "MOM" or middle of month, terms usually permit the discount to be taken on all purchases made to the fifteenth, if paid by a stipulated date, usually the twenty-fifth of the month. These terms are used in connection with "EOM" or end-of-month billing, which permits the buyer to take a discount if payment is made before the tenth of the month following, on purchases made between the fifteenth and the end of the month. It is the practice of allowing a discount for each payment that makes trade credit on an open account basis so expensive. While terms of sale vary in different trades, perhaps the terms, 2 per cent 10 days, net 30, sometimes expressed 2/10,n 30, are most common. On this basis, the buyer has thirty days from the invoice date or from a stipulated date to pay the bill, but may deduct 2 per cent if he pays the bill within the first ten days. Should he take the full thirty days, he is in effect sacrificing 2 per cent on the face of the bill in order to keep his money twenty days longer. Two per cent for twenty days is equivalent to approximately 36 per cent per annum, a really high rate for the privilege of using the purchased goods or their proceeds as working capital. In many businesses where profit margins are low and competition great, failure to take advantage of each discount may mean the difference between profit or loss. Nevertheless, for the small businessman, trade credit may be easier to obtain than bank loans and may permit a larger volume of business to be transacted with a much smaller investment in net working capital.

Few lines of business make use of an ordinary promissory note to support trade credit transactions. Sometimes delinquent debtors are required to sign promissory notes for the amount of the unpaid account. Credit analysts are inclined to view the presence of a notes payable item on a concern's balance sheet with suspicion and the notes receivable item on a vendor's balance sheet as possible evidence of unwise credit extension or a poor collection policy.

Trade acceptances are time drafts drawn by a seller of merchandise on the buyer for the amount of the invoice and *accepted* by the buyer. Acceptance consists of the drawee writing and signing across the face of the draft the words, "Accepted, payable at the ———— Bank" on a stipulated date. The acceptance is then returned to the seller, who may hold it to maturity and ask his bank to collect it or discount it before maturity at his bank. Discounting before maturity gives the effect of increasing the rate of turnover of receivables, thereby reducing the amount of net working capital necessary. While the acceptor, by his acceptance of the draft, becomes the primary obligor, the seller who discounts the note is secondarily liable to the bank should the buyer fail to pay the acceptance, upon presentation. Where the buyer is unknown or has no credit standing, it may be assumed that the discounting bank looks chiefly at the seller's endorsement rather than at the buyer's acceptance for security. Although the use of trade acceptances has been vigorously advocated, they have not been generally used as a credit instrument in the domestic trade of this country. Buyers are inclined to look upon the instrument as a device to aid the seller only, and competitive conditions have prevented vendors from insisting on its use. It is, therefore, not one of the important ways of obtaining working capital through trade credit.

Bank loans as a source of working capital. The principal source of short-term working capital required to meet seasonal needs, other than temporary conditions requiring additional working capital, is the short-term bank loan. Short-term bank loans are those repayable within a year. Most banks require that the short-term or liquid nature of such a loan be demonstrated by repayment at a maturity short of a year and that the business be out of debt to the bank at least one month out of the year. As a matter of practice, loans are usually for a shorter period than eleven months and are renewed within that period as required. The term *self-liquidating* is often used in describing the nature and utilization of short-term bank loans. This means that the proceeds of the loan will be used for a purpose which is expected to provide funds for repayment of the loan at maturity. An illustration would be a loan to a retailer to stock additional goods for the holiday trade, the sale of which automatically provides the means of repayment.

Proper use of bank loans may greatly increase a concern's profit and make it unnecessary to maintain as large a net working capital investment as would be necessary if such a short-term source were not available.

Bankers' acceptances. This method of short-term financing which is used as a method of financing the acquisition of inventories is more common to exporters and importers than it is to the domestic field. By the former it is used to finance imports and exports of all types of goods whether finished manufactured articles or bulk raw materials. In domestic trade, it is more likely to be used to finance large shipments, usually carload lots of raw materials such as cotton. To a vendor, it represents a method by which he obtains cash for his goods immediately upon shipment and to the purchaser a method of obtaining inventory with payment deferred until later, perhaps until he has sold the goods or converted them ready for sale.

Reduced to its simplest terms, a transaction involving the use of a banker's acceptance is accomplished in the following manner. Having ascertained that a supplier has the goods or commodity meeting the desired specifications in the quantity desired but requires payment at time of shipment, the buyer goes to his bank and makes application for a commercial letter of credit to be established in favor of the seller covering the proposed shipment. If the application is favorably considered by the bank, an agreement is drawn up and signed whereby the bank agrees to permit the vendor to draw drafts for the amount of each shipment which will be *accepted* by the buyer's bank. This acceptance makes the bank the primary obligor and responsible for the payment of the draft when due. The agreement will specify the terms of the shipment and the papers to accompany the draft, usually the invoice, government inspection certificate, if required, evidence of insurance, and an order bill of lading frequently naming the bank as the consignee. The buyer also agrees to pay the bank the amount involved in time to meet the draft. Frequently, additional matters are included, such as providing that the goods will be stored in a public warehouse upon arrival until required or sold, the bank in the meantime retaining the warehouse receipts as security. The bank then notifies the seller either directly or through a correspondent bank in the place of shipment that shipments may be made according to the terms specified. The seller draws the draft which he may discount with the correspondent bank. The buyer's bank has usually issued to the local bank an irrevocable credit in which it has agreed to honor all drafts drawn according to the established terms. Sometimes the local bank adds its promise to honor the drafts in any event, whether the issuing bank does or not. This is called *confirmation* and the credit is thus said to be irrevocable and confirmed.

No money has actually been advanced to the buyer. The funds obtained by the seller came from the sale or discounting of the draft. What the buyer has obtained is working capital in the form of goods; he has borrowed the use of his bank's credit on the basis of his own credit or the value of the goods. Because the drafts are obligations of banks, the discount rate is normally lower than that on any other type of commercial paper. The buyer pays his bank a charge or commission for accepting, which may be about ¼ of 1 per cent for a ninety-day draft equivalent to 1 per cent a year. It would appear that the use of a banker's acceptance, where feasible, is a very economical method of financing inventory. However, as is very often the case, where the goods have to be stored in a public warehouse and the receipts given to the bank as security, the storage fees and handling charges may amount to considerably more.

Commercial paper as a source of working capital. The term *commercial paper* is applied to unsecured promissory notes which, instead of being discounted with the borrower's bank, are sold to or discounted with a commercial paper dealer. Concerns dealing in commercial paper are called *commercial paper houses*. They may operate in this market exclusively or this function may be carried on by a department of a financial house primarily engaged in the security business. The large finance companies handling automobile installment paper are large users of this market but place much of their paper directly with banks rather than with dealers (see Federal Reserve Bulletin).

This type of financing is not usually utilized by other than medium and large sized concerns, with well established reputations for stability and generally accepted credit standing. Because the dealer does not endorse the paper, he must sell it on the reputation of the issuer only. Therefore, to command a speedy market, the issuer's credit must be widely accepted. Discount rates are usually quoted as applicable to "best names" and "other names." "Best name" paper is also referred to as prime commercial paper and is that issued by concerns quite well known and of high credit rating. "Other names" represent concerns of excellent credit rating but not as well known, perhaps smaller and possibly engaged in a business activity not regarded as sufficiently stable to command the highest rating.

Negotiations with a dealer for the sale of commercial paper brings about a careful credit investigation on the part of the dealer. While the dealer does not guarantee the paper through an endorsement, his reputation in the business depends upon the care and the thoroughness of the credit investigation of those concerns whose paper is purchased. The dealer charges a fee for handling the paper, usually ⅛ to ¼ per cent. He may also profit from disposing of the paper at a slightly lower rate of discount than that at which it was acquired.

The dealer sells the paper promptly, most of it to banks, some of whom rely entirely upon the credit investigation of the dealer. Other banks may demand and receive the right in the contract of purchase to return the paper to the dealer within ten days if upon their own appraisal they are dissatisfied with the credit of the issuer.

The notes usually bear a three to six months' maturity. The agreed-upon total amount to be discounted may be divided into notes with denominations in round numbers varying from $2,500 to amounts as high as $100,000. The dealer, in specifying the denomination, has in mind, of course, the probable desires of his customers. If the customer clientele consists of small and medium sized banks, he will ask the borrower to prepare notes of the smaller denomination.

Advantages of using commercial paper as a source of working capital. Users of commercial paper may anticipate the following advantages over the use of ordinary bank loans.

1. The amount borrowed may be larger than that obtainable under the usual bank "line of credit" agreement. Banks are limited by banking law as to the amount that may be lent to one borrower. Even were there no such restrictions, banks prudently seek to diversify their loans and might deem the desired loan too large an amount to risk in one type of business. Commercial paper issued by the business will probably be placed by the dealer among a number of banks.[3]

---

[3] It should perhaps be noted that some large loans are negotiated with a number of banks. Usually the borrower's bank aids in obtaining the participation of other banks.

(2) The borrower received the full amount borrowed less the discount and the dealer's fee, whereas his bank might insist that he maintain a non-interest demand deposit of from 10 to 20 per cent as a compensating balance.

(3) The discount rate, on prime paper at least, is usually less than the rate on ordinary bank loans and usually always less than the net cost of bank loans when the compensating balance requirement is considered (see Chapter XIII).

(4) The credit standing of the borrower is enhanced by the use of comercial paper. As it would be futile to try to market such paper unless the buyer had an excellent credit standing, the presence in the market of a concern's paper advertises to all users the good credit of the issuer.

(5) Borrowing through the sale of commercial paper is not subject to local or regional credit stringencies which might interfere with or make bank borrowing expensive. Commercial paper enjoys a national market not likely to be affected by regional conditions.

(6) There is no obligation to clean up all loans periodically. The sale may be continuous.

Disadvantages. Not withstanding the above, it is generally understood that commercial paper may offer some disadvantages to the user.

(1) It is discounted in what may be termed a "fair weather" market. When trade conditions are poor or credit conditions stringent, it may be practically impossible to sell commercial paper. It is then that it may be realized that good banking connections are valuable. A concern's bank, where relationships with the firm extend over a considerable period of time and which have been profitable to the bank, will even in adversity be likely to continue to try to finance a customer whom it knows well and in whom it has a high degree of confidence.

(2) Banks which buy commercial paper expect and demand prompt payment at maturity. The personal relationship between borrower and lender is absent. If the borrowing concern lacks funds to pay, it probably will have to endeavor to sell a new issue of commercial paper to retire the maturing obligations. Should it appear that the concern's financial condition has deteriorated, this may be difficult or the discount rate may be higher than the rate on prime paper.

(3) It is a source not open to the small concern and often not to concerns of medium size. For successful operations, it generally is restricted to large concerns with a wide reputation. The disadvantage is, of course, one not applicable to those concerns which make use of this medium of financing, rather it points out a lack of availability to many who might wish to use it.

Methods of increasing turnover of inventories and receivables. It has been shown that the rate of turnover of receivables and inventories has a direct bearing upon the amount of working capital a concern should

have. If turnover can be speeded up, these assets are more rapidly converted into cash and the proceeds available to pay the concern's bills.
Some of the methods used in accomplishing such action are the following:

1. Special sales.
2. Discounting of trade acceptances and customers' notes.
3. Hypothecation of accounts receivable.
4. Commercial factoring.
5. Inventory financing.
6. Granting discounts as a reward for cash payments on goods sold.
7. Discounting installment paper.

Each of these methods will be discussed briefly.

1. *Special sales*. Retail merchants constantly use this method of keeping their stock moving. Special sales at reduced prices are advertised in
the papers daily, since rapid turnover not only helps out the working
capital situation, but also increases profits. Department heads and buyers
pride themselves on maintaining a rapid merchandise turnover. The
practice is not limited to retailers, however. Many manufacturers facing
large, accumulated inventories or wishing to speed up business in slack
seasons reduce prices and advertise unduly. A period of declining business is especially marked by such sales, when merchants and manufacturers attempt to liquidate inventories that are becoming *frozen* from
lack of demand.

2. *Discounting of trade acceptances and customers' promissory notes.*
The use of a promissory note as a means of paying for inventories is not
generally used in this country where the unevidenced open-book account
is so widely used in buying goods on a credit basis. In fact, the presence
on a balance sheet of any considerable amount of notes payable might,
as suggested previously, lead a credit analyst to suspect that because
prompt payment of bills was not forthcoming, the purchaser had been
asked by the vendors to sign notes for overdue accounts. Promissory notes
are used in some instances by vendors of commodities in large quantities
where the terms granted may be long and the vendor desires a credit
instrument which he may discount with his bank, thus increasing the
turnover of accounts receivable.

Although the use of trade acceptances has from time to time been
vigorously advocated as a better way of selling goods on credit than the
present almost universal use of the open book charge account, it is not,
as previously pointed out, found in many lines of business. To the buyer,
it is a means of obtaining working capital in the form of merchandise. To
the seller who discounts the acceptance, it is a means of speeding up his
accounts receivable turnover.

3. *Hypothecation of accounts receivable.* Finance companies and some
commercial banks will lend funds against pledged accounts receivable.

Depending upon such factors as the nature of the product, the past collection record, the character of the management, and the volume of receivables, amounts up to 90 per cent of the face value of receivables may be borrowed at costs ranging from an annual rate 8 to 18 per cent on average advances. Customers are usually not notified of the pledge of the accounts, and the borrower agrees to turn over all receipts on pledged accounts to the lender as soon as received.

4. *Commercial factoring.* Accounts receivable may be sold to concerns known as *commercial factors.* Such sales are usually made without recourse and on a *notification* basis, *i.e.*, the customer is notified to pay to the factors. Originally chiefly used in the textile industry, this method of financing has had a much wider use in the last two decades. Factors perform a variety of services for the concerns they serve, such as rendering invoices, checking credit of customers and the like. Total costs for such services may vary and are a matter of private contract. However, the practice of charging 6 to 7 per cent on actual funds advanced is usual, with a typical additional charge of 1 to 2 per cent for such services as those mentioned above. The factor contracts to pay the vendor for the accounts within ten days of the average due date.[4] If desired, the factor will advance money at the time of sale at an agreed-upon rate. This rate is almost always noncompetitive and the same with all factoring concerns. Many of a factor's clients do not require advances at the time the sale of the accounts receivable is made and are willing to wait until 10 days after the average due date for their money. In such circumstances, they are charged only a factoring service fee. The concern using this service has shifted to the factor the risks inherent to sales on a credit basis and the cost of billing, ledgering and collecting accounts receivable.

5. *Financing of inventories.* Inventories may be pledged as security for loans running from 60 to 85 per cent of the value of the goods pledged. In order to give the lender adequate security, the goods may be placed in a *bonded warehouse* and the warehouse receipts of the warehousing concern endorsed over to the lender by the borrower. A growing practice is that of *field warehousing,* which has the advantage of keeping the goods on or near the premises of the borrower. For example, certain space in the borrower's factory or warehouse may be turned over to the field warehousing concern, which, through a representative on the spot, issues warehouse receipts as the goods are deposited in a segregated space. These receipts are frequently nonnegotiable in form and are made out to the lender.

The representative is frequently a former employee of the borrower who is temporarily transferred to the payroll of the warehousing com-

---

[4] Computed on the basis of the earliest credit terms specified. For example, if terms are 2 per cent 10 days, net 30, the computation will be based on the 10-day period.

pany. Field warehousing costs seldom exceed 2 per cent of the value of the goods per annum and loans against receipts may be as low as 4 and seldom higher than 7 per cent, where the lenders are banks. Commercial finance companies and factors usually charge more, depending of course on the size of the loan and importance of the customer. In some fields, the advances made by factors and finance companies are secured by a lien usually referred to as a factors lien in favor of the lender. Trust receipts may be used in much the same manner, the borrower in effect declaring himself trustee for the goods and the proceeds for the benefit of the lender.

Bills of lading issued by steamship lines and common carriers when made out in *order* form may be used as security for advances. This is usually accomplished by attaching the bill of lading to a draft drawn upon the customer for the amount of the invoice. Insurance protecting against loss while the goods are in transit is usually required.

6. *Liberal cash discounts.* It is an almost general practice in this country to find discounts of from 2 to 5 per cent allowed for cash payment within 10 days of the date of the invoice. Although this reward is a large one, it probably has been allowed for in the selling price, and those who take the full credit period for payment fail to reap the advantage granted to others who pay cash. Since the taking of cash discounts offers a considerable saving, the effect is to reduce the number of credit sales and, hence, increase the accounts receivable turnover.

7. *Financing installment sales.* In many lines of business, a large part of retail sales are made on what is properly referred to as the installment plan. Ordinarily sales made on this basis, which are paid for in monthly installments spread over periods ranging from three months to extremely long terms of two or three years, would require tremendously large amounts of working capital. Certainly, this popular method of doing business depends for its success upon the means which have been developed for financing a more rapid turnover of funds initially committed by the business to installment sales.

A retailer sells goods to a customer on an installment contract which is in effect a conditional sales contract, in which the buyer has obligated himself to make periodic installment payments on the purchase price. Failure to meet such payments automatically reverts title to the merchandise sold in this manner to the vendor or his assignee and the whole may be repossessed.

The vendor making installment sales normally requires a cash down payment and assesses an additional charge against the purchaser known as the finance charge. By prior arrangement, such contracts are usually immediately sold to a sales finance company or bank. The vendor receives the amount of the contract less the discount or finance charge of the finance company. Because the vendor usually adds the finance charge to the amount of the purchase contract on all installment sales, the net amount received by the vendor is equivalent to a sale for cash.

Several types of arrangements are made by installment vendors and the finance companies. If the installment paper is taken by the finance company "without recourse," then the latter has no claim on the vendor upon default. If "with recourse" upon default, the contractual obligation of the buyer is returned by the finance company to the vendor for the unpaid balance. Another type of arrangement, especially found in the automobile business, is the so-called "repurchase" contract. Here the finance company must repossess the article upon default of the purchaser and then may return it to the vendor for the unpaid balance of the purchase price.

Until recent years, vendors had to depend upon the sales finance companies to market their installment contracts. Of recent years, banks, large and small, have entered the business and many commercial credit companies and factoring companies have established departments which handle sales finance paper.

Department stores and mail order houses making many sales of general merchandise on a budget or time payment plan are usually unable to discount or sell such contracts to a finance company in the usual way. Customers make payments directly to the vendor who maintains the accounts. Sales on these terms may include all types of merchandise and are not limited by vendors to durable goods. Receivables of this type are financed by pledging them for loans similar to the non-notification process discussed under *hypothecation of accounts receivable.* Large merchandisers often obtain what in effect is a sort of revolving credit, with continuous outstanding loans covered by an ever-changing portfolio of outstanding sales contracts.

Advantages of sufficient net working capital. The proprietor of a business or the officials of a corporation who can go home at night and sleep in peace and comfort without worrying about how wages and salaries are going to be met the next day enjoy a position in business that can come only as a result of efficient management that has provided adequate working capital. Consequently, while perhaps the most important advantage of sufficient net working capital—the feeling of security and confidence that should come to every well-managed and successful business —is more or less intangible, there are, nevertheless, a number of really tangible advantages open to the business with sufficient ready working capital and strong lines of credit that may be drawn upon when needed. These may be briefly enumerated as follows:

1. A real sense of security, resulting from a sufficient amount of working capital on hand, will create confidence and loyalty not only throughout the business itself, but also among its customers, creditors, and business associates.

2. Advantage may be taken of cash discounts in the purchase of raw materials or merchandise, resulting in a saving in interest charges on the amount of working capital employed.

3. A strong credit position can be maintained, enabling the company to rest securely in the confidence of its bankers, who, in turn, will be more willing to lend the cash for seasonal working capital needs at favorable rates and on liberal terms without guaranty or indorsement.

4. The necessity of raising cash in periods of emergency makes it advantageous for a company always to carry a reasonable amount of surplus cash.

5. Advantage may be taken in purchasing raw materials, coal, or other factory supplies in a sharply advancing market, or in off-season periods, resulting in substantial savings where storage costs are not prohibitive.

Administration of current assets. The whole problem of the administration of cash and working capital is intimately and closely tied up with the almost limitless problems of cost accounting, organization, and management, but there seem to be certain guides that may be laid down. These general points, if they may be so called, may be summarized as follows:

1. Fixed administration expenses should be reduced to a minimum in order that the business may be as nearly elastic as are the business conditions affecting it and the country in general.

2. All processes of the business should be analyzed, logically synthesized, and applied to future plans and budgets.

3. The units in the several departments should be of such size that each department will be used to its full capacity. Thus, no unnecessary waste will occur.

4. Unnecessary and unproductive fixed operating assets should be salvaged and turned into cash.

5. The business should provide a dividend policy that will readily attract new capital.

6. The management must keep the credit of the company at the bank good for seasonal and emergency demands for cash.

7. The concern should use supplementary financial agencies (commercial paper broker, trade acceptance, factoring, etc.) for raising cash when expedient.

8. The management must provide enough initial working capital for every step in expansion to permit regular capital to perform its ordinary functions without undue strain.

9. The management must, also, provide ample regular working capital, through the sale of stocks and bonds, or through the plowing in of surplus earnings.

10. It is necessary to keep a cash budget, in order to forecast the demands for cash funds and the sources from which cash may be derived.

Sources and application of funds. Naturally every dollar of net profit and every dollar retained out of gross profits in the nature of reserves for depreciation will not reflect an increase in net working capital at the end of the period of operations concerned. Some of the earnings are disbursed as dividends, some expended for plant and equipment and other fixed assets. Earnings may be applied to a reduction of bonded indebtedness or used to retire preferred stock. This is clearly shown in the Summary of 1956 Financial Operations of the United States Steel Corporation printed in the 1956 annual report of the corporation. Working capital, as shown in this summary, represents the net working capital according to our definition. This would have shown an increase but for $225,000,000 reserved in the nature of a fund for additions and replacements. Other sections of this annual report show that this fund was invested in government securities, a fund which, including $300,000,000 reserved in previous years, totaled $500,000,000. The working capital summary for the following year of 1957 shows an increase in net working capital and also that the $500,000,000 funded reserve for plant and equipment has been reduced by $100,000,000, expended for this purpose. It may also be of interest to notice that this company does not include its holdings in government securities for the replacement fund among its current assets. It prefers to treat this fund, even though available for working capital, as though it had already been expended for fixed asset replacements. However, excess cash has also been invested in government securities and is shown as part of the current assets. There being nothing to indicate that the item of $269,185,070 in government securities shown in the 1957 financial position summary has been set aside for a particular purpose, it can for purposes of analysis be treated as part of the cash on hand.

Two items shown in the additions to working capital illustrate the shift from fixed assets to current assets which is normal in most business concerns. Wear and exhaustion of facilities (depreciation) are treated as expenses of operations and, like all other expenses, are charged against gross income in arriving at net income for the period. They also represent a deduction from the book value of plant and equipment, as shown at the beginning of the period. There has therefore been an internal change. The amount by which the plant and equipment has declined in book value has been offset by a charge against income of a similar amount resulting in an addition to the net working capital.

Likewise the proceeds from the sale and salvage of plant and equipment worn out and no longer needed is also a transfer of part of the fixed investment, as shown at the beginning of the period to net working capital.

The financial position and working capital summary of the operations of the United States Steel Corporation should demonstrate quite clearly that an analysis and management of the working capital of a business require study of the flow of funds throughout the business if a true picture is to be obtained.

Some cash expenditures do not decrease the assets but are represented by corresponding increases which may be found among the current assets—for example, inventories or, among the fixed assets, plant and equipment. Likewise, declines in current assets may represent only that the amount has been used to increase plant and equipment and proceeds from sale and salvage of plant and equipment may increase the current assets.

To gain a clear picture of the problems facing the management and particularly of the general flow of funds as represented by the total business investment and their effect upon cash flow, a comparative summary of balance sheet changes taken at various times, perhaps quarterly, during past years is helpful. This may be followed by estimates of changes anticipated in various balance sheet accounts in the future which will result if planned operations are carried out. Detailed studies such as this should go hand in hand with the preparation of the cash and financial budget discussed below. As a mechanism for financial management, comparison of actual results accompanied with careful investigation of the deviation of actual results from estimates is necessary if full value of these laborious analyses and forecasts is to be realized.[5]

SUMMARY OF 1956 FINANCIAL OPERATIONS

(from the annual report of the United States Steel Corporation, Dec. 31, 1956)

Additions to working capital		
Income		$348,098,916
Add—Wear and exhaustion of facilities		277,598,963
Proceeds from sales and salvage of plant and equipment		29,812,853
Proceeds from sale of common stock under Stock Option Incentive Plan		4,760,696
Total additions		660,271,428
Deductions from working capital		
Expended for plant and equipment	$311,792,037	
Set aside for property additions and replacements	225,000,000	
Reduction in total long-term debt	42,674,975	
Dividends declared on preferred and common stocks	170,103,878	
Miscellaneous deductions	2,102,834	
Total deductions		751,673,724
Reduction in working capital		$ 91,402,296
Working capital per consolidated statement of financial position		
December 31, 1956	$603,739,028	
December 31, 1955	695,141,324	
Reduction		$ 91,402,296

[5] See Howard and Upton, *Introduction to Business Finance* (New York: McGraw-Hill Book Co., Inc., 1953), Chapter 5.

CONSOLIDATED STATEMENT OF FINANCIAL POSITION

(from the annual report of the United States Steel Corporation, Dec. 31, 1957)

	Dec. 31, 1957	Dec. 31, 1956
Current assets		
Cash	$ 257,189,783	$ 267,909,652
United States Government and other marketable		
securities, at cost (approximates market)	269,185,070	242,239,366
Receivables, less estimated bad debts	255,690,189	314,498,132
Inventories *(details on page 38)*	650,990,865	501,283,785
Total	1,433,055,907	1,325,930,935
Less		
Current liabilities		
Accounts payable	387,818,400	389,281,706
Accrued taxes, less United States Government		
securities of $298,700,000 at December 31,		
1957 and $272,700,000 at December 31,		
1956	292,208,745	254,843,551
Dividends payable	46,620,736	46,591,835
Long-term debt due within one year	26,793,533	31,474,815
Total	753,441,414	722,191,907
Working capital	679,614,493	603,739,028
Miscellaneous investments, less estimated losses ..	41,451,217	42,416,361
United States Government securities set aside		
for property additions and replacements	415,000,000	525,000,000
Plant and equipment, less depreciation		
(details on page 37)	2,109,587,398	1,877,994,847
Operating parts and supplies	50,465,488	45,424,240
Costs applicable to future periods	24,510,008	19,484,070
Total assets less current liabilities	3,320,628,604	3,114,058,546
Deduct		
Long-term debt *(details on page 38)*	216,547,272	245,023,677
Reserves for insurance, contingencies and accident		
and hospital expenses *(details on page 37)*	106,262,155	105,062,063
Excess of assets over liabilities and reserves	$2,997,819,177	$2,763,972,806
Ownership evidenced by		
Preferred stock, 7% cumulative, par value $100		
(authorized 4,000,000 shares; outstanding		
3,602,811 shares)	$ 360,281,100	$ 360,281,100
Common stock (authorized 90,000,000 shares;		
outstanding 53,753,622 shares at December 31,		
1957, and 53,699,617 shares at December		
31, 1956)	2,637,538,077	2,403,691,706
Par value $16⅔ per share .. $ 895,893,700		
Income reinvested in business		
(see page 33 for addition		
of $232,946,288 in 1957) . 1,741,644,377		
Total	$2,997,819,177	$2,763,972,806

SUMMARY OF 1957 FINANCIAL OPERATIONS

(from the annual report of the United States Steel Corporation, Dec. 31, 1957)

Additions to working capital

Income		$419,406,956
Add—Wear and exhaustion of facilities		276,008,777
Proceeds from sales and salvage of plant and equipment		7,276,659
Proceeds from sale of common stock under Stock Option Incentive Plan		2,100,175
Total additions		704,792,567

Deductions from working capital

Expended for plant and equipment	$514,877,987	
Less—Use of funds set aside in prior years	110,000,000	
	404,877,987	
Reduction in total long-term debt	33,157,687	
Dividends declared on preferred and common stocks	186,460,668	
Miscellaneous deductions	4,420,760	
Total deductions		628,917,102
Increase in working capital		$ 75,875,465

Working capital per consolidated statement of financial position

December 31, 1957	$679,614,493	
December 31, 1956	603,739,028	
Increase		$ 75,875,465

The cash or financial budget. One of the best means not only of conserving working capital, but also of anticipating actual cash requirements of a business, is to prepare a cash budget. In principle, this budget is made up of two parts: (1) an estimate of the expected monthly cash receipts for a future period, and (2) an estimate of disbursements for the same period. One is matched against the other, the balances cumulated, and the result is the monthly cash position. One form of such a statement is reproduced on page 232.

The preparation of a cash or financial budget is one of the final steps in budgetary procedure. Before an estimate of cash balances or requirements can be arrived at in this manner, considerable work must be done. Monthly sales must be estimated, expected collections computed, and receipts from all other sources estimated. Budgets, based on the sales estimate, are prepared to cover the expenses of the producing department. Each and every department estimates its expenditures, and all of these are summarized in their proper places in the cash budget.

A few of the many advantages of such procedures are stated below:

1. A standard of performance is established for every department of the business.

FINANCIAL BUDGET

PERIOD
FROM _____ TO _____

	Jan.	Feb.	Mar.	Apr.	May	June	July	Aug.	Sept.	Oct.	Nov.	Dec.
Estimated sales												
Receipts:												
Cash sales												
Accounts receivable												
Notes receivable												
Other income												
Security sales												
Total receipts												
Disbursements:												
Direct labor payroll												
Indirect labor payroll												
Purchases												
Administrative salaries												
Insurance												
Taxes												
Miscellaneous expenses												
Dividends:												
Preferred												
Common												
Interest:												
Bonds												
Bank loans												
Total disbursements												
*Excess or deficiency**												
Cash balance beginning												
Borrow during month												
Repay during month												
Cash balance ending												

* In red.

Cash or Financial Budget of a Manufacturing Company

2. Since all plans are drawn at the same time and consolidated in one budget, needless wastes through duplication can be noted and eliminated.

3. Business plans can be modified to meet financial possibilities before it is too late to make requisite changes.

4. Budgeting, if not demanded by the bank, is an important element in favor of a business when it is seeking a bank loan.

5. A budget acts as a check on imprudent expansion.

6. Expenses are best controlled through a budget.

7. It is the only way that cash requirements can be determined in advance.

Questions for Study and Review

1. What distinguishes the fixed from the current assets of a business? Name two types of assets usually found in each of these classifications.

2. What is the current ratio? The quick ratio? Which of these ratios gives the best test of a concern's ability to pay its bills promptly? Why?

3. Compare regular and seasonal working capital as to type of sources used. Give an illustration of why a concern may need seasonal working capital.

4. State the formulas for accounts receivable turnover and finished goods inventory turnover.

5. Explain why increasing the rate of turnover of accounts receivable is important in the financial management of a concern.

6. Why may we count the allowance for depreciation of plant and equipment as one of the sources of working capital?

7. Why is the purchase of goods on time on terms of 2% 10 days, net 30 or similar terms an expensive source of working capital?

8. Should a concern rely upon bank loans as a source of its regular working capital? Explain.

9. How are term loans usually repaid? Why do we classify them as intermediate sources of working capital?

10. What is a *trade acceptance*? Is it an important way of obtaining working capital in the form of goods? Discuss.

11. Explain the terms 2%, 10 days, net 30, E.O.M. and 2% 10 days, net 30 M.O.M. terms of purchase operate. In each case, when does the bill have to be paid if the discount is to be earned?

12. What is meant by saying that the purpose for which short-term bank loans are used should be *self-liquidating?*

13. Are actual funds lent to a concern financing the purchase of goods by means of a banker's acceptance? How do the vendor and shipper of the goods get paid?

14. What is *commercial paper?* Is this type of financing available to all business concerns?

15. What institutions usually purchase and hold commercial paper to maturity? What advantages does it have to these institutions?

16. Contrast briefly the practice of hypothecation or pledging of accounts receivable for loans with that of factoring.

17. How does a vendor of goods on the installment payment plan finance such accounts? Who pays the cost of such financing?
18. State five advantages of having sufficient net working capital.
19. State at least five advantages of preparing and operating under a financial budget.

Problems

1. The Storm Manufacturing Co. plans to market a new machine which is to sell for $110. The following estimates of cost per machine were made:

Cost of production	$ 80
Selling and administrative expense	10
Total cost	$ 90
Profit	20
Sales price	$110

The terms of sale are 2% 10 days, net 30 E.O.M., and one-half the customers are expected to take advantage of the discount offered.

The estimated volume of business and production is as follows:
100 machines per month during the first month;
200 machines per month during the second month;
300 machines per month during the third month;
400 machines per month during the fourth month; and
500 machines per month during the fifth month and thereafter when capacity production is reached.
Show by the construction of a simple cash budget the additional demands for working capital which will be incurred before the business is "on its feet."

2. A corporation has accounts receivable equal to thirty days' sales. Terms of sale are 2/10, net 30. The management feels that by changing the terms of sale to 10 per cent down and the balance in twelve monthly installments sales will ultimately improve. If sales are now $120,000, what is the amount of accounts receivable at the present time, and what will it be seven months after the corporation changes its terms? How might the corporation finance the increase?

3. The Jones Corporation makes an annual profit of 10 per cent of sales and has an average inventory of $150,000 which it turns over four times a year. The annual cost of funds invested in inventory, insurance and storage are 6 per cent, 0.2 per cent and 1 per cent, respectively. The company has its choice of (a) reducing the average inventory to $100,000 by efficient inventory control, or (b) increasing the rate of inventory turnover to six times which, however, would reduce the profit margin to 9 per cent of sales. Which method is the more profitable?

4. The Balance Sheet of Sampson and Company, Inc., is as follows:

Cash	$ 10,000	Accounts payable	$ 50,000
Accounts receivable	15,000	Fixed liabilities	25,000
Inventory	75,000	Capital stock	150,000
Fixed assets	300,000	Surplus	175,000
	$400,000		$400,000

The corporation needs $100,700 additional working capital, $35,000 for inventory, $15,000 for accounts receivable and $50,700 additional cash. What would be the effect on each of the above if the funds are secured by means of (a) a bank loan payable within one year, and (b) a long-term loan?

5. In the situation above, what will be the effect upon (1) working capital; (2) net working capital; (3) current ratio, and (4) quick ratio if plan (a) is used and, if plan (b) is used.

6. If a firm borrows money at a rate of 6 per cent in order to take advantage of cash discounts, what yearly percentage of savings will be accomplished under the following terms of sale:

a. 1%/10, net 30.
b. 2%/10, net 60.
c. 3%/10, net 30.

Written Assignment

The annual sales of the Durable Machinery Manufacturing Co. are $900,000, cost of sales $600,000, selling and administrative expenses $200,000. An average inventory of $200,000 is maintained.

a. What is the present rate of turnover of inventory? ~ 4 i l
b. If the sales are increased to $1,350,000, cost of sales to $900,000, and the average inventory remains the same, what would be the new rate of turnover?
c. If sales remain at $900,000, and cost of sales $600,000, but inventory can be reduced by more careful control to $150,000, what would be the new rate of turnover?

CHAPTER XIII

Business and Banks

Business and commercial banks. The various services performed for business concerns by commercial banks are important and essential. Indeed, it is difficult to conceive of a business concern in this country which does not in some way depend upon commercial banks for one or more services required in the conduct of day-to-day business affairs. While many of the services obtainable today had their origins in antiquity, other have been designed to meet needs not known a half a century ago. Banks are business institutions operating for profit. Just as merchants not only stock merchandise in response to existing demands but also new merchandise in an endeavor to create new demands, so have the banks advertised new services and entered fields of activity not previously associated with commercial banking.

American banks. From England, whence we directly inherited our legal system, we also received a heritage of commercial practices. Many of these practices are very old and had been known and used in Europe in the middle ages. Indeed, some may be traced to usages found in the Middle East antedating the birth of Christ. Today many of these services are performed by commercial banks, although when these commercial practices first developed no such institutions existed.

After the American revolutionary war, banks in the original thirteen states were chartered by the various state governments with the exception of the First Bank of the United States and the Second Bank of the United States which were created by special legislation of the Federal Government. From 1836, when President Jackson vetoed the renewal of the charter of the Second Bank of the United States until 1863, all banks in the country were state banks. These banks performed the general banking services common to the period in which they operated, creating currency, loaned and paid out in exchange for various commercial bills and other orders through the issuance of their own bank notes. These notes circulated as currency, usually at full or par value in the nearby territory served by the banks, but often at considerable discount at places more remote. In fact a traveler from one locality to another in the United States faced great inconvenience and financial loss because of the difficulty of carrying a widely accepted medium of exchange.

Beginning in 1863 when the National Currency Act became a law,[1] national banks could be chartered upon application to the Comptroller of the Currency of the United States. Since that time, we have had both state and national banks operating throughout the country, often serving the same community. One of the main purposes of creating national banks was to establish a currency of general acceptability at face value wherever offered in this country. Accordingly, national banks were authorized to issue their own bank notes which readily circulated at full face value, as the law required that they be secured by 100 per cent in government bonds deposited with the Treasurer of the United States plus a 5 per cent redemption fund also placed with the Treasurer. State bank notes were rapidly retired by the imposition of a federal tax upon their issuance and, in 1866, upon such notes in the hands of individuals. The result was that many state banks applied for and received national bank charters as their ability to issue notes at that time was thought essential to profitable banking. With the passage of the Federal Reserve Act of 1913, it was planned to gradually retire national bank notes but this was not completely accomplished until 1935. The principal reason for retirement of national bank notes, although they represented a sound currency, is that the issue lacked elasticity, that the amount of notes outstanding did not rise or fall as did the needs of business. Conditions of currency shortage frequently occurred, to the embarrassment and inconvenience of business generally.

During the long period between 1836 when the Second Bank of the United States went out of existence until the passage of the Federal Reserve Act in 1913, this country had no central bank. Fear of concentration of financial power in one single district in the United States probably dominated Congress. The deposit business of banks had become increasingly important and no adequate system of providing reserve protection against such deposits existed. The Federal Government, through subtreasuries located in different parts of the country, was with difficulty trying to be its own banker and perform its own fiscal services, often having to call upon private bankers for assistance, especially when monetary transactions with other nations were concerned.

To overcome the fear of concentrated financial power referred to above, the Federal Reserve Act divided the United States into twelve districts and established a Federal Reserve Bank in each to act as a banker's bank, to hold banks' reserves against deposits, issue currency as

---

[1] Became known as the National Bank Act with amendments made in 1874.

required and serve as bankers and fiscal agents of the Federal Government.

A Federal Reserve Board was set up in Washington, D.C. to act as a coordinating agency between the twelve banks and to maintain a gold settlement fund deposited by each of the twelve banks. This makes it possible to transfer balances between the banks as daily transactions might require. Until 1935, the Federal Reserve Board could exercise very little power or control over the policies of the twelve banks but the exigencies of the depression brought about amendments to the Federal Reserve Act in that year. The Federal Reserve Board now has the power to direct many of the operating policies and procedures to be followed by the twelve banks. There still remains with each Federal Reserve bank sufficient independent authority to enable it to meet the peculiar needs of the district it serves.

Many people believe that the Federal Reserve banks are owned by the Federal Government. This is not true. Each member bank subscribes 3 per cent of its capital stock and surplus in stock of its Federal Reserve bank. The law permits the Federal Reserve to require up to 6 per cent but 3 per cent has proved ample. The Federal Reserve bank may pay its members dividends upon their investment up to, but not exceeding, 6 per cent. Earnings in excess of this amount are to go to the Federal Government. As the Federal Reserve banks perform a host of services for the Federal Government without charge, earnings of the Federal Reserve banks go in large part to defray the expenses of these services.

All national banks are required to be members of their district Federal Reserve banks. State banks may become members through meeting the same membership requirements as the national banks. Of the approximately 14,000 banks in the United States, about one-half are now members of a Federal Reserve bank. However, the importance of the one-half (or less) who are members may be judged by the fact that they represent 90 per cent of the demand deposits (checking accounts) in the country.

The many services performed on behalf of business concerns by the Federal Reserve banks are chiefly made available through the intermediary of the businessman's bank. His bank is without doubt enabled to serve him more efficiently through the various services rendered by the Federal Reserve banks to its member banks and through member banks, to a lesser degree, to non-member banks. A full discussion of these is beyond the province of this text. Nevertheless, it may be well to point out that through the clearing and collection system of the Federal Reserve banks a businessman is able to accept, at face value, checks drawn on banks in any part of the country and to know that, after the lapse of a definite number of days, his bank, in which he has deposited the check, will credit the proceeds to his account. In other words, the Federal Reserve banks conduct a nationwide clearing and collection system serving the entire country. <u>All banks using the Federal Reserve banks clearing and collection service agree to honor at par checks drawn on any bank in the country regardless of its location.</u>

It is also through the power of the Federal Reserve banks to issue Federal Reserve Notes that currency shortages prevalent at certain seasons in different parts of the country prior to the creation of the Federal Reserve banks no longer exist.

Choosing a bank. Whether a bank has a state or a national charter has, as a practical matter, no real bearing on the choice of a bank with which to do business, regardless of the size of the concern seeking such a connection. The convenience of location, the size of the bank in terms of its capital and surplus, services it is prepared and willing to offer, and the loan limits or line of credit (a term more fully discussed later in this chapter) which may be obtained by the business concern are usually the most important factors. <u>Banks are limited by Federal and state laws as to the amount in proportion to the individual bank's capital and surplus which may be lent to one borrower.</u> A large business expecting to borrow heavily should choose a bank able to give the desired loan accommodations. In larger cities, large banks have many branches, and in some states, where permitted, branches throughout the state. This enables a business to have available all the resources of a large bank at a branch often but a few steps from its door.

Sometimes some special services are desired. A concern meeting a large payroll with checks may wish to establish a check-cashing service for its employees at a bank nearby. A business with considerable foreign trade may require a bank with foreign connections to facilitate the handling of drafts, ocean bills of lading and cable transfer of funds common to such business.

The proper approach to the problem of choosing a bank is to list the probable services required and discuss these needs with one of a bank's officers. It may be well to visit a number of banks, if necessary, so that one may be measured against another, as to the desire and ability of each to meet the probable needs for various services.

Services Rendered Business by Commercial Banks

The list of services which may be performed by commercial banks for their customers is a long one. Many businessmen are not acquainted with the facilities for various valuable services which are placed at their disposal when they establish banking relationships and maintain a good balance with a commercial bank. Needless to say, all of these services cannot be listed here, but businessmen should be familiar at least with the following:

1. As a depository and safe-keeper of his money.
2. As a collection and discount agency.

3. As a source of short-term loans.

4. As an agency for the transfer of domestic and foreign funds.

5. As a trustee.

6. As a source of credit information.

7. As an aid in the conduct of foreign trade.

8. As an expert financial consultant and adviser.

1. The bank as a depository and safekeeper of money. The bank is a convenient place to deposit cash for safekeeping. A businessman deposits his cash regularly, and the bank places each deposit to the credit of his account. If the depositor wishes to transfer any portion of his cash on deposit to a creditor, he simply draws a check payable to the creditor which can be used by him as the payee. A deposit may be placed in the bank either as a *special* or a *general deposit*. A *special deposit* is one consisting of money or valuables of any kind, for which the bank acts merely in the capacity of a warehouse: to care for and protect the deposit, and to return it to the depositor upon demand. The depositor always retains his title to the special deposit and can demand the return of the identical items deposited. The bank is in no sense the owner of the special deposit; it is merely its trustee. The banks usually maintain on their premises safe deposit vaults and for a small rental, make available safe deposit boxes to their customers, thus obviating the cumbersome handling of special deposits. The *general deposit*, consisting usually of cash, checks, notes, drafts, and coupons, is turned over to the actual ownership of the bank, which becomes a debtor to the depositor. In the transaction, the latter becomes a creditor of the bank: he has a claim against it to the amount of the deposit and has the right to demand the payment of all or any part of it. These general deposits may be made payable on demand (*demand deposits*) or after a specified time (*time deposits*). Businessmen's accounts are mostly on a demand basis.

2. The bank as a collection and discount agency. The businessman uses the credit he has established through his deposits as a means of paying his bills by check. A *check* represents the depositor's order on his bank to pay a certain sum to a third party. The bank, in the usual course of business, will pay the check upon presentation by the payee or his endorsee, and will charge the amount against the depositor's account. Payment by check is general in the United States. It is estimated that at least 80 per cent of the business transacted outside of New York City is paid by check and in New York City, 90 per cent.

The depositor's bank presents the checks drawn on other banks and arranges the method of remittance. This service is known as "collection." The bank merely serves as agent for its depositors in collecting checks drawn on other banks but deposited with it. It is one thing to collect a check and quite another thing to make the funds available to the depositor. Suppose that a merchant in San Francisco buys merchandise in New

York and remits by a check drawn on his local bank in San Francisco. The New York manufacturer will deposit the check in his bank, which, in turn, will return it for collection. Not until the check is actually presented to the drawee bank, charged against the account of the maker, canceled, and the settlement made with the presenting bank is the collection process complete. The agent now has the funds. The process of getting the funds back to the New York bank is the "exchange" function.

Businessmen occasionally accept *promissory notes* from their customers in settlement of accounts and carry them on their books as Notes Receivable. If the business is in need of funds, such notes may be endorsed and discounted with the bank, and the businessman receives either credit on the books of the bank or cash for the face value of the note, less the discount. At maturity, if the bank has not rediscounted the note with some other bank, it will proceed to collect it from the maker. Only when the maker does not honor the note will the businessman hear of it again, for in such a case he is liable as an endorser. Should the businessman not be in need of cash, he may hold the note until shortly before maturity and then deposit it in his bank for collection. The bank then acts as his agent in collecting it. Sometimes this service is rendered without charge, especially if the note is to be collected from someone in the vicinity. If, however, the maker lives out of town, a charge will usually be made for collection.

Occasionally a seller of goods will draw a *draft* for the proceeds. A *draft* is an unconditional order in writing—addressed by one person (drawer) to another (drawee) and signed by the drawer—which requires the drawee to whom it is addressed to pay on demand, or at a fixed or determinable future time, a certain sum of money to, or to the order of, a specified person, or to the bearer (payee). The draft may be payable on demand. In that case it is called a *demand* or *sight draft*. Should it be payable at some future time, it is called a *time draft*. When a time draft based on a commercial transaction is sent by the seller (drawer) to the buyer (drawee) for acceptance and the drawee accepts it by writing on the face of the draft *accepted*, affixing his signature and designating the place of payment, the instrument is called a *trade acceptance*. The accepting of a draft means that the drawee—now called the acceptor—has acknowledged on its face that he will pay the draft at maturity.

Sight drafts are sometimes used in an attempt to enforce the collection of overdue accounts and are not discounted by banks. The banks act merely as agents for collection, and often charge for the service.

Time drafts and trade acceptances are often discounted by a bank for its customers. The bank advances the face value less the discount, figured at current interest rates to maturity. The bank may either hold the draft until maturity and then present it for payment, or it may rediscount it with another banking institution, probably the Federal Reserve Bank.

Drafts are also useful as a means of making C.O.D. shipments. Bills of lading are drawn in negotiable form to order, and a draft for the value of the shipment is attached. The businessman's bank will forward both documents to a bank in the buyer's locality. Since the carrier will deliver the goods only upon presentation of the bill of lading, the buyer must obtain the bill of lading from the bank by payment of the draft. Occasionally, the terms will provide for the delivery of the shipping documents upon acceptance of the draft for payment at some future date.

Businessmen also make use of banks to finance shipments of commodities and goods by means of bankers' acceptances, which were discussed in some detail in Chapter XI. Here two banks are normally involved, the bank of the buyer which authorizes the shipper to draw a draft for the amount of money involved in the shipment and agrees to *accept* the draft, thus lending bank's credit to the buyer, and also the seller's bank which discounts the draft and thus provides the seller with cash for his shipment.

3. The bank as a source of short-term loans. Of all the functions performed by the commercial bank, the most important is that of supplying the needs of business for short-term capital in the form of _bank loans_. Banks, in time of normal business, derive a large portion of their earnings from interest charged on loans. From the standpoint of business in general, the lending function is an extremely useful one. Through the medium of the deposits of those who are not in immediate need of funds, a bank obtains the basis for extending credit to those who do need them. It is to be noticed, also, in this connection that many businesses have seasonal needs for additional capital which can be properly supplied by bank loans; whereas, it would be uneconomical to use long-term loans or owned capital for the purpose, as it would not be in use all the year round.

We have seen how a business may obtain cash or bank credit through the discounting of various types of *customer paper* at the bank. In order to borrow at the bank, a business discounts its own promissory note. This procedure includes the usual discount operation: the bank discounts the note when it is presented; that is, the interest is deducted to maturity, and the account of the borrower is credited only with the net proceeds. If, however, the loan is a *demand loan* (as most loans against collateral security are likely to be), the borrower's account is credited immediately with the face value of the note, and interest is charged against the account on a monthly basis.

Borrowing from a bank, either when the business possesses good credit or when it can offer acceptable collateral as security, should be a simple operation. Borrowing, when obligations are promptly met, enhances the credit of a business and makes the account of such a business a very desirable one from the viewpoint of the bank. A business that preserves a clear borrowing record and that is in the habit of making use of bank loans often finds that it is in a far better position to obtain bank loans in times of stress than is the business that looks upon the bank only as an emergency reservoir of funds, to be tapped when times are hard, inventories frozen, and the business itself short of cash.

Interest rates are based on the basic going or prime rate, which represents the rate to large borrowers of high credit standing. It may almost be considered a minimum rate and most borrowers will pay a higher rate dependent upon the risk, size of the loan and other pertinent factors. Because most banks require that the borrower maintain a *compensating balance* in his checking account equal to about 20 per cent of the loan, the actual cost of the loan to the borrower is higher than the loan rate, as banks may not under the law pay interest on demand deposits. This practice is discussed further under "Line of Credit."

Unsecured loans. It has been variously estimated that from 60 to 70 per cent of bank loans are *unsecured:* no collateral is deposited with the banks; and such loans are made with no other security than the general credit of the borrower, which is pledged when the promissory note is signed. Banks have learned through long experience that unsecured loans may be made safely where proper care is exercised in investigating the credit standing of the borrower. "Good banking is not pawnbroking or collateral lending but is the recognition or cashing of current titles based upon values growing out of ordinary trade and unaccompanied by detailed or particular evidence of ownership of goods."[2] Since business in the United States is largely conducted on the *open book account method,* it would be almost impossible for the average business to obtain loan accommodations at banks on anything but an unsecured basis. Open book transactions do not give rise to negotiable paper, which could be used for collateral, and the goods themselves have passed from the possession of the seller. Then, too, the practice of selling goods on open book account often makes it necessary for the seller to borrow to finance his accounts receivable.

It should be mentioned here that, in recent years, banks in some sections of the country have established departments to engage (so far, in a limited manner) in accounts receivable financing, competing with factoring organizations and commercial finance companies. Loans are made to business houses against an assignment of accounts receivable. Under this plan, the proceeds from the collection of accounts receivable must be forwarded to the bank in the actual form in which they are received by the borrower. Accounts receivable financing by banks is expected to show considerable growth in the future.

---

[2] H. P. Willis and G. W. Edwards, *Banking and Business* (New York: Harper & Brothers, 1925), p. 117.

Establishing credit at the bank. Before a bank will lend on an unsecured note, the borrower must establish his credit. The bank must be assured that the loan will be paid when due. Great emphasis is placed on the character of the management. In addition, depending upon the circumstances, the bank may conduct careful investigations and require considerable information as to the borrower's credit standing. Banks may use any, or all, of the following means of obtaining information as to the advisability of granting a loan:

1. Personal interviews of the borrower by the bank officers.

2. Financial statements of the business with supporting schedules explaining items appearing on these statements. Statements covering a period of two or three years are desirable so that trends may be noted.

3. Reports of commercial agencies: those of general scope offering reports on all businesses everywhere, and those specializing on concerns in a particular line of business.

4. Statements from other banks in which the borrower carries, or has carried, accounts, or with which he has had other business dealings.

5. General data from other concerns in the same line of business.

6. Records of the bank itself, since the borrower is usually a regular customer of the bank from which he seeks to borrow.

When making application for a loan, it is quite usual for a business to be called upon to furnish considerable information as to its financial standing. Income, profit and loss statements, and balance sheets, not only for the present but also for previous periods, are usually requested by the bank. Supporting schedules of information are often required if the figures shown by the statements are not self-explanatory. Frequently the bank will supply forms to be filled out by the businessman. Forms vary for different banks, but supplementary information is usually required regarding officers and directors, reserve and depreciation policies, bad debt losses, inventory valuation, contingent liabilities, real estate owned, auditing and trade discount practices. It is impossible in this text more than to touch upon the principles underlying the analysis of a *credit risk.* There are four primary factors that must be considered in the analysis of any credit risk. These factors are: (1) the character of the debtor, (2) the capacity of the debtor or the management of the debtor business, (3) the capital investment in the debtor business, and (4) the economic conditions of the industry. In an analysis of these factors, the banker is interested in one question: Will the borrower pay the loan when due?

Character is an essential element of any credit risk. If the character of the applicant be poor, the credit man seldom proceeds further. The character of the management of a concern is known by reputation and is ascertained through information received directly or indirectly from those who have had dealings with it. Honesty and intention to pay must exist; otherwise, there would be no object in going into the question of ability to pay.

From the bank credit man's point of view, *capacity* means ability to manage the business for which credit has been asked. It extends to all the factors that may make for the failure or the success of the business itself. For instance, in addition to investigating the ability of the management, the credit man would be interested in knowing whether or not the business is favorably located and whether its methods are up to date.

The *capital* or *financial strength* of the credit risk comes in for very careful investigation. It includes the amount of capital invested, borrowed, and owned; the portion invested in fixed assets; and the amount already in current assets. It is indicative of the resources available for the settlement of any claims against the business.

Economic conditions affect the credit risk and always have a bearing on the problem. In particular, the manner in which current economic conditions affect the industry of which the business is a part may indicate probable trends in the future of the concern whose credit is being analyzed. It should also be borne in mind that conditions, such as rapidly falling price levels, extreme booms, labor troubles, and similar fundamental factors, are points that the credit man must not overlook in passing upon the risk.

In recent years, it has become common practice for banks not only to require figures on past operations, but to insist that the business furnish a budget showing the expected receipts and disbursements for the ensuing period and often, also, an estimated statement of its income, profit, and loss.

By such procedure, the bank is able to see when the loan can be repaid and whether the expectations of the businessman are reasonable. The banker also knows that in making up such a budget, the businessman has had to plan in advance all the details of his operations, and thus the chance of mistakes through hasty judgment is largely eliminated.

The line of credit. With all the information concerning the borrower in hand, the bank will complete its investigation and determine how much the customer may borrow and for how long a time. The maximum amount that may be borrowed is known as the *line of credit.*

The customer is expected to borrow from time to time against this credit in the amounts necessary to see him through his successive needs. The sum of all the loans that he has outstanding at one time will not be allowed, of course, to exceed his line of credit. It sometimes happens that a firm may obtain from the bank a line of credit and apply for one loan to cover the entire amount, but this practice is unusual. As long as the business pays up its various loans promptly, occasionally cleaning them all up, and observes the various rules and standards of the bank, the line of credit remains *open* and the bank does not make new investigation of each application. Periodically, however, the bank will institute an investigation to ascertain whether the business, at its present size, is still in condition to justify the line of credit, or whether it should be cut down. Of course, applications to increase the line of credit will always lead to reinvestigation.

It is not uncommon for businesses to arrange for concurrent lines of credit with several banks. Such a practice will, generally, if the firm is sound and prosperous, expand or increase the credit standing of the business and make it somewhat independent of any one particular bank. It is understood, of course, that the business does not have at each bank a line equal to the line it might have doing business with only one bank, but that each bank is cognizant of the customer's line at the other banks and extends to him a line that, when combined with the lines at the other banks, will not exceed his rating.

It is customary for banks to require an annual *clean-up* of customers' loans, and sometimes businesses make this clean-up at one bank with funds borrowed from another. When there are several lines of credit with different banks, a sort of *revolving credit* is thus set up. Good business demands that this be done only with the knowledge and, at least, the tacit consent of all concerned. Smaller businesses, however, and those whose credit is not particularly strong will find it better policy to devote all of their efforts to strengthening their credit and building up a satisfactory line with one banking house.

Where a business finds that it has a constant need of funds obtained from short-term bank loans, steps should be taken to increase the net working capital. In times of credit stringency, bank loans are likely to be difficult to renew. Also a concern which is adequately supplied with regular working capital obtained from long-term or permanent sources will find that a larger line of credit may be obtained for such proper use of short-term loans as seasonal financing. Short-term bank loans should primarily be used for self-liquidating purposes. That is, the purpose for which the funds are used should provide for the repayment of the loan when due.

When a line of credit is once obtained, it must be *kept open*. This can be done only by the borrower's observing all the rules and requirements of the bank. Various institutions have different minor regulations, but the principal ones usually found are:

1. That the customer must maintain a deposit equal to a specified percentage of the line of credit. The percentage usually required is 20, though in some cases it may be 25 and occasionally it may be set as low as 10. Bankers refer to this as the *compensating balance*. The businessman should realize that maintaining a substantial deposit is one of the surest ways of retaining the confidence of his banker.

2. That the customer must clean up all loans periodically, usually once

a year. By insisting on this annual clean-up of loans, the bank makes certain that it is lending only to prosperous concerns and for temporary working capital. Only in exceptional cases and for good reasons should a bank countenance a customer's cleaning up his loans by the use of funds borrowed for the purpose from another bank at which he has established a line of credit.

Once a line of credit is granted, the borrower may expect the bank to watch the manner in which it is used. The bank may require additional financial statements from time to time and occasional interviews with the borrower. The bank is also usually cognizant of the business deals of its customers, and its officers are often able to observe without formal investigation whether money lent is being properly used. Should the bank become doubtful of practices followed by the borrower, it probably would call for an explanation; and should the explanation be unsatisfactory, the line of credit may be curtailed or canceled entirely.

There is normally no charge for the line of credit itself. Each time a loan is obtained under the line of credit, a promissory note carrying a definite maturity is signed by the borrower and discounted with the bank. Sometimes where a line of credit of large amount is agreed upon, committing the bank for a number of years in the future, the bank will charge a commitment fee on the amount of the credit not being used. This fee is not large, usually not in excess of ¼ of 1 per cent and represents compensation to the bank for standing ready to lend a large amount whenever requested during the period covered by the credit. Such loans have been made to public utilities as a temporary means of financing expansion costs preliminary to more permanent means of financing.

Personal loans. The making of personal loans on an installment basis is a business developed by banks to a point where many banks have established separate departments to handle the volume. These loans are made on the basis of the borrower's signature alone, on his signature plus the signature of a co-maker and against different types of security, frequently chattel mortgages. Some banks will lend as much as $10,000 in this way, but the majority of the loans are relatively small.[3] As of December 31, 1957, outstanding personal loans made by banks totaled $2,379 million or 30 per cent of the total in the United States.[4] This type of loan is sometimes obtained by small business concerns which cannot borrow from the regular loan department of a bank in the usual way. Big city banks make unsecured personal loans, sometimes at 4 per cent. Banks in smaller communities may charge 6 per cent. This, however, is not the net cost of the loan. Because interest is usually taken out in ad-

---

[3] Based on figures obtained from the Federal Reserve Bulletin, March, 1958.

[4] The Manufacturers Trust Co. of New York finds that personal loans made by the personal loan department average $1,100.

vance and because, for example, a loan repayable in twelve equal installments in effect gives the borrowers but six months' use of the total proceeds, his net cost will be slightly in excess of 8 per cent. Loans made against some security other than signatures are usually at lower rates.

Secured loans. Some loans are made only against collateral security of some kind. These loans are usually termed _collateral loans_. Banks require this sort of security when the risk is such that it would not be prudent to lend on an unsecured basis. In some businesses it is practically always necessary to offer collateral as a basis for obtaining loans. For example, practically all loans to stock brokers for the purpose of financing customers' margin accounts are handled in this way; stocks and bonds are pledged as collateral.

Banks greatly prefer collateral which is readily marketable, because that feature adds to the liquidity of the loan. Where possible, a variety of collateral is more acceptable than all of one kind, for, obviously, there is likely to be greater safety where this principle of diversification can be followed. Banks reserve the right to sell the collateral in case of default; and the loan is made due and payable at once if the collateral depreciates in value, unless additional collateral is deposited. These requirements will be made clear by a study of the following typical collateral loan agreement.

Typical Collateral Loan Agreement

.... Dollars   .... 19 ....
ON DEMAND, for value received, ... promise to pay to THE NATIONAL BANK of .... or order, at its banking house .... Dollars with interest at the rate of ...... per centum per annum, ... having deposited with said Bank, as Collateral security for payment of this or any other direct or indirect liability to said Bank, due or to become due, or that may hereafter be contracted ....
....

In case of depreciation in the market value of the security hereby pledged, or which may hereafter be pledged for this loan .... agree to furnish, on demand, satisfactory additional security, so that the market value thereof shall always be at least .... per cent more than the amount of this note. And failing to deposit such additional security, this note shall be deemed to be due and payable forthwith, anything hereinbefore expressed to the contrary notwithstanding and the said Bank, or its assigns, may immediately reimburse itself by the sale of the security, as hereinafter authorized. And authority is hereby given to the said Bank, or its assigns, to sell, assign and deliver the whole or any part of the said Collateral, also any security, substituted therefor or added thereto, without notice or advertisement, either at public or private sale, at the option of the said Bank, or its assigns, on the non-performance of this promise; any balance of the net proceeds of such sale remaining after paying all sums, whether then or thereafter payable, due from .... to the said Bank on account of this note or otherwise, to be returned to ......

.... And it is further agreed that the said Bank, or its assigns may bid and become purchasers of such sale, and no other purchaser shall be responsible for the application of the purchase money.

(Signature) ....

....

Collateral for loans. There are scores of items that may be used as collateral; but the principal ones only are mentioned here, and they may be set forth as follows:

A. Financial type.

1. *Stocks.* Certificates of stock in business organizations are acceptable collateral if they are marketable and may reasonably be expected to remain so till the expiration of the time of the loan.

2. *Bonds.* Corporate, municipal, or government bonds are acceptable if they are sound and marketable.

B. Merchandise type.

1. *Warehouse documents.* A warehouse document is a receipt for goods stored in a warehouse. Goods may be stored in a public warehouse or on the owner's premises subject to a field warehousing arrangement. Both types were briefly discussed in Chapter XI. Public warehouses are sometimes called bonded warehouses because of the custom of such warehouse companies purchasing a bond from an insurance company protecting against any financial loss to one who has stored goods in the warehouse which may be due to negligence on the part of the warehouse companies. This is not a substitute for insurance, which should be carried by the owner of the goods against the risks of fire, theft, etc. In some states, public warehouses are considered to be public utilities and subject to regulation by state agencies as to rates and operating procedures.

Field warehousing is a far more recent practice that has grown very rapidly, especially since the end of World War II. An independent warehouse company will, for a nominal rental, lease premises from a manufacturer or distributor, segregate the premises leased from the others with suitable partitions (or fences if outside storage is used), place its own employees in charge of receiving and receipting for goods stored and releasing the same just as though operating a public warehouse. The premises are well posted with signs indicating that they are under the control of the warehouse company.

This practice saves trucking and storage charges and, if the material stored is to be required for manufacturing, it prevents delay because it is close at hand.

In both public and field warehousing, two kinds of receipts can be used. A negotiable receipt carries with it title to the goods. A non-negotiable receipt does not. Where stored raw materials are withdrawn at frequent intervals for processing or where finished goods are withdrawn as sold, the non-negotiable receipt will be used as security for loans. This type of receipt will be made out to the lending bank because it cannot be transferred by indorsement. By prior arrangement, the bank can authorize the release of the goods from storage merely by notifying the warehouse man in the agreed-upon manner. Negotiable receipts must be presented for release of the goods because whoever legally owns the receipt has title to the goods. Therefore, they are not suitable for use where part of the goods are likely to require release at frequent intervals. Where bulk commodities such as grain which is to be sold in large quantities are involved, negotiable receipts are usually used.

2. Transit documents. The *bill of lading* is the principal transit document. It is a receipt issued by a carrier certifying that he has received the therein-described goods from the within-named consignor for transportation to a certain destination, to a specified consignee, or to the order of any person. It serves as a receipt for the goods, a contract to transport, and a document of title. There are *straight* bills of lading and *order* bills of lading. The *straight bill of lading* states that the goods are consigned or destined to a specified consignee, and is intended primarily for domestic shipments; while the *order bill of lading* consigns the goods to the order of any person, and is intended for both domestic and foreign shipments. A straight bill of lading must be marked "Non-Negotiable," and duplicates must be so characterized. Title to the goods rests with the consignee; while he may transfer his title by indorsement and delivery, he can transfer no better title than he holds, and a bank that lends on a straight bill of lading to a wrongful person has no protection. An order bill of lading, however, may be negotiated; and, when it is properly indorsed, any holder in good faith has title to the goods. This document, therefore, is good bank collateral.

3. Trust receipts. With a bank in possession of a warehouse receipt, bill of lading, or other such document, it is impossible for the merchant to get possession of his goods so as to dispose of them and pay off the loan. The bank will, therefore, often release the document held as collateral if the borrower signs a *trust receipt*, whereby the bank obtains the title to the goods and the borrower pledges to turn over to the bank the first proceeds from the sale up to the amount of the loan. Goods like automobiles which are easily identifiable may be transferred to a bank on a trust receipt basis, while remaining on the dealer's showroom floor as security for a loan. As the cars are sold, the loan is paid off. This practice is known as "floor plan financing."

C. Personal type.

1. Real estate. Deeds, deeds of trust, mortgages, leases, and similar rights in good real estate may constitute good bank loan collateral, though, as a rule, commercial banks do not favor this type.

2. Chattels. Deeds, deeds of trust, bills of sale, and similar rights in movable goods capable of transfer—such as, portable machinery, furniture, livestock, crops, and many similar things—may constitute acceptable collateral. Many banks, however, decline to accept them as such on the ground that they may lack marketability.

3. *Bank books.* Savings bank pass books, which serve as vouchers or receipts for deposits made, and without the presentation of which withdrawals cannot be made, are often assigned to a bank as collateral for a loan. Some savings banks, however, prohibit the assignment of their pass books.

Bank requirements as to collateral

A. *Margin.* Banks will demand that the market value of the collateral exceed the amount of the loan, so as to safeguard the bank in case of possible shrinkage of the value of the collateral. The excess margin usually required is about 20 per cent. When, through a decrease in the value of the collateral, it falls below this percentage, the borrower may be required to deposit additional collateral.

B. *Character of collateral.* Banks will not depend entirely on a margin for their protection; they will also insist that the collateral be of a satisfactory character. On a large loan they may demand *mixed collateral,* consisting probably of railroad, industrial, and other securities, rather than *straight collateral,* consisting of securities of only one class. Likewise, they will not grant too many small loans, each secured by the same type of collateral. When corporate securities are used, they should be conservative, rather than speculative, issues; they should be active on the market, rather than inactive; and they should have good delivery— that is, they should be negotiable in form and indorsed in blank by the borrower. Property other than securities is not acceptable as collateral, unless it has a determinable value and a potential market.

Commercial banks should not be expected to furnish long-term capital. Not only is it poor banking for the commercial bank to make short-term loans for investment in the fixed assets of a business, but it is also a dangerous practice for the business. As previously emphasized, short-term bank loans should be self-liquidating; that is, the assets in which they are invested should be regularly converted into cash in the usual course of business so that the loans may be repaid when due. If a business places funds derived from bank loans into fixed assets, there is always danger that cash will not be available to repay the loan when due. Then, if the bank refuses to renew, the business may face serious financial difficulties, perhaps bankruptcy.

The same danger may result if bank loans are used to speculate in inventories. Large inventories may be slow to liquidate and hence become almost the same as fixed assets. If bank loans invested in this manner come due, it may be necessary to reduce the inventory through sales at cut prices; this practice involves severe losses.

4. The bank as a source of intermediate or term loans. Since about 1935, banks with ample reserves have made loans to business known as term loans (see chapter on Financing Working Capital Requirements). These loans run for longer than the short-term loan and are not self-liquidating in character, for they are used for fixed assets, as well as for working capital. As previously indicated they are repaid in installments sometimes extending for five years or more. Occasionally single large loans are participated in by several banks and also by insurance companies. Because these loans extend for such a long period that business conditions may radically change before the loan is fully repaid, much attention will be paid by the lenders to the stability of the business in the various stages of the business cycle and the loan contract may contain restrictions upon the management designed to safeguard the loan. Some bankers are opposed to this type of business on the ground that it is not sound banking policy to deviate from the long-established policy of making self-liquidating loans only. However, as long as banks have more than enough reserves to take care of short-term loans required by their customers, we may expect term loans to be made. There is no evidence to indicate that banks have engaged in the practice beyond the limits of safety.

5. The bank as an agency for the transfer of domestic and foreign funds. Practically all commercial banks have correspondent banks in other cities in the United States and will sell drafts on their correspondent bank, which may be used in remitting funds. A bank draft has better acceptability than a personal check, or the check of a small corporation, and may be more desirable for that reason. A merchant in Chicago may wish to pay a debt to a New York firm in New York funds. This may easily be accomplished through the aid of a Chicago bank that maintains a balance in some New York bank. The Chicago bank will sell a draft on the New York bank, which may be used for the remittance. Banks also remit funds by telegraph for their customers to different cities.

The larger banks in New York and a few other large financial centers have foreign correspondents and are able to render the same services in connection with the transfer of funds internationally, as are described in the preceding paragraph with respect to domestic payments. This does not mean that the small bank or banks without international connections cannot assist business in this way. The smaller banks invariably have balances in larger banks and, through these connections, are able to render practically the same service.

6. The bank as a trustee. Many commercial banks have trust departments. A bank acting as a trustee may care for various funds, including such a fund as an employees' pension fund, which the business management may not wish to care for itself. Through its corporate trust department, the bank will act as a trustee for mortgage bond issues, as a depository for stocks and bonds held under trust agreements, and often as a registrar or transfer agent for the corporation's securities. The latter service, however, is not a trust function but is more in the nature of a fiscal agency service, although it is usually handled by the corporate trust department.

7. The bank as a source of credit information. Banks, of course, are not commercial credit agencies, but they do keep files of credit information. In fact, large banks maintain separate credit departments. The collected information serves the bank's own purposes in its dealings with those businesses with whom the bank may have relations, and usually the bank will give credit information upon inquiry by its depositors. Large city banks with foreign connections are frequently the only easily available sources of information on the credit standing of foreign houses. Banks are often named as references by their customers who are seeking credit accommodations elsewhere and will usually give information as to their customer's credit standing. The confidential relationship existing between the bank and its depositors is, however, seldom violated, as the information given is usually general and such as not to violate any trust reposed in the bank.

8. The bank as an aid in the conduct of foreign trade. Almost all foreign trade transactions require the services of a bank. The bank forwards and collects drafts drawn against the consignee and delivers the bills of lading upon payment or acceptance of the draft. An importer may arrange for a letter of credit with a bank and instruct the bank to make payment against it upon presentation by the exporter of the shipping documents evidencing shipment of the specified goods. A shipper of goods to far-off lands may obtain funds immediately by drawing a draft against the buyer and, after attaching the bill of lading and other shipping documents, by discounting the draft with his banker. The bank will then proceed to collect the draft through its foreign correspondent. A few large banks have branches or agencies abroad, which may be used for this purpose. Banks also sell drafts and cable transfers in foreign exchange so that remittances may be made in the currency of the country to which the payment is to be sent. Interior banks, which are not equipped to give full service in connection with foreign trade, may usually do so with the assistance of their connection with large banks that have foreign departments.[5]

9. The bank as an expert financial consultant and adviser. No businessman should overlook the splendid assistance that may often be rendered by his banker in the way of timely financial advice. The confidential relationship of the banker to his many customers gives him a very

---

[5] A discussion that would fully cover the various services performed by banks in connection with foreign trade is beyond the province of this text.

thorough insight into business affairs in general. The banker sees the errors made by businessmen who are his customers. He sees the results of these errors and may use this knowledge to prevent others from making the same mistakes. He is financially trained and is often able to guide a businessman into more prudent financial practice through giving him the benefit of his wide financial experience. It is not to be implied that the banker is infallible—that he does not err as do other humans. His advice is, however, always worth seeking, and a discussion of business plans with the banker is always advisable, since he may not only save losses but may also contribute some valuable profit-making ideas.

The attitude of the businessman toward his bank

In the foregoing discussion, an effort has been made to touch upon some of the many services a business may expect to find its banker willing and able to perform. The businessman who keeps his character above reproach and his credit good, and who shows reasonable capacity and aptitude in his business, need have no fear that the banker will not be glad to do business with him. Bankers are interested in helping their customers to success if they can do so with no more than a normal risk. They are anxious to sell the services of the bank as a merchant is to sell his goods. They must, of course, be careful to maintain their own integrity, through sound judgment in making loans. Banks are, in a sense, trustees of their own credit, which has been pledged to the community. Care in the exercise of their banking functions is more than a mere phase of the dealings with their customers; it is a community trust.

Questions for Study and Review

1. State eight services performed by the commercial banks.
2. Discuss the functions performed by the bank as a collection or discount agency.
3. What is meant by a draft, a sight draft, a time draft, a trade acceptance?
4. Distinguish between a trade acceptance and a bank acceptance.
5. What is an unsecured loan; a secured or collateral loan?
6. State six sources of information available to the bank seeking credit information for the purpose of granting a loan.
7. Four primary factors in analyzing a credit risk are known as the 4 C's. Explain the meaning of each.
8. Explain how the *compensating balance* requirement results in an effective cost of borrowing from the bank greater than the interest rate at which a concern's notes are discounted by its bank.
9. What is meant by a line of credit? State two rules usually enforced by the bank if the line of credit is to be kept open.
10. Name the various kinds of collateral acceptable as security for bank loans, classifying them as financial type, merchandise type, personal type.

11. What are the usual bank requirements as to collateral?

12. *a.* Discuss the service performed by the bank in transferring funds.

   b. Discuss the functions of the bank as a trustee.

Problems

1. A corporation estimates that it will need $2,000,000 additional working capital each year for the next five years. It does not wish to incur funded debt as a means of financing its needs. Explain the arrangements which it may make with commercial banks to raise the needed funds.

2. The Willis Hotel Co., Inc., bought supplies from the Famous Furniture Corporation in the amount of $6,795 and agreed to settle by means of a trade acceptance due in 90 days.

   (a) Draw up the instrument in complete form with the acceptance endorsement.

   (b) If the Famous Furniture Corporation needs cash 30 days before the due date of the acceptance, what disposition can it make of the instrument?

3. A New York importer purchased goods from a Mexican firm. The Mexican exporter drew a sight draft, with bills of lading attached, which is now in the hands of a New York bank. Explain how the importer may arrange with his bank to finance this shipment until the goods have been sold and payment for them received.

4. A New York manufacturer has secured an order from Buenos Aires. His foreign customer desires 90 days' credit, which the New York manufacturer does not wish to grant. How may the transaction be handled so as to give the desired extension of time without requiring the assumption of credit risk by the New York shipper?

5. The Willate Corporation has outstanding $20,000,000 notes payable to banks which was borrowed to finance long-term working capital needs. The corporation now proposes to change this short-term, or floating, debt into long-term, or funded, debt. Explain how this could be handled, and the part which a commercial bank with trust powers would play in the operation.

6. A corporation needs $50,000 additional working capital to carry it until the end of the selling season, but it has exhausted its line of credit with the commercial banks. What other source of short-term borrowing is open to it?

Written Assignment

John Elton owns a successful retail novelty and gift store which he established ten years ago in a small industrial city. His store and stockroom occupy the first floor and basement of a three-story building which he owns. Being well located, he has had no difficulty in renting the second and third floor for office space to professional tenants at an annual rental of $10,000. Total income from rental and the store has averaged $35,000 after federal income taxes for the past three years. His credit is excellent. He usually discounts all bills.

The city has been growing rapidly. There are several new industrial plants and population has been increasing as workers and their families have moved to the city because of excellent employment opportunities. Mr. Elton believes that with an increase of $60,000 in normal inventories he could increase his income $10,000 a year. In addition to this amount, he would like to have $25,000 to acquire additional stock for Christmas gift business.

After some thought, he discussed his needs with his banker. The banker has great confidence in the ability of Mr. Elton and also in Mrs. Elton, who actively participates in the business, although she is not a partner. He tells Mr. Elton that he will lend him the full amount required on the following basis:

1. The bank will discount a four-month note for $25,000 on October 15. Interest 5 per cent.
2. The bank will discount a two-year note for $60,000 repayable in equal monthly installments but will require that Mr. Elton give a first mortgage on his building as security. Interest 4 per cent.

Assume that these terms are acceptable to Mr. Elton and the loans are made.

  a. Suggest a reason why the term loan was at a lower interest rate.
  b. What was the effective interest rate of each loan.

NOTE: Although Mr. Elton's bank usually requires that a 10 per cent compensating balance be maintained, this balance would not be greater than that normally maintained by Mr. Elton and may therefore be ignored in computing the effective rate.

CHAPTER XIV

Surplus, Dividend, and Reserve Policies

Introduction. The primary purpose of a business is to make a profit for its owners, and a business which does not return a profit sufficient to compensate the owners for the risks incurred is said to be an economic failure. Surprisingly enough, it is difficult to determine what *profit* is. The accountant thinks of profit as that amount remaining after deducting from gross revenue all of the expenses incident to the operation of the business. The cost of goods produced for sale or purchased for resale is a cost of doing business. So are salaries, insurance, cost of maintaining the property and the plant, as well as a charge for the use of the plant and equipment. The latter is called depreciation and will be discussed later in this chapter. Building, tools, and machines wear out or become obsolete and this loss in value must be counted as one of the costs of doing business to the same extent as are the salary of the foreman in the factory or the typist in the office. Computing these costs mathematically is not difficult.

What is difficult, however, is giving a dollar value to some of the costs. Salaries, insurance, raw materials and maintenance are simply billed and paid currently and in current dollars. Other expenses do not seem to be quite as easily computed. For example, in the chapters on working capital, problems arising from the valuation of inventories were discussed. The difference between using "lifo" and "fifo" (see footnote page 316) can amount to many thousands of dollars' difference in the annual profits reported by the accountant each year. The problem of depreciation is equally, if not more, complex. Suppose, for instance, a corporation bought a machine for $100,000 and expected it to last ten years. How much should the accountant charge each year for the use of that machine? Suppose after he came to a decision, the machine became obsolete in the third year. Have the profits of the firm for each of the first three years been erroneously computed? Suppose further that the machine which the company bought at the end of the ten years to replace the now worn-out machine, cost $150,000, should the charge to expense over the ten years' life of the old machine be recomputed to allow for the higher cost of the new machine?

A further problem arises out of the changing value of the dollar. If Mr. Jones bought a house for $12,000 in 1941 and rented it for $1,200 annually, he earned 10 per cent on his investment. Suppose, however, that the value of the house increased by 1958 to $25,000 and the fair rental had increased to $2,500 net. Is Mr. Jones still earning 10 per cent on his investment, or is he earning 20 per cent? If a corporation acquired land, property, and equipment when prices were low, now that prices are higher (and the purchasing power of the dollar low) is that corporation earning a high profit or not? The difficulty arises out of the necessity of using as a measuring device or yardstick of profits a dollar which is changing in value. It is somewhat the same difficulty you might experience in measuring distance if the government changed the number of inches to the foot each year.

Income. From the point of view of the businessman, income is always defined in terms of money. He considers as income the money receipts or claims to money derived from three sources: (1) the revenue from regular operations; (2) revenue from outside operations; and (3) income from miscellaneous sources such as investments. Since it is from these three sources that surplus and dividends chiefly originate, a brief discussion of each may be helpful.

Income from operations. The income statement of Sinclair Oil Corporation and its subsidiaries, reproduced on page 260, does not break down the gross operating income by dollar amounts. A footnote, however, specifies that gross operating income arises from the sales of purchased crude oil, and the sale of refined oil products, petrochemicals and natural gas. The income statement of a railroad considers the gross operating income to be that income derived from freight handling, passenger service, mail and express. In an electric utility, the gross income for operations would include revenue from the sale of electricity and in some from sale of gas.

Income from outside operations. Income may arise not only from direct operations but also from operations not directly connected with the main business of the company. A railroad company, in order to attract tourists and thereby increase its revenues from passenger traffic, may operate hotels. The Canadian Pacific Railroad in Canada, for example, operates a chain of hotels in the beautiful Canadian Rockies. The Missouri Pacific Railroad Co., for example, owns the Missouri Pacific Freight Transport Co., which operates some ten thousand miles of truck routes. This truck company operates primarily for the handling of less than carload shipments in the territory served by the railroad.

Income from other sources. Other income earned by a company may be included under the heading of "other sources" in the income statement. Such income comes from a variety of sources and is somewhat of a catch-all. Income derived from investments owned by the company is often termed "other income." Often, too, this item is of considerable importance. In the Sinclair statement referred to, interest and dividends amounted to $6,685,849 and $1,222,649 respectively. These items, together with a miscellaneous item of $1,137,917, account for 6¼ per cent of the total income. A pure holding company has as its only source of income that obtained from the securities of other corporations which it owns. The item of dividends and interest then becomes income from operations in the holding company financial report.

Why does not the accountant lump all of these sources of income together inasmuch as they are all sources of income and cash? The answer is that it makes analysis of the financial statement and therefore of the company operations much easier not only for the management, but for the creditor, and for the stockholder. When the business operation is divided into its component parts, it is only logical to divide the financial operations into the same components so that these components may be analyzed more easily and the success or failure of the venture judged. Where a railroad operates hotels or a trucking company, in addition to the railroad, management is interested in knowing how well the railroad is operating compared with other railroads, and whether the hotel is profitable compared with other hotels, or the success or failure of the trucking company measured with other such companies. By segregating the income into the various sources and charging the expenses of producing the income to the source of the income, the corporation is in effect making up several income statements. It must not be supposed, however, that if one of these ventures compares unfavorably with that of other like companies that it should be discontinued. The hotels operated by a railroad might be operated at a loss, but still might be the means of increasing the income of the railroad far beyond what it would be if the hotels were not being operated.

The income statement. Income statements were formerly prepared in a very dry and technical fashion so that only a person fairly well trained in accounting or analyzing statements could comprehend them. In more recent years, those companies which submit statements to security holders have endeavored to make their statements more understandable to the stockholder or bondholder who has little if any training in accounting or finance. Many companies go even further than merely presenting figures in a conventional form and describe the operations in narrative style illustrating the report with simple charts and graphs.

STATEMENT OF CONSOLIDATED INCOME

	Year 1956		Year 1955	
1. Gross Operating Income ...		$1,180,101,830		$1,110,066,902
2. Costs and Expenses:				
Costs, operating and general expenses	$944,527,339		$895,579,948	
Depreciation, depletion and amortization	74,902,217		67,703,046	
Leases and concessions cancelled, dry holes and property retirements ..	26,284,978	1,045,714,534	30,413,978	993,696,972
3. Operating Income		134,387,296		116,369,930
4. Other Income:				
Interest	1,222,694		1,010,756	
Dividends	6,685,849		5,973,568	
Miscellaneous—net	1,137,917	9,046,460	1,424,325	8,408,649
		143,433,756		124,778,579
5. Other Deductions:				
Interest	9,018,637		9,050,557	
Net income applicable to minority interests in Venezuelan subsidiaries	344,307	9,362,944	293,068	9,343,625
6. Income—Before U. S. Federal Taxes on Income		134,070,812		115,434,954
7. Provision for U. S. Federal Taxes on Income		43,000,000		34,725,000
8. Net Income		91,070,812		80,709,954
9. Net Income per Share (based on average number of shares outstanding during the respective years)		$6.17		$6.01
10. Special Credit:				
Profit on sale of stock of Westpan Hydrocarbon Company (no provision required for U. S. Federal taxes on income) (Note 3)		4,835,355		—
11. Net Income and Special Credit		$ 95,906,167		$ 80,709,954

STATEMENT OF CONSOLIDATED EARNINGS RETAINED
IN THE BUSINESS

	Year 1956	Year 1955
28. Balance at Beginning of Year	$512,756,674	$468,624,853
29. Net Income and (in 1956) Special Credit	95,906,167	80,709,954
	608,662,841	549,334,807
30. Dividends Paid on Common Stock—(1956—$3.00; 1955—$2.70)	44,316,742	36,578,133
31. Balance at Close of Year	$564,346,099	$512,756,674

CONSOLIDATED BALANCE SHEET
(December 31, 1956 and 1955)

ASSETS

		1956	1955
1.	Current Assets:		
2.	Cash	$ 224,693,526	$ 124,887,100
3.	U. S. Government and other short term securities, at cost which approximates market	712,583	25,490,589
4.	Accounts and notes receivable, less allowance for doubtful accounts	104,309,671	109,324,671
5.	Inventories:		
	Crude and refined oils, at cost following the last-in first-out principle (lower than aggregate market) ..	122,651,587	102,389,232
	Materials and supplies, at cost or fair value	29,706,838	23,838,953
	Total Current Assets	482,074,205	385,930,545
6.	Investments:		
7.	Richfield Oil Corporation (1,223,581 shares), at cost ..	12,518,425	12,518,425
8.	Texas Pacific Coal and Oil Company (1,091,692 shares), at cost	47,564,384	—
9.	Other investments, at cost or less	16,262,218	10,768,516
		76,345,027	23,286,941
10.	Properties, Plant and Equipment:		
	At cost, less accumulated depreciation, depletion and amortization	884,307,069	812,893,649
11.	Other Assets and Deferred Charges:		
12.	Notes and accounts receivable due after one year, less allowance for doubtful accounts	13,096,495	13,019,780
13.	Due from officers and employees under Amended Stock Purchase and Option Plan (Note 4-c)	7,040,414	9,094,971
14.	Prepaid expenses and other charges	10,405,793	5,899,426
		30,542,702	28,014,177
		$1,473,269,003	$1,250,125,312

LIABILITIES

		1956	1955
15.	Current Liabilities:		
16.	Accounts payable	$ 101,148,560	$ 100,678,022
17.	Long term debt due within one year	18,732,257	8,764,449
18.	Accrued interest and taxes (including provision for U. S. Federal taxes on income)	50,217,630	44,774,004
	Total Current Liabilities	170,098,447	154,216,475
19.	Deferred U. S. Federal Taxes on Income (Note 2)	10,800,000	6,900,000
20.	Long Term Debt Due After One Year	355,168,755	248,676,951
21.	Reserves—Insurance and Miscellaneous	9,720,814	9,207,454
	Total Liabilities and Reserves	545,788,016	419,000,880

STOCKHOLDERS' OWNERSHIP

22. Minority Stockholders of Venezuelan Petroleum Company ..	2,419,476	2,075,169
23. Sinclair Oil Corporation Stockholders:		

24.   Common stock: (Note 4)
    Authorized—20,000,000 shares—par value $5 per share
    Issued—15,487,555 shares at December 31, 1956,
        14,528,428 shares at December 31, 1955 ....
	77,437,775	72,642,140

25. Other paid-in capital	287,151,748	248,374,927
26. Earnings retained in the business	564,346,099	512,756,674
	928,935,622	833,773,741
27. Less: Cost of common stock in treasury (264,957 shares at December 31, 1956)	3,874,111	4,724,478
Total (applicable to 15,222,598 shares out- standing at December 31, 1956)	925,061,511	829,049,263
	$1,473,269,003	$1,250,125,312

STATEMENT OF OTHER PAID-IN CAPITAL

	Year 1956
32. BALANCE AT BEGINNING OF YEAR	$248,374,927
33. ADDITIONS:	

34.   Excess paid in over par value of shares issued upon conversion of $42,295,400
    principal amount of 3¼% Convertible Subordinated Debentures less net
    expense applicable thereto ....
	37,059,328

35. Excess paid in over par value of shares issued upon conversion of 4⅜% Con- vertible Subordinated Debentures	593
36. Excess of sales prices over cost of treasury stock delivered under amended stock purchase and option plan	1,716,900
37. BALANCE AT CLOSE OF YEAR	$287,151,748

LONG TERM DEBT AT DECEMBER 31, 1956

	Payable in 1957	Payable in Later Years	TOTAL
20-Year 2¾% Sinking Fund Debentures, due August 1, 1965	$ 2,750,000	$ 1,750,000	$ 4,500,000
25-Year 2⅞% Sinking Fund Debentures, due December 1, 1972	2,600,000	36,550,000	39,150,000
25-Year 3% Sinking Fund Debentures, due November 1, 1974	—	50,000,000	50,000,000
25-Year 3⅜% Sinking Fund Debentures, due August 1, 1976 (Sinclair Pipe Line Company)	3,400,000	61,300,000	64,700,000
3¼% Convertible Subordinated Debentures, called for redemption January 3, 1957 (Note 4-a)	4,570,000	—	4,570,000
4⅜% Convertible Subordinated Debentures, due December 1, 1986 (Note 4-b)	—	167,246,900	167,246,900
3⅛% (maximum 3¼%) Instalment Notes Payable to Banks, due April 1, 1957 to October 1, 1961 (present interest rate 3¼%)	5,000,000	23,000,000	28,000,000
3% Instalment Notes Payable to Banks, due September 1, 1958 to September 1, 1962 (Venezuelan Petroleum Company)	—	15,000,000	15,000,000
Purchase Money and Other Obligations	412,257	321,855	734,112
Total	$18,732,257	$355,168,755	$373,901,012

PROPERTIES, PLANT AND EQUIPMENT AT DECEMBER 31

	GROSS		NET (After accumulated depreciation, depletion and amortization)	
	1956	1955	1956	1955
Properties and equipment for oil and gas production	$ 681,019,020	$ 594,863,947	$384,850,170	$329,609,500
Natural gasoline plants and equipment	37,274,092	31,865,048	18,794,678	14,965,112
Crude oil and products pipe line facilities	177,424,880	170,245,388	120,467,504	116,987,428
Oil tankers and other marine equipment	24,240,253	24,415,495	9,121,991	10,266,505
Refineries	349,832,664	332,053,505	193,244,401	189,016,341
Terminals, bulk distributing stations, service stations, tank cars and other marketing facilities .	237,798,400	225,085,977	145,806,044	140,762,553
Research laboratories and equipment	10,564,886	9,811,918	6,863,973	6,554,450
All other	10,658,097	9,573,696	5,158,308	4,731,760
Total	$1,528,812,292	$1,397,914,974	$884,307,069	$812,893,649

NOTES TO FINANCIAL STATEMENTS

•

NOTE 1—Gross Operating Income includes sales of purchased crude oil amounting to $212,800,793 and $184,065,276 in 1956 and 1955, respectively. The cost at which such crude oil was purchased closely approximated the sales price.

NOTE 2—Under Certificates of Necessity, portions of the cost of certain properties, plant and equipment are being amortized for U.S. Federal income tax purposes over a period of five years, whereas in the financial statements depreciation on these facilities has been accrued at normal rates. To offset the resulting temporary tax deferment, the estimated provision for U.S. Federal taxes on income includes $3,900,000 in 1956 and $3,600,000 in 1955 (no portion of which is applicable to common carrier pipelines) representing the consequent tax liability which it is expected will arise in later periods.

NOTE 3—The sale in 1956 of the Company's interest in Westpan Hydrocarbon Company, on which a profit of $4,835,355 was realized, completed Sinclair's divestment of holdings which it received under the corporate simplification plan of Southwestern Development Company, a company which was subject to the provisions of the Public Utility Holding Company Act.

NOTE 4—(a) Subsequent to December 31, 1956, 76,946 shares of common stock were issued upon conversion of $3,398,800 principal amount of 3¼% Convertible Subordinated Debentures. The remaining debentures amounting to $1,171,200 were redeemed on January 3, 1957.

(b) There were 2,573,029 shares of common stock reserved at December 31, 1956 for conversion of the 4⅝% Convertible Subordinated Debentures (initial conversion price, effective until December 1, 1961, $65 per share).

(c) At the beginning of the year, options (all exercisable) were outstanding to purchase 1,700 shares at $39.50 per share, 26,335 shares at $34.00 per share, and 63,200 shares at $41.25 per share. During 1956 options were exercised for the purchase of 1,700 shares at $39.50, 18,000 shares at $34.00, and 45,800 shares at $41.25, leaving options outstanding at December 31, 1956 for 8,335 shares at $34.00 and 17,400 shares at $41.25. The options were granted under the Company's Amended Stock Purchase and Option Plan on July 2, 1951, November 24, 1953 and April 14, 1954, respectively, at prices per share which were not less than "closing market" on the day preceding the dates of grant. The options expire five years from the dates of grant, or prior thereto in certain contingencies. No further options may be granted pursuant to the Plan under which the authorization to grant options expired May 18, 1954. The Company holds 192,675 shares as collateral security for amounts outstanding at December 31, 1956 under options exercised for the purchase of said shares.

NOTE 5—Annual rentals on certain office buildings held under long-term leases approximate $2,700,000, and annual expenses for tankers under long-term charter, expiring in 1960 and thereafter, are estimated at $9,500,000. The Company estimates that rentals paid less rentals received in respect of service stations held under long-term leases will be approximately $4,800,000 in 1957, which estimate excludes, however, service station rentals based on volume of gasoline sold.

Under long-term agreements with companies in which it has stock investments the Company might be required under certain conditions to provide them with additional funds through advances against future charges for transportation and merchandise. No loss is anticipated by reason of such agreements.

The Sinclair Oil Co. statement (pages 260-63) is a typical statement. The many items going to make up both the income statement and the balance sheet must be understood by every student of finance. While a textbook on accounting should be consulted for a comprehensive understanding of the principles involved in their preparation, a brief discussion of the various items here will aid in a better understanding of corporation finance.

Item 1. Gross operating income has been discussed above.

Item 2. Costs and Expenses. All of these expenses were incurred in obtaining the operating income. The expenses included in this section therefore are operating expenses and not financial expenses. That is, these expenses arose out of the effort to procure and sell the company's products.

Item 3. This is the difference between item 1 and item 2. Stated in another way, it is the profit derived from operations before financial expenses have been considered.

Item 4. This item has already been discussed.

Item 5. This classification contains two expense entries. The first, interest, represents the cost of the money borrowed by the company. The amount of the long-term debt appears as item 20 on the balance sheet, the short-term portion of the debt as item 17. The company has included as a part of its annual statement the details of the amount of each bond issue, the year payable, and the breakdown between that portion of the debt due within the current year and that portion due in the future. A simple calculation here will show that the company paid an average interest rate of 3.36 per cent for its borrowed money during the year. The second deduction represents that portion of the income of a Venezuelan subsidiary which was earned by the minority interest. Inasmuch as this is a consolidated report, the total income from the Venezuelan company was included as belonging to Sinclair. However, since the Sinclair Oil Co. does not have a 100 per cent interest, the share of the income equal to the proportionate share owned by the minority interest is presented here as a deduction.

Item 6. This represents the income earned by the company from all sources and after all deductions. It is the sum of items 1 and 4 less the sum of items 2 and 5.

Item 7. It is virtually impossible to compute the corporate income tax from figures published in annual financial reports for many reasons. Depreciation, for example, may be treated one way for tax purposes and another way for the company's own records. Certain items may be carried forward or backward from one tax computation to the next which are not ascertainable from the annual report—and indeed there is no reason to include them as the company is reporting the financial operation to those concerned, not the income tax report. Frequently a footnote to the financial statement will explain certain items such as depreciation. In the footnotes which accompanied the Sinclair statement, the management indicated in a summary form the differences between the income reported for tax purposes and the income reported in the financial statement.

Item 8. This is the result obtained after subtracting the income tax in the previous item from the net income shown in item 6.

Item 9. is not properly a part of the income statement. Nevertheless, it is added so that the stockholders and others concerned can compare the earnings per share this year with the earnings per share in the previous years.

Item 10. This might well have been labeled *non-recurring* income. It is capital gain and therefore should not be included in an income statement. It might well have been set apart to distinguish profit on the sale of capital assets from income. However, like all profit, it is a part of the income of the company for this year. It was placed after item 9 so that an analyst would not wonder in later years why the "income" behaved so erratically in 1956. It also puts the stockholder on notice that this is not to be expected again in future years.

Item 11. represents the total income, including all money earned by the company after giving effect to all the expenses incurred in earning the money.

The balance sheet. The balance sheet is a statement of the assets, liabilities and capital of the business as of a given date. It is a static picture of the business as opposed to the movement portrayed by the figures in the income statement. In the balance sheet of the Sinclair Oil Corporation and subsidiaries, the assets are classified into four categories: current assets; investments; property, plant and equipment; and other assets and deferred charges. Current assets are composed of cash, United States Government and other short-term securities, notes receivables, and inventories. Government securities are, to all intents and purposes, cash as they can be converted to cash on almost a few moments' notice. The inventories have been valued on the principle of last-in, first-out. However, a parenthetical statement makes it clear that such value was lower than aggregate market value. For a detailed analysis of inventory is necessary if an adequate appraisal of the company's current position is to be made. Inventory is further divided into two portions. The first represents the products of the company to be sold to customers in the regular course of business, the second the materials and supplies on hand required in the production processes. Often this latter portion of the inventory is carried separately, outside of current assets.

The second classification of assets (items 6, 7, 8, 9) represents the parent company's ownership in its subsidiaries, and in other companies over which it may have little, if any, control. This is a consolidated balance sheet, therefore the total earnings from the subsidiaries are reflected in the earnings statement.

The third classification is that of properties, plant and equipment. The value assigned to these assets are the cost to the company when it originally acquired them less accumulated depreciation, depletion and amortization. Stated in this form, it is of limited use since it is too general for detailed analysis. To assist the analyst, the company has enlarged this figure by means of a detailed table of the cost and the accumulation of depreciation on each item of their major properties.

The fourth classification is a catch-all of items which cannot logically be placed in the other groups. In the aggregate, it is usually of minor importance.

On the liability side of the balance sheet, the current liabilities are largely self-explanatory from the terms used. In addition to the accounts payable for the ordinary purchases of the company of raw materials and supplies, the company owed interest to creditors and taxes to the government. The long-term debt due within the year and the long-term debt not due within the year are itemized in a separate schedule. The total debt of $373,901,012 consists of sinking fund debentures, convertible subordinated debentures, and installment notes payable to banks. Of the total debt, $18,732,257 matured within the current year; hence it is considered a current liability. The remaining amount will mature in varying amounts from 1958 to 1986. Notice that the tax liability of the company is carried in two separate lines (items 18 and 20). The company received *certificates of necessity* from the government which permitted it to write off, or depreciate, certain of its properties over a five-year period. For tax purposes, therefore, the company computed the depreciation rate at 20 per cent each year. For its own purposes the company depreciates these properties and equipment over what it considers to be the normal life of the equipment. The accelerated rate of depreciation permitted under the certificate of necessity provides that the entire cost of the property may be depreciated at the rate of 20 per cent a year and charged off against income for tax purposes, at that rate. Therefore, after five years, although the assets are still in use, there can be no further charge against income for depreciation. If the company did not adjust the accounts so that the normal rate of depreciation could be applied throughout the life of the asset, the income would be understated during the first five years and overstated for the balance of the asset's useful life. In footnotes the company refers to the rapid rate of depreciation as a temporary tax deferment.

The stockholders' ownership or capital section of the balance sheet is important, not so much for the portion which concerns the common stock outstanding and in the treasury, as for the portion which reflects changes in the surplus. The change in the item "earnings retained in the business" from one period to another, links the balance sheet and the income statement. In fact, it has been said that the entire income statement exists principally to show the changes which have occurred in this section of the balance sheet. Of course, this is an oversimplification which is misleading. From the statement, it appears that by December 31, 1955, the company had retained in the business over the years the sum of $512,756,-674 (item 28). The consolidated income statement discloses that $95,906,-167 was earned by the company during 1956, and this was added to retained profits at the beginning of the year. From the sum of the two, the company paid dividends of $44,316,742 to the stockholders, leaving a balance at the close of the year of $564,346,099. Similarly, changes in capital surplus during the year are accounted for. These changes are set forth in the table on page 262. The major increase arose out of the conversion of the debentures. Since the par value of the common stock is $5.00 a share and the bonds were convertible during the year into common stock at a price of $44 per share, a capital surplus of $39 a share is created each time a bond is converted into stock. The sum of $37,059,328 represents the total difference between the $5.00 par and the $44 purchase price upon conversion, subject, however, to an adjustment for the expenses incident to conversion and an adjustment of interest on the bond and dividend on the stock. The sum of $1,716,900, shown arising from the sale of treasury stock delivered under the stock purchase and option plan, works in the same fashion. The company sold the stock for a price exceeding the $5.00 par value to the purchasers.

Adequacy of income. The income of any business must of necessity be sufficient to pay all operating expenses, including the upkeep of the property, and still leave enough money over to pay interest on borrowed capital and a fair return on the owners' investment. If this cannot be done, the business is not a financial success. Money is invested in a business solely to produce profits; it is this feature that distinguishes business from philanthropic activities.

No standard can be established as to adequacy of revenue. That point is determined by the nature of the business. As it has been shown in the chapter on capitalizing the corporation, investors are more inclined to be content with a small return when the safety of the business is reasonably assured than they are with a big profit when there are many hazards.

Relation of income to fixed charges. The directors must take care that their company does not issue bonds calling for interest payments likely to exceed the available gross income. As observed below, when the operating revenues are stable and the operating expenses are fairly constant, the business may incur a larger percentage of fixed charges. If the margin above the interest is too narrow, relief must be sought by: (1) reducing fixed charges, (2) reducing the operating expenses without a corresponding reduction in the operating revenues, or (3) increasing the operating revenues more rapidly than the operating expenses.

The reduction of the funded debt is usually a difficult task requiring the consent of the bondholders, or, if the bonds are redeemable, requiring cash or occasionally a refunding issue of either stocks or bonds. The difficulties involved in the adjustments of such debts of a company are treated in Chapters IX and XVII.

The second expedient, that of reducing the operating expenses without a proportionate decline in operating revenues, is equally hard to achieve. It will be remembered that attention was called to the fact that a large percentage of operating expenses is fixed; also, that a reduction would be likely to disrupt the organization, which would result temporarily in inefficiency and loss. Industries that have as their chief item of expense the wages to unskilled labor and that have little fixed capital can most readily adjust their operating expenses to correspond with their operating revenues.

Perhaps the third method is the most feasible. Greater concentration on advertising and selling, with special attention given to customers and the careful and expeditious filling of orders, may produce the desired effect. Attention is called to the advantage of large-scale production, which, when possible to apply it, results in lower unit operating costs.

Desirability of stable income. There are many reasons why steady revenues are desirable. Chief among them are the following:

(1) A larger percentage of the capitalization can be composed of bonds with fixed charges, but with lower interest rates. This feature makes possible larger returns to the owners; that is, the stockholders.

(2) More definite production and financial plans may be devised, because of the relative certainty of the requirements.

(3) A permanent organization can be maintained, a factor that will result in economies to the business.

(4) The credit standing of the company is improved. This point applies

particularly to the sale of securities, which makes possible cheaper financing.

⑤ Stability of dividends follows, giving investment characteristics to the stock.

Depreciation. No one could question the fact that the business must incur expenses for wages, for if the employees are not paid they usually do not care to continue working. But what is not so obvious, perhaps, is the fact that the use of buildings and equipment owned must be paid for too. Accountants refer to the latter cost as *depreciation* and treat it as an expense of doing business just as the worker's salary is an expense of doing business. Gone are the days when a human laborer did most, if not all, of the work. Today, as automation becomes more feasible, increased amounts of expensive machinery and equipment must be furnished to each worker. The number of persons employed has increased steadily each year since the end of World War II. The capital investment per worker has grown at an even greater rate. At the end of 1956 Sinclair Oil Corporation, for example, had an investment of $51,798 for each employee. Ten years prior to that date, the investment per employee was $25,788. Although there is no cash outgo required to "pay" the "wages" of this machinery which is working side by side with the human employee, its use constitutes a cost which must be met out of gross income of the company. Should the gross income be insufficient to meet this cost in addition to other costs, then the business is a failure.

Depreciation may be defined as the loss in value of tangible assets arising from physical, functional, and accidental causes. Not all tangible assets are subject to depreciation in the accounting sense, however. Inventory might depreciate in value on the shelves from physical, functional, or accidental causes. This loss must be acknowledged in arriving at the profit or loss for the year but, since it arises out of sales in the ordinary course of the business, it is more appropriately considered in the computation of the cost of goods sold. Land does not wear out if it is being used to support a building, or for the landscaping of the area around the factory or office. It may wear out, however, if it is used for farming or other purposes than support. The term depreciation applies to assets whose duration might be prolonged by repairs, renewals or replacements. It has no relation whatsoever to the replacement cost of the item at such time as the item becomes worn out. That is, the depreciation is a charge for the wearing out or loss in value of assets now owned rather than a means of providing for their replacement at such future time.

Many persons argue that this is not wise. In a period of rising prices such as has prevailed since World War II, it does not seem to some realistic to charge depreciation based on the original cost of building and equipment when the cost of replacement will most certainly be much more. Some argue that the charge should be based on the estimated replacement value and that if the annual charge for depreciation over the life of the machine or building is not sufficient to replace the machine when it wears out, then the company is using up its capital. The accountant, on the other hand, maintains that the concept of depreciation is one of cost, not replacement. If the business uses today's machine, it is to be charged for this and not for the machine that the company may buy tomorrow or the day after that. The two concepts are each logical and yet irreconcilable.

Depletion. The term *depletion* is employed in connection with assets that cannot be replaced, or the duration of which cannot be lengthened by repairs or renewals. It is thus a loss in quantity. Such assets are sometimes referred to as wasting assets, as they are constantly being converted from a fixed property investment to stock in trade and are sold. Oil fields, mines, and forests are subject to depletion; buildings and machinery depreciate.

Deterioration. Deterioration is a term used to designate a loss in quality of an asset. Such loss may arise through wear and tear in the normal use of the asset, or it may be due to decay through the action of the elements, such as rust. Deterioration renders the asset less valuable, hence it depreciates it.

Cause of depreciation. Depreciation may be the result of many causes, operating sometimes jointly and at other times singly. It must always be remembered that the effect is not cumulative, and that the cause that will result in complete depreciation in the shortest time will dominate. The cause may never, for instance, be both inadequacy and obsolescence at the same time; one predominates. The cause resulting in the earliest abandonment of the asset is known as effective depreciation, and serves as a basis for the depreciation charge.

CAUSES OF DEPRECIATION

I. TANGIBLE PROPERTY:

A. *Physical.*
$\begin{cases} \text{1. Wear and tear.} \\ \text{2. Decrepitude—age.} \\ \quad \text{a. Action of time.} \\ \quad \text{b. Action of elements (normal).} \end{cases}$

B. *Functional.*
$\begin{cases} \text{1. Inadequacy.} \\ \text{2. Governmental requirements.} \\ \text{3. Obsolescence.} \end{cases}$

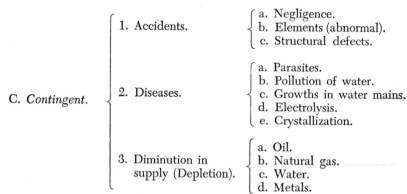

II. Intangible Property Rights:[1]
    A. *Limited in time.*
    B. *Abandoned.*

Depreciation policy. The depreciation policy of a business is evidenced by the rate at which depreciation is charged off each year. It must be remembered that depreciation is a cost of doing business that must, along with other expenses, be considered in determining net profits. A concern that is liberal in the amount charged off each year is said to have a conservative depreciation policy. In considering a depreciation policy, a concern must include a maintenance policy. A concern that is on the alert to repair and renew its equipment to the point of efficiency prolongs the life of its assets and thereby reduces the amount necessary to charge to depreciation each year. Maintenance, therefore, is directly connected with depreciation, and both together constitute a concern's expenses for depreciating assets. At this point, however, it must be recalled that although maintenance involves a cash outlay, depreciation is a bookkeeping charge against the profits.

Calculating the amount of the depreciation charge. There are several methods of calculating the amount of depreciation to be charged off each year. The soundest methods are based on three elements, namely: (1) the original, or cost, value of the asset, (2) the length of time it may be profitably used by the business, and (3) the scrap or trade-in value at the end of its useful life. Under the provisions of the current federal income tax law, three methods of computing the depreciation allowance are permitted. In each method, consideration of the three elements of cost, life and junk value may be considered. The most popular method because of its simplicity is the *straight-line* method. To compute the annual depreciation charge, simply divide the total cost of the item less scrap value

---

[1] In modern accounting practice, intangible assets are not usually included in computing depreciation, the cost being amortized over an appropriate period. Accidents may be covered by insurance or by contingency reserves or, more often, by purchase of insurance policies.

by the number of years of useful life. Thus, if a machine cost $1,100 and has an estimated scrap value at the end of five years of $100, then the annual charge for depreciation is: $1100 - 100 = 1000 \div 5 = \$200$. Depreciation is often expressed as a percentage of the value of the asset. An asset that lasts a long time will, of course, have a smaller percentage of its value charged off each year. Typically the depreciation following the straight-line method is based on the following annual rates:

Buildings (including improvements and equipment)	2½ to 7½%
Machinery and equipment	5 to 15%
Furniture	6⅔ to 10%
Automobiles and trucks	20 to 33⅓%

In the 1952 Code of Internal Revenue, two additional methods of computing depreciation were permitted. One method is called the fixed percentage of a declining balance method. It is so-called because each year a fixed percentage is applied to the original cost less the scrap value, the result subtracted from the starting figure, and the same percentage applied to the remaining balance. This procedure is followed each year for the useful life of the equipment or machine being depreciated. The percentage to be applied is determined by formula but the percentage may not be more than twice the percentage employed in the straight-line method. In this method, salvage value is not deducted prior to determining the annual rate. Assuming, for example, that an asset acquired for $1,000 is to be depreciated over five years by this method, the following computation will illustrate the practice:

1st year $1,000 ÷ .40 equals $400; remaining value $600
2nd year $600 ÷ .40 equals $240; remaining value $360
3rd year $360 ÷ .40 equals $144; remaining value $116
4th year $116 ÷ .40 equals $46.60; remaining value $69.60
5th year $69.60 ÷ .40 equals $19.84; remaining value $49.76

The amount remaining will ordinarily be recovered from salvage.

The second method permitted under the new code is termed "sum of the digits." Again the original cost less the scrap value is computed as in the straight line method above. Then the sum of the number of years in the life of the machine is procured. In the above illustration, where the life of the machine is five years, the sum of 5, 4, 3, 2, 1 is 15. The amount to be charged for depreciation each year would then be found by taking 5/15 the first year, 4/15 the second, 3/15 the third, 2/15 the fourth, and 1/15 the fifth year.

1st year 5/15 of $1,000:	$ 333.33
2nd year 4/15 of $1,000:	267.67
3rd year 3/15 of $1,000:	201.00
4th year 2/15 of $1,000:	133.33
5th year 1/15 of $1,000:	66.67
	$1,000.00

The straight-line method makes it possible for a company to recover half of the value of the item during the first half of the useful life of the item. In each of the other two methods, about two-thirds of the value of the item is recovered in the first half of its life. Where there is a danger of a machine becoming obsolete before its useful life has run it is, of course, an advantage to secure the maximum recovery before the advent of the new machine makes the old one uneconomical to operate. Likewise, an expanding industry will find it an advantage to secure higher recovery in the early years to provide funds for additional capital acquisitions. An industry which is stable, or which has no great need for funds, will probably adopt the straight-line method, as it evens out profits over the life of the machine through the regular and similar charge against profits each year. The company which makes a liberal depreciation charge in the early years finds its tax lowered as the income is lower. Conversely, in latter years when the depreciation charge is less, its profit is consequently higher. On the increased income, it stands to reason that the income tax will be higher.

Cash flow. The owners of a business are primarily interested in the profits. But the financial manager of the business faces the task of administering not only the profits, but all the cash which comes into the company as well as the cash which is paid out. Most of the cash is utilized for the raw materials, for rent, supplies, and wages. One of the expenses, however, which the accountant charges against gross income, as we have seen, is the expense for depreciation of assets. Nevertheless, there is no cash outgo for this expense. The treasurer writes no check on the corporate bank account. The cash flowing through the corporate bank account must be adjusted to reflect the fact that some of the items which the accountant charged against gross income in fact never left the company. A simple illustration will serve to demonstrate this. Suppose the XYZ Corporation starts its corporate life with the sale of $1,000 worth of stock. The balance sheet will then appear:

ASSETS		LIABILITIES	
Cash	$1,000		
		Stock	$1,000
Total Assets	$1,000		$1,000

Now suppose the company buys a machine with this thousand dollars and that this machine is going to produce a thousand parts and then become worthless. To simplify matters, let us suppose that there will be no scrap value whatever for the machine. The balance sheet will change to look like this:

ASSETS		LIABILITIES	
Cash	0		
Machine	$1,000	Stock	$1,000
Total	$1,000		$1,000

Let us suppose further that the company makes the first of its products—a wondrous widget. If the selling price is $5.00, the profit and loss statement might look something like this:

Sales			$5
Raw materials	$1		
Wages	1		
Overhead	1		
Depreciation	1	4	
Profit			$1

If the treasurer writes checks to cover expenses and profit, he will write four checks of $1.00 each. One dollar for raw material, a second dollar for the direct wages, the third for the various items of overhead, and the fourth for the owner as his profit. One dollar of the five still remains in the bank and the balance sheet will now look like this:

ASSETS			LIABILITIES	
Cash		1		
Machine	$1,000			
less depreciation	1			
		999	Stock	$1,000
		$1,000		$1,000

The depreciation charge has been the means of putting cash into the business. This cash may be used for anything—new equipment, adding to the inventory, or replacing old equipment, to suggest a few uses. Sometimes the amount recovered for depreciation and depletion (which works in the same fashion) exceeds the profits of the company. From the profit statement of Sinclair Oil Corporation and subsidiaries on page 260, it appears that the profit for the year 1956 was $9,070,812 compared to the charge for depreciation and depletion of $74,902,217.

What is surplus? The surplus of a corporation may be defined as the excess of its assets over its liabilities and capital stock. It appears on the balance sheet of the business. Usually it is divided into earnings retained in the business and paid-in or capital surplus.

The word "surplus" is not always fully understood by those unfamiliar with accounting practices. In fact, sometimes it is thought to represent cash on hand. Perhaps its real meaning would be better understood if it is pointed out that a corporation could be in serious financial difficulty and unable to pay its bills or interest charges and still have a substantial surplus. All of the many railroad corporations which went through Federal bankruptcy reorganization procedures in the period extending from 1932 to 1946 had substantial surpluses in their balance sheets at the time such legal proceedings were begun. Many large corporations, despite large surpluses, have suspended or reduced their dividends during periods of business recession because to continue payment at previous rates in the face of declining income would have reduced the cash on hand to a dangerous point.

Sources of surplus and availability for dividends. Surplus is not necessarily the result of accumulated profits, that is, profits retained in the business. Since surplus merely represents the excess of assets over liabilities, any upward revaluation of assets not resulting in an equivalent increase in liabilities, or any reduction in liabilities that does not also involve a reduction in the amount of the assets, results in increased surplus.

Profits constitute the most general source of surplus. However the fact that surplus arises from many other sources should not be overlooked. These sources must be understood by the financial administrator in order that he may accurately determine the real net worth of the corporation. Moreover, the sources of surplus should be taken into careful consideration when the declaration of dividends is contemplated by the directors. At this point, and before going any further, it must again be emphasized strongly that surplus is not entirely in the form of cash. A reference to the Sinclair Oil Corporation statement will show that the cash is only about one-half of the amount of the earned surplus. The statement is often made that "dividends must be paid out of surplus." This statement may be misleading. Cash for the payment of dividends cannot come out of surplus. The balance sheet of a business is just what the name implies —a balancing of the assets on the one side with the liabilities and capital account on the other side.

Therefore, any transaction must involve two accounts. There may be an increase in an asset, as for example cash, offset by a decrease in another asset, for example, accounts receivable. Or there may be a decrease in the asset "cash" and a decrease in the account "surplus." When the laws of some states provide that dividends can be paid only out of surplus, it means that a dividend in cash (or property for that matter) may be paid only if there is a surplus existing which can be decreased by the same amount as the cash or property disbursed. Therefore, if there is insufficient cash but an adequate surplus, no cash dividend is possible. On the other hand, if there is plenty of cash but no surplus on current net earnings, no dividend could be declared.[2]

A moment's reflection will show the reason for this rule. If cash dividends were distributed to stockholders, what account on the liability side would be charged? There are only three possibilities, *viz.*, a liability,

---

[2] In some states, Delaware for example, dividends may be declared out of current net profits even though a deficit exists. In others, profits must be applied to erase a deficit before any dividend may be paid. This is the case in New York.

capital stock, or surplus. It can't be a liability since obviously the debts are not decreasing; therefore it must be capital stock. Court decisions have stated that the capital stock account is in the nature of a "trust fund" for creditors. That is, the creditors have accepted the credit of the corporation based on the existence of a "cushion" of stockholders' contributions. For example, if the creditors of a new corporation are asked to sell a thousand dollars' worth of merchandise on credit, they might well ask, "Well, how much are you, the owners, putting up?" If the owners reply, "We, too, are putting up $1,000," the creditors can easily figure that for every dollar they put up the owners are matching it. Now if the owners withdraw part, or all, of their thousand, where do the creditors stand? The same thing would happen if the owners now declare a dividend from the capital stock.

Although the directors may have the legal right to declare a dividend from any surplus (there are some exceptions to this statement) that may appear on the balance sheet, it is not always good financial policy to do so. Accountants follow the policy of separating the earned surplus, that is, the surplus built up from accumulated earnings, from other sources of surplus. It is primarily from the accumulated earnings that dividends are paid even where the law governing the distribution of dividends may permit the declaration and payment of dividends from any surplus.

The principal sources of surplus are:

1. *Current earnings from operations and from outside operations.* These certainly are the primary sources to which business should look for the building up of its surplus. Surplus derived from both of these sources may be properly used for dividends in all states. Income from outside operations coming from rentals, interest and dividends accruing to the business from bonds and stocks held may also be properly used for dividends. Some companies lease out all of their properties, and the rental from the property constitutes the entire income of the company. Parent companies, operating with a number of subsidiaries, often receive a large part of their income in the form of dividends on the stock of the subsidiaries, and non-operating holding companies obtain virtually all of their income from dividends and interest.

2. *Sale of securities above stated value.* Whenever a company sells its own stocks or bonds at a price above the par value, the asset side of the balance sheet would be greater than the liability side inasmuch as the cash would increase by the selling price, but the capital stock or bonds would be carried on the opposite side of the balance sheet at par. The difference between the cash received and the par value is capital surplus. Where no par stock is sold, many states permit an arbitrary division of the consideration received into the capital account and the capital surplus account. Surplus derived from this source should ordinarily not be

used for dividend purposes. Obviously it is merely returning to the stock-holder part of his original investment.

(3.) *Sale of assets for more than book value.* Companies that carry their assets at a conservative valuation sometimes have an opportunity to dispose of parts of them, especially unused real estate, at an advantageous price. Such a procedure, of course, increases the surplus by the amount by which the sale price exceeds the book value.

A surplus created by selling assets above their book value makes, in reality, a capital surplus, and should ordinarily be kept in the company. If there is apparently no possibility of ever having to replace the asset, the excess, provided it is properly explained, may in such cases be disbursed to stockholders.

(4.) *Upward revaluation of assets.* When it is found that any asset is actually worth more than the valuation at which it is carried on the books, it may, in some instances, be revalued at its worth. Such revaluation, of course, increases the amount of the total assets without creating any offsetting liability, and so helps to build up the surplus. Unscrupulous operators may write up the value of the assets beyond their worth. This practice creates a surplus on paper, which, of course, arises from an unrealized profit, and the practice is entirely unjustifiable. Where, for some reason, the value of assets is written up, the best accounting practice is to offset the increase with a reserve for revaluation of assets and not increase the surplus account.

A surplus created by the upward revaluation of assets is not usually distributed as dividends. The assets revalued later may prove to have been unjustifiably written up, or, if they were justly written up, they may again fall off in value.

(5.) *Donated surplus.* Any donation of value made to a business may be added to its surplus. The most common form of donation is that of stock donated to the treasury by one who has received stock in return for property, patents, services, etc. The real value of such treasury stock as an asset, however, is in most cases very questionable.

Surpluses caused by donations to a business should, of course, be used for the purpose stipulated by the donor. When stock is donated to the treasury, it is seldom good policy to use the surplus thus created for dividends. This surplus is capital surplus, rather than earned surplus, and the questionableness of the value of the treasury stock makes the surplus created thereby of dubious value.

(6.) *Surplus inherited from constituents of consolidation.* Surplus turned in by one or more of the businesses forming a consolidation goes toward building up the surplus of the consolidated company.

A surplus appearing in the balance sheet of a consolidated company as a result of its taking over the surpluses of constituent companies should be used by directors in whatever manner will best serve the interests of the consolidated company. However, directors should be guided in the use of such surplus by a careful consideration of the purposes and sources of the surpluses in the companies from which they were respectively derived.

7. *Conversion of unnecessary reserves.* Reserves, as will be shown later in this chapter, are, in reality, portions of the earnings set aside from the surplus for what are deemed necessary purposes before either the dividends or the surplus is determined. If one of these reserves is found to be unnecessary, it is perfectly proper to abolish it and to put the amount that had accumulated in the reserve back into the surplus.

Surplus from the conversion of unnecessary reserves is properly available for dividends, if it is not more urgently needed for some other purpose in the business. This reserve was originally held back out of earnings the entire sum of which would otherwise have been available for dividends. If no longer needed, it may properly be made available to the stockholders.

8. *Surplus derived from the purchase of the corporation's stock below par or stated value or its bonds below face value.* The purchase of stock below the value at which it appears in the capital account gives rise to a capital surplus similar in nature to that arising from the sale of stock at prices above par or stated value. It is not a profit and should not be used for dividends. Purchase of bonds below face value is somewhat different in that a real gain has been realized; still it ought to be treated as capital surplus. Presumably the proceeds of the bonds, when originally sold, has been invested largely in fixed assets and the purchase has not produced a presently realized cash profit. Proper and prudent financial management would not consider it available for dividends.

9. *Surplus from reduction in value of capital stock.* By various recapitalization processes, surplus is sometimes created through reduction in the stated value of a corporation's stock, such as the reduction in par value or reduction in the number of shares with the consent of the stockholders, and reduction in the stated value of the company's non-par stock.

Surplus derived through such recapitalization processes should not be used for dividend purposes. Such practice may result in rendering directors liable for impairment of the capital of the corporation.

Why surplus? The question often arises, "Why does a company hold back some of its earnings? Why doesn't it pay all of the profits out to the stockholders?" There are many sound reasons for this practice. Banks build up surplus for the protection of their depositors. And, by offering increasing security to the depositors, the bank hopes to attract additional deposits and over the years to increase its earnings. Insurance companies increase surplus for the same reason, that is, to add to the protection afforded the policyholders.

Industrials follow the same reasoning in part and increase surplus as a protection to creditors and increase their credit standing. However, the chief reason for retaining earnings is to expand the business. Expansion through the retention of earnings is often the most feasible way to keep pace with the growth of the economy. It is less costly than going to the financial market. The stockholder loses nothing if the profit of the business keeps pace with the increase in the surplus retained. If management has been wise in the expansion program, the retained profits should increase the market value of the stock.

Reserves. Until a few years ago, accountants almost universally classified reserves as *valuation reserves, liability reserves,* and *surplus reserves.* Original practice was to show these reserves on the liability side of the balance sheet. Later practice found accountants placing the accumulated depreciation and the reserve or allowance for bad debts on the asset side of the balance sheet where they appeared as deductions from property and the accounts receivable. The three types of reserves may be described as follows:

a. *Valuation reserves.* A valuation reserve is set up to offset loss of value in an asset. Thus the reserve may be the accumulation of the annual charge for the use of a machine or piece of equipment such as the depreciation reserve. Or it may be set up to provide for a possible diminution in the value of an asset through failure to realize the full value of the asset, as a reserve for bad debts.

b. *Liability reserves.* Liability reserves are provided where a known liability exists though the amount of the liability is uncertain. For example, it is certain that a profitable concern will have to pay an income tax yet the exact amount cannot be computed until the end of the year when the final profits for the year have been computed. To provide for this, a reserve for income taxes is set up as a current liability.

c. *Surplus reserves.* Surplus reserves represent merely an earmarking of surplus for some purpose. It is a notice to the stockholders that at least that part of the surplus represented by the reserve will not be used as an offset against cash dividends. Such surplus reserves are reserves for contingencies, for pensions, for insurance, for working capital, and other things.

Remember that reserves do not represent a fund. That is, there is usually no cash set aside. If desired, a fund could be set up by segregating cash equal to the reserve. This is often done in the case of insurance reserves.

The term *reserve* like that of *surplus* discussed in a preceding paragraph is not usually understood by those unfamiliar with accounting practice. Perhaps at one time this was not a serious matter, because those investing in the securities of corporations were relatively few and likely to be businessmen familiar with financial statements. Today, however, it is generally considered that the terminology used by corporations in presenting financial information to their stockholders and the public should be clearly understandable to those not versed in accounting techniques. There are a number of reasons for this, some of which are:

1. The stock of American corporations is held by thousands of persons. (American Telephone & Telegraph Co. has over 1,500,000 stockholders.) Corporations mail annual reports to all stockholders on record.

2. Newspapers print excerpts from corporate financial reports.

3. Under the federal law, initial public sale of new issues of securities must be accompanied by a prospectus which contains financial statements.

Both the American Institute of Certified Public Accountants and the American Accounting Association have advocated the adoption of accounting terminology and practice which results in the elimination of the use of the word "reserve" or greatly limits its use in the balance sheets of corporations.[3]

Without becoming too greatly involved in the details of accounting practice which would lead us beyond the province of this text, the tendencies in present-day accounting practice relative to this subject may be summarized as follows:

1. *Valuation reserves.* These reserves are chiefly concerned with depreciation and bad debts. It is recommended that they be shown respectively as *depreciation* and *uncollectibles.* They are to be carried on the asset side of the balance sheet as deductions from the pertinent property accounts and from accounts receivable. The annual charge for depreciation may properly be referred to as *depreciation expense.*

2. *Liability reserves.* The amount of the liability (the exact amount of which is unknown) should be estimated and, if payable within a year, appear among the current liabilities with an appropriate description. If desired, the word "estimated" may preface the description. If the liability is contingent and if it cannot be estimated, a footnote to the balance sheet should state the facts.

3. *Surplus reserves.* This type of reserve which may reflect managerial policies such as *Reserve for Working Capital,* or *Reserve for Expansion* or required by contract such as *Pension Reserves or Sinking Fund,* should be separately shown in the proprietory section of the balance sheet and there grouped to make one total under the heading *Appropriations of Retained Income.*

For a time, at least, the student will find both the old terminology and

3 American Institute of Certified Public Accountants, *Accounting Terminology Bulletin,* No. 1. New York: 1953. Also see *Accounting Review,* Vols. 25 and 26, American Accounting Association, Ohio State University.

practices as well as the practices recommended above in use. Public utilities and railroads whose accounting procedures are prescribed by governmental commissions may be expected to continue old practices for a long time. The regulating commissions are reluctant to change the many forms, orders and instructions involved for these may have resulted from protracted public hearings or in some cases from court decisions.

Directors' responsibility for surplus policy and dividends. The directors have the sole power of declaring dividends in a corporation. They must not pay dividends out of the capital. That is, there must actually be a surplus available if dividends are declared. The surplus need not necessarily be an earned surplus to satisfy the legal requirements. It is possible to *create* a surplus by *writing up* the value of the tangible assets, or by including an intangible item of goodwill on the asset side of the balance sheet. If these values exist, there is, in the absence of a statute, nothing illegal in the practice, though it is usually not considered good financial practice to create a surplus in this manner. A surplus may also be created by reducing the stated value of no-par stock or by reducing the par value of par value stock. The same object could be accomplished by reducing the amount of stock outstanding. These latter practices are often difficult to accomplish, because they require in most states the consent of all, or a two-thirds majority, of the stockholders.

Directors have been forced to repay dividends when they have been paid out of capital. They have been forced, also, to pay dividends when the stockholders have been able to show in court that they were being treated inequitably through the failure of the directors to declare certain dividends. The Dodge Brothers forced the Ford Automobile Company to distribute dividends to them as stockholders.[4]

Forms of dividend payments. Dividend payments may be made quarterly, semiannually, or at year end. Large corporations usually pay dividends quarterly. Quarterly payments, while more popular with the stockholders, are costly to the corporation because of the clerical and mailing expense involved. The postage alone to mail a dividend check to each of the American Telephone and Telegraph stockholders is over $48,000.

Dividends may be paid in:

1. cash	4. bonds
2. stock	5. property
3. scrip	

(1) *Cash dividends.* Cash payment of dividends is the most common. Such form of dividend is practically always desired by the stockholders in preference to dividends of any other kind. It is only when the stock-

---

[4] See *Dodge v. Ford Motor Co.*, 204 Mich. 459; 170 N.W. 668; 3 Am. L. Rep., 413-449.

holder is in the high income tax brackets that he might find some other type of dividend more to his liking.

(2.) *Stock dividends.* A stock dividend represents a capitalization of reinvested earnings of the corporation for, from an accounting point of view, a stock dividend results in the transfer of the amount of the dividend from the surplus account to the capital stock account. The result from the shareholder's point is the same as though he were paid a cash dividend and then compelled to invest his dividend in additional shares of stock in the company. The primary reason for paying a stock dividend is the desire on the part of the directors of insuring the retention of accumulated profits in the business. Stock dividends do not increase the equity of the stockholder; rather, his equity remains the same. If the stockholder sells the stock he received as a stock dividend, he parts with a portion of the equity he had in the business before the payment of the dividend. Theoretically the price of the stock should decline proportionately upon the payment of the stock dividend. A share of stock selling on the market at $120 before the payment of a 100 per cent stock dividend should decline to approximately $60 upon payment of the dividend. If, however, as is the case during prosperous times when most stock dividends are paid, the corporation is able to maintain the same cash dividend per share it customarily paid prior to the declaration of the stock dividend, the stock will advance in price because of the desirability of its increased cash dividend.

A stock dividend is nontaxable if, after the dividend is paid, the proportionate interest of the stockholders is not essentially different from their former interest.[5] The practical effect, therefore, of stock dividends is to withhold permanently from the stockholders the amount of earnings so capitalized.

Among the reasons for paying a stock dividend is that of pacifying stockholders who, if they did not receive any dividend, would be discontented. Corporations may also wish to increase the stock outstanding for the purpose of making the dividends appear smaller through being distributed over a greater number of shares or through large distributions to bring the price of their stock down to a more popular market level.

There is no doubt that stockholders regard stock dividends with almost as much favor as cash dividends. They do not seem to realize that a stock dividend represents a mere division of the stockholders' equity in a corporation into a greater number of units. From the standpoint of corporations, a stock dividend may point the way to a permanent retention of earnings for the purpose of expansion. It means practically the same thing as obtaining new capital from the stockholders in the amount of the stock dividend, and eliminates the expense of having to conduct

---

[5] *Eisner v. Macomber*, 152 U.S. 189.

a marketing campaign. The corporation's directors should not, however, declare stock dividends without bearing in mind the fact that the tendency will be to increase the aggregate amount of dividend disbursement necessary to keep stockholders satisfied.

(3) *Scrip dividends*. Sometimes companies have sufficient earnings to justify a dividend and sufficient cash to pay it in cash form, but do not do so because they believe it expedient to conserve the cash in the business for a certain period of time. Also, they may withhold the payment because of a temporary lack of cash. In such cases, resort may be made to the *scrip dividend*, which is the payment in scrip of a dividend, or the company's promise to pay. The scrip usually bears a definite date of maturity or payment, but this date may be contingent. Sometimes the time of payment is left to the discretion of the board of directors, and in such cases it must, under the law, be paid within a "reasonable time."

The scrip is sometimes interest-bearing and sometimes non-interest bearing; and it really consists of promissory notes of the company. The declaration of scrip dividends, however, is comparatively rare.

4. *Bonds used as dividends.* A very rare practice is to issue bonds to the amount of the proposed dividend in the place of cash and to keep the latter in the business. This practice serves very much the same purpose as a scrip dividend, except that it postpones the time of the payment to a more distant date and gives the holder of the bond a stronger claim against the company than he would obtain through the scrip.

(5) *Property dividends*. Property that is unnecessary in the conduct of the business and is in divisible and distributable form may be divided among stockholders as a *property dividend.* This kind of dividend is quite unusual and, when resorted to at all, is generally in the form of securities of subsidiaries owned by the distributing company.

Extra dividends. The directors of a corporation that has established a regular rate of dividend are often reluctant to increase the rate until they are convinced that the new rate may be maintained. Increased profits may give the concern more cash than it needs: Non-recurring profits, such as those arising from the sale of unnecessary fixed assets at a price in excess of book value, or a decision to disburse profits accumulated from previous years, if paid out as part of the regular dividend, would interrupt the stable rate. Under such circumstances the regular rate is declared as usual and an additional amount is declared as an *extra dividend.* Thus the stockholders are in effect told that the larger amount may not be repeated and that their directors have not deemed it expedient and proper to change the regular rate.

Factors affecting declaration of dividends. Before the directors can safely declare a dividend, they must consider several factors.

(1) *The legal factor.* In the majority of the states, it is illegal to pay a dividend if, after its payment, the capital would be impaired (using the

legal rather than the accounting concept of capital). As was stated above, this requirement might be met if only capital surplus existed. An upward revaluation of assets, however, would create a capital surplus, but at the same time might operate as a fraud on creditors and for that reason be illegal. The corporate law of the state must be examined carefully by the directors before they declare a dividend.

2. *The tax factor.* Stockholders in the high income tax bracket find that very little remains to them from a cash dividend after their income tax is paid. For that reason, the additional income they would derive from dividends paid in cash is little incentive for them to invest in common stock. A person with taxable income of $100,000 would have to receive a cash dividend of 22.73 per cent to equal a yield to him of 2.5 per cent on a tax-free municipal bond. It would be far better for them if the directors would use the profits to expand the corporation; they could then hope that the price of the stock would rise on the exchange. Then, instead of income, the stockholder might sell out and receive a capital gain which would be taxed at a much lower level than the income would be. At the same time, such a policy of reinvestment of profits might be a wise one for the corporation to follow.

3. *Working capital needs.* The payment of cash dividends naturally reduces the working capital, as the cash is disbursed in the form of dividends. Whether this payout of cash for dividends rather than for other corporate purposes is wise depends upon the conditions within the corporation and economic conditions in general. If it appears that the business is entering upon a period of recession, conservatism should be followed, for the business may need all of its cash resources to carry it safely through the period of decline. On the other hand, a business which is following a policy of expansion in boom times may likewise find that it needs all of the cash it can get.

4. *Other needs and purposes.* Care should be exercised by directors always to make sure that there is really a surplus; that is, that all necessary reserves have been set aside and that the surplus has been derived from sources available for dividends.

To whom do dividends belong? Dividends belong to the owners of the stock of the company in proportion to their holdings. This amount, however, may be regulated by contract, as it is in arrangements to pay special preferential rates to preferred stocks. Generally, though, stock changes hands often; and, when the same shares are held by several persons during the course of a dividend period, there arises the question: To whom, of these several holders, does the dividend belong?

When a dividend is decided upon, a company will usually announce a date for the closing of the transfer books or, if the books are not closed, a date upon which a list of stockholders will be prepared. Stockholders whose names appear on the books of the company as holders of stock are the ones to whom the company will send the dividend. If a person owned certain stock on this date but did not have it in his name on the books of the company, he would not receive the dividend check from the company. He could, nevertheless, claim it from its recipient— the person whose name was on the company's books at the time the dividend list was compiled. In other words, the actual owner of the stock on the day of the closing of the books, or the making up of the dividend lists, is entitled to the dividend; but the company has discharged its full liability when it sends dividends to those whose names appear as owners on the books at that date, whether they are the actual owners or not.

When a share of stock sells close to the record date, the question arises as to whether the seller or buyer is entitled to the dividend. The rule of the New York Stock Exchange (*Constitution and Rules of the Board of Governors,* effective May 16, 1938, Rule No. 210) is the commonly accepted practice relative to ownership of dividends in these circumstances.

Regular-way transactions in shares are ex-dividend on the third full business day preceding the record date fixed by the corporation. Regular-way delivery means that securities are purchased for delivery on the fourth full business day after the date of the contract. The seller whose name is recorded on the books of the corporation receives the dividend and, accordingly, the amount of the dividend is deducted from the price paid by the buyer.

In the case of cash transactions, which require delivery on the date of the contract, however, securities become ex-dividend on the day following the record date. If, for example, a corporation closes its transfer books on May 21, all stocks to be paid for and delivered that day are sold cum-dividend, since the buyer has time to have his name registered as owner before the expiration of the record date. Upon rare occasions, the New York Stock Exchange may permit a stock to sell cum-dividend after the record date. This means that the buyer is paying a price that includes the dividend, even though the corporation pays the dividend to the seller. In such circumstances, the seller is required to furnish a due bill stipulating that the dividend belongs to the buyer.

As soon as a dividend is declared, provided there is an adequate surplus, it becomes a debt of the company to the stockholders. If the company should fail before the payment of the dividend, the stockholders would, in respect to the dividend due, take position with the other unsecured creditors of the company.

If, at the time of the declaration, a fund is set aside to pay the dividends, this fund becomes the property of the stockholders, and they have first claim upon it, even in case of a failure of the company.

Questions for Study and Review

1. Distinguish between income from operations, income from outside operations, and other income.
2. State five reasons why a stable income is desirable to a business.
3. Define depreciation, and distinguish between deterioration and depletion.
4. What is meant by the depreciation policy of a business? Why should the maintenance policy be considered along with the depreciation policy?
5. Describe three methods of calculating the annual depreciation charge.
6. What is meant by surplus?
7. State several sources of surplus and indicate in each case whether or not the surplus so obtained should be used for dividend.
8. Why does a business need a surplus?
9. State several purposes served through setting up reserves.
10. In what forms may a corporation pay a dividend? What factors affect the declaration of any dividend by a corporation?

Problems

1. A corporation submitted to its stockholders the following income statement for the fiscal year:

Net sales	$230,385
Operating expenses	164,087
Operating profit	$ 66,298
Other Income	1,037
Total income	$ 67,335
Fixed charges	2,286
Net income before federal taxes	$ 65,049
Provision for federal taxes	25,565
Net income	$ 39,484

Explain (a) the sources of income, (b) the operating and financial charges, and (c) the earnings available for the bondholders and the stockholders respectively.

2. Explain the purpose for establishing reserves or similar accounts for the following balance sheet items: (a) plant and equipment, (b) accounts receivable, (c) patent rights, and (d) taxes. What effect does the establishment of these reserves have upon the net income of the company for the fiscal year?

3. The following balance sheet is submitted to a board of directors at the meeting at which the payment of a dividend to stockholders is to be considered:

ASSETS		LIABILITIES	
Current assets	$4,892,763	Current liabilities	$2,687,425
Fixed assets	2,464,647	Funded debt	1,250,000
Miscellaneous assets	432,879	Reserves	752,864
		Capital stock	2,500,000
		Surplus	600,000
Total	$7,790,289	Total	$7,790,289

Would capital be impaired by the payment of a dividend of (a) $300,000, (b) $600,000, or (c) $650,000?

4. The treasurer of Lampon Corporation prepares the following balance sheet for the board of directors of the corporation:

ASSETS		LIABILITIES	
Current assets		Current liabilities	$ 2,892,763
Cash	$ 1,500,000	Funded debt	1,000,000
Receivables	1,892,645	Reserves	423,324
Inventory	2,392,881	Capital stock (1)	5,000,000
Fixed assets	8,754,629	Surplus	8,672,922
Investments	2,807,092		
Miscellaneous assets	641,762		
Total	$17,989,009	Total	$17,989,009

(1) 200,000 shares outstanding; par $25

Explain the effect upon the respective balance sheet items of the payment to stockholders of (a) a cash dividend of 5 per cent, (b) a stock dividend of 10 per cent, (c) a scrip dividend of 6 per cent, and (d) a distribution of securities owned by the corporation and valued at $1,500,000.

5. On May 1, the board of directors of the Marden Manufacturing Co., Inc. met and declared a dividend of 6 per cent on all stock of the company as of May 15, payable June 15. Mr. Alden was the owner of 50 shares of this stock on April 30, and sold it on May 5 to Mr. Babcock, who sold it to Mr. Cutchens on June 1. Who is entitled to the dividend?

Suppose Mr. Babcock had sold it to Mr. Cutchens on May 15. Who would receive the dividend and why?

Written Assignment

DESIGNED PRODUCTS, INC.

BALANCE SHEET, SEPTEMBER 30, 1958

ASSETS			LIABILITIES	
Cash	1)20,000	$ 200,000	Accounts payable	$ 300,000
Securities owned		100,000	Accrued payroll	18,000
Accounts receivable	$82,000		Preferred stock (1)	400,000
Less: Reserve for bad			Common stock (2)	1,000,000 1,200,000
debts	1,640	80,360	Capital surplus	500,000 490,000
Inventories		400,000	Surplus	1,062,360
Plant and equipment	$2,000,000			642,360
Less: Reserve for				
depreciation	500,000	1,500,000		
Land		1,000,000		
		$3,280,360		$3,280,360 3,172,0,360

(1) 5%, $100 par value per share
(2) No par value, 100,000 shares outstanding

At the close of the fiscal year, the directors make the following decisions:

1. The value of securities owned is to be written down by 10 per cent because of a decline in market value, the write-down to be charged against capital surplus;

2. The regular 5 per cent dividend on the preferred stock is to be declared;

3. Because of the low cash position and large surplus, a 20 per cent stock dividend is to be paid to the common stockholders, valuing the stock at $20 per share (approximately book value) for the purpose.

Problems

a. Reconstruct the balance sheet to give effect to the directors' actions, showing also any change in the number of shares of common stock outstanding.

b. Without reconstructing the balance sheet, state the effect upon common stock, surplus account, and number of common shares outstanding if, instead of a stock dividend, the directors had decided to order a two-for-one split of the common stock.

c. What was the book value per share of the common stock before the directors declared the 20 per cent dividend?

d. What was the book value per share after the 20 per cent stock dividend? Have the stockholders gained or lost in the total book value of their holdings? What would be the probable effect on the market price of the stock caused by the 20 per cent stock dividend?

CHAPTER **XV**

Forms of Business Combination

Combination of business units. In earlier chapters, the formation of various types of business organizations was discussed somewhat in detail. We were concerned in those chapters with the organization of one business unit only, and we dealt chiefly with the ways by which men seek to associate with one another in a single concern. In this chapter, we shall study the various forms of combination, not of individuals, but of two or more business units. We shall undertake to study not only those forms of combination that result in a complete union or fusing of two or more businesses into one *de jure* or *de facto* whole, but also those forms of loose agreement whereby separate concerns agree to act in concert to achieve some particular purpose.

Is business too big? The people of the United States have always taken pride in its "bigness," and understandably so. Where other countries quite naturally took pride in their thousand years of history and of the development of art, music and architecture, we took pride in our pioneering and swift development of a great country. It is a big land, it has a big population and it requires a big industrial development to make available to its citizens the high standard of living they enjoy. China and Russia are larger in area and older in history, yet most of their citizens are on barely more than a subsistence level. But there is always the danger that "bigness" in business will work to the detriment of the country; that it will become tyrannical over its competitors, its employees—in fact over the entire community. To bridle the excesses brought about by monopoly, laws were enacted starting with the Sherman Anti-trust Act in 1890.

Monopoly, unreasonable restraint of trade and bigness, however, are not simple concepts and the solution of these problems is not easy. Laws enacted to prevent such abuses are difficult both to administer and to interpret and the legal and economic arguments used by lawyers and the courts in one period are not always valid and logical in another period as economic conditions change. The debate over whether big business is a blessing or a curse will probably never end. The answer to the question becomes more difficult to arrive at, too, because some of the problems of size are social in nature, some are political, and some are economic. These divergent political, social and economic theories cannot always be reconciled though it is the function of the lawmakers and the courts to make the attempt.

The courts particularly have been hard pressed to set standards for businessmen and lawyers to follow. At what point does a corporation become "big" and constitute a danger to our economy? At what point does a restraint of trade become an unreasonable restraint? At what point does monopoly become a fact? When the first anti-trust laws were enacted, few companies could boast of assets totaling $100,000,000. Today there are many with assets totaling more than a billion dollars.

The principal arguments against big business today may be summarized as the fear that:

(1) The concentration of power in the hands of a few persons is not to the ultimate welfare of the nation.

(2) The large companies tend to congregate in one section of the country, leading to an imbalance of power as between the sections of the country.

(3) There is a loss in efficiency as business becomes big.

(4) Big business becomes sterile as it becomes loath to venture new capital and make change.

(5) Big business stifles competition and our system of free competition by driving the little fellow out of business.

(6) Big business destroys the individual and robs him of his individuality.

It must be conceded, however, that business and business conduct have changed since the early 1930s, and those who favor big business stress this change and point to the recent record of business. They are frank to admit its past mistakes and its evil deeds. The conduct of the directors and officers who control the large (and even the small) corporations today is certainly different from that of their predecessors at the turn of the century. The age of absolute and dictatorial power in the few to rule with little or no regard for stockholders and labor is gone. Today a deep awareness of the social responsibility of management toward the community, labor and the stockholders is very much in evidence.

Business has changed in other ways, too. Whether large or small, business has become infinitely more complicated than it was even twenty-five years ago. Giants such as United States Steel, General Motors and many, many others have become so complex in character that a team of experts must operate them. The chief executive's role today is more of a coordinator among the tax experts, the labor experts, the production engineers, the sales executives, and the financial experts, than it is decision maker.

Proponents of big business point out also that both the Federal Government and the state governments have become more powerful and exercise more control over business and business decision making. Today hardly a business decision of any importance is made without first considering the effect on the corporate tax or the impact of the various administrative agencies such as the Securities and Exchange Commission or the Federal Trade Commission. Even a small local shopkeeper has to maintain detailed records for social security payments on unemployment insurance, and sales tax. He must consider the various methods of depreciation with an eye to the tax picture and his method of inventory valuation will change as the tax law changes. The government is equipped to handle big business—or any business for that matter—much more ably than it could fifty years ago.

Labor unions have become large and more powerful since the beginning of the century. They are a match for even the giants of industry. In fact it is sometimes said that they are more powerful than any single corporate business ever became. No longer do the workers fear exploitation.

On the more positive side, it may be pointed out that large companies can offer a stability of employment and other fringe benefits not always possible in small companies. Also only large companies can spend the enormous sums necessary today for the research required to produce new products cheaply. Radio Corporation of America is reputed to have spent $50,000,000 on black and white television before it was perfected and a still-to-be-determined sum on color television in addition. The cost of developing a product like nylon would be far beyond the resources of a small business. And it can be pointed out that only a large company could afford the huge capital investment required for automation in industry.

All of this makes it possible for us to own all those things such as automobiles, television, air conditioners, and countless others which make life enjoyable. The United States, with less than 10 per cent of the world's population and land area, produces more than the rest of the world combined. It must also be conceded that the great productivity of the United States is the bulwark between the forces of freedom and the forces of communism. Well-fed, well-clothed, well-housed people are not interested in the lures of the communist. Nor can the products of war, such as airplanes, tanks, trucks, guns and guided missiles, be produced in great numbers by small companies.

Internal growth versus external growth. Growth or expansion may come from within the existing organization, in which case it is called *internal growth*. Or it may come from without, through some form of combination or existing organizations. The latter is termed *external growth*. Corporations seldom follow a policy either of internal or external growth to the exclusion of the other form, although examples may be cited where a large company grew almost exclusively by following one method. General Motors and United States Steel are usually cited as examples of predominantly external growth while Ford Motor Co. serves as an example of predominantly internal growth.

Internally, expansion may come through the proceeds from the sale of stock, of bonds, from short-term borrowing, or through retained profits. Less appreciated perhaps is internal expansion, which results from the development of new patents or processes exceeding in value the cost of their creation.

Whether management will choose to expand through internal or external means is a matter of objective and expediency. Its decision is the result of choice among the advantages and disadvantages of each. Among the advantages of internal expansion may be listed:

(1) With funds to spend on expansion, a modern plant can be erected in the desired location close to the labor supply, the supply of raw materials, or the market area, whichever is most desirable.

(2) All plans for expansion can be geared to the economic conditions as such conditions develop. If the economy undergoes a change, further expansion plans may be amended to conform to such changes.

(3) Management is able to remain in control throughout, since it is they who decide where funds will come from and when, and where funds will be expended and when.

Among the disadvantages may be listed:

(1) Expansion into new products or new territories is a form of promotion. There is always a great risk attached to any promotion. Unforeseen costs in building even an addition to an existing building can mean the difference between profit and loss. Development of new territories, new products, and new machines is filled with uncertainties. By contrast, the acquisition of a presently going concern substitutes certainty for uncertainty.

(2) The increase in the cost of construction and of equipment today as compared with costs ten years ago. A modern plant may operate much more efficiently than a fifteen-year-old plant and result in production economies over the old plant. If, however, the cost of the new plant is appreciably more than the cost of acquiring the older plant it may be the older one that is cheaper in the long run.

(3) Internal expansion is apt to be a slower process than external expansion. It takes time to construct a factory, purchase special equipment, train a labor force and push into new markets and new territories. During this promotion period, a great amount of capital is employed with little if any increase in profits. Bondholders and bankers must be paid interest and stockholders look for dividends on the money which

they have advanced for this purpose. In external expansion the return on capital is immediate as all units are in full operation.

(4) The creation of a new plant adds to the capacity of the industry. Overproduction or unstable market conditions may result as each company strives to hold its place in the market.

External expansion, too, has its advantages and disadvantages. Among the advantages are:

(1) A plant, equipment, marketing territory and production staff are acquired, immediately permitting the acquiring company to take advantage of a market that is in existence at the time of the acquisition.

(2) The productive capacity of the industry is not increased so that stability is not threatened by overproduction.

(3) The acquiring company obtains another company's plant with a known capacity and with known costs. The range of future uncertainty is thus reduced and planning is simplified.

(4) The cost of acquiring an existing company is apt to be less than the cost of erecting a new plant. This is probably true at any point in the economic cycle.

(5) The cash outlay is usually lower when an existing company is acquired through combination than when a new plant is erected. This is so because a combination is frequently consummated by means of an exchange of stock.

(6) A combination of two or more companies may offer several tax advantages by reason of a more favorable treatment of exchanges of securities than sale of assets. Whether this would be so in each case depends upon the facts and circumstances at the time. In general, consolidations are tax-free.

Like everything else, external expansion has disadvantages.

(1) The acquiring company may be forced to accept many things it does not wish along with the product lines, territories, and personnel it wants. However, several companies have found that what might at first seem undesirable may turn into a profit as they sell the unwanted parts acquired in the deal.

(2) The acquiring company may discover that its capital structure is strained through being forced to assume a debt or preferred stock issue of the acquired company with the result that subsequent financing becomes difficult, if not impossible.

(3) External combinations, particularly those brought about through merger or consolidation, are likely to be permanent fusions. There is no retreat after the combination is executed. A faulty promotion, a change in economic conditions, as well as other factors, can have dire consequences to owners of the acquiring corporation when they have accepted stock in the newly formed company for their old stock. Of course, the same holds true for bondholders.

4. The management of the acquiring company may find itself limited in its freedom of action. A strong bloc of minority stock, or a large creditor, may force the management to comply with its requests.

5. New ideas in production and technological changes in buildings, machinery, and warehousing equipment often make it more profitable to build a new plant rather than acquire an old one. When a concern expands by building its own plant, it has a better opportunity to select a location having the greatest advantages and build a plant of the exact size desired.

Advantages of large-scale production. Several of the reasons for combination have been touched upon in Chapter XI, "Raising Long-term Capital." The more common reasons usually given for combination may be grouped conveniently under the headings of production economies, distribution economies, and financial and administrative economies.

1. Production economies
   a. Standardization of products, raw materials and supplies
   b. Utilization of by-products
   c. Increased efficiency of plant and equipment
   d. Equalized distribution of labor and production
   e. Control of sources of raw material and supplies
   f. Large-scale purchasing

2. Distribution economies
   a. Transportation economies
   b. Unification and consolidation of sales force
   c. Development of foreign markets
   d. Collective advertising

3. Administrative and financial economies
   a. Development of research
   b. Interchange of data and ideas
   c. Reduction in overhead, especially administrative
   d. Reduction in the cost of financing and financing on a large scale
   e. Ease in raising additional capital

What is the most profitable size? Some business units must be large because the plant must be large to produce the unit. A steel mill, for example, must be large in terms of size and investment of capital. Similarly, the automobile industry has found that to produce the number of automobiles demanded (close to eight million in 1955 and seven million in 1956) requires expensive automation. An electric utility which services the demands of a city the size of New York or San Francisco will need a tremendous capital investment. In other types of industry, large plants are not necessary. The manufacture of clothing furnishes an example. Nevertheless, even in those industries in which large size is not necessary it has been demonstrated that expansion by internal or external means may result in the achievement of some of the economies already referred to.

The question of the optimum size of a business, that is, the size which assures the maximum profit and greatest stability in the face of economic changes, has been the subject of much research. Contrary to popular belief, the largest companies are not always the most profitable nor are they always able to stand the onslaught of a depression. A comparison of the two hundred largest corporations thirty years ago with the two hundred largest corporations in existence today will make it evident that even the largest fall.

During the depression, the largest gas and electric holding companies failed. Among the factors which determine the optimum size of a business firm may be listed:

1. *Technical forces within the industry.* The greater the part played by machinery as compared to labor in production, the larger can be the firm before profits begin to diminish. A company which could utilize a machine costing several million (as some of the digital computers like Univac) dollars must have a large enough production to spread the cost of the machine over many units of production, yet a company which isn't large enough to incur a capital outlay such as this investment, may find its per unit labor cost so high that it cannot compete with its larger rival. Where expensive machines are utilized, they must be used to their fullest extent. Suppose a plant which manufactures electric refrigerators finds that the machine which produces one part has a capacity of 300 a day whereas the machine which produces a second necessary part produces 400 a day; the most efficient level of production is 1,200 units, so four of the first machines and three of the second would be required. Were production to be at any lower figure, one or the other machine would be operating at less than capacity. Thus, a production level of 400 would require two machines capable of producing 600 and, therefore, they would be operated only 66⅔ per cent of the time.

2. *Management.* Large-scale production has its economies, but only up to a point, although it is difficult to determine when the point has been reached. As the organization becomes larger, the services of high-salaried experts in the field of production, marketing, sales, labor and finance is justified. However, the same increase in size requires an ever-increasing staff in all ranks and of every description. Supervision and control becomes difficult and waste and inefficiency creep in. Difficulty in maintaining coordination between the different steps in operation or between widely separated plants may nullify any gains achieved through the economies of size.

3. *Obtaining funds.* Very often the greatest problem facing the management of a small firm is the difficulty of securing funds for both working capital and fixed capital. The costs per dollar of making a small loan are greater than those involved in a larger loan. Moreover, banks and other lending institutions are hesitant about making loans to smaller firms.

It is obvious that the optimum size of any given firm would be different in regard to each factor discussed. Reconciling these is a difficult task and is one which calls for an astute management team.

Motives for expansion. It must not be forgotten that a businessman, whether he operates a small hardware store or a vast corporation, is a human being first, last, and always. He has his likes and dislikes, fears and ambitions, just the same as anyone else. This personal motive cannot be overlooked in studying combination anymore than it can be overlooked in studying any phase of business. The gas station operator who enlarges his station may and frequently does so because he wants added profit. But he may do so also because he wants the social standing that seems to go with being a big businessman in the community. When an executive's salary is raised from $200,000 to $300,000, his increase in take-home pay is only $10,000 after income tax. Yet he feels the prestige of earning $300,000 gives him business and social standing.

There are many more tangible reasons why firms combine. So many in fact that it is difficult to classify them.

1. Many companies are forced to expand because the owners find that a business cannot remain static. A concern must move ahead with its competitors or it will fall behind, and perhaps even fail. Should the competitor enlarge its market, reduce its production costs, or achieve any of the economies of large-scale production, it may be able to cut prices. Today high sums are spent on advertising merely to keep the product name before a public which buys well-known brands. That these brands are superior or inferior to the unadvertised brand makes little difference. To increase the market, therefore, becomes the chief objective of the business.

2. Closely allied with the need for keeping up with competitors is the desire to reap the benefits of large-scale production. After the first year of merger the president of the Packard-Studebaker Co. was able to report to its stockholders tremendous savings through the utilization of a machine which would not have been justified for either company alone.

3. Some corporations which manufacture one product find that it is not only more profitable to add additional lines, but that diversification adds safety. Norma Electric Light Corporation, manufacturer of Christmas lights, had a season which extended from September until after Christmas. Success or failure lay in the perfect coordination of the manufacturing, the inventory and the selling departments as the retailers had a deadline to meet. Adding other products spread the work load, as well as the risk and profits. Corporations like Westinghouse Air Brake, which were specialists in air brakes for railroad cars, expanded by absorbing companies which manufacture air brakes for trucks and industrial machinery and so spread the risk incident to the close tie with the railroad industry.

4. In periods of prosperity as well as of recession, some firms see an advantage in acquiring companies which produce the raw materials they need. Others perceive the advantage derived from getting close to the consumer. American Cyanamid Co. has grown in recent years, and with growth has broadened its objectives and now is moving toward the consumer rather than maintaining its previous position as a research organization and manufacturer of raw materials and intermediate products.

5. One of the penalties of being small is the difficulty of raising capital. As sales increase, so must both working capital and fixed assets. Funds for modernization are needed to keep up with the swift technological changes taking place in many industries today. Combination of a smaller company with a larger one is one method of gaining needed funds through the substitution of the credit standing of the large company for that of the small one.

6. Owners of closed corporations with no one to carry on the business when they retire often find it wise to combine their company with a large company whose securities are widely sold on a national stock exchange. Combinations of this sort offer two advantages to the seller. He may possibly carry on for a period of years as manager of the division which was formerly his company. He simplifies disposition of his estate both by fixing a valuation through the substitution of shares with a market value for those whose value is difficult to determine. If desired, he may convert his estate to cash or diversify by acquiring other securities through ability to market his shares.

7. If the provisions and legal interpretations of the Code of Internal Revenue are precisely followed, there may be advantages to corporations and stockholders through accomplishing a merger with another corporation. Mergers are usually tax-free, not being considered a sale but merely a fusion of existing corporations into one. For example, in a closely held corporation, a considerable portion of the earnings may be retained by the corporation and hence not be subject to the individual income tax of the stockholders who may enjoy income subject to high rates. There comes a time when further retention of earnings cannot be justified under sections of the income tax law and distribution in the form of dividends may be necessary to avoid penalties. If the corporation is merged with another corporation and the stockholders receive stock in the merged corporation in exchange for their stock, they may in effect have received a distribution of the accumulated earnings in the form of new stock. No present tax need be paid and any gain realized when the stockholder eventually sells the stock will be at the lower capital gains rate rather than subject to income tax rates, which for persons with large incomes would be much higher.

Another advantage realized through combination with another corporation arises from tax law provisions permitting a corporation to offset profits currently realized against losses of the previous two years or against losses sustained for five years in the future. A combination of a concern with profitable operations with one which is losing and has lost money during the past two years, permits such an offset. Such mergers were common during World War II and subsequently when corporate income tax rates could reach the high rate of 82 per cent. Ironically, corporations which were losing money found themselves with a valuable asset—losses! So common did this method of tax avoidance become that Congress found it necessary to tighten up the laws relative to such so-called tax mergers.

(8) An old reason for combination which has become increasingly prevalent is the joining of two or more companies to form a third which performs some function for its two parents. The railroads and the bus companies have frequently cooperated with other such companies in the erection of bridges or terminals. More recently large corporations have combined to form a new company whose facilities are used jointly between them. Thus, Standard Oil Co. (Ohio) and Ashland Oil and Refining Co. organized the Ohio River Pipeline Co. as a joint carrier. American Cyanamid Co. and Texas Co. formed the Jefferson Chemical Co. to enter the new field of petrochemicals. In this fashion, companies are able to operate a joint facility too big for either one to operate, or to develop a new product market.

Some of these motives are as old as the history of business itself, others have motivated businessmen only in more recent years. During the period between 1885-1905 when such giants as United States Steel Corporation, American Tobacco Co. and International Harvester Co. were being formed, the chief motivating force seems to have been the desire to control the industry and to achieve something akin to monopoly if indeed real monopoly was not possible. United States Steel Corporation, for example, was a consolidation of 170 independent companies.

The second wave of combinations lasted about eleven years between 1918 and 1929. It was characterized largely by the common desire of management and investment bankers to make profits through the sale of the new securities resulting from the consolidation. Estimates of increased earnings because of the economies and advantages of the combination were frequently extremely optimistic. Capitalization of the total anticipated earnings resulted in a larger capitalization for the new company than that of the several constituents prior to the consolidation. The additional securities provided for liberal treatment of the stockholders of constituent corporations with enough left over to provide profit for the promoters. Naturally a rising and active stock market is a necessary background for such activities.

Since 1940, there has been a third wave of combination in which management, rather than promoters and bankers, have played the leading part. These combinations, which have been accomplished by merger, consolidation, stock control and occasionally by lease, have been motivated by the desire for tax savings, diversification, and the need for additional production or distribution facilities.

Direction of expansion. External expansion may be classified as (1) horizontal (2) vertical (3) circular or conglomerate. Horizontal expansion is the term applied to the combination of two or more firms engaged in the same phase of operation. Thus, the combination of two companies engaged in the production of fountain pens, or of three corporations in the retail trade is said to be horizontal. If the combination is of companies engaged in different phases in the line between the raw material production and the ultimate consumer it is called vertical. Both are sometimes called *integration in industry.* During relatively prosperous periods, vertical integration is likely to be backward. That is, the retailer, moved by the desire to assure himself a source of products, acquires the producer or the producer, wishing to assure himself of raw materials when every other manufacturer is clamoring for the same material, acquires the company producing the raw material. This is called vertical integration backward. In less prosperous times the reverse is likely to be the case. The profits of the middleman seem large to those all along the line and the producer absorbs the wholesaler or even the retailer and goes right to the consumer. Vertical integration is less likely to result in control or monopoly and is, therefore, less vulnerable to anti-trust actions.

The third type almost defies description because it is so varied in the form it may take. It is really a catch-all. The term *circular* has been used to describe a combination of firms aimed at achieving economies through distribution, or some common facility. Thus, a food company might gather to it other noncompeting food companies which had the same customers. One salesman taking orders for breakfast food, coffee, and beans can operate more economically than many salesmen from separate companies, duplicating traveling time and expense. Typical of such combinations is the General Foods Corporation. An organization such as E. I. du Pont de Nemours & Co. or Radio Corporation of America, which has excellent and extremely expensive laboratory facilities, may accumulate a number of companies that depend upon research but are unable to finance it individually.

The term circular was later broadened to *conglomeration* in a effort to fit new situations as they arose. These combinations in some cases seem to defy reason; for example, the combination of Solar Aircraft Co., which manufactures parts for jet planes, and Hubbard Casket Corporation which makes caskets. (The union was subsequently dissolved.) Others appear logical, serving the need for diversification, complementing the line of products manufactured and sold, or simply acting as a means of investing surplus cash in a profitable manner.

Usually a combination is relatively simple to classify, although there may be times when it is a borderline case. How, for instance, should the acquisition of a company engaged in the production of earth-moving equipment by a company manufacturing automobiles and trucks be classified?

Financial considerations in external expansion. The combining of two or more corporations is a difficult task. It is fraught with danger to all parties. Will the new company be unwieldy? Will the personnel mix to develop a new team? Will the expected market be there? These are but a few of the many questions to be considered. In many cases, a combination of companies is an isolated affair and none has expanded in this fashion before. Others may make a policy of continuous growth by this means. In either event both parties must be prepared. The financial structure of each company must be properly balanced. Heavy bonded indebtedness, arrears on preferred stock or overcapitalization may make a company less valuable at the bargaining table. Companies with preferred stock that is non-callable, or callable at a high price, find themselves in a strategically weak position. Preferred stockholders of American Radiator & Standard Sanitary Corporation who have a $100 par 7 per cent preferred, callable at 175, would have to receive an amount all out of proportion to the amount originally contributed to capital way back in 1929. Were they to receive common stock in exchange, they would get currently about 8 shares for 1. A company with a high proportion of mortgage bonds may find its credit strained when bargaining with a company which has nothing but debentures or no debt at all.

A sound working capital condition is essential for success at all times, but particularly during the period after the combination when adjustments are being made and all are reorienting themselves and the business. When Gruen Industries acquired a 60 per cent stock interest in L. E. Waterman Pen Co. Ltd. of Canada and its subsidiaries, and the Waterman Pen Companies of the United States and England, it found that the cash it would have to contribute to the pen companies was more than Gruen could raise. Fortunately, however, it was possible to dispose of this stock a few months after acquisition.

Due regard must be given to the business cycle. It is cheaper to acquire another company during a recession when prices are low. But sales and profits are at a low ebb too. It is expensive to acquire another company when prices are high. But sales and profits are high, also. The true measure of a bargain is the return on the investment. A bargain picked up during a period of business recession may pay off when times improve. But the risk of high losses before that time comes, or the risk that obsolescence will depreciate what otherwise might be efficient machinery, must not be overlooked. Conversely, a combination just before a prolonged dip in earnings may lead to failure. Seasonal, cyclical and secular changes must all be considered.

Types of combinations. There is considerable confusion in terminology regarding combinations. The popular term of any type of combination that results in a complete union is *consolidation*. The word is often applied regardless of whether two or more corporations are actually fused together into one legal unit or whether one has gained control of another through stock ownership. The various terms describing the different types of combinations discussed in this chapter will now briefly be defined.

1. *Consolidation.* The term *consolidation,* as originally used, meant the complete fusion of two or more corporations into a single new corporation accompanied by the filing of a new certificate of consolidation, similar in form to an original certificate of incorporation. The constituent corporations lost their identity. The stock of the new corporation was exchanged for the stock of the old companies. The statutes of most states provide definite instructions for accomplishing a fusion of corporations in this manner. In the absence of such statutes, the same result was achieved by a purchase of the assets and assumption of the liabilities of the combining corporations by a new corporation formed for the purpose and paying for the assets with the latter's stock. The constituent corporations could then be dissolved and the stock distributed to their stockholders.

2. *Merger.* A *merger* is a combination of one or more corporations with an existing corporation. It is a statutory method providing for the taking over by one corporation of the powers, assets, and liabilities of one or more corporations. The identities of the absorbed corporations are merged in the one. The name may or may not be changed. However, the terms merger and consolidation are now used almost interchangeably by the statutes of several states and by the press in reporting such combinations. Some states, like New York, list the creation of a new corporation or the use of one of the existing corporations as the absorbing concern under the single heading "consolidation." The word *merger* is reserved to cover a situation when one corporation owns at least 95 per cent of the stock of another, in which case a fusion can be accomplished by mere resolution of the board of directors of the possessor corporation. In either case the name of one or both of the corporations may be changed. The advantages of merger and consolidation may be listed as follows:

1. Each constitutes a permanent form of combination in the form of a complete fusion, as contrasted to a holding company or lease, and management obtains complete control of both companies inasmuch as they are now one.

2. Generally there is no tax to be paid at the time of combination. Al-

though called a "tax-free" exchange, the term is apt to be misleading. Any tax imposed upon the capital gain or loss resulting from the combination is postponed until the gain or loss is actually realized rather than imposed when the consolidation takes place and when nothing happens other than an exchange of securities.

3. The cost of operation is lower as after fusion there need be only one board of directors, one group of officers, one set of records and one income tax paid. Contrast this with a holding company or lease where duplicate organizations are maintained.

The disadvantages are:

1. Both merger and consolidation require the consent of at least two-thirds of the stockholders of each corporation involved (the proportion required is governed by state corporation laws which differ among the states). In contrast, the lease and the purchase of assets require only the consent of the stockholders of the lessor corporation or the vendor corporation.

2. It is extremely difficult to determine the terms of merger or consolidation. Since both stockholder groups must acquiesce, the terms in the last analysis must be attractive even at the risk of being somewhat less than wise. Stockholders are not specialists in corporation finance and tend to react toward market price, price earnings, ratios and rate of dividends. None of these may be a fair measure of the worth of a company, yet they are important criteria in arriving at merger terms. A sound valuation can only be arrived at after a thorough analysis of the companies. Different accounting systems must be reconciled to make them comparable. An engineering analysis and an economic analysis must also be made. Frequently startling facts are uncovered. The valuation problem is less of a stumbling block in the path of combination by means of a holding company or a lease.

3. The merger or consolidation is a permanent form. Once the two or more companies are combined, it is difficult if not impossible to undo the process. Often unwanted divisions or product lines are acquired and unless they can be sold or otherwise disposed of, it can become a drag on profitable operations.

4. Not the least of the disadvantages is the creation of personnel problems occasioned by a combination. What happens to the two boards of directors, the two sets of officers or other executives? This is often a "behind the scenes" problem that frequently prevents a proposed combination before it gets into the public discussion stage.

3. *Purchase of assets.* This method of combination is brought about by the outright purchase of all or a part of the assets of one business by another. The business organization making the sale may or may not go out of existence. A purchase of the assets of one company by another has certain advantages over other forms of combination.

1. It is usually easier to purchase the assets rather than merge or consolidate inasmuch as the stockholders of the purchasing corporation do not have to be consulted. Stockholders of the selling corporation, of course, would have to agree to the sale and the terms of the sale. In most states approval of the holders of two-thirds of the stock is necessary.

2. A sale makes possible the purchase of a portion of the corporation's assets if that is all that is needed rather than the entire business. Today corporations have spread their activity over many fields and the modern corporation may manufacture a wide variety of products. General Motors Corporation, for example, manufactures automobiles, trucks, diesel locomotives, refrigerators, and earth-moving equipment, to list only a few of the widely known products. A merger or other complete combination of two units might lead to an undesirable and unprofitable union. A company that manufactures and markets television may wish to combine with another company which manufactures television sets but cannot see a profit in the second company's radar manufacturing division or its household appliance division. Terms of purchase may be worked out which may result in the acquisition of only the division desired. The vendor corporation may continue to operate the remainder or seek a purchaser interested.

3. There may be tax advantages, particularly if one corporation has capital losses to offer.

4. It may be the only feasible method of combination in states where an outright merger or consolidation of domestic and foreign corporations is prohibited by law.

It is not without its disadvantages, however:

1. Dissenting stockholders in several states may demand cash for their stock. If a substantial number of stockholders (10 to 20 per cent, for example) made such a demand, the cash drain on the company might weaken the working capital position.

2. There may be a heavy tax liability to the selling corporation if capital gains are realized unless such a sale qualifies as a tax-free exchange under the Revenue Act.

4. *Lease of assets.* When the assets of a going concern are acquired by another corporation by means of a long-term lease, something very close to complete fusion has been achieved. Of course, not all of a concern's assets may be leased by another, but the effect, insofar as control of the property so acquired, is considered the same. Property of the lessor passes from control of the lessor corporation to that of the lessee. When all of a concern's assets are leased, the lessor corporation ceases to exist as an operating business and merely holds the lease and collects rentals under its terms. In some long-term leases, rent is paid directly to the lessor's stockholders by the lessee in the form of dividends, which are usually guaranteed at a stipulated amount by the terms of the lease. In-

terest on the lessor's bonds is frequently paid, or at least guaranteed, by the lessee, and taxes on the leased property are also paid by the latter. This reduces the lessor corporation's position to a mere nominal existence as a separate legal entity. Renewal provisions are usually so liberal as to leave the option of renewal completely with the lessee, making such leases in effect perpetual. ✓

Use of the lease. Railroads, urban street railways, oil, and mining companies have been the principal users of leases as a method of combining properties. Many sections of main line track of large railroads, especially east of the Mississippi river have been operated, some for more than half a century, under lease. Terms of ninety-nine years are fairly common and some are for much longer terms. An example of a very long-term lease is that of the West Shore Railroad to the New York Central, which has a term of 475 years. Typical of rental agreements is the guaranteed dividend on the common stock of the New York and Harlem Railroad provided in its lease to the New York Central. Leases on extractive properties usually provide for a royalty on production with a guarantee that a certain amount of development will be carried out by the lessee to insure the continued yield of the property.

Authority to make a lease. Whether the management has the authority to make a lease without the consent of the stockholders is, in the absence of state statutes, uncertain, with conflicting decisions in the courts of different states. As far as the lessee corporation is concerned, the power to expand the operations of the corporation rests clearly with the board of directors as being within their discretion. A decision to allow all of the corporate property to be taken over and operated by another corporation should not rest with the lessor's board of directors, but should have the approval of the stockholders. The stockholders should have the right (1) to have the corporation's property managed by directors whom they elect, (2) to have a vote in determining broad policies of management, and (3) to participate in the earnings of the corporation in proportion to its prosperity and not be compelled to accept a fixed rental. In New York an old decision of the highest court [Beveridge v. N.Y. Elev. R.R. Co., (1899) 112 N.Y. 1] would seem to be contrary to the principles set forth above and which appear to be in line with majority legal opinion. In this case, the court approved a lease accomplished by resolution of the board of directors. When a corporation is in bad financial straits or has been operating for some time at a loss, it seems generally agreed that directors could lease the property in line with their duty to protect stockholders against losses.

5. *Trusts.* The term *trust* is applied by the press and public to almost any large combination; and where it is so used, there is generally an implication that the trust is a monopoly capable of exerting control over prices and service. As a matter of fact, the trust as a form of combination

no longer exists. From 1885 to 1890, several groups of corporations, using the device of a voting trust, combined in the following manner. In the voting trust, the stockholders of a single corporation deposited their stock in the custody of designated voting trustees, who issued voting trust certificates in exchange. The stockholders retained all rights to their stock except that of voting power, which was delegated to the trustees temporarily; that is, during the life of the trust agreement. The trust was but the next step to increase the sphere of control. Two or more corporations formed voting trusts within their several independent organizations, but each designated the same individuals for voting trustees. This vesting of authority in a common management placed that management in a position to dictate policies for each of the several corporations that had as its primary purpose the welfare of all, rather than the welfare of itself.

Under this form of organization, it is necessary for the combining companies to surrender their entire control into the hands of trustees, and this action becomes subject to attack because it is *ultra vires*. Objecting minority stockholders may insist on their inherent right to help determine the broad policies by which their chosen directors shall be guided. As a method of forming combinations, the trust was abandoned with the dissolution by the courts of the Sugar Trust in 1890, and of the Standard Oil Co. of Ohio in 1892. The grounds for the decision in the North River Sugar Refining Co. case are interesting, for they hold the trust form illegal without reference to the question of monopoly. The chief points brought out by the court in its decision may be summed up as follows:

1. That, despite the allegation of the defendants that, although the corporation has become a member of a combination which possessed complete control over it, such a condition arose through the action of the stockholders and not of the corporation (and therefore the penalty of dissolution should not be visited upon the corporation), the court held that there might be corporate conduct without formal corporate action, and that the stockholders, in acting collectively as an aggregate body without a single exception, had reached results clearly corporate in character, and could not escape the consequence of their acts by pleading innocence of a convenient fiction, the corporation. This disposed of the question as to whether the North River Sugar Refining Co. had participated in the creation of a trust.

2. That the defendant had accepted from the state the gift of corporate life, only to disregard the condition under which it was given; and that it had received its powers and privileges merely to put them in pawn; that it had given away to an irresponsible board its entire independence and self-control.

3. That the stockholders of the corporation had parted with the control that the charter gave them and the state required them to exercise.

4. That the corporation, in helping to create an anomalous trust, that

was in substance a partnership of several corporations, was violating the law that forbids corporations to enter partnerships.

6. *Holding companies.* What constitutes a holding company is not subject to precise legal definition. It might be said that any corporation which holds stock of another corporation is a holding company. Usually ability of the stock owning corporation to control or materially to influence the control of the corporation whose stock it owns comes much closer to meeting most people's concept of the term *holding company.* Seldom would ownership of a majority of the voting stock be necessary to give control. A pure *holding company* is a corporation organized for the purpose of acquiring primarily the voting stocks and other voting securities of various corporations. The securities of the corporations to be controlled are obtained either by a direct exchange for those of the holding company or by a purchase for cash which has been obtained previously by the sale of the securities of the holding company to the security-buying public. The ownership of these voting securities gives to the holding company the right to elect the various boards of directors and thus control their policies just as successfully as if all had been fused into one corporation. The pure holding company is not an operating company. Its management is concerned chiefly with establishing policies, leaving the details of execution of those policies and the industrial operations of the properties to the experts in each company. From 1901, when it was formed, until 1951, the United States Steel Corporation was a pure holding company. Following a long series of mergers among its operating subsidiaries, it became a combination operating and holding company in 1951 in a merger with the United States Steel Co., the operating company into which its earlier operating subsidiaries had been merged. It remains a pure holding company with respect to the railroad corporations and a few other non-manufacturing subsidiaries. Other large holding companies are also operating companies; for instance, the American Telephone & Telegraph Co. operates its Long Lines Department directly, and the business from it in a recent year was over $465,000,000.

Advantages of holding companies. In the United States, the holding company has become increasingly important as a means of effecting combinations of corporations. It has been especially popular in the public utility field, but has by no means been limited to this business, being used extensively in large industrial combinations. This development of the use of the holding company has been due partly to the necessity of having some suitable means of uniting incorporated businesses that were domiciled in many states. As a method of combination, the holding company possesses many advantages, some of the more important of which are stated and briefly explained below.

1. Many states require the consent of two-thirds, three-fourths, and even greater proportions of the stock of a corporation to change the capital structure of the company. A minority of the stockholders of an exist-

ing operating company could easily prevent the expansion by withholding their approval. But if a bare majority of the stockholders were to incorporate a new holding company and exchange their share of the old securities for stock of the holding company, with a capitalization great enough to acquire the business in question, the objecting minority would be impotent to do anything legally to prevent the proposed combination.

2. No state allows a corporation to engage indiscriminately in many kinds of business. For example, New York State does not allow a business corporation to perform the functions of a bank, a trust company, an insurance company, or a railroad or other transportation company. Yet a holding company, specifically authorized as it always must be to hold stock of other corporations, is able to accomplish the same results through stock ownership of legally constituted independent units. This advantage will be discussed more fully later in the present chapter under the heading *Integration in industry*.

3. A holding company can be organized as a parent company to avoid adverse state legislation on *foreign corporations*. It is then in a position to organize separate *domestic corporations* in each of the states that have placed undesirable restrictions and burdensome taxation on corporations of other states.

Aside from the legal advantages, there are others of a financial or an economic character. Not the least of these is ease of formation.

4. No other form of combination, thus far discussed, (a) produces quicker results, (b) requires less legal entanglement, and (c) gives the same stability when weighed against time and legal requirements. All previous plans require the consent of large majorities of stockholders. Time, often in addition to prolonged effort, is required to get such permission. The holding company plan, on the other hand, requires not more than a majority of the stock, and frequently less gives control, as we have learned in a previous chapter. All plans thus far discussed are handicapped by possible litigation with a non-consenting minority protected by statutory rights; under the holding company plan, less than a majority of the stockholders can seldom effectively object.

5. The holding company provides a suitable organization for raising most of its funds. Through the device of collateral trust bonds, it is able to finance not only its own subsidiaries but also other corporations from which it obtains valuable contracts for its operating subsidiaries. It can appeal to investors more successfully than the average non-holding company: first, with probably the most fundamental of investing principles, "Don't put all of your eggs into the same basket" (the securities of a holding company are usually backed by a pool of the securities of many other corporations); second, with the effectiveness of its management.

6. This effectiveness of management or economy in the centralized control of large amounts of capital is probably the greatest advantage of the holding company. The executives of the holding company are the

most successful executives from the subsidiary organizations. The subsidiaries are the training camps where many executives are being trained
simultaneously, and the most efficient chosen. In the nonholding type of
corporation, only one set of executives can be trained at a time, and
this one set is in the position of the cowboy whom, once in the saddle,
the bucking bronco finds it difficult to unseat. The centralized control
of large amounts of capital gives to the holding company the usual economies of consolidation mentioned in the previous chapter. But, in addition to these economies, the holding company structure provides for a
centralization of financial control that is unparalleled in any other private corporate organization. The capital amassed by, and now under the
control of, the board of directors of the American Telephone & Telegraph Co., a holding company, is tremendous. The greater the number
of combinations effected within a holding company, the more concentrated the centralized control will become, yet the legal position is firm
as long as the organization is nonmonopolistic in character and not in
restraint of trade.

7. The holding company provides a better type of managerial organization for meeting varying local conditions, which could not be met as
easily through the line organization of a single corporation. The board
of directors of the distant subsidiary have the executive authority to
make changes that local conditions warrant, but that a branch office
superintendent would be unable to accomplish until authorized by a
distant management. The distant management, however, is looking at
the problem through glasses tinted with the local color of its own territory and cannot readily be persuaded to approve plans that seem inconsistent with its own experience.

Disadvantages of the holding company. In spite of its advantages, the
holding company has come in for considerable criticism. Much of this
criticism may be traced to the general urge for economic reform brought
about by the business depression, which followed the stock market panic
of October, 1929. The failure of the tremendous Insull utilities combination and the depreciation in value of the securities of most of the large,
public-utility holding companies seriously disturbed public confidence
in this form of combination and caused agitation for strict governmental
control of public utility holding companies. After investigation and public hearings, Congress passed the Public Utility Holding Company Act
of 1935, regulating public-utility holding company systems in the electric
light and power and gas industries. The disadvantages of holding companies may be roughly classified into three groups: (a) disadvantages of
the holding company as a method of corporate combination, (b) disadvantages to creditors and minority stockholders of the subsidiary corporations, and (c) disadvantages to the consumer. Some of these disadvantages will now be stated under their appropriate classifications.

A. Disadvantages of the holding company as a method of combination.

1. *Overcapitalization.* Holding companies often acquire control of other companies by purchasing stock in the market at current market values, and if the acquisition is made in a period of stock market boom, serious overcapitalization of the holding company may result. Failure or capital reorganization is almost sure to follow as soon as earnings decline.

2. *Duplication of taxes.* The subsidiary corporations pay a Federal income tax upon their profits, and the holding company will also pay a Federal income tax upon its profits, which are represented by the dividends received from the subsidiary corporations. In addition, a foreign holding company, licensed to do business in a state in which one of its subsidiaries is incorporated, will in all probability be called upon to pay some form of state income or stock tax, although the subsidiary is also paying taxes to the state government.

3. *High overhead costs.* Maintaining separate corporations requires separate officers and administrative forces. Moreover, each subsidiary must render reports to governmental bodies.

4. *Legal restrictions.* The provision of the Clayton Act, which prohibits the holding of stock of one corporation by another if the result will be "a substantial lessening of competition," has largely restricted the use of holding companies to combinations of noncompetitive corporations, such as public utilities. The latter in the electric and gas industries are now regulated by the Securities and Exchange Commission, charged with responsibility of carrying out the provisions of the Public Utility Holding Company Act of 1935.

B. Disadvantages to creditors and minority stockholders.

1. *Excessive dividend disbursements.* The holding company's earnings are dependent upon dividends paid by the subsidiaries. In times of business depression, the board of directors of the subsidiary, since it is controlled by the holding company, may vote larger dividend disbursements than the condition of the subsidiary will warrant in order that the holding corporation may be able to pay interest on its bonds and dividends on its preferred stock.

2. *"Upstream" loans.* "Upstream" loans are loans to the parent company made by the subsidiary. Using its power over the subsidiary, a holding company may force the subsidiary to loan money to it. Such loans are sometimes made when the subsidiary needs all the cash it has, and in most cases, the loan itself is an *ultra vires* act on the part of the subsidiary management. In respect to holding companies affected by this law, Section 12 of the Public Utilities Act forbids such loans. In fact, almost all intercompany financial transactions are now subject to regulation by the S.E.C. if part of a registered holding company system.

3. *Diversion of subsidiaries' business.* In order to bring about unification of operations that will achieve the greatest efficiency and economy,

a holding company management may find it advisable to discontinue certain operations of a subsidiary or to confine the subsidiary to one product. However advantageous this may be from the standpoint of the holding company, it may result in loss of goodwill and reduced profits, to the detriment of the subsidiary's creditors and minority stockholders.

4. *Influence on prices.* The holding company may, through its control over the subsidiary management, fix prices on subsidiaries' products to other subsidiaries at a discount, causing lower profits for the subsidiaries' minority stockholders.

5. *Management and service fees.* Holding companies occasionally have management departments, and sometimes separate management subsidiaries, and make contracts with a subsidiary for management services. Section 13 of the Holding Company Act subjects such contracts to regulation by the Securities and Exchange Commission which has largely resulted in ending pernicious aspects of these practices. If the fees for these services are reasonable, there are decided advantages to having them performed by the skilled staff of the management corporation. In some cases, however, excessive fees are charged merely as a means of extracting further profits from the subsidiary. Since such fees represent operating expenses of the subsidiary, they provide a means of increasing the income to the parent corporation without the necessity of sharing it with the minority stockholders.

C. Disadvantages to the consumers.

1. *Lack of local management.* Although holding corporations usually emphasize the fact that the locality of the district served is represented in the management, the necessity for uniformity of operating policies means that the local management must operate within limits established by the central management. Proper expenditures for improvements and extensions of service are usually subjected to the approval or concurrence of the holding company and may be delayed because of the financial needs of other subsidiaries in no way serving the local community. Naturally, the private holding company management is less likely to have the grasp of local problems and needs possessed by an independent, local board of directors.

2. *Interference with local rate adjustments.* The highly paid legal department and legislative lobby of the holding company is always at the service of the subsidiary in resisting any attempt on the part of the customers to obtain lower rates for service.

3. *Diversion of funds to other localities.* The dividends on the stock of local subsidiaries are sent to a distant city where the main office of the holding company is located and therefore do not increase local purchasing power. Often, all the subsidiary's surplus cash is kept by the holding company, instead of the local bank.

Federal regulation of public utility holding companies. In 1935, Congress enacted the Public Utility Holding Company Act, which, after defining a holding company as being one that holds 10 per cent or more of the voting securities of a public utility company engaged in the electric or gas business, required all such holding companies to register with the Securities and Exchange Commission, prohibited the issuance of any new securities or changing the rights of existing securities until such registration was completed. The purpose of the Act was to bring about a simplification of complicated holding company structures and to limit holding companies to a single integrated system. The Act defines an integrated system for electric light and power public utilities as "one or more units of generating plants and/or transmission lines and/or distributing facilities, whose utility assets, whether owned by one or more electric utility companies, are physically interconnected or capable of physical interconnection and which under normal conditions may be economically operated as a single interconnected and coordinated system confined in its operations to a single area or region, in one or more States, not so large as to impair (considering the state of the art and the area or region affected) the advantages of localized management, efficient operation, and the effectiveness of regulation." It also prohibits a subsidiary from extending credit to a holding company and prohibits a holding company from making service, sales, or construction contracts with an associate public utility company. It subjects any subsidiary to regulation of the Commission in making any such contracts with an associate company. A major purpose of this legislation was to correct the complicated structures of existing holding companies, but note that, here, voluntary simplification had been in progress well before 1935.

It is probable that even without Federal legislation, considerable simplification of the top-heavy and complicated holding company systems would have taken place. Put together rapidly, expediency, opportunities for promoters and bankers profits, and a careless receptiveness of almost any type of security issues by speculative markets, resulted in many holding company structures being grossly over-capitalized. The overhead costs of operation must have been so great as to completely offset any advantage gained. But voluntary adjustment and reorganization would have been slow and complicated by legal difficulties. The results from many compromises with security holders would likely have fallen very short of those that have been achieved under the Federal law. One has only to study the painful process of railroad reorganization over a period of seventy-five years and to survey the present situation to realize what might have been expected from voluntary attempts to simplify the public utility holding company structures. Properties controlled by individual holding companies were scattered all over the United States and, in some cases, other nations. Inter-company stock-holding, holding company upon holding company, interlocking directorates, management and service contracts, and the use of every known device of control presented a problem to the Security and Exchange

Commission that seemed almost beyond comprehension. That the task of simplification and integration was nearly accomplished in a decade and during a period of national emergency and war without interruption of utility service or necessary expansion, and without disastrous effects upon the nation's economy is a tribute to the S.E.C. and to those leaders of the industry who through their cooperation made it possible.

In carrying out orders of the S.E.C., some of which were contested in the courts before becoming effective, a reasonable time was given to the holding companies in order that orderly procedures could be followed and losses minimized. Difficult problems resulted from orders requiring holding companies to divest themselves of ownership of scattered companies in order to integrate in one territory. Stock of such campanies was usually sold in large blocks through secondary offerings outside stock exchanges and also distributed as property dividends (sometimes called "spin-offs") to the holding companies' own stockholders.

7. *Pools, gentlemen's agreements.* In contrast to others, agreements to accomplish some particular purpose or purposes, such as *trade associations* and *pools,* are loose types of combination. *Pools* are usually formed to accomplish the control of prices through agreements (1) to limit the supply, (2) to divide up territory, and (3) to regulate competitive bidding. These purposes are illegal as far as domestic trade is concerned, though they are encouraged by legislation as far as export trade is concerned. These are mere agreements between businesses to act in harmony in certain matters to attain a common end.

8. *Community of interest.* This term generally is used to refer to a state of close harmony in the operations of two or more corporations brought about through the same person or persons on the boards of directors of several corporations, or merely through the influential stock ownership of two or more corporations by one person or closely associated group, for example, a friendly banking interest.

Factors in choosing the form of combination. Just as there is no one method of business organization suitable for all business organizations, there is no one method of combination suitable to all situations. Management will have some objective in view and so will choose the method of combination which best achieves that objective. Factors such as the following must be carefully considered and answers found to each.

1. *How easy or how difficult is it to bring about each of the forms of combination?* Merger and consolidation require a great deal of preparatory work concerned with valuation, personnel and preparation of stockholders. In most states two-thirds of the stockholders of each corporation must assent to the plan. Management will contrast this with a combination through the purchase of assets, or the lease which requires the consent of a proportion of the stockholders of the selling corporation or leasing corporation but not of the acquiring corporation. Management will

contrast all of these forms with the holding company where no stock-holders' consent, voting as a group, may be necessary.

2. _Problem of valuation._ Merger, consolidation and purchase of assets all involve complicated questions of valuation, in order to arrive at a fair ratio of exchange or of a purchase price. The lease presents problems of rent which may be far more difficult to solve than problems concerning the value of the business for merger or purchase. For example, how is a fair rent to be arrived at when the lease is for ten years or a hundred years? Will ever-changing demand render the leased premises more valuable or less valuable or even worthless? The holding company probably offers the least problems of valuation.

3. _Method of financing the combination._ The amount of cash, bonds or stock required to finance the combination will often be a major factor in choosing the form of combination. Purchase of assets often requires an outlay of cash also needed for expansion of inventories or modernization of facilities. On the other hand, the financing of such a purchase through the creation of bonded indebtedness may strain the credit standing of the new corporation, seriously limiting either or both its short-term and long-term credit needs. The lease is the most desirable from this point of view since a cash outlay is seldom required.

4. _How flexible will the fusion be?_ Mergers and consolidations, once consummated, are difficult to undo. What if the fusion should prove unfortunate, or economic conditions change? Perhaps the two organizations cannot be combined harmoniously, or the product lines are not complementary. Although unwanted properties may be disposed of, it may cause difficulty, or be possible only at great loss. Purchase of assets of one company by another eliminates part of the difficulty, as only those assets desired are purchased. It doesn't solve all of the problems, however. The lease is less permanent than complete fusion, but may prove inflexible short of avoidance in a bankruptcy or reorganization proceeding. Probably the holding company is the most flexible, if flexibility is the paramount consideration. It may offer permanency by a later fusion of the companies, if that is desired.

5. _Taxation._ There are very few business combinations which can be made today without serious consideration of the effects of taxes. In fact, in many cases it is the deciding factor. In general, there is no federal or state tax arising solely out of the exchange of stock in a merger or consolidation. As a result, the merger or consolidation is said to be tax-free. Whether or not a combination would be subject to any taxes at the time of the combination must be left to the tax experts. On the other hand, where one company purchases the assets of another company, there may be two taxable transactions. Result, the first tax may be levied on the selling corporation if it realized a capital gain—that is, if the corporation sells the assets for an amount greater than the value of these assets in its

possession. Second, the stockholders of the selling corporation pay a capital gain tax on what they receive, should the amount be greater than the cost of their share in the corporation. Similarly, the stockholders may have a capital loss if the amount received is less than the cost of their share in the corporation.

The Bureau of Internal Revenue will render its opinion in advance of a merger or consolidation as to whether or not it qualifies as a tax-free exchange. Corporations are taxed on the income received from stock held in other corporations just as an individual must pay income tax on dividends he receives from stock he owns. In addition, if one corporation owns a sufficiently large block of stock of another corporation, it may qualify to file a consolidated return. This may result in some tax savings. This saving leads some companies to merge or consolidate their subsidiaries rather than continue as a holding company and declare intercorporate dividends which are taxable.

Legal requirements for fusion. Before going further with a study of business combinations, we must briefly consider the practical and legal steps necessary to consummate the fusion in a satisfactory manner.

In a merger and consolidation these steps are four in number, as follows:

1. There must be the conception of the idea of merger or consolidation by someone. In the 1920s this was most often a professional promoter or group of investment bankers who spent a great deal of time investigating possible mergers. These men would take options on likely companies, or approach the management with a plan of combination. In either event, the management and the promoters expected to make profits through the sale of securities of the new companies to the public. Sometimes legitimately, the economies derived from the combination would result in profits which were capitalized at a fair rate of return. Thus, if Company A earned $1,000,000 and Company B earned a similar amount, the combination of the two companies might result in the creation of a new company with earnings, not of $2,000,000 but of $2,500,000. Capitalizing this excess at the rate of 10 per cent permitted the bankers to sell $5,000,000 worth of securities to the public over and above the securities of the two companies outstanding before the combination. Often, as previously noted, unscrupulous promoters and investment bankers overestimated the amount of increased profits which could be derived from the combination and overcapitalized the new venture. Others arbitrarily increased the book value of the properties of the two companies and sold additional securities or bonds on the basis of this fictitious value. Today most mergers and consolidations are brought about by the management of the companies involved with little or no outside aid. Sometimes the management of a company will enlist the aid of investment bankers or others to be on the lookout for a company which

they might reasonably acquire. Once the idea is presented, those in control of each business involved must be persuaded of the advantages of the proposed combination. A plan must be formulated that will be incorporated into a resolution to be adopted by the several boards of directors. This resolution will incorporate the details of the plan which must subsequently be submitted to the stockholders of the respective companies.

2. The assent of the stockholders of each company must be obtained either by their unanimous approval, evidenced by signatures in person or by proxy, or by the approval of at least two-thirds (in most states) of all outstanding shares. This vote must be taken at a special meeting called for the purpose of considering the fusion. It may not be taken up at the annual or general meeting of the several corporations. The statutes provide this for the protection of the stockholders, who might not otherwise be specifically apprised that the meeting would vote on this proposal.

3. As required by the state statutes in the states involved, for the corporations may be incorporated in several different states, the contract of agreement, duly executed, must be filed in the proper office.

4. To complete the merger or consolidation, the actual exchange of the old certificates of stock for the new certificates must be made in accordance with the plan specified.

Where one corporation purchases all or part of the assets of another the first step must take place. However, the stockholders of the purchasing corporation need not be consulted. If the property sold by the selling corporation constitutes a substantial part of the total assets, then the stockholders of the selling stockholders must be called to a special meeting to vote upon the sale. The proportion necessary to effectuate the sale is fixed by the state statute governing such sales. The lease of all or a substantial part of the assets of one corporation by another, in the main, follows the same requirements as in the case of sale. Step three in the merger outlined above would not be necessary in either a purchase of assets or a lease. It might be necessary to complete step four at least partially in the event of a purchase of assets through exchange of stock. It would not be necessary in the lease.

The basis of exchange in merger and consolidation. In bringing about a consolidation or merger, the usual method is to exchange the stock of one corporation for that of another. If a new corporation is to be formed, then the stock of the old companies must all be exchanged on some suitable basis for the stock in the new corporation. In either case a security holder must be convinced that he is getting dollar for dollar value or he will not be inclined to vote in favor of the proposed change. To make it as simple as possible for the stockholders to compute just what they are getting, and as a roughly fair basis of exchange, the market value of the several companies is often employed. As a simple illustration, if Company A stock is selling on the New York Stock Exchange for $50 per share, and Company B is selling for $25 per share, a two-for-one share of Company A, if they are being asked to accept B's stock, or a one-for-two exchange for B's stockholders, if they are receiving A's stock, might be a fair basis. When a new corporation is being organized, perhaps this method would not be entirely adequate, inasmuch as the various corporations might contribute assets more valuable than past earning power. When the stock of companies being united are not listed on a national securities exchange or, indeed, not traded at all (closed corporations, for example) some other method of evaluating the contribution of each must be arrived at. Of course, this is an oversimplification of a serious problem. What if Corporation A is paying $3 annual dividend and Corporation B is paying $1 a share, and suppose Corporation A is earning only $3 per share and Corporation B is earning $2 a share. One might have a heavy debt, while the other is debt-free. The sales trend of one might be upward, the other down—or supposing Corporation A uses "fifo" as a method of computing the cost of goods sold and Company B uses "lifo."[1] Or Corporation A uses the straight-line method of depreciation and Company B has taken advantage of the tax law which permits the use of the sum of the digits method of computation for this purpose. Many more factors must enter into the fair exchange. Those stated, however, indicate the complexity of the solution. Stockholders of each corporation need to know a great deal about the other corporation, as well as about their own. Financial statements should reflect the financial condition of a business but, until business employs a uniform method of accounting and of evaluating assets, financial statements alone are an inadequate means of comparing two companies. The method of arriving at inventory evaluation, the value to be given to patents, goodwill, trademarks and other intangibles, the present value of the fixed assets as compared to the book value, all of these adjustments and more must be made before the companies can be compared. In addition to the present market price, the following are likely to be important in the consideration of the exchange:

Book value per share.
Earnings per share, current year and last five-year average.
Working capital per share.
Debt per share.

All mergers and consolidations a matter of bargaining. It has been shown that all consolidations and mergers are worked out on the basis of mutual agreement. Since this is the case, it must be realized that no

---

[1] The terms "fifo" and "lifo" refer to *first in, first out* and *last in, first out* methods of valuing inventory.

established rule or standard procedure can be set down here regarding the practice to be followed. The general conditions at the time, the importance of the companies, the location of their plants, the desirability of obtaining the services of a certain executive, the condition of the stock market—all of these and many other considerations come up around the bargain table and result in compromises and special arrangements, which make it practically impossible for an outsider even to guess at the exact procedures followed and the real basis for the valuation placed on various properties.

Naturally, the offer to exchange stock cannot be made to each individual shareholder. It is arranged through an agreement between the directors of the combining companies, some of whom are often large stockholders. After the directors have bargained among themselves, often with the assistance of interested bankers, and have reached an agreement as to the basis of exchange, the proposal must be submitted at a special meeting called for the purpose. If the required number of stockholders consent, the absorbing corporation issues its stock in exchange and the fusion is consummated.

Rights of minority stockholders. The statutes of New York are typical of the rights of minority stockholders in consolidations, mergers, and purchase of assets combinations. These statutes provide that a stockholder who dissents within the time specified by the statutes shall be entitled to demand payment for his stock and, if a price cannot be agreed upon, to an appraisal by a board of appraisers appointed by the Supreme Court. The fees and expenses of such appraisal are to be borne by the corporation. (See Sec. 20, 21 and 87 of N.Y. Stock Corporation Law.) In New York these provisions apply to voting stockholders only. (See In re Harwitz 80 NYS 2d 570, Supreme Court, Special Term.)

There is no way in which a minority of the stockholders may prevent acquisition of majority control of their corporation by another corporation. They may, however, obtain an injunction against the operation of their corporation's business for the sole benefit of the holding company, when such operations result in provable damages to the minority. In some cases, the abuse of majority power has resulted in outside stockholders of a subsidiary receiving priority of claim in the assets in a dissolution proceeding over the claims of the holding company. ["Deep Rock" case, Taylor v. Standard Gas and Electric Co., 306 U.S. 307 (1939)]

There are numerous cases when fusion has been bitterly fought by minority stockholders, sometimes with success. A few years ago, the Bethlehem Steel Corporation attempted to purchase the assets of the Youngstown Sheet and Tube Co. At a special meeting of stockholders of the Youngstown Sheet and Tube Co., the necessary consents required by statute for the sale of assets were obtained. Nevertheless, minority stockholders obtained an injunction preventing the consummation of the sale on the ground that complete information had not been provided to stockholders prior to the vote. The validity of some of the proxies held by those voting in favor of the merger was also questioned.

Questions for Study and Review

1. What are the arguments for and against big business? Do you consider big business a danger to the welfare of the country? Support your position.
2. Distinguish between internal growth and external growth. In what manner may internal expansion be financed?
3. What are the advantages and disadvantages of internal expansion?
4. What are the advantages and disadvantages of external expansion?
5. Discuss the factors which determine the optimum size of a business firm.
6. What are the motivating forces behind expansion? Which would you think most important? Why?
7. Describe the three classifications of external expansion and give an example of each.
8. Name and explain the various types of business combinations.
9. Discuss the advantages and disadvantages of merger and consolidation.
10. What are the advantages and disadvantages of the purchase of assets as a form of business combination?
11. What is a holding company? List several advantages of the holding company.
12. Discuss the four legal steps that are necessary to consummate the fusion of two business companies.

Problems

1. The *A, B & C* Corporation desires to merge with *X, Y & Z* Corporation. While two-thirds of the *A, B & C* stockholders consent to the merger, it appears that only a bare majority of the *X, Y & Z* stock will be voted in favor of the merger. (The statutes require the consent of two-thirds of the voting stock for a merger.) How can the two corporations be brought under unified control? Would your answer be changed if only one-third of the stock of a desired corporation could be acquired?

2. A large holding company has a number of subsidiaries, which, with the holding company itself, are engaged in approximately the same type of operations and utilize the same equipment and supplies. All find it necessary to engage in a great deal of research and development, not only to improve and make more economical services now being rendered to their customers, but to keep up with development of new material and devise new ways to increase income. Suggest a way of saving costs in the procurement of material and supplies, insuring the availability of such supplies as needed, as well as making sure that they will meet desired specifications. Also suggest means by which research and development may be increased and duplication of effort and expense now existing may be avoided.

3. Two large metropolitan department stores desire to combine their delivery systems. Assuming that their forms of organization may not be the same,

advise them of methods by which they can accomplish their purpose, and show the advantages or disadvantages of each plan.

4. On November 15, 1906, the United States Government brought suit against the Standard Oil Company of New Jersey, a holding company with 70 subsidiary corporations, charging violation of the Sherman Anti-trust Act. On May 15, 1911, the Supreme Court confirmed a decision of the circuit court enjoining the Standard Oil Company of New Jersey from voting the stock of 37 of the defendant companies (the case against 33 having been dismissed) and enjoining the defendants from entering any like combination which would restrain interstate commerce in petroleum and petroleum products. Discuss the later merger of the Standard Oil Company of New York and the Vacuum Oil Company, bearing in mind that both of these companies were defendants in the above suit.

5. Corporations A, B, and C are being consolidated into a new Corporation X. Common stock of the X Corporation is to be offered to the three corporations in payment for their assets. The promoters and bankers will retain ten per cent of the total stock for their services. The corporation will be capitalized at 12 per cent, which in the judgment of the bankers represents a fair rate of return on the business. It is estimated that the present earnings of the three corporations will be increased as a result of economies of consolidation by $80,000.

A study of the income statements of the three corporations disclosed that the average earnings over the past five years were: Corporation A, $200,000; Corporation B, $125,000; and Corporation C, $75,000.

How much stock will be given to each corporation if: a. Shares are to have a par value of $100? b. No-par value stock is used and shares are marketed at $50?

Written Assignment

Representatives of Corporation A approach the directors of Corporation B with the suggestion that the two companies combine through statutory merger. The directors of A are agreeable and say that the consent of the required majority of the voting common stockholders can be obtained. Corporation B, however, has a relatively small issue of non-voting 7 per cent preferred stock outstanding which is not redeemable and which is preferred as to assets in case of involuntary dissolution at par value ($100), and in case of voluntary dissolution at $110. Corporation B stipulates that Corporation A, which has no preferred stock, create a stock with the same provisions as the preferred stock of Corporation B with a view to exchanging it on a share-for-share basis. This A refuses to do as it does not want any preferred stock in its capital structure. Assume that sufficient cash now possessed by Corporations A and B together is available to pay off the preferred; a proposition is now made to the directors of Corporation B whereby complete fusion could be accomplished and the preferred stockholders taken care of by being paid off.

a. What type of combination do the directors of A have in mind and how would it accomplish the desired objective concerning disposing of the preferred stock? *consolidation*

b. How much cash per preferred share would be required? *7/10*

c. Would the consent of the stockholders of both Corporation A and Corporation B be required? *yes only A*

d. Would there be tax problems involved which would not be present in the statutory merger first proposed? Explain fully.

CHAPTER XVI

Insuring Against Business Risks

Business risks. Every venture in life is attended with risk. Every human activity faces the danger of becoming a failure as the result of unfulfilled promises or as the result of catastrophes, such as fires, cyclones, or floods. For practically every type of business risk, however, there is some form of insurance that furnishes partial, if not complete, protection against loss.

The difficult problem for the businessman is to determine exactly what the outstanding risks of his business are. The solution to it is, then, at as low a cost as possible, to protect himself against those catastrophes that may unexpectedly occur. The determination of the outstanding risks of a business is a matter of careful analysis. For example, authorities claim that no part of this world is immune from earthquakes. For instance, London experienced in 1931 for the first time in a thousand years an earthquake of noticeable severity. But if earthquakes come only once in a thousand years, it is hardly advisable for a London businessman to carry earthquake insurance. In other parts of the world where earthquakes are a very common event, it is advisable to carry such insurance. The following list includes common risks of loss against which insurance may be taken:

1. Loss due to death of an invaluable employee or partner.
2. Fire loss.
3. Loss of income from rents due to fire.
4. Loss of profits due to fire.
5. Water damage from sprinkler leakage.
6. Water damage.
7. Damage or loss of goods in transit.
8. Riots, civil commotions and malicious mischief.
9. Explosion damage.
10. Earthquake damage.
11. Windstorm damage.
12. Hailstorm damage.
13. Flood damage.

14. Loss due to rain.
15. Automobile collision, fire and theft, automobile accidents,
16. Aviation accidents.
17. Building accidents.
18. Elevator accidents.
19. Loss of wages due to injury to employees.
20. Boiler explosions.
21. Flywheel breakage.
22. Engine breakdown.
23. Plate glass breakage.
24. Mysterious disappearance of property.
25. Defects in land titles.
26. Forgery losses.
27. Infidelity of employees.
28. Unfulfilled contracts.
29. Credit losses.

Although the above do not include all of the risks to which a business is subject, the list presents the main causes of loss.

Risk-bearing plans. There are two ways by which risks can be offset and the business protected against the danger of losses. The first is to transfer the risk to an insurance company, and the second is to carry self-insurance.

Before the significance of the risk-bearing plans can be thoroughly grasped, it is necessary for the reader to understand the theory of insurance. Professor Ackerman, in his work on *Insurance*,[1] describes the theory of insurance as follows:

Insurance distributes the cost of the risk over a large group of individuals subject to the same risk, in order to reimburse the few who actually suffer from the risk. For example, a study of past statistics in a city of 2,000 houses, each valued at $10,000, may indicate that each year there are losses by fire amounting to $10,000. Every owner, therefore, knows that some of the houses will be damaged by fire and it is possible that his house may be one of those which will be burnt. Theoretically, if the owners annually contributed to a common fund $5 for each owner, the risk would be covered, and each owner would be freed from the fear of financial loss through fire. This principle of distributing risk is the basis of all insurance.

Insurance is a social device whereby one party, the *insurer* or insurance company, agrees to meet certain stated risks in return for a money consideration paid by a number of other parties, the *insured*. The money consideration is called the *premium*. A fire insurance company, for example, will, in consideration of the payment of a premium, issue a contract called a *policy*, in which the insurance company agrees to reimburse the insured for a fire loss but not in excess of the amount stated in the policy and with the provision that the loss must occur during the period through which the policy runs.

Self-insurance operates though the setting aside of funds over a period of time to cover possible losses. To be practical, there should be a large

---

[1] Saul B. Ackerman, *Insurance* (New York: The Ronald Press Co., 1951), p. 3.

number of similar risks, all subject to the same hazards. To build up a reserve to equal the aggregate value of all the units would require in effect that the plant investment be doubled. A corporation with a single plant would not find it practicable to be a self-insurer for the reason indicated; to be fully protected, the insurance reserve must equal the value of the plant, even more if it is desired to insure against possible damages and personal injuries. However, if the property is scattered to such an extent that only a relatively small part is likely to be lost at one time, the concern may be a self-insurer without building up a reserve fund equal to the total plant investment. Railroads, because of scattered units, are usually self-insurers for at least part of the protection required. Because of the heavy investment in terminals and the possibility of huge personal injury claims in case of a train wreck, most railroads also carry insurance covering such large risks with insurance companies.

It should be pointed out that a concern is not self-insured until the insurance reserve fund has been built up to a size deemed adequate to cover reasonable loss likely to occur. Until that point is reached, the concern would be inadequately protected and should provide adequate insurance through regular underwriters.

Loss prevention should be an important part of any risk-bearing plan, because it enables insurance companies to charge lower premium rates and to diminish the cost if insurance is carried. "Safety first" is one of the best types of insurance. Risks can be reduced to a minimum by installing loss prevention equipment, by avoiding risks, and by educating those concerned to guard against all possible loss.

There is a definite limit as to how far accidents can be reduced by purely mechanical means. Most authorities today believe that accidents are due primarily to *human faults*, not mechanical faults. The answer lies principally in improving worker education and morale, and supervision at the foreman level. Insurance companies have been leaders in developing scientific safety programs, especially in connection with workmen's compensation insurance.

Contingency reserves or a large surplus account may be used for protection against possible losses, but this is actually *non-insurance*. If this plan is followed, the reserves and the surplus must be in liquid form in order that, when the contingency arises, the money will be available to cover the loss. Mr. O. V. Rodriques, writing many years ago, made a very fine distinction between non-insurance and self-insurance in connection with the fire hazard; his explanation reads as follows:[2]

Self-insurance. Self-insurance is the assumption of the risk by the owner of property, who lays aside periodically sums estimated as adequate to provide in

---

[2] R. H. Montgomery, *Financial Handbook* (New York: The Ronald Press Co., 1927), p. 657.

time a fund sufficient to reimburse him for any losses which may occur. Where plants are scattered over the country, isolated in most cases, and the class of business, together with the construction of the property, is such that fire hazards are greatly minimized, such insurance may be successfully undertaken by the owner. The chances for the success of a self-insurance plan would be greatly enhanced if, during the period of accumulation of the fund, insurance in other organizations were used to supplement the plan, this supplemental insurance being gradually reduced as the fund is increased.

Non-insurance is not self-insurance. Self-insurance should not be confused with the assumption of risks without any provision for losses when they do occur. Every man who does not insure his property carries this latter so-called self-insurance, but if he is in business, the interest of his bankers, creditors, customers, and employees must be considered. The essence of insurance is the provision for prompt indemnification of losses; and where this principle is not observed, insurance cannot be said to exist. Even where reserves are set aside but no actual segregation of promptly convertible assets is made, the principle of insurance is not properly observed. A sound business would require, not merely a bookkeeping entry, but also the accumulation of a fund invested in quickly convertible securities, kept virtually in trust.

Insurable interest. There are several important principles of insurance. One of these refers to *insurable interest*. If a person insures a building in which he has no financial interest, he will not be able to collect on his policy in case a loss occurs. The reason for this is that the principle of insurable interest requires that, *in order for the insured to be able to recover in case of loss, he must be able to show that he suffered a monetary loss when the property was damaged*. If the insured has no financial interest, he would be unable to show such a monetary loss. Important examples of insurable interest are:

1. The interest of an actual owner.
2. The interest of a lessee.
3. The interest of a mortgagee.

The *insurance contract* or *policy* is a contract between the company or insurer and the insured. In order to enable the reader to understand the characteristics of a policy, reference will be made to the fire contract, which is known generally as the standard fire insurance policy. The latter contains the following main provisions:

1. The parties.
2. A description of the property.
3. Amount of insurance.
4. The rate.
5. Total charge or premium.
6. The protection given.
7. Provisions affecting commencement and termination of insurance contract.
8. Provisions which void the contract.
9. Procedure in settling for a loss.

It is important that the insured know when the contract is legally in force. *The risk must have been accepted by the insurance company*. The delivery of the policy is not essential to make the insurer liable. Frequently, a *binder* is used in insurance covering property to indicate an acceptance of the risk by the insurance company. This is a temporary agreement that binds the company prior to the issuance of the policy.

Insurance contracts are usually terminated by the expiration of the term for which the policy was issued, cancellation by the insured or cancellation by the insurer. In most instances, the insurance contract may be voided if the insured commits a fraudulent act. The loss in many policies is payable within sixty days after a proof of loss has been received by the company.

Because of certain legislative requirements, in many states an insurance company cannot issue a policy unless the provisions have been approved in advance by the State Insurance Department. In addition, insurance rates, duties and obligations of representatives of insurance companies, investments, and treatment of policyholders are very closely supervised by the state. Generally, the law requires that insurance companies file financial statements annually, and these statements are open for inspection by the public.

The various forms of insurance that can be obtained are divided into five groups:

I. Life insurance.
II. Fire insurance.
III. Casualty insurance.
IV. Marine insurance.
V. Fidelity and surety.

I. Life insurance. This is the most important branch of insurance. Its primary purpose is to protect dependents. There are four important life insurance policy contracts. These are: (1) *term insurance,* (2) *whole life insurance,* (3) *limited payment life insurance,* and (4) *endowment insurance.* A term insurance policy provides protection for a definite number of years, and the policy becomes a claim provided the insured dies within the period stated in the policy.

The annual *premium* for a term policy is lower than for a whole life policy, since the term policy does not contain any cash surrender value. The *actual cost* (premiums less cash surrender value) of a whole life policy is less than that of a term policy; for this reason the whole life policy is the most popular form of contract sold.

The whole life insurance policy provides protection for the insured's dependents during the life of the insured: the policy matures at the time that the insured dies. A limited payment life insurance policy requires the insured to pay premiums for a definite number of years, for example, 20 years: after the twentieth year, the insured pays no more premiums; however, whenever the insured dies, the claim matures. An endowment policy requires payment of premiums for a definite number of years, for example, 20 years: if the insured dies before the twentieth year, his dependents will receive the face value of the policy; if he survives the twentieth year, he will receive the face value of the policy.

The insurance law regulates the provisions that must be inserted in every policy contract issued by a life insurance company. The important clauses of a life insurance policy are those relating to:

1. *Grace period,* requiring that the insured be permitted to pay his premium within thirty or thirty-one days after the premium is due without lapsing the policy.

2. *Incontestability,* providing that, after a certain period of time that varies from 1 to 2 years, the policy is incontestable by the insurance company except for the nonpayment of premium or the misstatement of age (if there has been a misstatement of age, the amount payable will be modified according to the insured's age).

3. The *beneficiary,* providing that the policy shall be payable to the person named in the policy by the insured. There are two forms of beneficiaries: _revocable_ and _irrevocable_. If the beneficiary is revocable, the insured can substitute the name of a new beneficiary at all times. If the beneficiary is irrevocable, the insured gives up his right to substitute a new beneficiary during the beneficiary's life without the consent of the irrevocable beneficiary.

4. *Nonforfeiture values,* that is, cash surrender value, extended insurance, and paid-up insurance. Premiums paid under certain policy forms, such as whole life, limited payment life, or endowment, are used partly to pay current claims and expenses and partly to create a reserve to help meet future claims. By statute, the purchasers of these policy forms are entitled to a share in the reserve, which share is designated as the cash surrender value available to the policyholder after he has paid a definite number of premiums. The cash surrender value at the end of each year must be printed in the policy. If the insured desires, he can surrender his policy and receive his share in the reserve. If he accepts this amount, he thereby surrenders all his rights under this policy. However, he has the privilege of borrowing the cash surrender value from the insurance company and paying interest on this amount: in the meantime, the policy remains in force for the face amount of the policy reduced by the amount of money that has been borrowed by the assured.

5. *Extended insurance option.* If the assured does not desire to continue his policy and does not demand the cash surrender value, he has two options. He may ask the company to grant extended insurance for the face amount of the policy for a specific number of years, which is stated in the policy, or he may request a paid-up insurance option.

6. *Paid-up insurance option.* If he desires, the assured may use his cash surrender value to purchase paid-up insurance for an amount smaller than the face value of the policy.

Business life insurance. An important use of life insurance is to protect business against the loss of an invaluable employee or partner, or a stockholder, in a corporation that has a very limited number of stockholders. This is called _business life insurance._ Business experience tends to show that manpower, executive ability, leadership, vision, and personality in members of an organization are qualities that can be built and developed, but not bought over the counter. Many successful concerns have found themselves seriously handicapped by the loss of one or more of their best employees, partners, or executives. Many a partnership has found it very difficult, on the death of one of the partners, to raise enough money to settle with the heirs of the deceased. The advantages of carrying business life insurance were very well stated by the late John Wanamaker, who said, "Twenty years ago I had a capital of about a half million dollars. I then realized that a businessman with a half million dollars of capital and one million and one half of insurance on his life would have better credit in his business than one with a half million capital and no insurance—and so I took the insurance. I now find that, by trading on the credit it created, I have made more profit than I would have made if the money which went into insurance had gone directly into my business."

Business insurance may be purchased especially to accomplish one definite end, but generally it will accomplish at least one of the following:

1. Furnish funds to replace an invaluable employee or partner who has been lost by death.
2. Supply the money needed to retire the interest of a deceased partner or stockholder.
3. Provide an emergency reserve, since money can be borrowed on the policy.
4. Stabilize and strengthen credit.
5. Retire individuals at old age.
6. Retire business obligations.

Life insurance trusts. A life insurance trust is a trust established by the insured to place the proceeds of life insurance policies in the hands of a trustee, to be distributed according to definite terms established in the trust agreement. This procedure may also be used in business. If life insurance is purchased to retire a partner's or a stockholder's interest, care should be taken in the naming of the beneficiary. If A and B are partners, it is inadvisable to make B the beneficiary of A's policy and A the beneficiary of B's policy. If A should predecease B, B would be entitled to the money under the life insurance policy in which he was named beneficiary. However, there is no guarantee that he would use this money to purchase from the estate of A the interest of A in the partnership of A and B. In fact, if he were in a poor financial condition, creditors might levy on the money that he had collected from the life insurance company. In order to avoid this contingency, it is advisable to prepare a special agreement called the *life insurance trust*. Under this agreement, which is signed by the partners, a third party is named the beneficiary; for example, *C* is made the beneficiary of *A's* policy and *B's* policy. The beneficiary under the terms of the agreement is usually required to collect the money from the life insurance company and to pay the money to the estate of the deceased partner, in consideration of which the estate of the deceased partner assigns its interest in *A's* and *B's* partnership to the survivor. Similar practice should be followed in connection with the life insurance policy purchased to buy the interest of deceased stockholders.

Group insurance. To develop loyalty among employees, businessmen have purchased group insurance to protect the dependents of the employees who die while on the payroll of the employer. The premium may be paid by the employer, or the employee may contribute with the employer. The policy is issued to the employer and each employee receives a certificate stating the amount of insurance protection to which his beneficiary is entitled. All rights under the certificate terminate as soon as the employee ceases to work for his employer. However, the former employee is entitled to a policy in his own name, provided he pays the rates charged by the insurance company at the age of the employee when the employment was terminated.

Industrial pensions. Some firms have introduced industrial pensions. These pensions provide protection for employees when they reach a certain specified age. Some of the factors upon which the payment of pensions depends are: (1) the length of service of the employee before retirement, (2) the amount of the annual wages of the employee. Funds to pay the pension may be accumulated by the employer and set up as a reserve. Of course, there is the danger that the reserve may be inadequate to meet all pension payments. In addition, all interest that the employee may have in the pension fund ceases as soon as the employee leaves his employer. There has been a tendency, in some cases, to purchase a contract with a life insurance company whereby the employee obtains the right to a certain amount of the deferred pension for each year that he works, payment by the life insurance company to commence at the retirement age. Under this arrangement, the right of the employee to the pension from the life insurance company continues whether or not he remains in the same employment.

II. Fire insurance. The most important policy in this group is the standard fire insurance policy, from which coverage the group takes its name. In this group are included policies covering damage to property owned by the insured, such as losses due to sprinkler leakage, water damage, windstorm, tornado, earthquake, explosion, riot, civil commotion, hail, and rain.

It is hardly necessary to say much concerning the fire risk. The continual clang of fire bells and the shrill call of the siren constantly remind everyone that fire losses are occurring every day. The annual fire loss is estimated to be in excess of $1 billion. Fire prevention authorities believe that the financial loss could be reduced if proper care were exercised in enacting adequate building laws that required the elimination of fire hazards, and in the maintenance of an efficient fire department.

Fire policy provisions. The standard fire policy embodies the following:

1. A description of the property.
2. The risk that the company assumes.
3. Duties to be performed by the insured in the event of loss.
4. Contribution to be made by each company if several companies have insured the same property.
5. Method of determining the amount of loss.

Risk that company assumes. Perhaps the most important provision, as far as the insured is concerned, is the risk assumed by the company. The company has to pay for any fire loss, unless the hazard has been increased after the policy becomes effective. The insurance company does not agree to pay for losses due to all contingencies. The policy provides that losses due to certain circumstances are not covered, including: (1) losses occurring as a result of war, riot, civil commotion, (2) losses incurred by act of civil authority, and (3) losses caused by theft. Losses due to explosion are not covered unless fire ensues, and then the policy covers for the loss due to fire. The new standard fire policies differ from the older ones in providing against loss by lightning so that it is no longer necessary to have a special endorsement covering this risk.

Duties to be performed by the insured in the event of loss. After a loss has occurred, the insured must notify the company immediately. He must separate the damaged goods from the undamaged goods, and then prepare a statement of loss, which he must file with the insurance company.

Contribution. Frequently an insured obtains several policies from various companies, as one company may not be willing to insure his property for the amount that the insured desires. For example, suppose the cash value of his property were $160,000. The insured might obtain policies from four different companies: from Company A, for $50,000; Company B, for $40,000; Company C, for $10,000; and Company D, for $60,000. Now, assume that the property is damaged by fire to the extent of $20,000. In accordance with the terms of the policy, each of the companies must pay the owner in proportion to the amount of insurance that each company carries. The amount of insurance will be determined as follows:

$$\text{Company } A \frac{\$50,000}{\$160,000} \times \$20,000 = \$6,250.$$

$$\text{Company } B \frac{\$40,000}{\$160,000} \times \$20,000 = \$5,000.$$

$$\text{Company } C \frac{\$10,000}{\$160,000} \times \$20,000 = \$1,250.$$

$$\text{Company } D \frac{\$60,000}{\$160,000} \times \$20,000 = \$7,500.$$

Method of determining amount of loss. The insurance company may send a representative to determine the amount of the loss. If the insurance company cannot agree with the insured as to the amount of loss, the insured cannot commence a suit to recover the amount he claims. However, the policy provides that the insured must appoint an appraiser and the company must appoint an appraiser. After these appraisers are appointed, they must meet and appoint an umpire. The two appraisers must then determine the amount of the loss. If they agree on an amount, the insurance company is required to pay the amount so determined. If the appraisers are unable to agree, it is the duty of the umpire to ascertain the amount of the loss; this amount must then be paid to the insured.

Coinsurance clause. An endorsement that is frequently attached to the fire insurance policy is known as the _coinsurance clause_. This clause requires the insured to carry a certain amount of insurance, which is measured by a percentage of the cash value of the property. A common percentage is 80 per cent. The reason for the insertion of this clause is that rates quoted by insurance companies covering the fire risk vary because they are based upon the certain percentage of his property on which the insured is required to carry insurance. The higher the percentage required by the insurance company, the lower will be the rate. In other words, if 100 per cent insurance is required, the rate will be lower than if 80 per cent insurance is required. Obviously, the rate will be lower if 80 per cent of insurance is required than if, for example, only 20 per cent of insurance were required to be carried. The effect of the operation of this clause may be seen from the following illustration. Assume that the cash value of the property is $175,000 and the rate paid by the insured is based upon the assumption that he will carry insurance up to 80 per cent of the valuation of his property. The insured has a policy for $120,000. A fire occurred, and the damage amounted to $35,-000. In view of the fact that the amount of insurance required was $140,000, that is, .80 × $175,000, and only $120,000 was carried, the insurance company will pay the loss determined from the following arithmetical computation:

$$\frac{\$120,000}{\$140,000} \times \$35,000 = \$30,000.$$

Modern business has seen the rise of many industrial organizations which have factories and warehouses in various parts of the United States. The standard fire insurance policy does not meet the need of these organizations, since the standard fire insurance policy covers goods at a specific location. If a firm has 60 branches, it would be expected to require 60 policies. Furthermore, it would be necessary to take great care in order to be certain that the policyholder was fully protected for the stock which might be in any branch at any one time. For example, stock might be received in a branch although the central organization might not have the notice of the receipt of additional stock. In the meantime, a fire might occur with loss to the policyholder on account of insufficient insurance. To meet the need of these organizations, fire insurance companies issue a special policy form, which, subject to limitation, will protect the assured, since the premium is determined by a report from the insured at the end of each month for the various locations where the insured has property.

The fire insurance policy is generally a contract of indemnification. If the insured is manufacturing an article for which the total cost is $10 and the selling price $11, the manufacturer is entitled under the policy to $10 for loss by fire. No consideration is given to the fact that the article was manufactured under contract for sale at $11 or could have been sold at $11. However, the insurance company will issue a policy agreeing to pay the loss of profit for goods ready for sale but destroyed by fire.

In addition to the loss of profit on goods manufactured, the manufacturer may suffer additional loss, since his plant cannot operate until it has been repaired and he has again obtained materials in order to start manufacturing operations. The loss resulting from inability to operate may be far greater than the loss to the articles damaged by fire. Although the fire has occurred and the assured has been reimbursed for the articles damaged, there are certain expenses that continue after the fire even though the plant cannot operate. Some of these are interest payments on bonded indebtedness, taxes on real estate, salaries to employees under contract, and payments on advertising contracts. In addition, there may be a loss on profits not earned owing to inability to manufacture. To cover such losses, the fire insurance companies issue a *business interruption policy*, which will indemnify the assured for loss of fixed charges and profits that could not be earned during the period after the fire and before operations could again be commenced.

Sprinkler leakage and water damage insurance. In order that the fire hazard and also the fire insurance premium may be reduced, automatic sprinkler systems have been installed in many establishments. These systems have water pressure outlets located throughout the buildings. Their outlets or taps open automatically when the temperature reaches a danger point. Sometimes they open accidentally. Protection against damage from this cause can be obtained through *sprinkler leakage insurance.*

Water damage insurance protects property owners against loss due to damage to property resulting from the use of water in buildings. This policy excludes damages caused by automatic sprinkler systems. The most common hazards are damage done by:

1. Bursting water pipes, due to defective plumbing.
2. Leaking system pipes.
3. Overflowing tubs and basins.
4. The collapse of supply tanks.
5. Rain water damage from defective roofs, spouts, open windows, or skylights.
6. Frozen pipes.

Hail insurance is written primarily for the farmer. It protects against damage done to crops by hail. Most policies provide that the insurance ceases when the crop has been harvested. Liability usually accrues to the company when the damage exceeds an agreed percentage of the total insurance carried.

Rain and hail insurance. Rain insurance is not primarily for protection against the damage actually done by rain water; rather, it aims to protect businessmen and promoters against financial loss on account of rain. Types of business which need protection against the losses that rain may cause are:

1. Baseball games.
2. Football games.
3. Prize fights.
4. Auction sales.
5. Races.
6. Carnivals.
7. Fairs.
8. Rodeos.

Windstorm, tornado, and earthquake insurance. Windstorm and tornado insurance protects the insured against loss directly due to windstorms, cyclones, and tornadoes. In some sections of our country, this is a very important form of insurance, since hardly a season passes without some damage from these causes. The policies usually exclude losses due to blizzards, snowstorms, fire, explosions, lightning, cloudbursts, tidal waves, or high water. Fire insurance should also be carried under such circumstances, because very often fire completes the damage started by a windstorm or a cyclone.

Earthquake insurance policies, like most insurance policies, protect against any loss which is the direct result of one or more causes. In this case, it is an earthquake or volcanic eruption. The exclusions are almost identical with those included in the windstorm and tornado policies. It is advisable, again, to properly supplement an earthquake policy with a fire clause.

Riot, civil commotion, and explosion policies. These policies cover destruction of property as a result of riot, strikes, insurrection, civil commotion, and explosions.

III. Casualty insurance. Insurance companies that write this branch of business confine themselves mainly to the following kinds of insurance:

1. Automobile insurance.
2. Workmen's compensation insurance.
3. Accident and sickness insurance.[3]
4. Burglary, larceny and theft insurance.
5. Miscellaneous public liability insurance.

Automobile insurance. The principal hazards due to the operation of an automobile are injuries to the public and damage to their property. In order to protect himself, the owner of an automobile should purchase an automobile bodily injury policy and an automobile property damage policy. The *automobile bodily injury policy* protects the insured against financial loss on account of the liability of the automobile owner to others for bodily injuries accidentally sustained, including death resulting from the accident injury.

In addition to agreeing to pay for any financial loss sustained by the owner of the automobile, the insurance company will defend any action against the insured, investigate and settle claims, and pay first-aid expenses without regard to the ultimate liability of the insured. Usually one clause of the policy provides that the insurance company is responsible for injuries caused by anybody who is driving the automobile with the permission of the owner.

Most companies today issue policies for a minimum of $10,000 to $20,000. The $10,000 is a per-person limitation, and means that the company will not pay more than this amount to any one person involved in an accident for which the insured is responsible. The $20,000 is a per-accident limit, and means the company will not pay more than $20,000 for any one accident, regardless of how many people were injured. These minimum limits are *not adequate* in view of the sharply increased jury verdicts today; increased limits of liability may be obtained for a very small additional cost, and should be requested by the insured.

The insurance company is not responsible if the accident was caused

---

[3] While originally written chiefly by casualty companies, this type of insurance has become in recent years an extremely important part of the business of the life insurance companies.

while the automobile (1) was used in connection with any prearranged race or speed contest; (2) was operated by any person under the age limit fixed by law or, in any event, under fourteen years of age; or (3) was used for any purpose other than that mentioned in the policy.

Automobile property damage insurance protects the insured against loss on account of his legal liability for damage done to the property of others. In addition to indemnifying for damage to the property of others, the policy also covers liability for the loss of the use of the property of others due to the accident.

It is the practice of insurance companies to write automobile property damage insurance in the same policy with the automobile bodily injury insurance. The standard limit for automobile property damage coverage is $5,000 for any one accident. Upon payment of an additional premium, higher limits can be obtained. In connection with the two coverages previously described, the owner of an automobile sometimes purchases _automobile collision insurance_. This form of insurance indemnifies the owner of the automobile on account of damage done to his own car as a result of collision, including upset. The insurance company will repair the car or pay the cost of the damages.

Frequently, collision coverage is issued with a _deductible clause_; for example, the $50 deductible clause. In the event that an insured, who has purchased collision coverage, suffers damages to his car to the extent of $175 as a result of collision, the insurance company will pay $125; that is, $175 less $50. The assumption of part of the risk of loss by the insured of $50 or $100 through acceptance of a deductible clause substantially reduces the cost of this type of coverage.

Workmen's compensation insurance. This form of insurance protects an employer for injuries to his employees arising from, and in the course of, his employment. The insurance company agrees to pay any award that may be made against the employer under the Compensation Law. (All states have a compensation law.) By virtue of this law, which disregards the question of negligence of the employee, employees are awarded payments for injuries caused during their employment.

Because the introduction of workmen's compensation insurance provides protection to injured workers during the course of their employment, many have felt that various other hazards which employees face should be covered by insurance taken out by their employer. As a result, most employers today must pay the entire cost of unemployment insurance for their employees, and must bear half the cost of the social security program (old age and survivors' insurance program). In addition, accident and sickness programs are now a subject for collective bargaining, and in some industries employers are compelled or expected to provide accident and sickness benefits for their employees.

Accident and sickness insurance. This form of insurance has grown rapidly in recent years and is now the most important type of insurance from the standpoint of premium volume (except life insurance). Accident and sickness policies are issued both by casualty companies and life insurance companies, and are designed to pay for (a) loss of income due to the inability to work because of an accident or illness; and (b) expenses incurred because of accident or illness. Accident and sickness policies vary widely in their provisions, and must be carefully examined to see the exact nature of the coverage given. Some policies, for example, cover only automobile accidents or airplane accidents, or certain specified illnesses. The majority of accident and sickness insurance is now written on a group basis to cover employees.

Burglary, larceny, and theft insurance. Because of the frequency with which thefts occur, insurance companies have developed policies that protect against such contingency. Two forms of this insurance are used extensively by businessmen:

1. Mercantile open stock burglary policy.
2. Robber policy.

The *mercantile open stock burglary policy* protects the businessman against burglary when his place of business is closed. In order to be able to recover for any loss, the insured must show that entry was made by the burglars with actual force and violence and that they left visible marks on the premises at the place of entry as a result of the use of tools, explosives, electricity, or chemicals.

Robbery insurance, as distinguished from *burglary insurance,* protects the insured during the regular course of business. There are three different forms of robbery policies:

1. Messenger robbery policy.
2. Paymaster robbery policy.
3. Office or store robbery policy.

The *messenger robbery policy* insures against loss due to robbery from the person in charge of the property while he is outside of the premises of the insured.

The *paymaster robbery policy* insures against loss due to robbery of the paymaster outside or inside the premises of the insured.

The *office or store robbery policy* insures against loss from a custodian while on duty within the premises.

Miscellaneous public liability insurance. As a result of the operation of any business or any undertaking, the owner or his employees may cause injuries to others for which the owner may be held responsible. For example, a piece of iron may fall from a building during the course of its erection and injure a passer-by. The contractor would be held responsible if it could be shown that the accident was due to negligence on his part. Protection against this hazard can be obtained by the purchase of *public liability insurance.* Some of the common forms of public liability insurance are:

1. Manufacturers' and contractors' public liability insurance.
2. Owners', landlords', and tenants' public liability insurance.
3. Elevator public liability insurance.

IV. Marine insurance. This form of insurance, which is similar to fire insurance, protects owners of cargoes against loss while the property is being transported on boats. The *marine insurance policy* offers coverage against numerous hazards instead of a single hazard, as is the case in fire insurance. It is not merely confined to protection against loss on account of fire, but also against a number of other risks and is sometimes written on an all-risk basis. Marine policies are also issued to cover the loss of the hull, as well as the loss of the freight charges.

Many insured have objected strenuously to the fact that they have to purchase many policies in order to cover the various risks from which they might suffer losses. This is especially true when goods are transported to various parts of the country. To meet this objection, many insurance companies issue policy contracts known as *inland marine policies* which are very often written on an all-risk basis. An important inland marine policy form is the *transportation policy.* This policy is in many respects very similar to the marine insurance policy. While marine insurance essentially provides protection on the high seas, the transportation policy provides protection for goods in transit by rail, express, airship, and coastwise steamers.

V. Fidelity and surety. Every businessman who engages an employee to handle funds or goods is confronted with the possibility that such an employee may steal the funds or the goods. Frequently, an employer has found after many years of employment of a trusted employee that the latter has violated his trust. An employer can obtain a fidelity bond, which protects him against loss due to defalcation by his employees. The essential purpose of a fidelity bond is to guarantee the honesty of the one who is bonded. If an employer desires, he can have a separate bond covering each of his employees. On the other hand, he can obtain one bond covering all employees, which is known as a *schedule bond,* listing all employees in a schedule attached to the bond. In addition to guaranteeing the honesty of individuals, fidelity and surety companies undertake to guarantee the performance of contracts. For example, a city may desire to construct a building. The lowest bidder may be awarded the contract. However, before the contract is issued, the municipality generally demands that the contractor must agree to finish the building for his bid. In order to guarantee to the city that he will complete the work, the contractor can obtain a surety bond called a *completion bond.*

The purpose of a surety bond is to guarantee performance of an act.

Social Security Legislation. The Federal Government passed the Social Security Act in 1935. The act was to provide for old-age pensions, unemployment benefits, and other social aids.

It provided for a Federal contributory old-age insurance plan. Employers were to be taxed on their payrolls and employees taxed a like amount on their wages, up to $3,000 per year. The rate of tax to each was to start at one per cent annually on January 1, 1937, and to be graduated upward to reach three per cent for each group in twelve years thereafter. Monthly benefits were provided for the worker who would reach the age of 65 on or after January 1, 1942, provided he had earned not less than $2,000 since December 1, 1937. If the worker reached the age of 65 prior to January 1, 1942, or if he reached the age of 65 after January 1, 1942, and had not earned $2,000 since December 31, 1936, he would receive a lump sum benefit depending upon the amount contributed by the employer and the worker.

Amendments to the act in 1939 postponed the tax increase to the 1½ per cent then due for three more years, expecting to jump the rate to 2 per cent in 1943. Since this, however, the original 1 per cent rate has been successively frozen each year until 1950, when it was increased to 1½ per cent. It is anticipated that the rate on employer and employee will ultimately reach 4¼ per cent on each.

Increasing social security benefits, including increased rates of employee payroll deductions matched by equivalent employer contributions, have become important political objectives. Nor have the increases been limited to increasing the rates more rapidly than provided in the original law. The basic salary on which the tax rate is computed has been increased to $4,200 and on January 1, 1959, it was established at $4,800. Meanwhile benefits have been extended to many new workers, including domestic servants and the self-employed. The cost to the latter is, of course, higher, than that of an employed person, because there is no employer to contribute. The rate for employees and employers, which has been 2¼ per cent, was increased January 1, 1959 to 2½ per cent.

A man at age 65 may begin to receive his benefit in the way of a survivor annuity and a woman may, if desired, at 62. There are other features, a full discussion of which is beyond the province of this text, such as wages earned after 65, or 62 in the case of women, disability and the like. A thorough knowledge of these is essential to businessmen, not only from the standpoint of their individual rights and obligations but because this subject is closely related to employee pension plans which today are included in many wage agreements.

Unemployment insurance. Another type of social insurance with which most businessmen have to be familiar is unemployment insurance. Unlike the program described above, this type of insurance, while covered

by Federal law, is administered by the various states with the cooperation of the Federal Government which contributes funds. Because there
are wide differences in state legislation relative to this form of insurance,
detailed discussion is impracticable here. Businessmen should study
carefully the laws and regulations of their own states so that all requirements may be met. It might be pointed out that many contracts
with labor unions stipulate unemployment provisions exceeding those
required by law in the amount of payment and length of the period of
unemployment covered.

The agent and the broker. Insurance is frequently purchased through
an agent or a broker. There is a legal distinction between an agent and
a broker. An agent is appointed by a specific insurance company to
represent the company. When the insured places an order for a policy
with him, he collects the premium and receives the commission from the
insurance company as a reimbursement for his efforts. Legally, he does
not represent the insured. The insured is not held responsible for improper acts of the agent. Legal responsibility for the proper performance of the agent's duties rests with the insurance company. Nevertheless, the agent makes an analysis of the prospect's needs for the purchase of insurance similar to the analysis made by a broker. The latter
does not represent any insurance company. Whenever he has to obtain a
policy for a client, he communicates with the offices of the various
companies that issue such contracts and tries to induce one of these
companies to issue the required insurance coverage. If the broker obtains a policy, the insured must remit a premium, usually to the broker.
The broker is reimbursed by a commission from the insurance company
that has issued the policy. It must be remembered that the broker is
not appointed to represent any specific insurance company. Therefore,
in most instances, the acts of the broker do not bind the insurance company, but bind the insured.

Every purchaser of insurance should examine each policy when it is
received from the agent or the broker. It is incumbent upon him to read
the policy and to note the contents. He will generally be held responsible for all obligations he has assumed, as stated in the policy. If there
is any misstatement in the policy and a loss occurs at a later period, he
may not be able to collect as a result of the misstatement. He should
have read his policy when it was received. In addition, there are four
important considerations that the insured should decide upon before
accepting a policy from an insurance company and paying the premium.
These are: (1) Is the company admitted to the state? (2) What is the
capital and surplus of the company? (3) What is the claim service record
of the company? (4) What inspection service does the company offer?

It is generally inadvisable to purchase insurance in a company that is
not admitted to the state in which the assured is doing business. In case

of loss, the assured may find it necessary to go to the state in which the company was organized in order to prove a claim, thus causing unnecessary expense. There should be sufficient capital and surplus in possession of the company to satisfy the assured that it will meet its outstanding claims. The value of the assured's contract will depend upon the company's claim settlement policy. A past history of prompt and just settlement of claims is an important factor in the determination of the insurance company's value to the insured. Many forms of insurance rates depend upon the condition of the insured's plant. These rates can be reduced by inspection of the plant by the insurance company; therefore, the person or corporation placing insurance on a plant should be certain to choose a company that will give adequate inspection service.

Questions for Study and Review

1. Name at least twenty risks to which a business may be subject.
2. Discuss two methods of assuming risks.
3. What constitutes an insurable interest?
4. When is an insurance contract legally in force?
5. How may insurance contracts be terminated?
6. What supervision has the state over insurance companies?
7. Name six branches of the insurance business. What kinds of protection are afforded by each?
8. Explain four types of life insurance contracts.
9. What is business life insurance?
10. For what purpose are life insurance trusts created?
11. List the essential clauses in the standard fire insurance policy.
12. What is meant by *contribution* with reference to the distribution of a risk among several companies?
13. What is coinsurance?
14. What is rain insurance?
15. Name and explain the principal branches of casualty insurance.
16. Who is required to carry workmen's compensation insurance?
17. How does the marine insurance policy differ from the common run of insurance contracts?
18. What is a fidelity bond?
19. What is the purpose of title insurance?
20. Contrast the insurance agent and broker.
21. What four matters should be considered before the insured accepts a policy from any company and pays the premium?

Problems

1. Mr. Anderson owned a filling station facing a summer resort hotel. His strategic location enabled him to do an excellent volume of business. Fearing

that the hotel would burn, he purchased a fire insurance policy on the hotel building for $5,000. Two months later, there was a fire and the hotel was completely destroyed. What are Mr. Anderson's rights?

2. Mr. Barton bought a $10,000 ordinary life policy dated January 1, 1925. What are the beneficiary's rights under the following conditions:

(a) He paid only one annual premium and died on January 18, 1926.

(b) He misrepresented important facts in order to obtain the policy, but paid all premiums as they became due and died on January 1, 1930.

(c) He paid premiums for ten years, but failed to pay the eleventh premium and died three months after the grace period.

3. Messrs. Chandler and Dodge, partners in a wholesale produce business, have invested $50,000 each in the business, which represents practically all of their personal assets. Outline an arrangement whereby the survivor will be able to continue the business without financial embarrassment and without admitting the heirs of the deceased into the business.

4. Mr. Andrews bought a $10,000 fire insurance policy from the Bee Company covering his building. Discuss his rights under the following circumstances:

(a) He waited several weeks before notifying the insurance company that he suffered a fire loss.

(b) A boiler exploded and caused $500 damage.

(c) He also had $5,000 insurance on the same building with the C Insurance Company, and a fire caused $600 damage.

5. Mr. Atkins bought a $50,000 fire insurance policy on his apartment house. The policy was subject to the 80 per cent coinsurance clause. What will be the liability of the insurance company for the following losses:

(a) The building had a cash value of $60,000 at the time of the fire, and the damage was $4,000.

(b) The building had a cash value of $125,000 at the time of the fire and the damage was $4,000.

(c) The building had a cash value of $60,000 at the time of the fire and there was a total loss.

(d) The building had a cash value of $125,000 at the time of the fire and the damage was $50,000.

CHAPTER XVII

Business Failures and
Reorganizations

Business failures and financial difficulties. Many concerns become involved in financial difficulties from which they may recover, or which may cause them to fail. Financial difficulties are usually indicated by inability to pay bills or continued failure to earn a profit. Either situation requires a reorganization of some kind if the business is to be made a going concern again. This reorganization may be administered voluntarily by the owners or managers, or may be brought about through action taken by the creditors.

Not every business that finds itself unable to meet its current liabilities or pay interest on its bonds is allowed to fail completely—that is, its assets liquidated for the benefit of creditors. Sometimes skillful readjustment on the part of its management is accomplished with such speed that creditors are willing to forbear until the affairs have changed for the better. The creditors themselves are usually far more interested in seeing the business continue as a going concern than they are in having its affairs wound up and its assets liquidated. This attitude results from recognition of the fact that the assets of a business often have little value when divorced from a going concern. To get their money out of a business, creditors often find it to their interest to give the business an extension of time in which to pay its bills, or even to take the initiative in gaining control of the business and in striving to put it on its feet again.

When there is a great public interest involved, such as in the case of railroads or public utilities, it is imperative that the company be reorganized so that the service upon which the public depends may be continued by the reorganized company. But the company must be maintained during the period of reorganization.

When there is no chance of rehabilitating a business, it must be liquidated. If there are debts, they, of course, must be paid before any liquidating dividends are paid to the stockholders. If the assets appear to be less than the amount due the creditors, or if the firm has been unable to pay its bills, it is likely that bankruptcy proceedings will be instituted, either voluntarily by the owners or necessarily by the creditors.

The purpose of this chapter shall be to discuss not only the causes of failure and the detection of impending failure but also, briefly, the manner in which various readjustments and reorganizations are brought about and the procedure followed when complete failure brings the business before the courts in bankruptcy proceedings.

Types of business failures. A business is an enterprise organized for profit. It may be said therefore, that a business that does not pay a profit and has no reasonable expectancy of profitable operations is a failure. This is true even though it has been successful in meeting its obligations to creditors. Such failures are sometimes termed *economic failures*. The causes of such failures are numerous and will be discussed more fully in this chapter.

Any attempt to classify failures as to type cannot result in arbitrary or clear cut definitions, for the separation of one type from another is merely a matter of degree. The types follow a chronological sequence, one gradually leading to the next, unless suitable remedies are found and applied. Furthermore, just as human ills are more likely to respond to treatment at the beginning, rather than in an advanced state, the more advanced the degree of business failure, the more drastic the remedy and the more difficult the cure. The classification of business failures that follows relates to difficulties of a concern with its creditors. These could very well be termed *legal failures* in that the business has difficulty in meeting, or cannot meet, the legally enforceable obligations due its creditors.

Financial embarrassment. A concern that, because of slow moving inventories, poor collections, or other cause of reduced turnover of current assets, is having difficulties in meeting its current liabilities, may be termed financially embarrassed. There need be no implication of insolvency, but the situation, if not improved, will result in drastic action by creditors.

Financial insolvency. When there has been a decline or dissipation of current asset values to an extent requiring new money, the conversion of fixed assets into cash, or sacrifices by creditors to correct the situation, a concern is sometimes called financially insolvent. The concern has no possibility of realizing enough from its current assets to meet obligations to creditors.

Total insolvency. Total assets, tangible and intangible, are less than obligations due creditors. Obviously, the most drastic remedies are necessary here. Perhaps the only hope of creditors is to bring about a liquidation and forced sale of assets under a bankruptcy proceeding. In many situations, such action is not legally feasible or the losses would be too great, and a drastic reorganization must be accomplished with creditors bearing losses or making sacrifices in proportion to their interest. A study of the failure and reorganization of many of the large railroad corporations during the period extending from about 1932 to the early 1940s will appropriately illustrate the types of sacrifice forced upon creditors by total insolvency.

Causes of failure. The causes of failure in a specific situation are, like the reasons for success, difficult to isolate. Failures seem frequently to occur from a "complication of diseases," rather than from one outstanding cause. Lack of working capital is often named as a cause for failure. It is, however, merely a symptom of some more deeply-rooted ailment that has brought about the resulting condition.

Although incompetence on the part of the management may in general be cited as the cause of practically all business failures, more detailed analyses indicate that the management probably lacked the skill and knowhow or the perseverance to succeed. Lack of capital, so often cited as the immediate cause, usually indicates lack of skill in planning. Nevertheless, it must be remembered that it is always comparatively easy to see at hindsight the steps that might have been taken to avert failure. It must also be realized that many times the foresight that should be exercised to prevent failure is more than could reasonably be expected from most businessmen. Students of finance find themselves interested in studying the various problems that have caused failures and the remedies for them, since, if businessmen have been inefficient in meeting such problems successfully, much can be learned through studying their mistakes.

A brief classification of the causes of business failures, which will form the basis of our discussion, follows:

1. Uneconomic or defective initial promotion.
2. Weak production or distribution policies.
3. Unwise dividend policy, and paying dividends from capital.
4. Overexpansion.
5. Cutthroat competition.
6. Poor financial planning.
7. Unforeseen and severe economic readjustment, brought about by a sudden cessation of demand for the product, revolutionary or unusual legislation, wars, radical tariff changes, and so on.
8. Operation of the business cycle.
9. Disasters, such as earthquakes, fires, floods.
10. Dishonesty and fraud.

A brief discussion of the various causes of failures listed above may be helpful.

1. Uneconomic or defective initial promotion. Failures resulting from defects in initial promotion sometimes occur even years after a business has started. Railroads have been pushed into sections of a country years before the traffic of that area could afford sufficient revenue to pay operating expenses. During the period from 1900 to 1914, hundreds of small electric interurban railways were built through the northeastern part of the United States. Most of these have disappeared today. Many of them were virtually failures from the outset. Day by day, we find examples of promotions that have misjudged public taste and demand. It is not to be implied here that there is any sure way to forecast the success of a business being promoted, but it is true that many failures would be avoided if a proper *discovery* were made in the early stages of promotion.

2. *Weak production or distribution policies.* Businesses that should have succeeded often fail because of waste and inefficiency in production. Modern competition effects lower profit margins, and the result is that the greatest of efficiency must be shown in the field of production so that costs may be kept at a minimum. Great progress has been made in the field of production in recent years, especially in regard to increasing general efficiency. Cost accounting systems have been installed; these show costs with accuracy. Much can still be done in the way of proper planning and budgeting, for one of the largest sources of loss arises through the improper scheduling of production to meet demand and through heavy inventory losses that follow overproduction.

In the field of distribution, losses occur through ineffective and misdirected advertising policies and, sometimes, from too little advertising. With competitors constantly striving toward dominance in the market, no concern can afford to rest idly upon its laurels or general reputation, but must constantly keep its name and product before the public. Many style changes add nothing of material value to a product. Wide-awake concerns, however, make such changes in order to have something to talk about, as they attempt to keep their product continually before the public. A concern's profits come from the sale of goods and from services, and, since under ordinary conditions a large proportion of its expense is likely to be fixed in nature, the smallest decline in gross income may be disastrous. Alert concerns strive not only to retain old customers, but also to broaden their markets into new territories.

3. *Unwise dividend policy, and paying dividends from capital.* The income of industrial companies is often extremely variable. In the prosperous years, it is usually prudent to set aside a certain amount of earnings to take care of the deficiencies of the lean years. This is especially important when capital has been derived from bonds with attendant fixed charges. Concerns contemplating expansion programs will also find it expedient to set aside funds in periods of prosperity, in order that funds may be available for expansion in periods of depression. At such a time, building costs are cheaper, and, if mergers are contemplated, the existence of large cash reserves will help maintain the price of the com-

pany's securities. This arrangement places the corporation in a better position to trade its securities for those of the company it may wish to absorb. The cost of expansion is an important factor when the future welfare of the concern is being considered. The obligation of the directors of a corporation to the corporation itself ranks equally with their obligation to the stockholders; if the welfare of the corporation demands a conservative dividend policy, not only should the directors act for the best interests of the corporation, but, in so doing, they protect the capital investment of the stockholders.

Payment of dividends out of capital often results through payment of dividends from unrealized profits. Payment of dividends from the paper profits shown by the enhanced value of investment trust portfolios was a practice followed by certain investment trusts in 1928 and 1929. As a result that, when such securities were not liquidated prior to the market recession in the fall of 1929, stockholders found their capital investment impaired not only through decline in the value of portfolios, but also through disbursement of capital.

4. *Overexpansion.* Overexpansion and unwise expansion may lead to serious financial difficulties. Concerns may expand without regard to their working capital position. In fact, the working capital position may be impaired through the investment of too large a proportion of the cash on hand in fixed assets. The ambition of the management to expand its business and achieve a dominating position often meets with failure, because markets have not been developed to take care of the increased capacity. The larger the plant, the greater the overhead that must be met. Increasing the capacity of a plant is foolish if markets will not, in the near future, absorb the increased output. The desire to expand often leads to the buying up of plants of weak or failing competitors and requires considerable capital expenditure before they can be placed on a paying basis.

Expansion of any sort should be the result of a well-developed plan and should take place only when it appears that the profits of the expanding concern will be increased, or the present profits protected. With the advent of the radio, many concerns manufacturing electric equipment and some in entirely different lines entered the radio business. The majority of these were not equipped successfully to push this side line to success. Those concerns that achieved the greatest success were obliged practically to divorce the radio business from their other businesses and to spend prodigious sums in research and advertising to establish their products. One of the main reasons for the failure of many concerns to maintain and develop their new radio business was the fact that no definite plan was laid and no effort was made to look beyond the immediate opportunity for profit that the public interest in radio seemed to offer.

5. *Cutthroat competition.* Ordinary competition should not be classed as a cause for failure, for it is one of the common problems that all businessmen have to meet. Occasionally, however, larger concerns with abundant resources have deliberately forced smaller concerns out of business by cutting prices far below cost. Examples of this may be found in the "gas wars" experienced in almost every community which drive gasoline stations out of business.

6. *Poor financial planning.* A poorly balanced capital structure, with so much borrowed capital that the margin of safety is continually low, is always in danger of failure. A small decline in the volume of business may result in insufficient funds to pay fixed charges and may cause foreclosure by the bondholder. Poorly balanced capital structures may result from the lack of a proper financial plan at the time of promotion, or may result from piecemeal financing at later dates. The fact that borrowed money may often be secured cheaply, thus giving an opportunity to trade on the equity, leads some businessmen to sacrifice safety in order to gain this advantage. The cardinal principle of successful financial planning dictates not only that the capital be obtained as cheaply as possible, but that it be obtained as cheaply as is consistent with safety.

7. *Unforeseen and severe economic readjustment.* Severest readjustment may be brought about by a change in demand or styles that may entail more expense than a business can afford. Henry Ford was forced to close his factory for many months when he found that the public demanded a car more up to date in style than his Model T. The Ford Motor Co. was so strong that it was able to finance the readjustment successfully; a weaker concern might have failed. Readjustments because of change in demand are frequent. Wagon or carriage manufacturers lost much of their business to tractor and automobile producers. Most of those who did survive have gone into the automobile or some similar business. Concerns that enter businesses in which style is an important factor, such as clothing, should be prepared to cope with this factor as one of the natural hazards of such businesses. But, in a business in which style is not a principal factor, the complete falling off in demand for the product may result in the tragedy of failure. Things that have been in great demand for years have been almost entirely displaced by new inventions. The motion picture industry is worrying about how to meet the competition of television as a means of entertainment. Truck, air and private automobile transportation competition has seriously affected railroad income. New methods of waving hair have done away with permanent wave machines. The bus, has completely supplanted the electric street car. World War II and subsequent political and economic disturbances ruined many foreign trade concerns.

It is not always convenient for a concern to make the change to another product. Often machinery adapted to one product must be entirely scrapped if that product is to be abandoned. Putting out a new product creates new marketing problems. Consumer goodwill must be built up all over again. Frequently, after a few attempts in this direction, the concern must be liquidated.

Legislation may definitely ruin a prosperous business. Radical tariff changes may injure not only an importing business, but also a domestic concern dependent upon foreign supplies in the manufacture of its product. These factors are unnatural hazards of a business and are, therefore, difficult to guard against.

8. *Operation of the business cycle.* Business forecasting is not an exact science. We are unable to predict with certainty the height and the degree of the slope, or the depth of the valley or the duration of business prosperity or decline. We have observed that the state of business is not always the same, that periods of prosperity seem to alternate with periods of depression. We have learned from experience to know some of the signs that seem to indicate that business has reached a dangerous degree of expansion, and we recognize some of the signs that point to recovery from periods of depression. Nevertheless, we have not been very successful in predicting exactly when a period of prosperity will end, or how greatly and for how long business will be depressed. The result is that businessmen are often caught unprepared and are unable to adjust their businesses to these severe economic changes in time to avoid losses. Prudent businessmen, however, are not discouraged over the lack of accuracy in business forecasting, but are always trying, through the careful study of their own experiences and those of others, to increase the accuracy of their forecasts.

9. *Disasters, such as earthquakes, fires, floods.* Although a business may usually obtain insurance to cover losses occasioned by disasters, the insurance usually covers only the property loss. If the disaster has a severe effect on business conditions, the business may not be able to return for years to its former position. The Mississippi River floods in 1927 and the Missouri River floods in 1951 practically paralyzed many business activities in these districts for many months because of the losses suffered by the community, as well as outright injury to business properties in those districts. Failures from these causes cannot well be charged to incompetence, for often, in such instances, even superhuman efforts would not be able to continue a business successfully.

10. *Dishonesty and frauds.* Banks, in particular, suffer failure from fraud. The costly Bank of the United States failure in 1930 and the McKesson and Robbins' difficulties in 1938 were brought about through fraudulent acts on the part of its management. Other businesses, too, suffer from such things as the sale of property to a corporation by its own directors at a price greatly in excess of its real value, or the fraudulent disbursement of unearned profits and the outright theft of funds and

property by those interested. Again, such losses may be insured against in part by bonding employees. Often, however, when the theft is by someone high in office in the business, no bond has been obtained for such protection.

The detection of failure tendencies. It may be gathered from the foregoing discussion that causes of failure may be external to the business or internal in origin. The causes are often difficult to detect. They are often present and inactive, or building up to consequence even when a business is enjoying what appears to be unparalleled prosperity. The sky may be cloudless with not even a rumble of thunder beyond the horizon to warn of an approaching storm. Detecting failure tendencies goes far beyond the mere reading of so-called business barometers, for like the barometric instruments of the weather man, the conditions causing the barometer to fall have been building up in the distance before any significant change is to be noticed on the instrument hanging on the wall. Business forecasting, like accurate weather forecasting, usually requires appraisal of conditions often quite remote in both distance and time from the present scene.

The weather man has an advantage over the businessman. He is dealing with natural phenomena or forces which at least to some extent can be weighed and the probable effect estimated and forecasted with reasonable accuracy. Furthermore, he deals with a fairly small number of causes, most of which are well known. There are so many economic forces which may be difficult even to comprehend and, if known, difficult to weigh and their importance hard to determine.

The advantage, however, is not all on the side of the weather forecaster. He is unable to control the natural forces that produce each day's weather conditions, no matter how forehanded he is in their discernment or skillful in forecasting the result. In the face of impending storm, he is limited to telling us what to be prepared for. The businessman, on the other hand, can often do much more than batten down the hatches and wait out the storm; if he, through proper alertness, study and analysis is successful in detecting failure tendencies, he may be able to head them off. This is basically the real purpose of trying to discover long in advance a developing situation that may spell future trouble.

Analysis of external factors. Any extended discussion of external factors would lead into a treatise on business forecasting and a study of statistical methods. Fortunately for the businessman, much of what he needs to know may be gleaned by study of trade journals which specialize in and constantly study and report on economic, political and physical factors affecting the industry. The daily newspapers and usually the Sunday editions have some pages devoted to matters affecting business.

In addition to the regular daily newspapers, there are well-known commercial and financial newspapers published daily, most of which are available at newsstands in business sections of the cities. The Federal Reserve Bulletin and many studies and timely talks made on business conditions by members of this organization are easily available to businessmen. In addition, such Federal publications as the *Survey of Current Business* publish data on current business progress and comparisons with earlier figures, so that trends may be ascertained. Numerous private services may be subscribed for in which will be found charts of business trends accompanied by an array of useful information. With so many sources available and the maintenance of adequate records within the business itself, there is little excuse for a business management not knowing what is going on in the world that may affect its business. There are at hand analyses made by experts to whom no salary need be paid, the only cost being the price of a magazine or newspaper or perhaps a subscription to a private business service or dues to an association of businessmen in their own field of activity.

Some business executives, it is true, employ statistically trained subordinates to study and digest for them material from sources such as those named above and prepare regular reports, sometimes daily. Others may have a clerk clip or blue-pencil items to be laid on a busy executive's desk so that he may keep himself well informed in a minimum of time.

Analysis of internal factors. Many of the conditions observed in a study of factors external to the business are quickly reflected within the business. If first discovered within the business, the reasons for a favorable or unfavorable situation may be found in sources outside of the business itself. Assuming careful and adequate records are maintained, the facts shown by such records should be constantly studied in connection with information obtained from external sources so that proper and timely measures may be taken, not only to try to head off or minimize the effect of some external unfavorable development, but to take quick steps to realize upon or "cash in" on any favorable opportunity. Analyses of internal and external factors are complementary and both are necessary.

Internal records referred to above will vary greatly because of the nature of different kinds of business. They begin with the accounting department. This department should serve financial management to a far greater extent than that of showing what bills to pay, what accounts to collect, and the preparation, periodically, of profit and loss statements and balance sheets. Today most industrial business concerns maintain cost accounting records which follow the process of production, recording costs at all stages. With modern machine methods, these figures can be made readily and quickly available so that executives may investigate any deviation from plans and make proper adjustments. The records should be prepared in such a form that necessary comparisons may be made, relationships between departments studied, and actual performances checked against budget estimates.

In addition to the basic accounting records, daily summaries such as sales by different items or product groups, stocks on hand and on order, turnover of receivables and average length of receivables outstanding, turnover of inventories, length of process period, cost of procurement of various components of the products and others are necessary and should be provided for. All of these, many of which come from the accounting records, should be prepared with the purpose in mind that the executives who must use them will not lose hours trying to find the information they need and more valuable time trying to recast the information in a more useful form. Above all, the information must be timely. Most of this information is historical but *ancient* history is of little help in the daily problems of control. On the other hand, recurring reports of the type referred to above consume much expensive time in preparation and the usefulness of such should be constantly studied and, if not worthwhile, immediately discontinued.

The use of ratios. One of the most important means of checking progress and detecting tendencies in a business is through the preparation and study of significant ratios, which indicate relationships between important items reported in the balance sheets or profit and loss statements of a business. It will be noted that the plural is used throughout the last sentences. Usually a number of ratios must be used and to be of value must be compared with the same ratios which have been prepared from financial statements for several periods in the past. In this way, changes may be observed, their causes analyzed, and trends detected. The use of ratios goes beyond their application to the financial statements of the business concerned. Similar studies should be made of important competitors' statements, if available, and average ratios for the industry should be prepared. By comparison, the management can see how it is holding up in competition and whether any of its own ratios are out of line with the industry. This does not necessarily mean that the result may be unfavorable, it may show that the concern is doing better than the industry as a whole. But here too, it is usually profitable to analyze the situation, so that the reasons for the more favorable showing may be understood and the good work continued or accelerated.

Some of the ratios normally studied with a view to self-analysis by a business concern follow;

(1) *The current ratio* (current assets divided by current liabilities). This ratio has been discussed in Chapter XII. It is a quantitative ratio indicating the ability of a concern to pay its current debts.

(2) *The quick ratio* (current assets minus inventory divided by current

liabilities). Generally considered a better test than the above because inventory turnover may be slow or could unexpectedly become slow.

3. *The turnover of receivables* (credit sales divided by average accounts receivable outstanding). This ratio is discussed in Chapter XII, and is usually used in connection with the average collection period obtained by dividing the average accounts receivable for the period by the average daily sales. Both are checks upon the validity of the current and quick ratios. They indicate quickly any difficulties experienced in collection of accounts and often reflect a decline in business conditions and a tighter bank borrowing situation.

4. *The turnover of merchandise or inventory* (cost of goods sold divided by average inventory). It indicates the number of times the inventory or stock is sold out during the period (usually a year). It quickly reflects conditions of good or poor demand and such internal management policies as inventory control, pricing, poor merchandising or failure to dispose of or write down in value slow-moving or perhaps obsolete merchandise stocks.

5. *Current liabilities to tangible net worth* (current liabilities divided by stock plus surplus minus intangible assets). This ratio indicates the extent to which a concern is relying on short-term capital for its operations. This ratio is used in connection with the ratio of total debt to tangible net worth. This, of course, would indicate the extent that borrowed capital is used as part of the business investment.

6. *Net working capital turnover* (net sales divided by average net working capital for the period). A low ratio here may indicate that the sales volume does not warrant the amount invested in current assets. Perhaps inventories are too large, or credit terms too long. A high ratio may not necessarily be favorable. It may indicate that the net working capital is not large enough properly to finance the business volume and provide for the usual margin of safety.

7. *Sales to fixed operating assets.* This ratio is a measure of the amount of capital invested in fixed assets in relation to sales. It is sometimes referred to as indicating the *fixed asset turnover.* It may be expressed as the amount of fixed assets per dollar of sales or the amount of fixed assets per some unit of production, such as tons, kilowatt hours, etc. It is of doubtful value where the relationship is expressed in terms of sales dollars, because fixed assets as carried on the books are at acquisition cost less depreciation, while sales reflect price fluctuations which may be the result of changes in the purchasing power of money. This ratio nevertheless should be expressed both in terms of sales dollars and of assets. The effect of these fluctuations on fixed asset turnover may then be accurately observed.

8. *Sales to net working capital.* As in the ratio just discussed, this ratio provides a measure of the efficiency with which the current assets are

utilized in producing sales. It is not, however, subject to the same limitations, because current assets normally express current market values.

9. *Turnover of net worth* (sales divided by tangible net worth). This is, of course, a measure of the efficiency with which the concern's investment is used in producing sales. It, too, should be worked out in terms of sales units as well as sales dollars in order that the effects of price fluctuations may be allowed for.

10. *Net profit to net sales.* This ratio indicates how much of the sales dollar is profit for net owners. It is frequently made public as justification for price increases and to show to stockholders and others the effect of increased operating costs. It is often graphically shown in the form of a pie chart, each segment representing the amount of outgo for some cost required in producing a dollar of gross income. The net profit segment may be divided between dividends paid and profit retained in the business. Of all the ratios discussed here, this is the one usually best understood and watched by the stockholders.

11. *Net profit to net worth.* This ratio is really an acid test of the efficiency of the management in employing the owners' investment. Profits being the motive behind all business investment, this ratio reflects the result of the efforts of the management to that end. It is also a test of the wisdom of the management in ploughing back some of each year's profits into the business.

12. *Current liabilities to tangible net worth.* This ratio shows the extent to which the day-to-day operations are being financed through reliance upon short-term sources. In a seasonal business, this ratio will show considerable variation, and properly so, for the management will rely upon short-term sources to finance peak requirements rather than have too much idle cash on hand in slack seasons. It is also used to indicate the extent that the short-term creditors are protected by invested capital contributed by the owners.

13. *Long-term liabilities to tangible net worth.* This ratio, used with that just above, completes the picture of the reliance of the owners upon borrowed capital. This ratio will vary according to the stability of the earnings of the owners. A concern fortunate in being able to maintain stable earnings may trade on the equity to a much higher degree than those businesses which are more vulnerable to cyclical declines.

Ratios are often warning flags of possible danger. The regular use of ratios in a systematic comparison of present and past operations and with competitive concerns and averages for the industry, when obtainable, inform the management of changes and trends some of which might be overlooked if these relationships between key operational accounts were not computed. Comparison of absolute figures can be deceptive, especially when the detection of trends is important.

Sources, flow and application of funds. In Chapters XII and XIV financial analyses through the use of studies of changes in balance sheet accounts were briefly discussed. Such studies play an important part, along with ratio studies, in helping to show up weak spots in the business as well as favorable developments which may be exploited. It is almost trite to observe that failures occur not only because of failure to note adverse trends in time to do something about them but also because the management "missed the boat" in not seeing some possible new development or opportunity for profitable expansion. The value of study of balance sheet changes is apparent from the very nature of double entry bookkeeping. An increase in liabilities finds an offset in the assets, a decrease in the assets, a decrease in a liability account.

Changes may also occur between asset accounts, leaving total assets the same. For example, cash may be expended for additions to plant. Shifts between liability accounts may take place also. A stock dividend, for example, results in a debit to surplus and a credit to capital stock. The changes in balances of individual accounts record the flow of funds within the business and in and out of the business. The channeling of this flow and keeping it in the proper volume is perhaps one way of stating the principal problem with which not only the financial management but all phases of management are concerned.

Because a business exists to produce profits, business activities whether in the field of production, distribution or finance are naturally dominated and justified by the profit motive. Most activities in some way affect the balance sheet accounts and a study of the changes in these accounts from period to period tells the story of business activities. It is a dynamic rather than a static portrayal. A single balance sheet, like a mirror, reflects only a present situation. When rearranged in comparison with previous balance sheets to reflect periodic changes, management has the means of reflecting movement. The funds invested in the business from whatever source are seen at work and to a large extent accomplishments and failures may be ascertained and measured. Through familiarity with the usual changes which take place, those who analyze the statements will be quick to observe any extraordinary deviation and investigate its cause.[1]

Bankruptcy and reorganization. To many persons the two terms are very confusing. Bankruptcy is in a sense the legal death of a business concern. The assets may be distributed among the creditors, if subject to equitable division and in accordance to priorities provided by law. The sale may be piecemeal or, as occasionally happens, all of the assets

---

[1] A thorough exposition of the preparation of and historical flow of funds analysis requires a much more extended treatment than the authors feel appropriate here. Those wishing to pursue the subject further are referred to Howard and Upton *Introduction to Business Finance* (New York: McGraw-Hill Book Co., Inc., 1953).

may be sold to a single highest bidder. The process usually discharges all the debts of the bankrupt, but does not necessarily mean that the business as such is dissolved. It may in many cases start all over again without any of its original assets, but requiring the contribution of new capital. Reorganization, on the other hand, contemplates the continuance of the business after a period during which the creditors agree to certain forbearances and sacrifices. True, the owners, if the business is insolvent, may lose all their interest and creditors assume ownership of the business, or the original owners may be permitted to participate again, provided they contribute new capital, or in effect buy back into the business again.

The confusion of those unfamiliar with the law is increased by the fact that, since 1933, the Federal Bankruptcy Acts have contained sections providing methods of reorganization leading to rehabilitation instead of being restricted as formerly to liquidation for the benefit of creditors. Hence we hear today of a concern being "reorganized in bankruptcy." No wonder people are often confused.

Insolvency and bankruptcy. These terms are not synonymous. A concern may be insolvent; in other words, its liabilities may exceed its assets and it still will not be bankrupt. The latter status requires a court proceeding, initiated either voluntarily by the debtor or brought about by unpaid creditors. A concern may be insolvent and still able to pay its bills, the losses in effect having been charged against the owners' capital investment. This is actually done in partnership accounting but not in corporation accounting. There it may show up as a *deficit* on the asset side of the balance sheet. Before such a capital adjustment could take place in corporations, the amount of stock would have to be reduced, through a *split-down* of the stock requiring stockholders' consent and usually an amendment to the certificate of incorporation. Such a proceeding does not require bankruptcy or reorganization proceedings; it is called a *recapitalization*.

Federal bankruptcy regulation. Bankruptcy was originally conceived as a proceeding against fraudulent debtors (actually those who did not pay their debts were considered fraudulent and debtors were imprisoned). The first statute was enacted in England in 1542 (Statute 34 and 35, Henry VII, c.4) and remained the law until 1845 when it was repealed (Statute 6, George IV, c.16). Subsequent statutes were enacted, tending more and more to the relief of debtors but, until 1861, were restricted to those engaged in trade. The new law enacted in 1825 permitted voluntary bankruptcy (see reference last stated) but Parliament withdrew this privilege in 1869. In 1883 the English law recognized that bankruptcy could be the result of misfortune as well as misconduct.

Probably motivated by a general feeling against harsh treatment of debtors, such as imprisonment which carried over in some sections

of this country from England, framers of the Federal Constitution conferred upon Congress the right to make uniform laws of bankruptcy for
the United States (Art. I, Sec. 8, cl. 4). Nevertheless, Congress took very
little action during the greater part of the nineteenth century. Short-
lived statutes were enacted in 1800, 1841 and 1867, during periods of
business recession, and repealed respectively in 1803, 1843 and 1878.
However, a comprehensive Federal Bankruptcy law was enacted in
1898 and has been with many changes and additions actively administered by the Federal courts since that date. The law states who is
entitled to such relief and provides for voluntary and involuntary proceedings, stockholders' priorities and procedures for claims and defines
certain acts which may be used by creditors to support their initiation
of bankruptcy proceedings against a debtor in the district Federal court
having jurisdiction.[2]

Reorganization. The term *reorganization* usually implies a change in
the financial plan of the corporation that is in financial difficulties. In
the case of a railroad reorganization, this change usually results in a
reduction of fixed charges, for that is commonly the chief problem of
adjustment. In industrials, the obtaining of new money is the serious
problem. Reorganization may leave the industrial corporation with
heavier fixed charges than before, or may leave it with an issue of preferred stock, although, at the time of its financial embarrassment, the
corporation may have had neither bonds nor preferred stock.

In addition to the change in the financial plan, the reorganization
seeks to remove or overcome the cause of failure. This may result in the
abrogation of leases, the sale of unprofitable property, or the replacement of an inefficient management with a better one. Often all of these
things must be accomplished before any new money can be obtained.
While reorganizations naturally will differ in the emphasis upon certain
objectives sought in each case, the general objectives may be stated as
follows:

(1) *Reduction of fixed charges.* Reduction of interest charges or, at
the least, the placing of interest charges on a contingent rather than a
fixed basis is quite likely to be the objective where financing has been
accomplished with large issues of bonds. The railroads having in the
various stages of construction and expansion relied heavily on bonds,
sometimes to the extent of 60 per cent of the capital structure, usually

---

[2] The Federal Bankruptcy Act extends voluntary bankruptcy to all persons, partnerships, and corporations (broadly defined to include joint stock companies, limited
partnerships, associations and business trusts) capable of contracting and owing debts,
except municipal, railroad, insurance, banking corporations and building and loan
associations. In involuntary bankruptcy, creditors may file petitions against any person,
partnership or corporation owing debts of $1,000 except: (1) wage earners, (2) farm-
ers or persons chiefly engaged in tilling the soil, and (3) municipal, railroad, insurance, banking corporations, and building and loan associations.

went into reorganizations with reduction of interest-bearing debt and substitution of income for fixed-charge bonds as the principal objectives.

(2) *Improvement of working capital position.* Obviously the raising of new money through public financing when a concern is in a failing condition would have little chance of success. If there are heavy fixed charges the reduction of interest charges, either through reduction in the rate or substitution of stock for bonds, may help some. Sometimes it is possible to dispose of properties not essential to the business or through the sale of an entire department to raise some money. Under the reorganizations in equity described below it was not unusual for stockholders who otherwise would be left with nothing when all creditor adjustments had been made, to be permitted to receive stock in the reorganized company only if an assessment on a per share basis was paid. Such assessments were voluntary but many stockholders would rather pay them than lose their ownership completely. Under some of the more modern reorganizations accomplished under the Bankruptcy Act described below, stockholders, having been eliminated in cases where the creditors' claims could not be met, were given the opportunity to purchase warrants entitling them to purchase stock at some future time.

(3) *Disposal of unprofitable properties owned under leases.* Receivers and trustees, often with the approval of the court which usually held hearings before taking action, sought to sell properties that were not making money, gaining working capital in the process as well as reducing working capital requirements for future operations. The court might also be asked to disaffirm leases that were unprofitable in the hope of eliminating future losses and again reducing the working capital requirements for operation.

(4) *Providing a new or correcting deficiencies in management.* As a condition of consenting to sacrifices of some of their claims, creditors may insist that the management whom they blame for the concern's difficulties should be replaced or that someone in whom the creditors have confidence be placed in the concern in a responsible position.

Reorganizations fall into four general types: (1) voluntary readjustments, (2) creditors committee reorganizations, (3) reorganizations with the help of the equity courts,[3] and (4) reorganizations under the Federal Bankruptcy statutes.

Voluntary readjustment. There are many directions a voluntary readjustment may take, dictated, of course, by the circumstances surrounding its necessity. It may take the form of a stock recapitalization in which the amount or par value of common stock is reduced by amendment of the certificate of incorporation, in order to create a capital

---

[3] Included because of historical interest and influence on present practices.

surplus against which reductions in value of assets may be charged. By this means, the concern may avoid showing a deficit, which, under the laws of many states, would prevent payment of dividends. The recapitalization may be for the purpose of eliminating a preferred stock with high dividend requirements or burdensome provisions. The latter, unless the preferred be callable, may be difficult to accomplish. Preferred stockholders are not likely to be willing to give up a favorable position unless well paid for it. Therefore, such readjustments may require high cash offers to preferred stockholders or offers of increased equity in the form of common stock. Sometimes, instead of eliminating the preferred stock, an effort is made to reduce the dividend rate by giving the stockholder some compensation in the way of conversion privileges, stock purchase warrants, or common stock. In the thirties, the business depression resulted in piling up dividend accumulations on many issues of preferred stock. The presence of such arrearages was a handicap to new financing; it stood between the common stockholders and any immediate realization of profits as business improved. Hence, many of the recapitalizations during this period aimed at either eliminating the preferred stock and its arrearages entirely or persuading the preferred stockholders to accept some offer of common stock and even bonds in settlement of the accumulated dividends.[4]

One of the simplest types of debt readjustments, when the financial difficulty is one of excessive floating debt, is a funding arrangement. A concern with a good reputation, engaged in an industry in which the demand is not likely to suffer permanent decline, may fund its floating debt by selling bonds through the usual channels. If this possibility is not open, creditors may be persuaded to take the concern's bonds in settlement of short-term debt. This is especially true if the only other alternative would seem to be liquidation or a long expensive reorganization proceeding.

A voluntary readjustment involving publicly held bonds is usually much harder to achieve. Such readjustments may seek an *extension of maturity,* a *temporary moratorium in interest payments,* or an *outright reduction of interest rates,* In most of such cases, some inducement may be offered. However, a concern in the position of not being able to meet its interest payments on bond issues has very little to offer that will have sufficient possibilities of value to interest bondholders. For example, the common stock of the concern in such difficulties is not likely to have much value in the market. The bondholders, however, are aware of the undesirability of expensive and long drawn out legal reorganization proceedings. This point is made much of in negotiations

---

[4] It should be understood that many recapitalizations are undertaken for other than financial difficulties. For example a "split-up" of stock may be for the purpose of reducing the price of individual shares to a more popular market level.

and is probably the best argument the concern can make for the bond-holder's acceptance of the proposed terms. Occasionally, it is also pointed out that such a reorganization proceeding in the courts would be very injurious to the goodwill of the business, whereas a voluntary readjust-ment would not have as bad an effect. The great difficulty in working out voluntary readjustments of the latter type springs from the fact that many bondholders hold out and even start legal proceedings in an effort to obtain a better deal. When the amount of bonds outstanding is relatively small and confined to but one or two issues, it is easier to accomplish than if there are many liens upon the property. Also, if the issue is held largely by institutional investors with whom a bargain may be struck before a public announcement is made, there is a better chance of success. One of the largest voluntary readjustments accomplished with-out the aid of the courts or legislation was that of the Boston and Maine Railroad in 1940.

Also to be classed as a form of voluntary readjustment because it can be accomplished only with the consent of the stockholders, is merger or sale of all the assets to a stronger concern or a merger with a pros-perous concern anxious to take advantage of the carry forward of tax losses to the extent permitted under the Internal Revenue Act.

Creditor's committee reorganizations. Especially characteristic of the severe price declines in the post-war depression of 1920 and 1921 was a type of reorganization that came to be known as *Creditor's committee reorganizations.* The circumstances were usually these. The concern was in debt to banks or other large creditors. Inventory values had greatly and rapidly declined. Collections on accounts receivable slowed up. Sales declined rapidly. Fixed assets in proportion to current assets were usually relatively small, and the business was well established with considerable goodwill. Obviously, creditors had little chance of avoiding loss if bankruptcy and liquidation were insisted on. By means of a voting trust or some type of contractual arrangement, the large creditors would take over or share in the management of the business. Business would go on as usual with small creditors being paid promptly so as to avoid danger of their bringing bankruptcy proceedings. Large creditors, through their representatives (sometimes called business doctors), would endeavor to reduce costs and to increase efficiency and would aid the concern in increasing its sales volume. The purpose was, of course, to get their money and get out as soon as possible. There was some fear of liability to stockholders of the business for mismanagement, but, on the whole, these creditors' efforts were, from their point of view, suc-cessful. Occasionally, money was raised by sale of fixed assets not needed or through sale of all of the assets to another concern for enough to satisfy the stockholders and pay off the debts. Although price declines in the early thirties caused some losses, they were more gradual, and this type of reorganization was not so common. A new section of the bankruptcy act, Section 77b (repealed in 1938), became law in 1934, permitting a management to obtain voluntarily the protection of the courts from its creditors while working out an adjustment. With the management remaining in power and creditors thus barred from legal action, it was not too hard to work out a settlement, which, when approved by the court, was binding upon all. Given a situation again like that in 1920 and 1921, something similar to the Creditors Committee type of reorganization may be used again.

Perhaps it might also be mentioned that under a Chapter XI arrangement discussed in greater detail below, the debtor, before initiating proceedings in accordance with the statute, may first approach its principal creditors and obtain tentative approval of a desired settlement before actually going to court with the plan. As a condition of accepting the proposed sacrifice, these creditors may stipulate that the ownership or control be sold to a purchaser meeting their approval or that a management satisfactory to them be installed under a long-term contract.

Equity receiverships. In many cases the best chance of general creditors realizing upon their bills and for holders of bonds not only to salvage part of their value but to hope for a resumption of defaulted interest payments, is not liquidation of the assets of a debtor corporation, but working out some type of reorganization, looking to the rehabilitation of the business. While there may be substantial sacrifices to be assumed on the part of creditors, especially those holding general and junior claims, a reorganization plan might be worked out which would give promise of salvaging far more than could be realized if the business were discontinued and the assets sold by a trustee in bankruptcy. Business assets may be of little value except in connection with a successfully operating business. Further the Federal Bankruptcy Act does not provide for outright bankruptcy of railroad corporations, a very important part of American business. The failure and liquidation of a large business affects many who are not creditors or owners. The loss of its trade may seriously jeopardize other concerns who were its chief suppliers of raw material and their creditors and employees. Some large corporations number their employees by several thousands and, were the concern to liquidate, these people would suffer greatly. In other words, there is a broad public interest in preventing the death and liquidation of some business concerns.

Where such conditions existed, relief was usually sought in an equity proceeding brought usually in the Federal courts. The Federal courts were compelled to develop orderly procedure for handling such cases because of the many railroad difficulties beginning in the nineteenth century and reaching great volume in the depression of 1890. Railroads largely operate in interstate commerce and therefore the use of Federal courts was logical. State courts can and have been used but the broad experience of the Federal courts led to their use in receiverships of large corporations other than the railroads.

While the use of equity receiverships largely ceased with the enactment of revisions to the Bankruptcy Act in 1933 and 1934, some knowledge of the procedure is necessary for a proper understanding of present practice.

For example, Chapter X of the Bankruptcy Act in Section 115 states:

The Court shall have and may exercise all the powers not inconsistent with the provisions of this Chapter, which a court of the United States would have if it had appointed a receiver in equity of the debtor on the ground of insolvency or inability to meet its debts as they matured.

Equity receivership procedure. While the powers of a judge sitting in an equity proceeding are sufficiently broad to permit adjustments to meet the equities involved in a particular case, the general procedure followed may be described as follows:

Equity receiverships ostensibly began as hostile actions, since it was necessary for a creditor or a group of creditors to present the petition to the court. Such actions, however, were usually the result of a prior arrangement made by the debtor with the creditor, who, as a result, lent his name to the proceeding. The term "friendly receiverships" was, therefore, frequently applied to describe the procedure. Usually, the court appointed the president or other officer of the corporation as receiver, and, occasionally in large cases, an independent co-receiver was appointed also. One defect apparent at the outset was the legal necessity of beginning action simultaneously in all Federal judicial districts wherein the property was located and the appointment of ancillary receivers in each. Later motions were made to consolidate all cases into one, which the courts, as a matter of practice, permitted. Voluntary protective committees, frequently headed by banking firms friendly to the corporation, were formed immediately upon the beginning of the action. These committees solicited the deposit of the securities owned by the group of claimants, which the committee had indicated they would represent, with power to the committee to act in their behalf. Representatives of the committees met as a reorganization committee to begin work on a reorganization. The first task was to arrive at a property value that could be used as a basis for determining the equities of each class of claimant. This value was the result of compromise and, in many cases, had little relationship to earning power, or even to book values. Once the court approved this agreed-upon value, it became known as the *upset price.*

The final plan might call for the incorporation of a new concern of about the same name, issuance of senior bonds of the new company, dollar for dollar, at the same interest rate to the senior bondholders of the old company. Junior bondholders were often compelled to make a sacrifice by accepting income bonds, preferred stock, and even common stock in exchange for their holdings. Stockholders frequently were required to pay an assessment in order to obtain any new securities in the reorganized company. Once the plan had been resolved, it was published, and a campaign ensued to obtain the consent of bondholders and other claimants. If substantial consent were received, the trustee of the senior defaulted bonds brought a foreclosure action and a sale was made to the highest bidder. Usually, there would be but one, which was the new corporation represented by the reorganization committee or reorganization managers appointed by this committee. The sale had to produce enough cash to pay off nondepositing claimants according to their proportionate interest in the "upset price," which was the amount bid at the sale. Underwriting bankers put up the cash and took over the securities refused by the dissenters. The new corporation then began operations. If money were needed to operate during the receivership, the courts might authorize the issuance of receivership certificates, which were normally sold to investing institutions and which had to be paid off also out of the proceeds of sale. Fees for protective committees were authorized by the court, as well as the salaries of receivers and referees whom the judge may have appointed to preside at hearings.

The entire procedure was often long drawn out. Protective committees and counsel were often allowed fees clearly in excess of deserved compensation. Bondholders received no interest during the receivership, and this fact was used as a method of coercion to force acceptance of the plan. A thorough investigation of railroad reorganization made by the U.S. Senate resulted in the adoption of Section 77 of the Bankruptcy Laws in 1933 to govern reorganization of railroads, followed a year later by Section 77B, providing for reorganization of other types of businesses. The latter section proved unsatisfactory and was replaced in 1938 with Chapters X and XI, which will be briefly discussed in paragraphs immediately following.

Federal reorganization statutes. As previously mentioned, the Federal government has broadened the scope of its bankruptcy laws to include provisions for corporate reorganizations. *Section 77* of the Bankruptcy Act was the first of these, and became law in March 1933. It applies to interstate railroads. An additional section has since been added to the Interstate Commerce Act, Section 20b, known popularly as the Mahaffie Act, which provides for readjustment of railroads' funded debt by a less complicated process than that established by Section 77. Brief discussion of this legislation will be found in subsequent paragraphs.

Railroad reorganization under Section 77. Section 77 made sweeping changes in the procedure for the reorganization of interstate railroads previously dependent upon equity processes. The Interstate Commerce

Commission was brought into proceedings at the very outset. When the management of a railroad finds further progress without reorganization impossible, the Interstate Commerce Commission is asked for permission to file a petition in a Federal court asking for the appointment of a trustee, under Section 77. If the permission is granted, the railroad begins the action, usually making an allegation that debts cannot be met as they mature. Insolvency could be stated as the reason, but an admission of insolvency would bar the stockholders from any participation from the outset. It may be that subsequent findings of insolvency will be made. In fact, the valuation finally set on railroad properties during the thirties usually showed the railroad to be insolvent. The court appoints one or more trustees, subject to approval as to choice by the Interstate Commerce Commission.

The trustee for the debtor corporation, or 10 per cent of any class of security holders, may submit a plan of reorganization to the Interstate Commerce Commission. The Commission may approve one of these plans or substitute one of its own. Hearings are usually held as required on the various plans submitted. The plan to be adopted must be approved by two-thirds of each class of claimant, including the stockholders if the corporation is not insolvent. When finally so approved, the court is asked to give final approval, which it must do if it is found that the law has been fully complied with. It will be noticed that the court's powers are greatly limited. It is the Interstate Commerce Commission that must approve the choice of trustee. Likewise, all fees for trustees, referees, protective committees, in fact practically all costs of the reorganization, must be approved by the Commission. Ancillary trusteeships are no longer necessary, for the Federal court taking original jurisdiction controls the entire property. The trustee may take no part in making the reorganization plan, his principal duties being to operate the railroad during the trusteeship.

From this brief discussion, it must not be assumed that railroad reorganizations are quickly accomplished. Many railroads that began proceedings shortly after the law went into effect, or changed from an equity proceeding to the new law as they were permitted to do, did not finally complete reorganization until after World War II. Costs were greatly reduced from those under equity, but they are still large because of the protracted nature of the proceedings. Reorganization of small railroads has sometimes cost slightly less than a million dollars, and that of larger ones, in excess of two million.

The Mahaffie Act. Because of the costs and the complicated nature of the above procedure, Congress has added a new section (Section 20b) to the Interstate Commerce Act in the hope that simpler methods would enable a railroad to accomplish recapitalization or readjustment of its funded debt without the formality of a Section 77 reorganization. In brief, the act provides that, with the approval of the Interstate Commerce Commission given after public hearings, a modification of indenture provisions may be submitted to security holders for approval. If 75 per cent of the affected security holders approve, the Commission may enter an order approving the change. This legislation has had what is, in effect, two previous trials. It is not substantially different from the so-called Chandler Act, a temporary measure enacted as Chapter XV of the Bankruptcy Act on July 28, 1939 to expire July 31, 1940, and a subsequent revival of the section as the McLaughlin Act, enacted in 1942 to expire in 1945. The experience of the Baltimore & Ohio Railroad, and the Lehigh Valley Railroad under Chapter XV demonstrated the feasibility of the simple procedure embodied in the Interstate Commerce Act referred to above. The new act not being part of bankruptcy procedure is free from many legal limitations resulting from court decisions relative to bankruptcy.

Reorganization under Chapter X. Under Chapter X, either the debtor corporation or creditors may petition a Federal court for a reorganization under the terms of the act. The act states the information that must be covered by the petition in either case. As a simplified manner of adjustment of debt has been provided by Congress in Chapter XI, a statement of the reasons why this procedure could not have been used must form a part of the petition. When the liabilities amount to $250,000 or more, the judge must appoint an independent trustee to manage the property during reorganization and also to work out a reorganization plan. If the technical operation of the property makes it advisable, the judge may appoint an officer of the debtor as an additional trustee. After the trustee has presented a plan of reorganization to the court, the judge will hold hearings. This presents an opportunity for creditor groups to criticize the plan or to present plans of their own. Following this hearing, the judge is required, when the indebtedness exceeds $3,000,000, to submit the plan to the Securities and Exchange Commission for an advisory report. The judge, at his discretion, may submit plans for corporations having a smaller amount of liabilities and may admit the S.E.C. as a party to the proceedings at any time, either upon its own motion or upon the request of the court. The S.E.C. advisory report discusses the feasibility of the plan and whether it is fair and equitable, *i.e.*, whether it is likely to enable the corporation to avoid financial embarrassment in the future and whether security holders and claimants have been treated fairly, according to their respective priorities.

If the judge now approves the plan, the various classes of claimants must vote on it and, as in Section 77, two-thirds of each class must approve, including a majority of the stockholders when the corporation is not insolvent. If the plan involves a public utility, the appropriate regulating commission of the state in which the utility is located must also approve before the plan can be put into operation.

Under Chapter X, a separate hearing is held on fees, allowances and expenses of indenture trustees, protective committees, attorneys, etc., who have been concerned in the reorganization. Frequently, the S.E.C. will, through its attorneys, appear at such hearings to question the statements of fees and expenses presented by the claimants. It may be added here that the judge does not have to accept the advisory opinion of the S.E.C. on the plan or its comment on the amount of fees. But experience has shown that the court will, as a matter of practice, place great weight on the findings of the S.E.C., because of the independence of the Commission's position and its members' expertness in such matters.

Proceedings under Chapter X have a better record of speed than those under Section 77, but here, too, an especially difficult case may take some years to accomplish. The proceedings are intended for reorganization, but it may be found as a fact that reorganization for profitable operation is impossible, and the court may then decree a liquidation. This was the final result in the reorganization of the Northeastern Steel Corporation of Connecticut. The Federal court having become convinced that the business could not be reorganized to operate profitably, ordered the assets sold in 1957.

The above treatment is very brief and one is advised to read the Act itself and to provide oneself with the record of some of the cases that have been adjudicated, in order to gain a more complete knowledge.

Arrangements with creditors under Chapter XI. In the country's previous experience with Section 77B, the courts were cluttered with small cases involving settlements with unsecured creditors only. To subject these cases to the longer and more complicated trusteeship under Chapter X would appear to be unnecessary, so in Chapter XI Congress established a comparatively simple method whereby the debtors' plan for settlement, or extension of the time for payment of his debts, could be presented to creditors through the orderly processes of the courts.

Proceedings under this chapter are initiated by a petition filed by the debtor either before or after adjudication in bankruptcy. The petition must state either that the debtor corporation is insolvent or that it is unable to pay its debts as they mature. It must also be accompanied by a statement of the debtor's affairs, including details of any executory contracts and, of course, a list of amounts owed to the various creditors. The petition will set forth the debtor's plan of settlement with creditors, either as a whole or by classes. The filing of the petition does not of itself act as a stay of an adjudication of bankruptcy, this remaining in the discretion of the court. The court may also appoint a receiver to take charge of the debtor's property and may, if it sees fit, appoint an appraiser to examine and inventory the property.

Upon at least ten days' notice, accompanied by copies of the debtor's plan and statement of affairs, a meeting of creditors is called by the court. At this meeting, creditors may accept the plan in writing. If all accept, the plan can be immediately confirmed, otherwise it must be accepted in writing by either a majority of all the creditors in number and amount, or, if the debtor has divided his creditors into classes, by a majority in amount and number of each class. The debtor must pay the money or securities due into the court before final confirmation. After this final confirmation, the arrangement is binding upon all creditors of the corporation.

Failure and liquidation. If reorganization is undesirable or impossible, it is necessary to *liquidate* the business for the payment of debts. Liquidation may take place without bankruptcy through an arrangement with the creditors whereby each agrees to settle for a certain amount of his claims. If a large number of creditors (not necessarily all) agree to the same terms of settlement and sign a mutual agreement to discharge the debtor upon his complying with such terms, a common-law composition is effected and is binding upon those who sign. Unless, however, such an arrangement can be made practically unanimous, as far as the creditors are concerned, it is usually abandoned. Creditors not joining may file a petition in bankruptcy at any time, or may attach a nuisance value to their claims in an endeavor to force the other creditors to buy them off.

An old method of settlement was to make an assignment for the benefit of the creditors. That is, the debtor would assign his assets to a trustee to be sold or otherwise disposed of for the payment of his debts. Since the debtor is not discharged of his debts by this procedure, and because the assignment is in itself an act of bankruptcy, this method is seldom used. Modern bankruptcy procedure accomplishes the same purpose through the appointment of a trustee in bankruptcy and has the added advantage that the debtor may be legally discharged of his debts by the court.

Bankruptcy. Bankruptcy actions are brought under the Federal law. Any person, except a municipal, railroad, insurance, or banking corporation or a building and loan association, may become a voluntary bankrupt.

Any natural person, except a wage earner or farmer, and every business corporation, except a municipal, railroad, insurance or banking corporation, may be adjudged an involuntary bankrupt, provided there is owing $1,000 or over. A petition may be filed within four months after the commission of any one of six acts of bankruptcy.

The six acts of bankruptcy by a debtor are as follows:[5]

---

[5] United States Bankruptcy Act, effective September 22, 1938, Chapter III, Sec. 3.

(1) "Conveyed, transferred, concealed, removed, or permitted to be concealed or removed any part of his property, with intent to hinder, delay, or defraud his creditors or any of them; or

(2) "Transferred, while insolvent, any portion of his property to one or more of his creditors with intent to prefer such creditors over his other creditors; or

(3) "Suffered or permitted, while insolvent, any creditor to obtain a lien upon any of his property through legal proceedings and not having vacated or discharged such lien within 30 days from the date thereof or at least five days before the date set for any sale or other disposition of such property; or

(4) "Made a general assignment for the benefit of his creditors; or

(5) "While insolvent or unable to pay his debts as they mature, procured, permitted, or suffered voluntarily or involuntarily the appointment of a receiver or trustee to take charge of his property; or

(6) "Admitted in writing his inability to pay his debts and his willingness to be adjudged a bankrupt."

Discharge in bankruptcy. Under the amended Bankruptcy Act, the adjudication of any person except a corporation shall operate as an application for a discharge. A corporation may, within six months after its adjudication, file an application for a discharge in the court in which the proceedings are pending. The debtor must have surrendered all his property to the custody of the receiver or trustee in compliance with the provisions of the Bankruptcy Act. Discharge by the court frees the debtor from the legal obligation of paying his debts. Creditors may oppose his discharge if they find that the bankrupt has not acted in good faith, that is, committed some fraud, such as concealing his assets, and so forth.

Priority of claims. The Bankruptcy Act specifies the order in which claims against the bankrupt estate shall be paid, as follows:[6]

(1) "The actual and necessary costs and expenses of preserving the estate subsequent to filing the petition; the filing fees paid by creditors in involuntary cases; where property of the bankrupt, transferred or concealed by him either before or after the filing of the petition, shall have been recovered for the benefit of the estate of the bankrupt by the efforts and at the cost and expense of one or more creditors, the reasonable costs and expenses of such recovery; the costs and expenses of administration, including the trustee's expenses in opposing the bankrupt's discharge, the fees and mileage payable to witnesses as now or hereafter provided by the laws of the United States, and one reasonable attorney's fee [sic], for the professional services actually rendered, irrespective of the number of attorneys employed, to the petitioning creditors in involuntary cases and to bankrupt in voluntary and involuntary cases, as the court may allow;

(2) "Wages, not to exceed $600 to each claimant, which have been earned within three months before the date of the commencement of the proceeding, due to workmen, servants, clerks, or traveling or city salesmen on salary or commission basis, whole or part time, whether or not selling exclusively for the bankrupt;

(3) "Where the confirmation of an arrangement or wage-earner plan or the bankrupt's discharge has been refused, revoked, or set aside upon the objection

---

[6] United States Bankruptcy Act, approved June 22, 1938, Chapter VII, Sec. 64.

and through the efforts and at the cost and expense of one or more creditors, or, where through the efforts and at the cost and expense of one or more creditors, evidence shall have been adduced resulting in the conviction of any person of an offense under this Act, the reasonable costs and expenses of such creditors in obtaining such refusal, revocation, or setting aside, or in adducing such evidence;

(4.) "Taxes legally due and owing by the bankrupt to the United States or any State or any subdivision thereof: *Provided,* That no order shall be made for the payment of a tax assessed against any property of the bankrupt in excess of the value of the interest of the bankrupt estate therein as determined by the court; *And provided further,* That, in case any question arises as to the amount or legality of any taxes, such question shall be heard and determined by the court, and

(5.) "Debts owing to any person, including the United States, who by the laws of the United States is entitled to priority, and rent owing to a landlord who is entitled to priority by applicable State law; *Provided, however,* That such priority for rent to a landlord shall be restricted to the rent which is legally due and owing for the actual use and occupancy of the premises affected, and which accrued within three months before the date of bankruptcy.

(6.) "Debts contracted while a discharge is in force or after the confirmation of an arrangement shall, in the event of a revocation of the discharge or setting aside of the confirmation, have priority and be paid in full in advance of the payment of the debts which were provable in the bankruptcy or arrangement proceeding, as the case may be."

Legal aid required in bankruptcy. Because of the technical legal nature of bankruptcy proceedings, attorneys should be engaged to represent both parties. Often one attorney will represent all the creditors, while the debtor will engage another attorney to represent his interests.

Questions for Study and Review

1. Explain briefly ten causes of business failures.
2. List some of the easily available sources of information on external factors which a businessman may wish to study in order to detect failure tendencies.
3. Name and briefly explain five ratios which may be studied in the analysis of a business concern.
4. Briefly explain the purpose of making studies of the sources, flow and application of funds as shown by the financial statements of business.
5. Do the terms, insolvency and bankruptcy mean the same thing? Explain.
6. What is the difference between bankruptcy and reorganization as treated in your text?
7. What is meant by the term *reorganization* as applied to a corporation?
8. Distinguish between four general types of reorganization.
9. Describe briefly procedure of reorganization under an equity receiver.
10. What are creditors' committee reorganizations? Under what circumstances are they appropriate?
11. By whom may a reorganization plan be filed for an industrial corporation under the United States Bankruptcy Act?

12. What is the function of the S.E.C. under a Chapter X reorganization?
13. How does the reorganization procedure for public utility corporations differ from that for industrial corporations?
14. What is an arrangement under the United States Bankruptcy Act?
15. In what essentials does railroad reorganization under Section 77 differ from industrial reorganization procedure?
16. Mention the four main objectives of reorganization?
17. What are the six acts of bankruptcy?
18. How may a debtor obtain his discharge in bankruptcy and what is the effect?
19. What is the priority of claims against a bankrupt estate under the United States Bankruptcy Act?

Problems

1. The Shelbourne Machinery Corporation has been established and operated successfully for a number of years. During the past three years, however, weak and incompetent management has resulted in a series of difficulties which have caused the company steadily to lose money and become insolvent. Prospects for a reorganization are good and, with a change in management, the company should in two or three years get back on its feet. The balance sheet prior to the reorganization is as follows:

BALANCE SHEET
(Prior to Reorganization)

ASSETS		LIABILITIES	
Current Assets:		Current Liabilities:	
Cash	$ 6,000	Notes Payable	$100,000
Notes Receivable	84,000	Accounts Payable	90,000
Accounts Receivable	65,000	Accrued Wages, Taxes,	
Inventories	36,000	etc.	10,000
Total	$191,000	Total	$200,000
Fixed Assets:		Fixed Liabilities:	
Plant and Equipment	110,000	1st Mortgage 8% Bonds	20,000
Deficit	59,000	Capital Stock:	
		6% Preferred Stock	100,000
		Common Stock ($100	
		par)	40,000
TOTAL ASSETS	$360,000	TOTAL LIABILITIES	$360,000

A. You are to prepare a reorganization plan together with a balance sheet giving effect to the reorganization.

The following changes in equities have been agreed upon by the creditors and the stockholders:

a. The first mortgage bondholders have agreed to accept in exchange for their present holdings 50 per cent in 6 per cent income bonds and 50 per cent in new common stock.

b. Notes payable (carried at 5 per cent interest rates) to banks are to be reduced 20 per cent; the new amount shall consist of 62½ per cent of 7 per cent prior preferred stock; and 37½ per cent shall be carried over by the new company as regular notes payable.

c. Accounts payable (non-interest bearing) are to be reduced 40 per cent; the new amount shall consist of 55½ per cent of 7 per cent prior preferred stock; and 44½ per cent shall be carried over by the new company as regular accounts payable.

d. The old 6 per cent preferred stock is to be exchanged par for par for new common stock which is to have the same par value as the old.

e. Common stockholders have agreed to subscribe at $34 per share for new common stock to the extent of one share of new common for two shares of old.

f. $15,000 worth of unused plant and equipment will be sold for $10,000 cash, and the proceeds used for new working capital.

B. Assuming that potential earnings in two or three years may rise to a maximum of $10,000, criticize the reorganization plan.

Index